# AAT

## INTERACTIVE TEXT

Intermediate Unit 21

# Using Information Technology

**In this May 2000 edition**

- Layout designed to be easy on the eye - and easy to use

- Icons to guide you through a 'fast track' approach if you wish

- Material up-to-date as at May 2000

**FOR 2000 AND 2001 DEVOLVED ASSESSMENTS**

BPP Publishing
*May 2000*

*First edition 1999*

*ISBN 0 7517 0218 8*

**British Library Cataloguing-in-Publication Data**
*A catalogue record for this book*
*is available from the British Library*


*Published by*

*BPP Publishing Limited*     *and*     *MACPA*
*Aldine House, Aldine Place*               *15 Jalan Medan Tuanku*
*London W12 8AW*                 *50300 Kuala Lumpur*
                                      *Malaysia*
*http://www.bpp.com*

                                        *03-2989622*

*We are grateful to the Malaysian Association of Certified Public Accountants for permission to reproduce in this text the syllabus of which the Association holds the copyright. We are also grateful for permission to reproduce past examination questions and solutions.*

**Page**

*BPP* PUBLISHING

# HOW TO USE THIS INTERACTIVE TEXT

## Aims of this Interactive Text

To provide the knowledge and practice to help you succeed in the devolved assessments for Intermediate Unit 21 *Using Information Technology*.

To pass the devolved assessments you need a thorough understanding in all areas covered by the standards of competence.

To tie in with the other components of the BPP Effective Study Package to ensure you have the best possible chance of success.

**Interactive Text**

This covers all you need to know for devolved assessment for Unit 21 *Using Information Technology*. Icons clearly mark key areas of the text. Numerous activities throughout the text help you practise what you have just learnt.

**Devolved Assessment Kit**

When you have understood and practised the material in the Interactive Text, you will have the knowledge and experience to tackle the Devolved Assessment Kit for Unit 21. This aims to get you through the devolved assessment, whether in the form of the AAT simulation or in the workplace.

## Recommended approach to this Interactive Text

(a) To achieve competence in Unit 21 (and all the other units), you need to be able to do **everything** specified by the standards. Study the text very carefully and do not skip any of it.

(b) Learning is an **active** process. Do **all** the activities as you work through the text so you can be sure you really understand what you have read.

(c) After you have covered the material in the Interactive Text, work through the **Devolved Assessment Kit**.

(d) Before you take the devolved assessments, check that you still remember the material using the following quick revision plan for each chapter.

    (i) Read through the **chapter learning objectives**. Are there any gaps in your knowledge? If so, study the section again.

    (ii) Read and learn the key terms.

    (iii) Look at the devolved assessment alerts. These show the sort of things that are likely to come up.

    (iv) Read and learn the **key learning points**, which are a summary of the chapter.

    (v) Do the quick quiz again. If you know what you're doing, it shouldn't take long.

This approach is only a suggestion. You college may well adapt it to suit your needs.

Remember this is a **practical** course.

(a) Try to relate the material to your experience in the workplace or any other work experience you may have had.

(b) Try to make as many links as you can to your study of the other Units at Intermediate level.

(c) Keep this Text, (hopefully) you will find it invaluable in your everyday work.

## INTERMEDIATE QUALIFICATION STRUCTURE

The competence-based Education and Training Scheme of the Association of Accounting Technicians is based on an analysis of the work of accounting staff in a wide range of industries and types of organisation. The Standards of Competence for Accounting which students are expected to meet are based on this analysis.

The Standards identify the key purpose of the accounting occupation, which is to operate, maintain and improve systems to record, plan, monitor and report on the financial activities of an organisation, and a number of key roles of the occupation. Each key role is subdivided into units of competence, which are further divided into elements of competences. By successfully completing assessments in specified units of competence, students can gain qualifications at NVQ/SVQ levels 2, 3 and 4, which correspond to the AAT Foundation, Intermediate and Technician stages of competence respectively.

Whether you are competent in a Unit is demonstrated by means of:

- *Either* a Central Assessment (set and marked by AAT assessors)

- *Or* a Devolved Assessment (where competence is judged by an Approved Assessment Centre to whom responsibility for this is devolved)

- Or *both* Central *and* Devolved Assessment

Below we set out the overall structure of the Intermediate (NVQ/SVQ Level 3) stage, indicating how competence in each Unit is assessed. In the next section there is more detail about the Devolved Assessment for Unit 21.

## NVQ/SVQ **Level 3 - Intermediate**

*All units are mandatory*

| Unit of competence | Elements of competence |
|---|---|

**Unit 5** Maintaining financial records and preparing accounts

**Central *and* Devolved Assessment**

| | |
|---|---|
| 5.1 | Maintain records relating to capital acquisition and disposal |
| 5.2 | Record income and expenditure |
| 5.3 | Collect and collate information for the preparation of financial accounts |
| 5.4 | Prepare the extended trial balance account |

**Unit 6** Recording cost information

**Central *and* Devolved Assessment**

| | |
|---|---|
| 6.1 | Record and analyse information relating to direct costs |
| 6.2 | Record and analyse information relating to the allocation, apportionment and absorption of overhead costs |
| 6.3 | Prepare and present standard cost reports |

**Unit 7** Preparing reports and returns

**Devolved Assessment *only***

| | |
|---|---|
| 7.1 | Prepare and present periodic performance reports |
| 7.2 | Prepare reports and returns for outside agencies |
| 7.3 | Prepare VAT returns |

**Unit 21** Using information technology

**Devolved Assessment *only***

| | |
|---|---|
| 21.1 | Obtain information from a computerised Management Information System |
| 21.2 | Produce spreadsheets for the analysis of numerical information |
| 21.3 | Contribute to the quality of the Management Information System |

**Unit 22** Monitor and maintain a healthy, safe and secure workplace (ASC)

**Devolved Assessment *only***

| | |
|---|---|
| 22.1 | Monitor and maintain health and safety within the workplace |
| 22.2 | Monitor and maintain the security of the workplace |

**BPP**
PUBLISHING

## UNIT 21 STANDARDS OF COMPETENCE

*What is the unit about?*

This unit is about using information technology as an essential tool when undertaking accounting activities. It involves being able to obtain any required information from the Management Information System (MIS) and being able to produce spreadsheets for the analysis and presentation of numerical information. The candidate has responsibility for observing the Data Protection Act, obtaining information from the MIS and correctly manipulating it in spreadsheets. Their responsibility extends to obtaining authorisation for its use, keeping confidential information secure and evaluating its appropriateness. The candidate will also be required to evaluate the quality of the MIS whilst using it and make appropriate recommendations for its improvement.

Elements contained within this unit are:

Element: 21.1    Obtain information from a computerised management information system

Element: 21.2    Produce spreadsheets for the analysis of numerical information

Element: 21.3    Contribute to the quality of the management information system

## Knowledge and understanding

**General information technology**

- Purpose and application of MIS (Elements 21.1 & 21.3)

- Relationship between MIS and other IT applications (Elements 21.1, 21.2 & 21.3)

- Range of MIS used in organisations (Element 21.1 & 21.3)

- A range of spreadsheet products (Element 21.2)

- Interfaces with other software packages: databases, word processors (Element 21.2)

- Purpose and application of spreadsheets (Element 21.2)

**The organisation**

- Types of information contained within the MIS (Elements 21.1, 21.2 & 21.3)

- Location of information sources (Elements 21.1, 21.2 & 21.3)

- Ways of organising, interpreting and presenting information (Elements 21.1 & 21.3)

- Relevant security and legal regulations, including the Data Protection Act, and their purpose (Elements 21.1, 21.2 & 21.3)

- Organisations' computer software, systems and networking (Elements 21.1 & 21.3)

- Cost benefit analysis techniques (Element 21.3)

BPP
PUBLISHING

**Element 21.1: Obtain information from a computerised Management Information System**

| | | Chapters in this Text |
|---|---|---|
| **Performance criteria** | | |
| 1 | The required information is correctly located within the MIS structure | 1-3 |
| 2 | Advice is sought where there are difficulties in obtaining the required information | 2-3 |
| 3 | Additional authorisation is obtained for sensitive or confidential information in accordance with the organisation's security regulations | 14 |
| 4 | Information is checked for its accuracy and completeness | 1, 6 |
| 5 | Information is stored in a format which helps others to access it and use it | 2 |
| 6 | Confidential information is kept secure and not disclosed to unauthorised people | 6, 14 |

**Range statement**

1 Information locations: database; unique reference codes

2 Information: obtained for own work and area of responsibility; obtained on request from others

3 Difficulties: costs incurred; time taken

**Evidence requirements**

- Competence must be demonstrated consistently, over an appropriate timescale with evidence of performance being provided from obtaining information from an organisation's MIS or part of an organisation's MIS

**Sources of evidence (these are examples of sources of evidence, but candidates and assessors may be able to identify other, appropriate sources)**

**Observed performance, eg**

- Obtaining information from an MIS

- Seeking advice

- Explore more cost effective methods of obtaining data

- Evaluating information

- Presenting information

**Work produced by candidate, eg**

- Advice that has been given

- Notification of methods not being cost effective

- Authorisation for information

- Print-outs obtained from the MIS

**Authenticated testimonies from relevant witnesses**

**Personal accounts of competence, eg**

- Report of performance

**Other sources of evidence to prove competence or knowledge and understanding where it is not apparent from performance, eg**

- Reports and working papers

- Performance in simulation

- Responses to questions

(x)

**Element 21.2: Produce spreadsheets for the analysis of numerical information**

| Performance criteria | Chapters in this Text |
|---|---|
| 1    The spreadsheet is titled in a way which clearly defines its use and purpose | 5-6 |
| 2    The arrangement of the spreadsheet is consistent with organisational conventions | 5-8 |
| 3    All rates and other numeric inputs and assumptions are stated to the correct number of decimal places | 5-8 |
| 4    Calculated values are checked for correctness when changes are made to the inputs | 5-8 |
| 5    The spreadsheet is used to carry out data modifications and for entry of related formulas | 5-8 |
| 6    Each cell is formatted clearly and accurately | 6 |
| 7    A method is selected to eliminate rounding errors which is suitable for the purpose of the spreadsheet | 6 |
| 8    Confidential information is kept secure and not disclosed to unauthorised people | 6, 14 |

**Range statement**

1    Spreadsheets produced by: modification; creation

2    Spreadsheets: which require possible rounding errors; which have conditions in some formulae; which are used to produce graphs

3    Spreadsheet produced: for own work and area of responsibility; on request from others

4    Information: numeric; alphabetic

**Evidence requirements**

- Competence must be demonstrated consistently, with evidence of performance being provided from the production of the full range of spreadsheets in one organisational MIS or part of an organisation's MIS

**Sources of evidence (these are examples of sources of evidence, but candidates and assessors may be able to identify other, appropriate sources)**

    **Observed performance, eg**

- Inputting data on a spreadsheet
- Checking calculated values
- Modifying data
- Entering related formulas
- Eliminating rounding errors

    **Work produced by candidate, eg**

- Formatted spreadsheets

    **Authenticated testimonies from relevant witnesses**

    **Personal accounts of competence, eg**

- Report of performance

    **Other sources of evidence to prove competence or knowledge and understanding where it is not apparent from performance, eg**

- Performance in simulation
- Performance in independent assessment
- Responses to verbal questioning

BPP PUBLISHING

## Element 21.3: Contribute to the quality of the Management Information System

| Performance criteria | Chapters in this Text |
|---|---|
| 1  Potential improvements to the MIS are identified and considered for their impact on the quality of the system and any interrelated systems | 9-14 |
| 2  Suggestions for changes are supported by a clear rationale as to how they could improve the quality of the system | 4, 9-14 |
| 3  The reliability of assumptions and judgements made is assessed and clearly stated | 9-14 |
| 4  The benefits and costs of all changes are described accurately | 1, 4, 9 |
| 5  Suggestions are presented clearly and in a way which helps people to understand and act on them | 4 |

**Range statement**

1    MIS: computerised system

**Evidence requirements**

- Competence must be demonstrated consistently over an appropriate timescale, with evidence of performance being provided from involvement with an organisation's MIS or part of an organisation's MIS

**Sources of evidence (these are examples of sources of evidence, but candidates and assessors may be able to identify other, appropriate sources)**

**Observed performance, eg**

- Evaluating an MIS

- Calculating benefits and costs

- Presenting suggestions

**Work produced by candidate, eg**

- Report of suggestions

- Rationale for suggestions

- Descriptions of costs and benefits

- Correspondence relating to the MIS

- Minutes from meetings

- Suggestions made

**Authenticated testimonies from relevant witnesses**

**Personal accounts of competence, eg**

- Report of performance

**Other sources of evidence to prove competence or knowledge and understanding where it is not apparent from performance, eg**

- Performance in simulation

- Responses to verbal questioning

## ASSESSMENT STRATEGY

This unit is assessed entirely by means of *devolved* assessment.

### Devolved Assessment (*more detail can be found in the Devolved Assessment Kit*)

Devolved assessment is a means of collecting evidence of your ability to carry out **practical activities** and to **operate effectively in the conditions of the workplace** to the standards required. Evidence may be collected at your place of work or at an Approved Assessment Centre by means of simulations of workplace activity, or by a combination of these methods.

If the Approved Assessment Centre is a **workplace,** you may be observed carrying out accounting activities as part of your normal work routine. You should collect documentary evidence of the work you have done, or contributed to, in an **accounting portfolio**. Evidence collected in a portfolio can be assessed in addition to observed performance or where it is not possible to assess by observation.

Where the Approved Assessment Centre is a **college or training organisation**, devolved assessment will be by means of a combination of the following.

(a) Documentary evidence of activities carried out at the workplace, collected by you in an **accounting portfolio**.

(b) Realistic **simulations** of workplace activities. These simulations may take the form of case studies and in-tray exercises and involve the use of primary documents and reference sources.

(c) **Projects and assignments** designed to assess the Standards of Competence.

If you are unable to provide workplace evidence you will be able to complete the assessment requirements by the alternative methods listed above.

# Part A
## Obtaining information

# Chapter 1    Information

---

## Chapter topic list

1    Information in this book

2    Why is information important?

3    Good information

4    Processing information

5    Management information systems: an introduction

---

## Learning objectives

On completion of this chapter you will be able to:

| | Performance criteria | Range statement |
|---|---|---|
| • Devise your own studying strategy for Unit 21 | | |
| • Check information for its accuracy and completeness | 21.1.4 | |
| • Appreciate the cost of obtaining information and the time taken | 21.1.6 | 21.1.3 |
| • Identify potential improvements to the MIS and consider them for their impact on the quality of the system and any interrelated systems | 21.3.1 | |
| • Make suggestions for changes supported by a clear rationale as to how they could improve the quality of the system | 21.3.2 | |
| • Assess and clearly state whether assumptions and judgements made are reliable | 21.3.3 | |
| • Accurately describe the benefits and costs of all changes | 21.3.4 | |
| • Present suggestions clearly and in a way which helps people to understand and act on them | 21.3.5 | |
| • *Understand some of the purposes and applications of MIS* | n/a | n/a |
| • *Identify types of information contained with the MIS* | n/a | n/a |
| • *Locate information sources* | n/a | n/a |

Italicised objectives are areas of knowledge and understanding underlying the elements of competence for Unit 21.

BPP PUBLISHING

## 1 INFORMATION IN THIS BOOK

1.1 This book is divided into three sections.

(a) **Part A** covers the topic of **information** in general: why it is important in organisations, where to find the information you need, and what to do with it once you've found it.

(b) **Part B** is mostly about **spreadsheets**, which are the tool most often used by accountants to handle information. It goes from very first principles to some quite complicated techniques. Part B also has an introduction to databases and database management systems, another type of information handling tool.

(c) **Part C** covers the remaining **knowledge and understanding** for Unit 21. It tells you about management information systems (MIS) and about the various components that make up a typical modern MIS: computer equipment and programs, networks and so on.

1.2 The emphasis in **Part C** is on understanding what makes up a system and understanding what else might be available to **improve** a system.

### Activity 1.1

You have just been appointed as accountant in an organisation that has a system made up of 10 stand-alone '486' PCs running Windows 95. The managing director has asked you to consider whether these PCs should be replaced with Pentium PCs in a network, running Windows 2000.

What do you recommend?

*Hint:* skim through Part C of this book.

### Working through this book

1.3 If you like you can start at Chapter 1 and work through each chapter in turn until you get to the end. However, don't feel you have to do this, just because the book is laid out in the way it is.

(a) If you want variety you may prefer to **switch between 'theory' and practical work**. If so, there is no reason why you should not work through the first chapter in Part A one week, the first chapter in Part B the next, and the first chapter in Part C the next.

(b) Perhaps you could do the theory when you are studying **at home**, away from a computer, and the practical material **at college**.

(c) Or you might prefer to work through all the **theory first** (Chapters 1 and 4 and all of Part C) and then all the **practical work** (Chapters 2 and 3 and all of Part B).

### Software needed to get the most out of this book

1.4 The illustrations in this book are mainly taken from Microsoft Windows 95/98, Microsoft Excel 97 and Microsoft Access 97.

1.5 If you have more recent versions this does not matter, although some of the **illustrations** in this book may look slightly **different** to what you see on your screen.

## Activity 1.2

Find out what software you are going to be using *now*. Ask your tutor at college, or someone at work, or see what you have available on your home PC.

## 2 WHY IS INFORMATION IMPORTANT?

2.1 Everything that we do **depends** upon information of some sort.

(a) If you want to phone somebody up you need to know their telephone number - information stored in your **memory**, or in an **address book**, or on a **letterhead**.

(b) If you want to see a film you need information about what cinemas are showing it and what time it starts. Perhaps you get this from a local **newspaper**.

(c) If you are simply getting dressed to go to work you use information about what is acceptable work-wear, what is clean and ironed in your wardrobe, what is currently fashionable, what you want others to think of you, what the weather is going to be like. Sources of this information may include **written rules** about standards of dress at work, **personal observation**, fashion **magazines**, the behaviour and dress of **others**, and the weather bulletin on **radio or TV**.

## Activity 1.3

Divide a sheet of paper into three columns headed 'Activity', 'Information used' and 'Sources'. List *five* different activities that you have done today or yesterday, and make a note of the information you used and where it came from. Try to include some work activities.

*Example*

| Activity | Information used | Sources |
|---|---|---|
| Food shopping | Current food stocks | Review of fridge, cupboards etc |
| | Personal likes and dislikes | Personal experience |
| | Advertisements | TV, newspaper, in-store display |
| | Recommendations | Friends and family |
| | Website | Website (on-line ordering) |

### Information requirements in organisations

2.2 A lot of the information that we use in everyday life can be stored in our own **memory**, because there is not a vast amount of it and because we use the same information repeatedly.

2.3 Business organisations, however, cannot rely on the memories of their employees. Take a sales team, for example.

(a) Individual members of the team may take orders from **hundreds** of different customers every day. Many of these customers will be new. All of them will have different needs. Nobody could possibly remember all the details of every order.

(b) **Different individuals** will deal with different aspects of a sales order. The person taking the order may know all the details, but unless these are recorded and **communicated** to the person who picks the product off the shelf, packs it and posts it, the customer will receive nothing.

(c) Individuals do not do the same job forever. Some leave to work for other organisations. Others are promoted to higher positions or moved to different roles. In either case they take everything in their memory with them. Businesses need **permanent records** to be left in place to allow a new person to carry on the job.

2.4 In other words, organisations need formal **systems** to manage information because of:

(a) The **volume** of information handled
(b) **Division of labour**
(c) The need for **continuity**

## Information management

2.5 Information must therefore be managed just like any other organisational resource such as people, machines or money. Information management entails the following tasks.

- Identifying current and future information **needs**

- Identifying information **sources**

- **Collecting** the information

- **Storing** the information

- Facilitating existing methods of **using** information

- Identifying **new ways** of using information

- Ensuring that information is **communicated** to those who need

- Ensuring information is **kept secure**

## Stakeholders

2.6 An organisation's information resources are very important to stakeholders. A **stakeholder** is a person or organisation that has an interest in an enterprise. Parties interested in an organisation's use of information are as follows.

(a) **Other businesses** for example, for common standards for exchanging data electronically.

(b) **Governments** (for example, data protection regulation).

(c) **Consumers** (for example in testing technology-based products such as teleshopping or Internet ordering).

(d) **Employees** and internal users (as information systems affect work practices).

## Competitors

2.7 An organisation can employ **three basic strategies** to obtain an advantage over competitors, and information resources are important to each of these strategies.

| Strategy | Comment |
|---|---|
| Overall cost leadership | This involves becoming the most cost efficient producer. Good **information management** can help **reduce costs,** for instance by cutting down clerical work or by better monitoring of raw materials usage to reduce wastage. |
| Product differentiation | This involves making a unique product or a product which appears different from your competitors', and hence more attractive. **Information** is used to **differentiate** some products. For instance customers may want itemised phone bills. They may appreciate glossy well-produced catalogues. They may like being informed about the progress of an order without having to phone up and nag. |
| Focus on a market niche. | A market niche is a group of consumers who have particular needs. **Information can be exploited,** for example, by using sales data to identify customer preferences and spot unusual trends. |

## 3    GOOD INFORMATION

### Distinction between data and information

3.1    First, some definitions: in normal everyday speech the terms **data** and **information** are used interchangeably. However, in the context of information systems the terms have distinct meanings.

> **KEY TERMS**
>
> **Data** is the raw material for data processing. Data relates to facts, events, and transactions and so forth.
>
> **Information** is data that has been processed in such a way as to be meaningful to the person who receives it.

### 3.2    EXAMPLE: DATA AND INFORMATION

A typical market research survey employs a number of researchers who request a sample of the public to answer a number of questions about a new product, say. Several hundred questionnaires may be completed. The questionnaires are input to a system. Once every questionnaire has been input, a number of processing operations are performed on the data.

| Operation | Example |
|---|---|
| Classifying | Male/Female; North/South/East/West |
| Sorting | Alphabetical order; descending numerical order |
| Calculating | Totals, averages and other statistics |
| Summarising | 'Most females in the north prefer X to Y' |

3.3    Individually, a completed questionnaire would not tell the company very much, only the views of one consumer. In this case, the individual questionnaires are **data**.

3.4    Once they have been processed, and analysed, however, the resulting report is **information**: the company will use it to inform its decisions regarding the new product. If the report revealed that consumers disliked the product, the company would scrap or alter it.

## Activity 1.4

Process the following data (by classifying, sorting and so on) to make information.

|  | Consumer 1 | Consumer 2 | Consumer 3 | Consumer 4 |
|---|---|---|---|---|
| Sex: | Male | Female | Female | Male |
| Age: | 24 | 53 | 19 | 49 |
| Rating for product X on a scale of 1 (dislike) to 5 (like very much) | 2 | 4 | 5 | 1 |

## Good information

3.5   The **quality of source data** affects the **value of information**. Information is worthless if the source data is flawed. If the researchers filled in questionnaires themselves, inventing the answers, then the conclusions drawn from the processed data would be wrong, and **poor decisions** would be made.

3.6   Different levels of management take different types of decision and often require different **types** of information. However, the information provided to them can be good or bad, and in fact information which is **good** information at one level can be **bad** information at another. We shall now go on to describe the factors which are important for the successful conversion of data to information.

## The qualities of good information

3.7   The qualities of good information are as follows.

(a)   It should be **relevant** for its purpose.

(b)   It should be **complete** for its purpose.

(c)   It should be sufficiently **accurate** for its purpose.

(d)   It should be **clear** to the user.

(e)   It should be prepared using **consistent** methods from one period to the next.

(f)   The user should be able to **rely** on it. The source should be **authoritative** or reputable.

(g)   It should be **communicated** to the right person, through the right channel of communication.

(h)   It should not be excessive - its **volume** should be manageable.

(i)   It should be **timely** - in other words communicated at the most appropriate time.

(j)   It should be provided at a **cost** which is less than the value of the benefits it provides.

### *Relevance*

3.8   Information must be relevant to the **purpose for which the user wants to use it**. Obviously, if someone wants to know the time there is no point in telling them the temperature as well. Sometimes it is not so straightforward, though. If somebody asks for information on, say, tea-drinking habits, they *may* also find information on coffee-drinking habits useful, depending on why they want the information.

**Activity 1.5**

How can you try to ensure that you get relevant information?

*Completeness*

3.9     An information user should have all the information he needs to do his job properly. If he does not have a **complete picture** of the situation, he might well make bad decisions.

3.10    Suppose that the debt collection section of a company is informed that a customer owes £10,000 and the debt is now 4 months old and overdue. The debt collection section therefore decides to write a **strongly-worded letter** to the customer asking for immediate payment. Now suppose that an important piece of information had been kept from the debt collection section, for example that the debt had already been paid or that the customer had negotiated special credit terms of 6 months. In these circumstances, sending a strongly-worded demand for payment would be a **mistake** and likely to create badwill that might harm the prospects of future sales to the customer.

*Accuracy*

3.11    Information should obviously be accurate because using incorrect information could have serious and damaging consequences. However, information should only be **accurate enough for its purpose** and there is no need to go into unnecessary detail for pointless accuracy.

(a)     **Supervisors and office workers** might need information that is accurate **to the nearest penny,** second or kilogram. For example, a cashier will do a bank reconciliation to the exact penny and purchase ledger staff will pay creditors exactly what they are owed. Much financial accounting information for day-to-day transactions must indicate amounts to the exact penny.

(b)     **Middle managers** might be satisfied with revenues and costs **rounded to the nearest £100 or £1,000,** since greater detail would serve no purpose. For example, in budgeting, revenue and cost figures are often rounded to the nearest £1,000 because trying to be more exact would usually only give a **spurious accuracy**.

(c)     **Senior managers** in a medium-sized to large organisation might be satisfied with figures to the **nearest ten thousand pounds,** or even hundred thousand or million pounds. Estimates to the nearest pound at this level of decision-making would be so inappropriate that they would seem ridiculous and so, oddly enough, perhaps undermine the user's confidence in the accuracy of estimates.

*Consistency*

3.12    An important quality of information in accounting is that it is prepared consistently. For instance if the June report of slow-paying debtors is prepared on the basis that 'slow-payers' are customers who have not paid within **60 days,** but the July report considers customers who have not paid within **30 days,** then it is not valid to compare the two reports. Often the problem is that different people take different approaches to the same basic problem.

*Clarity*

3.13  Information must be clear to the user. If the user **does not understand** it properly he **cannot use** it properly. Accounting information generally needs clear column headings and labels for each row, clear dates, clear totals and sub-totals, clear positives and negatives.

## DEVOLVED ASSESSMENT ALERT

Lack of features such as clear headings and sub-totals is likely to be a reason for failing your devolved assessment, too!

*Reliability*

3.14  Information must be **trusted** by the managers who are expected to use it.

    (a)  Information **sources** will not be used if they have proved **unreliable** in the past.

    (b)  Even if it has a good source, not all information is **certain**. Information relating to the **future** or to the **external environment** is uncertain. However, if the assumptions underlying it are clearly stated, this might make users more confident that they can rely on it.

*Communication*

3.15  Information that is needed might be **communicated to the wrong person**. In other words, it might be communicated to a person who does not have the authority to act on it, or who is not responsible for the matter and so does not see any need to act on it.

*Channel of communication*

3.16  There are occasions when using one particular **method of communication** will be better than others. For example, job vacancies should be announced in a **medium** where they will be brought to the attention of the people most likely to be interested. The channel of communication might be the company's in-house journal, a national or local newspaper, a professional magazine, a job centre or school careers office.

3.17  Some information is best communicated **informally** by telephone or word-of-mouth, whereas other information ought to be **formally** communicated in writing or figures.

*Volume and brevity*

3.18  There are physical and mental limitations to what a person can read, absorb and understand properly before taking action. An enormous mountain of information, even if it is all relevant, cannot be handled: it leads to **information overload**.

3.19  Usually this means that information should be **brief**, so long as this does not mean that it is incomplete or inaccurate.

*Timing*

3.20  Information which is not available until **after a decision** is made will be useful only for comparisons and longer-term control, and may serve no purpose even then.

3.21 Information prepared **too frequently** can be a serious disadvantage. If, for example, a decision is taken at a monthly meeting about a certain aspect of a company's operations, information to make the decision is only required once a month, and weekly reports would be a time-consuming waste of effort.

3.22 In a well designed information system, the frequency with which information is provided will depend on the needs of:

(a) The differing levels or status of persons to whom it is provided.
(b) The differing functional groups.

*Cost*

3.23 The **benefits** obtainable from the information must exceed the **costs** of acquiring it, and whenever management is trying to decide whether or not to produce information for a particular purpose (for example whether to computerise an operation or to build a financial planning model) a **cost/benefit study** ought to be made.

3.24 For information to have **value**, it must lead to a decision to take action which results in reducing costs, eliminating losses, increasing sales, better utilisation of resources, prevention of fraud (audit requirements) or providing management with information about the consequences of alternative courses of action.

3.25 The cost of **collecting** information does not give it value. An item of information which leads to an actual increase in profit of £90 is not worth having at all if it costs £100 to collect. The value of information lies in the **action taken** as a result of receiving it.

**Activity 1.6**

What questions might you ask in order to make an assessment of the value of information?

## ACCURATE

3.26 You might like to try a mnemonic to remember the points above. This does not fit the formal list in paragraph 3.7 exactly, but it should help you to remember the key issues.

Information should be:

**A** ccurate

**C** omplete

**C** ost-beneficial

**U** ser-targeted

**R** elevant

**A** uthoratative (in terms of source)

**T** imely

**E** asy to use

**DEVOLVED ASSESSMENT ALERT**

Use this mnemonic as a *checklist* whenever you are preparing your answers to devolved assessment tasks. For instance consider whether your answer is suitably *targeted* at the person you are meant to be providing it for. Have you included information that is not really *relevant?*. And so on.

## 4 PROCESSING INFORMATION

### Input-process-output

4.1 Data processing, whether it is done manually or by computer, follows a **cycle** of **input, process,** and **output**.

(a) Data is **collected**. There must be data to process and this may arise in the course of operations. There has to be a system or procedure for ensuring that all the data needed for processing is collected and made available for processing. The quality, accuracy and completeness of the data will affect the quality of information produced. We will look at sources of input information in the next chapter.

(b) Data is **processed** into information, perhaps by summarising it or classifying it and/or producing total figures. For example, a sales ledger system might be required to process data about goods despatched to satisfy customer orders so as to:

(i) Produce and send out invoices.

(ii) Record the invoices sent out in the customers' personal ledgers.

(iii) Produce a report of the total value of invoices sent out in the day/week etc.

(iv) Record the total value of invoices sent out in the debtors' control account in the nominal ledger.

(c) Files are **updated** to incorporate the processed data. Updating files means bringing them up to date to record current transactions. Updating the personal ledgers and the debtors control account are file updating activities to keep the sales ledger records up to date.

(d) Data is **communicated**. Continuing the example of the sales ledger system, the output consists of **invoices** and **statements,** and figures for sales totals and other management **reports**. Communication might involve the **routine** dissemination of information to users - for example regularly comparing actual and budgeted results each month. Communication also involves the provision of **non-routine** information to users on request, for example a list of all new customers in the Birmingham area, for a one-off marketing exercise.

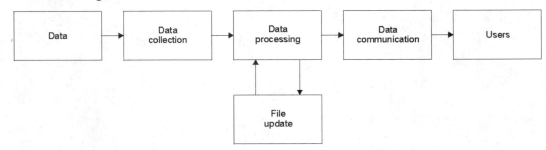

## Activity 1.7

You have two data processing tasks to do.

(a)  Write a letter replying to a customer's complaint.

(b)  Enter details of a purchase from a supplier into the accounting system.

What input do you need and where will you get it from? What does processing actually involve? What output will be generated?

## Data processing with a computer

4.2   In terms of **accounting** systems and databases, a data **file** is a collection of **records** with similar characteristics. Examples of data files include the sales ledger, the purchase ledger and the nominal ledger.

4.3   A **record** in a file consists of data relating to one logically definable unit of business information. A collection of similar records makes up a file. For example, the records for a sales ledger file consist of customer records (or 'customer accounts').

4.4   Records in files consist of **fields** of information. A field of information is an item of data relating to a record. For example, a customer record on the sales ledger file will include name, address, customer reference number, balance owing, and credit limit.

4.5   Within the file the records, or fields within records, may be of fixed or variable length.

(a)  **Fixed length records** will all contain the same number of characters and each record will have fields of fixed lengths too. Account numbers are fixed length records.

(b)  In a file with **variable length records**, each record may contain a different number of fields and corresponding fields may have a different number of characters. An example would be customer addresses.

## Key fields

4.6   Records on a file should contain at least one key field. This is an item of data within the record by which it can be **uniquely identified**. An example would be a unique **code** for each customer.

## Types of file

4.7   Files are conventionally classified into **transaction** files, and **master** files. These distinctions are particularly relevant in **batch** processing applications, described in a moment.

## Transaction files

4.8   A transaction file is a file containing records that relate to **individual transactions** that occur from day to day. For instance, as you know, when a company sells its goods day by day, the accounts staff might record the sales in a **sales day book,** which lists the sales made on that day, for which invoices have been issued. Eventually these transactions in the sales day book will be transferred ('**posted**') to the personal accounts of the individual customers in the sales ledger.

4.9   The sales day book entries are examples of **transaction records** in a **transactions file.**

13

## Master files

4.10 A master file in such a system is a file containing **reference data**, which is normally altered (updated) infrequently and also **cumulative transactions data**.

4.11 For example, in a purchase ledger system, the master file is the **purchase ledger** itself. This is a file consisting of:

    (a) **'Standing' reference data** for each supplier (supplier name and address, reference number, amount currently owed etc), and

    (b) **Transaction data for each supplier**, itemising purchases, purchase returns and payments to the supplier. This transaction data is built up over time.

## Old hat?

4.12 The terms transaction file and master file are not used much in modern processing, which prefers to talk in terms of **'databases'**. This is why we have not designated them as KEY TERMS.

## Data processing operations

4.13 Files are used to **store** data and information that will be needed again at some future time (eg next week, next month, next year) or to **provide** data or information for current use. The main types of data processing operations involving files are file **updating**, file **maintenance** and file enquiry or file **interrogation**

4.14 Computers, input, files and output can be brought together in a variety of different ways to provide a computer system. So how do we set about designing a computer system to do a particular job of data processing? Both manual and computer data processing can be divided into two broad types: **batch** processing and **real-time** processing.

## Batch processing

**KEY TERM**

**Batch processing** is the processing **as a group** of a number of transactions of a similar kind which have been entered over a period of time to a computer system.

4.15 For example the **payroll** work for salaried staff is done in one operation once a month. To help with organising the work, the payroll office might deal with **each department separately**, and do the salaries for department 1, then the salaries for department 2, and then department 3, and so on. If this is the case, then the batch processing would be carried out by dividing the transaction records into smaller batches eg **one batch per department**.

4.16 Transactions will be collected up over a period of time, perhaps in a transaction file, and will then be dealt with all at the same time. Some **delay** in processing the transactions must therefore be acceptable- ie in a payroll system, employees must agree to regular weekly or monthly payment.

4.17 Batch input allows for good **control** over the input data, because data can be grouped into **numbered batches**. The batches are dispatched for processing and processed in these batches, and printed output **listings** of the processed transactions are usually organised in **batch order**.

4.18 If any records go missing - for example get lost in transit - it is possible to locate the batch in which the missing record should belong. **Errors** in transaction records can be located more quickly by identifying its **batch number**. A check can be made to ensure that every batch of data sent off for processing is eventually received back from processing, so that entire batches of records do not go missing.

4.19 Bulk volume processing in batch mode allows the **processing** to be divided into separate stages, where each stage of processing is performed by a **separate computer programs**. (Long complex programs are more prone to error and take up more space in the CPU's internal store.)

## 4.20 EXAMPLE: BATCH PROCESSING OF SALES LEDGER APPLICATION

A company operates a computer based sales ledger. The main stages of processing are as follows.

*Step 1*    The **sales invoices** are prepared manually and one copy of each is retained. At the end of the day all the invoices are clipped together and a **batch control** slip is attached. The sales clerk allocates the **next unused batch number** in the batch control book. He or she enters the batch number on the control slip, together with the **total number of documents** and the **total value of the invoices**. The control details are also entered in the control book.

*Step 2*    The batch of invoices is then passed to the data processing department. The data control clerk records the batch as having been received.

*Step 3*    The invoice and control details are **encoded, verified, and input** to the computer. The first program is a **validation** program which performs various checks on the data and produces a listing of all valid invoices together with some **control totals**. It also produces **rejection listings** (exception reports).

*Step 4*    The data control clerk **reconciles the totals** on the batch control slip with the totals for valid and rejected data.

*Step 5*    The **ledger update program** is run to process the invoice data.

*Step 6*    Among the information, the computer prints out the **total of invoices** posted to the ledger and the data control clerk again **reconciles** this to the batch totals, before despatching all the output documents to the sales department.

*Step 7*    All **rejected** transaction records are carefully **investigated** and followed up, usually to be re-input with the next processing run.

## Real-time processing

**KEY TERM**

**Real-time processing** is the continual receiving and rapid processing of data so as to be able, more or less instantly, to feed back the results of that input to the source of the data.

4.21    Real-time processing uses an 'on-line' computer system (see below) to interrogate or update files as requested rather than batching such requests together for subsequent processing.

4.22    Transactions for processing might arise infrequently, and so it would take too long to build up a batch for processing at the same time. Instead, each transaction would be **processed individually** as it arises.

4.23    Alternatively, the information user might want to process a transaction **immediately**, and would not be prepared to accept the delay implicit in batch processing.

4.24    As each transaction is processed immediately on input (rather than in batches), all the batch processing stages of input, validation of data, updating and output are applied to that one transaction by a **single computer program**.

4.25    Real time systems are practically the **norm** in modern business. **Examples** include the following.

(a)    As a sale is made in a department store or a supermarket and details are keyed in on the **point of sale terminal**, the stock records are updated in real-time. Any customer wishing to buy a product can be informed as to whether the item is available or not (if not, an alternative might be offered).

Although the stock files are maintained in real time, other files (for example sales analysis or debtors) may be batch processed at a later stage with the accumulated sales details (for example stored on magnetic tape) from each point of sale terminal.

(b)    In **banking and credit card** systems whereby customer details are maintained in a real-time environment. There can be immediate access to customer balances, credit position etc and authorisation for withdrawals (or use of a credit card).

(c)    **Travel agents, airlines** and **theatre ticket** agencies all have to use real-time systems. Once a hotel room, plane seat or theatre seat is booked up everybody on the system must know about it immediately so that they do not sell the same holiday or seat to two (or more) different customers.

## On-line

4.26    On-line refers to a machine which is under the **direct control** of the principal **central processor** for that hardware configuration. A terminal is said to be on-line when it communicates interactively with the central processor. Modern computers such as PCs are **on-line by definition** (they have their own processor), and likewise PCs in a network have permanent access to the server, but terminals in mainframe-based systems may not be on-line.

### Activity 1.8

What are the implications, in processing terms, of the fact that some supermarkets are now open 24 hours a day?

## 5    MANAGEMENT INFORMATION SYSTEMS: AN INTRODUCTION

5.1    Organisations need not only information, but an information system to provide it.

## KEY TERMS

The word system is very hard to define because it is used in lots of different contexts: the underground system, the long-ball system, the blood system, and so on. Possibly the most useful idea to remember is that 'system' implies connections.

If you want a more formal definition of a system, one that applies to a business system is as follows.

> A collection of people, machines and methods organised to accomplish a set of specific functions.

A management information system (MIS) can be defined as:

> 'A system to convert data from internal and external sources into information and to communicate that information, in an appropriate form, to managers at all levels in all functions to enable them to make timely and effective decisions for planning, directing and controlling the activities for which they are responsible.'

> (Lucey, *Management Information Systems*)

5.2 A management information system, therefore, is simply a system that presents information to management!

5.3 However, this is not the only function of an organisation's information systems. A number of tasks might be performed at the same time.

(a) Initiating transactions (for example automatically making a purchase order if stock levels are below a specified amount).

(b) Recording transactions as they occur (for example a sale is input to the sales ledger system).

(c) Processing data.

(d) Producing reports.

(e) Responding to enquiries.

5.4 Ideally an MIS would satisfy **all the information needs of all levels of management**. Whether this is possible in practice will depend on the nature and type of information provided.

(a) An MIS is usually **good** at providing **regular formal information** gleaned from normal commercial data. For example, an MIS relating to sales could provide managers with highly accurate information on the following.

    (i) Gross profit margins of particular products.
    (ii) Success to date in particular markets.
    (iii) Credit control information (aged debtors and payments against old balances).

(b) It may be **less good** at presenting information which is relatively **unpredictable**, or **informal**, or **unstructured**. So, for example, an MIS could not provide completely accurate information about the impact on your organisation of a terrorist attack on the building next door or about precisely how much extra effort members of staff will make if they are given a 5% pay rise.

## More on information systems

5.5    We will discuss management information systems in more detail in Chapter 9 of this book.

---

### Key learning points

- Everything that we do, either in our personal life or as part of the activities of work, depends on information.

- Organisations need formal systems to manage information, because of the volume of information handled, the division of labour and the need for continuity. Information management entails identifying information needs and sources, collecting information, storing it, using it, and protecting it.

- Information is also important to the relationships organisations have with stakeholders and competitors.

- An important distinction can be made between data and information.

    ○ Data is the complete range of raw facts and measurements which exist within and outside an organisation.

    ○ Information is data which has been processed in some way so as to make it meaningful to the person who receives it.

- Good information has a number of specific qualities, for which ACCURATE is a useful mnemonic.

- Data processing follows a cycle of input-process-output. Output data is stored in files until it becomes the input data for the next session of processing.

- Computer files (in accounting terms) generally consist of records, which are themselves made up of fields and characters. Records are identified by key fields. Files are conventionally referred to as transaction files or master files for the purposes of processing.

- In batch processing, input transactions are collected in batches, before processing. It is suitable for large volumes of routine data, for which output is not required instantly. Batch processing helps with the control of data.

- In real-time processing, transactions are processed as they arise. It is suitable for processing data that arises irregularly and for which output is required very quickly. Real-time processing is becoming the norm.

- A management information system converts data from internal and external sources into information and communicates the information, in an appropriate form, to managers at all levels in all functions. It does so to help them make timely and effective decisions for planning, directing and controlling the activities that they are responsible for.

---

### Quick quiz

1    Why do organisations need formal information systems?

2    Name three 'stakeholders'.

3    Define information.

4    List six qualities of good information.

5    Why are management reports often prepared inconsistently from month to month?

6    What is information overload?

7    What is a record?

8    What is a field?

9    Is a word processing file a collection of records and fields?

10    What is the difference between batch processing and real-time processing?

18

11     A management information system (MIS) is only intended to be used by *senior* managers who are in charge of lots of junior staff. Is this True or False?

## Answers to quick quiz

1     Because of the volume of information handled, the division of tasks, and the need for continuity.

2     Suppliers, customers, employees, governments.

3     Information is data that has been processed in such a way as to be meaningful to the person who receives it.

4     Relevance, completeness, accuracy, clarity, consistency, reliability, timeliness, cost-effectiveness. It should be properly communicated and supplied in the appropriate volume.

5     Because different people take different approaches to the same basic problem.

6     More information than the recipient can read, absorb and understand properly.

7     Data relating to one logically definable unit of business information, for example a customer record.

8     An item of data relating to a record, for example a customer's name, or line 1 of their address.

9     It *could* be, but generally it is a document such as a letter, not obviously split up into records and fields (or at least not from the point of view of the creator and user of the file).

10    Batch processing saves up inputs over a period of time and then processes them as a group in one go. Real-time processing processes inputs one at a time, more or less instantaneously.

11    *False!* A MIS should provide information to help **everyone** to manage whatever it is they are responsible for, no matter how junior they are in the organisational hierarchy.

## Answers to activities

## Answer 1.1

This is the type of question that Part C of this book is intended to help you to answer. Have a skim read through it now and see if you can find out what the difference between a '486' PC and a 'Pentium' is.

## Answer 1.3

Here is another suggestion.

| Activity | Information used | Sources |
|---|---|---|
| Dealing with query from customer about products | Customer's requirements Product details | Phone call or letter Catalogues, computer databases, colleagues, own knowledge |

## Answer 1.4

*Summary*     Women like the product more than men. Younger people rate it slightly more highly than older people.

To arrive at this summary you need to **classify** by sex and age and **sort** according to the rating given. You could have included average scores. This is not really necessary with only four samples, but would be useful if you had 400.

| | |
|---|---|
| Average rating by women | 4.5 |
| Average rating by men | 1.5 |
| Average rating by under 30s | 3 |
| Average rating by over 30s | 3 |

## Answer 1.5

It is usually helpful to explain **why** you want a piece of information: 'I am doing some research into hot-drinks in connection with a new product we are developing' should get a different answer to 'I am trying to find out what type of tea is most popular'.

The same applies if you are asked to **provide** information: make sure you have an idea of why it is wanted. If you are still not sure, provide the precise information asked for, but add a note saying 'information is also available on X, if relevant'.

## Answer 1.6

(a) What information is provided?
(b) What is it used for?
(c) Who uses it?
(d) How often is it used?
(e) Does the frequency with which it is used coincide with the frequency with which it is provided?
(f) What is achieved by using it?
(g) What other relevant information is available which could be used instead?

An assessment of the value of information can be derived in this way, and the cost of obtaining it should then be compared against this value. On the basis of this comparison, it can be decided whether certain items of information are worth having.

## Answer 1.7

(a) | *Inputs* | *Source(s)* |
|---|---|
| Customer's name and address | Customer's letter or your company's own database of customer details |
| Customer account number | Sales ledger |
| Complaint details | Customer's letter or a note of a telephone call |
| Response to the complaint | Procedures manuals, explanations from colleagues, your knowledge of what went wrong |
| Date | Calendar |
| Letter layout | Procedures manuals |

*Processing* involves assembling the above information into letter format, typing up the letter, printing it out, checking and correcting it and possibly getting it approved by someone else.

*Output* is the final checked and approved letter, with a signature added, and an envelope.

(b) | *Inputs* | *Source(s)* |
|---|---|
| Supplier details | Supplier's invoice; details in your own accounting system |
| Transaction details | Supplier's invoice; your own order form |

*Processing* involves typing words and figures into the appropriate parts of the system and updating the records.

*Output* may be in the form of a day book listing and/or a list of suppliers' balances.

## Answer 1.8

If the supermarket wants all its records to be permanently up-to-date it will have to use a *real-time* system, whereas before it could have used a batch system and updated its records overnight.

In practice the system would probably operate in real-time locally (in each branch) and a mini-computer in each branch would send its transaction details to a central mainframe perhaps once per day: a combination of real-time and batch processing.

Most small modern systems (eg Sage Line 50) can operate either in batch mode or in real-time.

# Chapter 2    Obtaining information

## Chapter topic list

1    Information in files

2    Computer filing with Windows: a practical example

3    Computer searches

## Learning objectives

On completion of this chapter you will be able to:

| | Performance criteria | Range statement |
|---|---|---|
| • Locate the required information correctly within the MIS structure | 21.1.1 | 21.1.1, 21.1.2 |
| • Seek advice where there are difficulties in obtaining the required information | 21.1.2 | 21.1.3 |
| • Obtain additional authorisation for sensitive or confidential information in accordance with the organisation's security regulations | 21.1.3 | |
| • Check information for its accuracy and completeness | 21.1.4 | |
| • Store information in a format which helps others to access and use it | 21.1.5 | |
| • Keep confidential information secure from unauthorised people | 21.1.6 | |
| • Appreciate the cost of obtaining information and the time taken | 21.1.6 | 21.1.3 |
| • Identify potential improvements to the MIS and consider them for their impact on the quality of the system and any interrelated systems | 21.3.1 | |
| • Make suggestions for changes supported by a clear rationale as to how they could improve the quality of the system | 21.3.2 | |
| • *Understand the relationship between MIS and other IT applications* | n/a | n/a |
| • *Take advantage of interfaces between software packages* | n/a | n/a |
| • *Identify types of information contained with the MIS* | n/a | n/a |
| • *Locate information sources* | n/a | n/a |

Italicised objectives are areas of knowledge and understanding underlying the elements of competence for Unit 21.

 BPP
PUBLISHING

## 1 INFORMATION IN FILES

1.1 Much of the information used in organisations is obtained from its own internal records and these are kept in **files**.

1.2 Apart from records about, say, sales and purchases or stock, there are huge amounts of other information passing through organisations.

- Letters, memos
- Notes of phone calls and meetings
- Reports
- Procedures manuals
- Advertising material
- Mailing lists
- Important/routine addresses and phone numbers

1.3 Many of these items are created by **individuals** such as you, and you therefore have the responsibility for maintaining your own filing system.

1.4 General principles of **good filing practice** are covered in the Foundation topic *Business Knowledge*. The following paragraphs contain reminders of some key points.

### The features of a storage and retrieval system

1.5 Whatever form documents and recorded information take, if they are to be of any use, they must be kept in a suitable way so that:

(a) **Authorised** people (and **only** authorised people) can get to the information they require **quickly and easily.**

(b) Information can be **added to, updated** and **deleted** as necessary.

(c) Information is **safe** from fire, loss or handling damage for as long as it is required.

(d) **Accessibility, flexibility** and **security** are achieved as **cheaply** as possible.

### Computer filing

1.6 Most of the principles of **manual** storage and retrieval of information also apply in a **computerised** context: it is important to develop **good habits**. The computer does take some of the hard work out of such tasks, as we shall see, but it is still important to be careful, especially about keeping copies (back-ups) of your work.

*File names and extensions*

1.7 When you open a new file in a computer system the system will **automatically** give it a **working title** like 'book2.xls'. This means, quite simply, 'workbook number two', the second workbook that you have created during that working session.

1.8 The **three letters after the full stop** (the file **extension**) are to tell the computer what **type** of document the file is: in this case a spreadsheet workbook created with Microsoft Excel software. Here are some other common file extensions.

| Extension | File type |
|---|---|
| *123* | A spreadsheet created in a more **recent** version of **Lotus 1-2-3** |
| *apr* | A database created with **Lotus Approach** |
| *cdr, bmp, gif, jpg, wmf* | Various formats for **graphics** files (there are many others) |
| *dbf* | A database created with **dBaseIV** or Microsoft **FoxPro** |
| *doc* | A word processing document created in **Microsoft Word** |
| *exe* | A **program** of any type |
| *htm (or html)* | An **Internet** file |
| *lwp* | A word processing document created in **Lotus Word Pro** |
| *mdb* | A database created with **Microsoft Access** |
| *sam* | A word processing document created in **Lotus AmiPro** |
| *txt* | A simple text file created with (say) **Microsoft Notepad** |
| *wk4 (wk1, wk2, wk3)* | A spreadsheet, created in an **older** version of **Lotus 1-2-3** |
| *wpf* | A word processing document created in **Corel WordPerfect** |
| *zip* | A **compressed** file |

1.9 Names like 'book2' do not tell you what the file relates to. Also your collection of files will quickly become **unmanageable** unless you have a clearer method of identifying files.

1.10 You should follow the system of file-naming **prescribed by your organisation** if there is one. If not, try to give the file a name that would **enable someone else to find it** quickly, say, when you are on holiday.

1.11 Modern computer systems have sophisticated search facilities that allow you, for example, to build a list of all files of a certain type created or saved on a certain day (or from a certain day onwards) and to **preview** them without actually having to open each file individually. We shall look at some of these later in this chapter.

1.12 The number of ways you can search for a document depends on the information you give the computer when you save it. When you create a file in Microsoft Excel, for example, you are given the option to enter not just the file name, but also 'properties' such as **subject, author name** and **keywords**. (You might pick as a keyword a particular product name, say.) The computer will then be able to search for all files that fit any of these criteria: all files with the subject 'computers', for example, or all files that include the keyword 'product alpha'.

## DEVOLVED ASSESSMENT

You may be asked to recommend changes to improve a filing system that is described in the Devolved Assessment data.

You should, of course, follow good practice when creating your own files in answer to devolved assessment tasks. It would be a shame to fail because your hard work could not be located on disk!

## 2   COMPUTER FILING WITH WINDOWS: A PRACTICAL EXAMPLE

2.1 In this section we are gong to work through a **practical example** of file creation, amendment, organisation, deletion, recovery and so on. If this is something that you do all the time you can probably skip this section.

2.2 We shall be using a simple word processing application called **Notepad**. This is available as a utility in the Windows operating system.

2.3 We are assuming, from this point onwards, that **you are sitting at a computer** and following through all the things we describe, hands-on.

## Creating a file

2.4    Find the application called **Notepad** on your PC by clicking on **Start,** moving your mouse pointer up the menu to **Programs,** then across to **Accessories,** then down to **Notepad.**

Click or double-click on the icon or menu item to open up the Notepad program.

2.5    Simply by opening Notepad you have taken the first step in creating a file: this one is presently **Untitled** as you can see from the title bar of the Notepad window.

(a)    If you **do nothing** other than close down Notepad again nothing will have been created and so **no file will be saved.** Try this.

(b)    If you **type anything** at all, Windows will help you to **save your file.** Open up Notepad again and type in your name. Then, without making any active attempt to save the file, try to close down Notepad.

2.6    This time, instead of the window disappearing instantly you get a message.

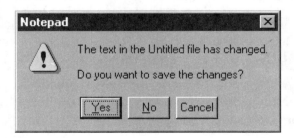

2.7　If you click on **Yes** when you get the above message a new window will appear.

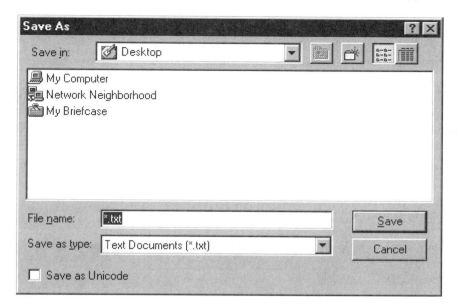

## Saving files

2.8　The **Save As** window is common to all Windows-based applications that have a facility for storing data in a file.

2.9　When the window first appears, the **File Name** box is highlighted. Don't type anything here yet. You can move from section to section of this window by pressing the **Tab** key. (This is the key above the Caps Lock key on your keyboard.) Each time you press this, a different item in the window becomes highlighted (or is surrounded by a dotted line). Try this out.

2.10　You can move back and forward between consecutive items if you wish. To move back you hold down the **shift** key – the one you would use for capital letters – and press **Tab**. Try this out too.

---

### Activity 2.1

**Everything** in Section 2 of this chapter is an Activity for you to do. The whole point is that you are sitting at a computer following through these instructions and experimenting for yourself.

---

2.11　We shall now conduct you on a **guided tour** of the Save As window. We do so in the order in which you should **make decisions** or check things, not in the order of Tabbing.

*Save in*

2.12　The **Save in** box will probably say **Desktop** when the Save As window first appears (alternatively it might say **Windows**). However you can find out all the possible locations in which you can save a file by clicking on the **arrow** at the right of the box. A list of the 'drives' available will then appear and you can select the appropriate drive by clicking on its name.

2.13　This is like deciding what **filing cabinet** you are going to keep a paper file in. When we talked about storage of information we mentioned that computers put their data into different 'drives'. There is a hard drive, where the data is written onto a disk which is part of the computer equipment itself, and there is a 'floppy drive', where the data is written onto a disk that can be removed and carried about. The hard drive is usually called **drive C**, and the floppy drive is **drive A**. There can be more drives than this – there may well be on your systems at work and at college – but this is the usual set-up for a stand-alone PC.

2.14 Typically a college is likely to prefer you to not to take up hard disk space, and you may therefore be told to save anything you want to save to the A drive on a floppy disk that is exclusively yours. If you have a floppy disk, put it in the A Drive and select the A Drive option in the Drive menu. When you click on A in the **Save in** menu you will see the details in the box below it change automatically. When you have done this change the drive back to C.

2.15 The result will be something like this.

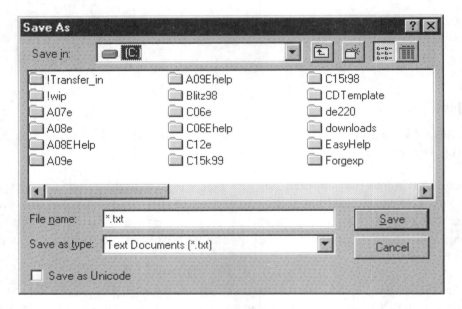

2.16 **Double-click** on any of the yellow folder like icons and the details in the box will change. For instance this is what happens if you double-click on the Windows directory folder.

2.17 The Windows directory is now the one named in the Save in box and you have the option of 'drilling down' to further **sub-folders** of the Windows folder, as listed in the box below, just by clicking on their yellow folder. Notice that the folder currently open (Windows) actually *looks* like an open folder: 📂.

2.18 If you were going to save your file you would search for an appropriate folder and sub-folder by **double-clicking** in this way until you found one. You might have a directory on your floppy disk in the A drive called 'Notes', say. To save the file there, you would need to **double-click** in the Save in and directories boxes until the Save in box said **Notes**. Remember: in Windows 95/98 it is the **Save in box that specifies where the file will be saved,** not any highlighting anywhere else on the screen.

*Save as Type*

2.19 As a rule you won't need to do anything with this box. It specifies the **format** in which the file will be saved, and it will always suggest the usual format for documents created in the application you are using. For the Notepad application the usual format is as a **Text (.txt)** file.

2.20 If you did want to change the format that Windows suggests here, you would click on the down arrow to see if data created by this application can be saved in another format. In the case of Notepad there are no real alternatives, but there *are* other possibilities in, for example, the Sage Line 50 accounting package, Microsoft Excel and Microsoft Word.

2.21 The file type shown in the Save as Type box determines what files are listed in the box above it. In our example, there are no txt files in the Windows sub-directory, so there is nothing listed in this box.

*File Name*

2.22 When the window first appears this box is highlighted. It shows an asterisk, a full stop and three letters. In place of the asterisk you must choose a name for your file. You are not actually going to save it on this occasion (unless you want to), but you should know the basic rules for file names.

(a) In versions of Windows earlier than Windows 95, file names must be **no more than eight characters long**. Characters can include numbers and letters but *not spaces*. This no longer applies but many people still regard it as a good discipline, forcing users to devise meaningful and well-organised coding systems.

(b) As we have already seen, the name should be something sensible that will help to identify the file if you want to find it again at a later date. Try to **avoid the names of applications** in your file names: for example you *can* call a file 'WINDOW01', but the system already has hundreds of files with names something like this so it could easily get lost.

(c) If you want to create a series of files of the same type and on similar subjects, it is helpful to **number them sequentially**. If you are sure there are going to be fewer than ten such files you can use 1, 2, 3, etc, but it is usually better to be safe and use 01, 02, 03, because the Windows filing system sorts numbers in order of the first digit. If you numbered some files 1, 2, 3, etc up to 10 they would be sorted in the order 1, 10, 2, 3, etc.

(d) The format of the file must always be reflected in the file name by the file **extension**. However, there is **no need for you to type an extension yourself**. You can just type something like **NOTES01** in the file name box and Windows will automatically give the extension specified in the File Type box, in this case **.txt**.

27  **BPP**
PUBLISHING

2.23 If there were existing files listed in the box you would be able to just click on one of them and it would appear in the File name box where you could edit it. This can sometimes save a bit of typing. If you try to save one file with the name of another, however, it will **overwrite** the old file. Windows warns you about this and gives you a chance to change your mind.

---

### Activity 2.2

You are going to save ten files, and your organisation stipulates that file names must be no more than eight characters long. Devise a file name for each file incorporating part of your name, or your initials, or something that identifies you, and consecutive numbers.

---

## Closing down

2.24 This concludes our guided tour of the Save As window. You can just click on the **Cancel** button, unless you want to save your Notepad file. (Save it onto a blank floppy disk if so. Pick an appropriate name and save it in the main A directory. Click on OK when you are ready to save the file. Unless there is *already* a file with the name you chose on the disk, the file will be saved.)

## Explorer

2.25 One of the most important applications in Windows 95/98 is one called **Explorer** (and an alternative called '**My Computer**'). Amongst other things, these applications allow you to see what directories and files are on a disk, make copies of files and disks, move files around from one directory to another, look at the files in a directory in date order, or name order, or file type order, and to search for files.

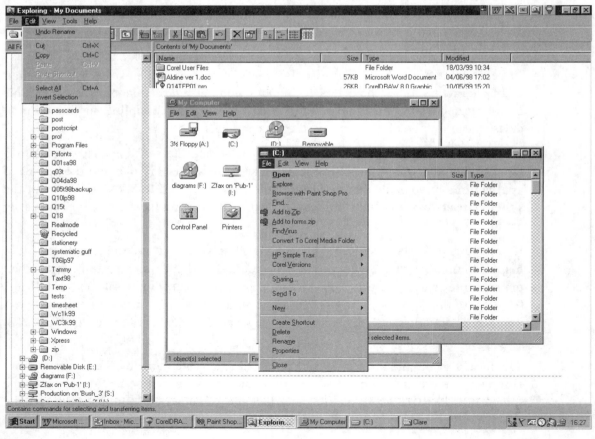

2.26   The next table sets out the main things that you are likely to want to do with Explorer (or My Computer).

From within Windows Explorer .....

---

### File management in Windows 95/98

---

*Creating a new main folder*

Click on **C:\,** then click on **File** at the top of the screen, then on **New,** then on **Folder.** A new folder appears in the right hand part of the screen. Type in a suitable name for the folder and press Return. Try this out and call your folder 000000 (six noughts). Press **F5** to 'refresh' the screen.

*Creating a sub-folder*

Click on your new folder (000000) in the left hand side of the screen and then click on **File ... New** etc as above. Call your sub-folder 000001.

*Looking at folder contents*

In the left hand part of the screen, double-click on any folder. Sub-folders and/or files within the main folder will appear in the right-hand part of the screen. Double-click on sub-folders to see their contents.

*Looking at folder size/free space*

Select a folder and look at the information displayed at the bottom of the screen.

*Opening a file*

Select the file and then double click on it. The relevant package (eg Notepad) will open your file.

*Moving a file*

Find the file in Explorer and click on it once. Place the mouse pointer over it and, holding down the left mouse button drag the file to the appropriate folder in the left-hand window.

*Copying a file*

Find the file in Explorer and click on it once. Click the **right** mouse button and choose **Copy** from the menu that appears. Select the location for the copy by clicking in the left hand side of the screen. Click the right mouse button and choose **Paste.**

*Deleting a file*

Select the file as before and **right click**. Choose **Delete** from the menu.

*Copying a file onto floppy disk*

Put a floppy disk with plenty of free space on it into the disk drive. Select your file and right click. Select **SendTo** and then **3½ Floppy (A)** from the menu.

*Sorting files*

Click on **View** at the top of the screen and choose **Details.** Select a folder. In the right hand part of the screen click on the headings **Name, Size, Type** and **Modified** successively to arrange and re-arrange the files in different orders. Click again to revert to the previous order.

*Recovering a file*

Close Explorer and find an icon labelled **Recycle Bin** on your desktop screen. Click on this to open it and locate the file you want to recover from the list that appears. Click on the file in question, then on **File** at the top of the screen. Choose the **Restore** option.

---

**BPP** PUBLISHING

### Activity 2.3

It is possible that your system at work or college prevents you from using Explorer/My Computer. This will be to stop people messing about with files and directories that do not belong to them. If so get a tutor or authorised colleague to demonstrate the following tasks to you. Otherwise, do them yourself.

(a)  Create two new main directories or folders using Explorer/My Computer. Call one 000000 and the other AAAAAA.

(b)  Create sub-folders in each of your new directories, called 000001 and AAAAA1 respectively.

(c)  Create four files using Notepad. Just type in a few words or numbers: the contents are not important. Use the following names and save the files to the directories/folders shown.

| Name | Location |
|------|----------|
| Myfile01 | C:\000000 |
| Myfile02 | C:\000000\000001 |
| Myfile03 | C:\AAAAAA |
| Myfile04 | C:\AAAAAA\AAAAA1 |

(d)  Close Notepad. In Explorer/My Computer , locate the files you have created and open each one in turn from Explorer/My Computer.

(e)  Move Myfile01 from C:\000000 into C:\AAAAA1.

(f)  Copy Myfile03 into C:\000000\000001.

(g)  Move all of your files into C:\000000. Delete all of the other directories/folders you have created.

(h)  Arrange the files in C:\000000 as follows.

   (i)    Name order
   (ii)   Date order
   (iii)  Size order
   (iv)   Type order

(i)  Copy C:\000000 onto a floppy disk.

(j)  Delete C:\000000.

(k)  Use the File menu to *rename* the A:\000000 directory as BPPCh02.

## Deleting files

2.27  It is very easy to delete files from a disk or to write over files that you meant to save in their existing form. Most systems will ask you to **confirm** that you want to delete a file if you give the computer this instruction.

## 3    COMPUTER SEARCHES

3.1  Most modern software packages offer a means of finding files and also finding information within them.

### Windows 95/98

3.2  In Windows 95/98 there is a searching tool that you can use by clicking on **Start**, then on **Find** then on **Files or Folders**. A dialogue box similar to the following will appear.

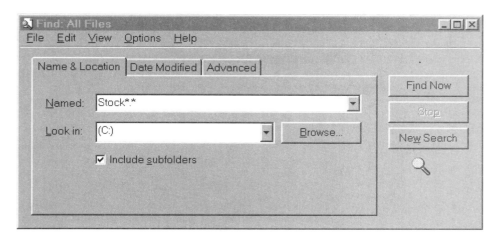

3.3 The extra tabs give you the options of entering a variety of criteria, depending what you can remember about the file you are searching for.

(a) If you know the file was worked on in the last week say, you can limit your search to files **created or modified** in the last seven days.

(b) At the very least you should be able to have a stab at a word that the text is likely to contain, or perhaps guess roughly how large the file is, in which case you can use the **Advanced** option.

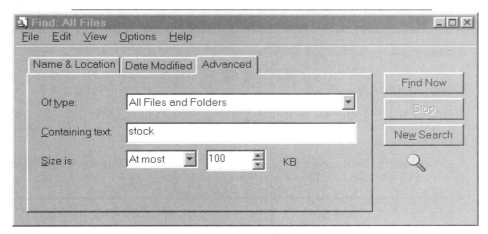

3.4 You can specify just **one criterion or several**. For instance you might simply search for any files containing the text 'stock', or you might restrict your search to Excel files created in the last 2 days containing the text 'stock'.

3.5 The result of a search like this would be a **list of files** that fit the criteria you specify. You can then **sort the list** in a variety of ways: by file name, by sub-directory name, by size, by type or by date of last update. You can also **open** any file directly from the list by double-clicking on its name. If you right click on a file's name there are other options such as **deleting** the file, **renaming** it or **copying** it.

## Searching for files when a package is open

3.6 Some software packages offer similar file searching options to the Windows 95/98 Find facility via their **Open** dialogue box. Here, for instance, are some of the opportunities you get in Excel 97 if you click on **File ... Open** and then on **Advanced**. (In earlier versions you click on a **Find File ...** button.)

**BPP**
PUBLISHING

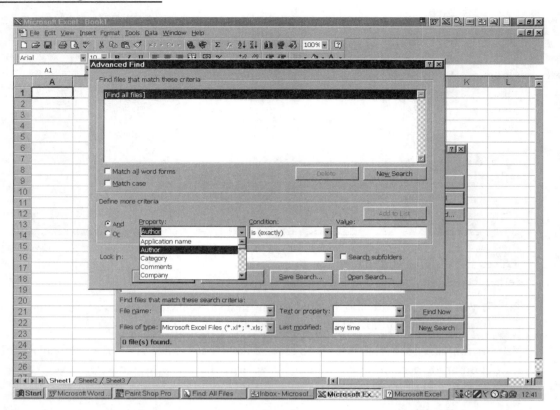

## Activity 2.4

Find 10 files on your PCs hard disk using Explorer/My Computer and note down the name, type, sub-folder, date modified and so on.

Now pretend that you do not have the full information and prove that you can use your PC's Find facility to locate these files using the various methods described above (eg just use a few letters of the name, or file type, or date last modified).

If you are working with others in class you could prepare a list that does not include all the essential details and then swap PCs with another person and challenge each other to find the files you want.

## Searching for information within files

3.7 The easiest way to find a specific piece of information in many packages is to use the **Find** option, usually on the **Edit** menu. Here is what you get if you do this in Excel.

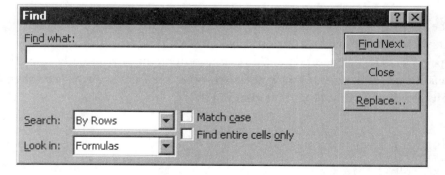

3.8 Here you type in the characters (words or figures or both, including spaces if necessary) that you want to find and click on Find Next. The **first** cell containing the characters you specified is **found and highlighted**. The find dialogue remains open and you have the option to find the next example if there are more than one in your file and the first one is not the one you want.

3.9     Obviously this is a bit **laborious** if there are hundreds of cells containing the characters you specified. In this case you either need to define your Find characters in another way or use one of the more **advanced data sorting** facilities offered by Excel. We shall be looking at these in Chapter 8.

3.10    An **accounting package** may have its own special search facilities. For instance Sage Line 50 software includes Sage's **Finder** button and **Criteria** button.

3.11    Sage software provides a **'look-up' tool** whenever users reach a point where they may have to **do a search** for the entry they need to make. At the right of the data entry field there is a button with a picture of a magnifying glass on it. This is called the **Finder** button, shown below next to the A/C box.

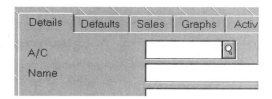

3.12    When the user is confronted with an empty box with the Finder button it will be because they have to choose one code from many possibilities. In Sage the user clicks on the button (or presses **function key F4** if they prefer to use the keyboard). Another alternative if they know, say, that the code begins with G, is to type G and then press Enter. In each case the user is then presented with a new little window as shown below.

3.13    If the account code wanted can be seen in the list immediately the user just clicks on it to highlight it and then clicks on OK or presses Enter to transfer the code into the A/C box. If not, the user can use the scroll bar or the cursor keys to **scroll up or down until they see the code they want,** then click on it and click OK.

3.14    The **Criteria** button at the foot of the Finder window offers a further means of searching for accounts that fulfil certain conditions. Let's say, for the sake of argument, that you are in charge of the purchase ledger for accounts of suppliers who come from Watford (unlikely for small companies but a quite possible way of organising work for a larger company). If you were to click on the Criteria button you would see the following screen.

*BPP* PUBLISHING

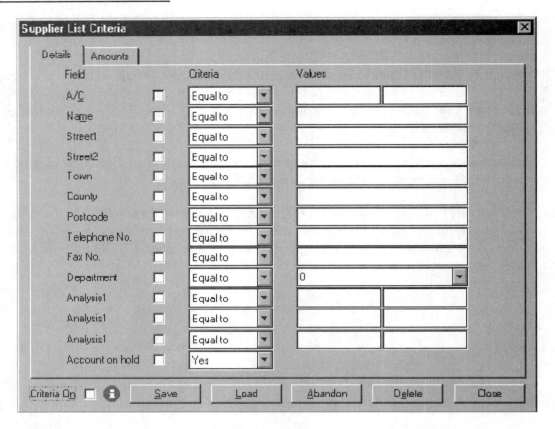

3.15 Click in the white square to the right of Town and an **x** will appear in it. Click in the 'Values' column alongside **Town** (after the 'equals' box) and a cursor will appear. Type 'Watford' and click in the white square labelled Criteria On. Then click on **Close**. You will be returned to a Finder list window which shows only the names of those suppliers whose records indicate that they are located in Watford.

3.16 As you can see from the Supplier List Criteria screen there are numerous other options. For example the **Amounts** index tab gives you another screen on which you could choose all accounts with a balance of *more than* £1,000. When you click on the arrow to the right of 'equals' a menu of options drops down.

| | |
|---|---|
| Equals | = |
| not equal to | != |
| less than | < |
| Greater than | > |
| Between | <> |

3.17 The problem with this is that you need to have a pretty good idea of the criteria that you want to use to limit the number of accounts that you are given to choose from. If, for example, you have a vague idea that the post code for Watford begins with W it is no use just typing W in the postcode box. You can, however, type 'W*': as we saw earlier, the asterisk is a '**wildcard**', standing for any other character or characters. (The question mark wildcard does not work in Sage.)

3.18 Besides making life easier for users to find their way around the system the criteria button is an example of a tool that takes advantage of the fact that the accounting records are a **searchable database** of useful information about customers. For instance an analysis of customers by **post-code** could be very useful for marketing purposes.

## Key learning points

- Most information used in organisations is kept in its own internal records.

- The key principles of internal record management are accessibility, flexibility and security. If these principles are followed it should always be easy to obtain the internal information you need.

- Files are generally created, amended and saved from within an application package such as a spreadsheet.

- Once this is done, an important tool in Windows 95/98 is the Explorer utility. This allows you to view what files you have stored on disks in any drive, create new directories for them, copy them, move them from one place to another, delete them, rename them or just open them up again for further amendment.

- Modern computer systems offer sophisticated searching capabilities, both for finding files in the first place and for obtaining information within them.

  o One example is the **Find** option on the Windows 95/98 **Start** menu, which allows searches by name, location, file type, file content, date, and file size.

  o Another example is the **Find** option that appears on the **Edit** menu of almost all software packages.

- Wildcard characters such as * and ? are very useful if you are not sure of the full details of the information you are searching for.

## Quick quiz

1. What do the file extensions 'htm' , 'txt' and 'exe' tell you about files?

2. How many drives and directories (or folders) are there on a typical PC?

3. List eight things that can be done using Explorer.

4. What should be shown on a disk label?

5. You have a word processed file which is 50 pages long. You know it contains a section with a title something like 'forthcoming legislation'. What is the best way of locating this information?

6. Explain the difference between the wildcard character ' * ' and the wildcard character '?'.

7. What does the symbol '>' mean?

## Answers to quick quiz

1. An 'htm' (or 'html') extension is used for Internet files. The extension 'txt' signifies that the file is a simple text file: it should be open-able by practically any text editor. The extension 'exe' is used for programs

2. There are usually three drives - the hard disk or C Drive, the floppy disk drive (A) and the (CD-ROM drive (D). There can be any number of folders or directories.

3. Create new folders or directories, look at folder contents, look at the size of files and folders, open files, move files from one place to another, copy files, delete files, copy files onto floppy disks, sort files, recover deleted files.

4. Contents, date, name/initials, place in set.

5. You could use your word processing package's **Edit ... Find** facility and type in the single word 'legislation', since there are not likely to be more than a few uses of this word. If it turns out that there are lots of examples of 'legislation' you could abandon your first search, return to the beginning of the document and try another option, such as '19??' (since the section in question is fairly likely to contain a date). Good searching requires you to think in an informed way about what the subject matter is likely to contain.

6. The asterisk can stand for *any number* of unknown letters or digits. The question mark stands for *one* unknown character or digit only.

7. 'Greater than'. For example, you might try to obtain information about debtors' balances that have been outstanding for a period '> 90 days'.

## Answers to activities_____

### Answer 2.1

There is no answer here, but we want to stress again that you will not get the full benefit from this book unless you try out all the things that it suggests for yourself, **hands-on**, on a computer.

### Answer 2.2_____

Here are some suggestions for people named Steve Morris, John Smith and Jamie Lee Curtis.

| | | |
|---|---|---|
| SteveM01 | SmithJ01 | JLC_001 |
| SteveM02 | SmithJ02 | JLC_002 |
| SteveM03 | SmithJ03 | JLC_003 |
| etc | etc | etc |

Notice the use of the underscore ( _ ) character in JLC_001. You can't have spaces in Windows 3.x.

### Answer 2.3_____

This is a practical activity. Try it as often as necessary on your own and then do it with your assessor watching and ask your assessor to sign below to certify that you can do it. You can use this as evidence towards your Devolved Assessment.

*The student named below has successfully completed Activity 2.3 in the BPP Interactive Text* Information Technology (5/99).

*Student Name (and ID no. etc):* _____

*Assessor name, position etc:* _____

*Date:* _____

### Answer 2.4_____

Again this is a practical activity, this time partly with the intention that you have the courage to explore what files there are on the PC you are using (ie what information you could obtain from it). And again, if you can do it successfully you should be able to use it as evidence towards your Devolved Assessment, so get the person in charge to sign you off.

*The student named below has successfully completed Activity 2.4 in the BPP Interactive Text* Information Technology (5/99).

*Student Name (and ID no. etc):* _____

*Assessor name, position etc:* _____

*Date:* _____

# Chapter 3 The Internet and other external sources

---

## Chapter topic list

1 External information

2 The Internet

3 Getting on to the Internet

4 Searching the Internet

5 Refining your search

6 Other Internet features

7 A practical exercise

---

## Learning objectives

On completion of this chapter you will be able to:

| | Performance criteria | Range statement |
|---|---|---|
| • Locate the required information correctly within the MIS structure | 21.1.1 | 21.1.1, 21.1.2 |
| • Seek advice where there are difficulties in obtaining the required information | 21.1.2 | 21.1.3 |
| • Obtain additional authorisation for sensitive or confidential information in accordance with the organisation's security regulations | 21.1.3 | |
| • Check information for its accuracy and completeness | 21.1.4 | |
| • Store information in a format which helps others to access and use it | 21.1.5 | |
| • Keep confidential information secure from unauthorised people | 21.1.6 | |
| • Appreciate the cost of obtaining information and the time taken | 21.1.6 | 21.1.3 |
| • Identify potential improvements to the MIS and consider them for their impact on the quality of the system and any interrelated systems | 21.3.1 | |
| • Make suggestions for changes supported by a clear rationale as to how they could improve the quality of the system | 21.3.2 | |
| • *Understand the relationship between MIS and other IT applications* | n/a | n/a |
| • *Take advantage of interfaces between software packages* | n/a | n/a |
| • *Identify types of information contained with the MIS* | n/a | n/a |
| • *Locate information sources* | n/a | n/a |

Italicised objectives are areas of knowledge and understanding underlying the elements of competence for Unit 21.

BPP PUBLISHING

## 1 EXTERNAL INFORMATION

1.1 There are many occasions when it is necessary to search outside the organisation's own records to find the information you need. In the first section of this chapter we **remind** you of the main **sources of external information**. In the rest of the chapter we go on to describe what is fast becoming the most important source of external information-the **Internet**.

### Organisations providing information

1.2 Organisations that provide information include the following.

(a) **Newspaper and magazine publishers**. Information is gathered from reporters, writers and photographers and goes to anyone who buys the resulting printed material. You ought to be aware of the many 'trade journals' that are available. You probably know about *Accounting Technician* for members and students of the AAT. Most industries are served by several such journals and magazines: your organisation probably subscribes to those that are appropriate to its sphere of operations.

(b) **Publishers of books,** for example BPP Publishing. Information comes from authors, artists or photographers, usually as hard copy, but possibly now on computer disk: it is passed on in printed form, occasionally supported by video and/or audio tapes. The government, and its various departments and agencies, especially the Office for National Statistics, also publish information through HMSO (Her Majesty's Stationery Office).

(c) **News agencies** such as Reuters or Associated Press. These organisations collect information from reporters and eye witnesses of events and sell it to newspapers and others on a commission basis.

(d) **Radio and television** stations. These often provide information about local services and activities, gathered from local organisations, as well as about the content of their own programmes. The information may be provided over a general radio or television transmission, or in answer to a particular telephoned or written enquiry.

(e) **Ceefax and Teletext** are the services provided by the BBC and ITV companies respectively (in the UK). They can be consulted by any owner of an appropriately adapted television set. The user simply calls up a 'page' on his screen, having found the relevant page number on an index. You can sometimes see 'Pages from Ceefax' demonstrating the service in between scheduled TV programmes. Information offered includes weather reports, news, sports results, recipes and other items of general interest.

(f) **Viewdata** is the term used for systems which provide information through the telephone network to a telephone or computer terminal screen. **Prestel** is the viewdata service set up by British Telecom to rival Ceefax and Teletext: a very large bank of information has been gathered from organisations such as the Office for National Statistics, newspapers and the British Library. Prestel also offers facilities for transmitting information back down the line as a means of communicating with other users. (Prestel is now available as in Internet service.)

(g) **British Telecom**. This organisation not only provides an information-transmitting service, but also provides information to users, such as the telephone's 'speaking clock' giving the time, and 'dial-a-?' recorded messages for weather information, sports results and so on.

Also, don't forget the **phone book** and '**Yellow Pages**' or '**Business Pages**' as a source of information about businesses. It is well worth getting to know your way about the introductory pages of the phone book. The introduction to the London Business Pages, for example, gives addresses and so on of trade associations, institutes and advisory bodies and brief descriptions of what they do, details of government offices, business libraries and foreign embassies, contacts for EC information, details of corporate entertainment venues and trade exhibitions, and travel information.

(h) **Advice or information bureaux**. These provide enquirers with information in their own particular field, in the form of advice or counselling from staff, or information leaflets and fact sheets. Examples include: a local Citizens Advice Bureau; a Consumer Standards Office; Offices of Fair Trading; Law Centres; arts or sports publicity organisations providing information on events to those who wish to participate; Tourist Information bureaux and so on.

(i) There are also private and public **Consultancies** of all sorts. Accounting firms have management consultancy divisions, insurance brokers offer various services - even your local GP can be seen in this light. Most organisations will have an information 'desk' which can be contacted for details of a non-confidential nature about themselves or their field: the tourism department of an Embassy is a good source of information about a country or city and so is a helpful travel agent.

(j) **Libraries and information services**. These usually buy in information in the form of books, audio/visual material, microfilm and so on, store it, and allow access subject to a number of conditions. They may be part of the free public library system, or associated with a learned or professional institution or other body, in which case access may be limited to elected members, specially recommended users, or suitably qualified persons.

(k) The **Internet** described in detail later in this chapter.

## Reference books

1.3 Reference books - which can be found in a local **public library,** or in your **college or office library** - are a rich (secondary) source of any item of information you might want to find.

(a) **Dictionaries**. There are various dictionaries available, some general, others covering specific subjects. They list words and phrases in alphabetical order, with a brief entry explaining them. You will be familiar with language dictionaries from schooldays. Make sure you always have access to a good dictionary of the English language and don't be ashamed to use it whenever you are in doubt about the spelling or the meaning of a word (or its pronunciation if you have to use it in a phone call). If you deal regularly with solicitors, have a dictionary of legal terms available; if you deal with chemical engineers or geophysicists a dictionary of science is handy.

(b) A **thesaurus** (*Roget's Thesaurus* is the best known) lists words categorised by topic, with indexed and cross-referenced synonyms. Have a browse through one, starting with the index at the back. They are very useful at helping you find the right word for a particular situation, but only if you know the meaning of the word to start with.

(c) There are also guides to **letter-writing,** English **usage,** titles and **forms of address, pronunciation** of names and so on which might be helpful to deal with specific problems.

(d) **Atlases and road maps** often contain more than the usual maps indicating physical geography. They may provide, in map or text form, information on land usage, population distribution, social trends, industry, commerce and politics. Check the date of publication of any atlas or road map you consult, as they do go out of date quickly.

*BPP* PUBLISHING

(e) **Timetables and itineraries**. Rail guides, air travel guides and various timetables will be important sources of information for you if you are making travel arrangements. Timetables are usually in tabular form, reading across and downwards, and make use of many different symbols to keep them as free of 'clutter' as possible. The symbols are explained in a 'key' on the table. Try and master the reading and interpretation of timetables: it is worth knowing how to draw one up for yourself or someone else.

(f) **Almanacs** are general sources of factual information; *Whitaker's Almanac* is useful for political and economic statistics. Consult the index, and make sure you are using an up-to-date edition.

(g) There may be **specific reference works** which you use in your particular line of work. In a tax department of a firm of accountants, for example, you would use published lists of dividends and fixed interest payments for publicly quoted securities. If you worked for a car dealer your 'bible' might be *Glass's Guide* which lists second-hand values for vehicles by make and model.

(h) Larger organisations usually have one or several **procedures manuals** which tell you how to go about your job and quite possibly specify how different sorts of information should be stored and retrieved.

## 2 THE INTERNET

2.1 The **Internet** is the name given to the technology that allows any computer with a telecommunications link to exchange information with any other suitably equipped computer.

2.2 Terms such as 'the net', 'the information superhighway', 'cyberspace', and the 'World Wide Web (www)' are used fairly interchangeably, although technically the '**web**' is what makes the 'net' **user-friendly** .

### DEVOLVED ASSESSMENT ALERT

Surprisingly, the Internet is not **specifically** mentioned as an area that you should know about.

It could, however, very reasonably be assumed to be included under a number of headings. In any case, we make no apologies for including extensive material and exercises on the subject: it is a key part of your future.

### Websites

2.3 As you are no doubt aware, most companies of any size now have a '**site**' on the Net. A site is a collection of screens providing information in multimedia form (text, graphics and often sound and video), any of which can be viewed simply by clicking the appropriate button, word or image on the screen.

### Internet Service Providers (ISPs)

2.4 Connection is made via an Internet Service Provider (ISP). The user is registered as an Internet subscriber and may pay a small monthly fee together with **local telephone call charges**, even if contacting other users on the other side of the world. Many ISPs now provide free Internet access, by which they mean no subscription fee. (Telephone charges still apply.) The United Kingdom ISP market is becoming more competitive. It is expected that 'free' Internet telephone calls will be available late 2000, although a flat rate subscription charge would be payable.

2.5 ISPs such as **America Online (AOL)** and **Freeserve** provide their own services in addition to Internet access and e-mail capability. For instance, AOL also offers a main menu with options such as Life, Travel, Entertainment, Sport, Kids. It is rather like a quality Sunday newspaper, except that the sections are updated at least daily, and it provides **much larger information resources** (one option in the travel section, for instance, is to find out about train and plane timetables throughout the UK or worldwide).

2.6 Other ISPs in the UK include **Demon, Virgin** and **CompuServe**.

## Browsers and search engines

2.7 Most people use the Net through interface programs called **browsers** that make it more user-friendly and accessible. The most popular and best known is **Microsoft Internet Explorer**.

2.8 Surfing the Net is done using a **search engine** such as Yahoo!, Excite or AltaVista. These guide users to destinations throughout the world: the user simply types in a word or phrase like 'beer' to find a list of thousands of websites that contain something connected with beer.

2.9 Companies like Yahoo! make money by **selling advertising space**. For instance if you type in 'beer', an advertisement for Miller Genuine Draft will appear, as well as your list of beer-related sites. If you click on the advertisement you are taken to the advertiser's website, perhaps just to be told more about the product, perhaps to be favourably influenced by the entertainment provided by the site, or perhaps even to buy some of the product.

2.10 The advertiser may get you to **register your interest** in the product so that you can be directly targeted in future. At the very least advertisers know exactly how many people have viewed their message and how many were interested enough in it to click on it to find out more.

2.11 An Internet development that has created a good deal of excitement is known as **'push' technology**, because instead of having to search for individual pieces of information the user simply accesses a **'channel'** and watches as information is sent down the line.

(a) For instance **PointCast** has attracted more than 1m regular viewers to its Web news channel, which automatically delivers content from newspapers and magazines at regular intervals. It retrieves information from selected sources on the net and presents it, with advertisements, headlines and stock prices, on a screen saver.

(b) **Marimba** allows users to download a 'tuner' and select content channels, very much like switching channels on TV.

2.12 Browser software packages provide a facility to **store Internet addresses** so that users can access frequently-visited sites without having to go through a long search process. Thus in business use, workers who **regularly need up-to-date information**, say, on stock market movements, or new government legislation, or the activities of a competitor, can simply click on the appropriate entry in a personal 'favourites' directory and be taken straight to the relevant site.

## Activity 3.1

Do you have access to the Internet? If not, and it cannot be arranged through work or college, start seeking out a friend or colleague with a suitably equipped PC who will let you get hands-on experience of using the Internet.

What **hardware** do you think you need to get onto the Internet?

Do you think it is used much in **business**, or is it just an alternative form of entertainment?

## 3 GETTING ON TO THE INTERNET

3.1 It should be no more difficult to get on to the Internet, once your computer is set up to do so, than it is to start up any other program. You will probably find an **icon** on your computer for a browser such as Netscape Navigator or an Internet Service Provider such as America Online (AOL), CompuServe or The Microsoft Network. Check with your tutor or system administrator which icon you should use, if necessary.

3.2 All you have to do to get started is **double-click** on the icon.

3.3 Depending how your system is set up you may then need to supply a **password**. Your tutor or system administrator will advise you about this too.

3.4 Once you have got past the password stage what will appear on the screen depends on **which ISP** you are using, and **what browser** is used within that ISP.

### America Online

3.5 The initial America Online **Welcome** screen has three main options: an option to pick up any **e-mail** you may have received, or to write new e-mail; a Member Services option, to check information about **your account** and so on; and a **Main Menu** option.

3.6 The Main Menu option displays another screen with a variety of further choices such as Chat, Entertainment, Sport, Computing and so on. The option you want is the one that says **Internet**. Clicking on this and then on the **Search** option will give you the following screen.

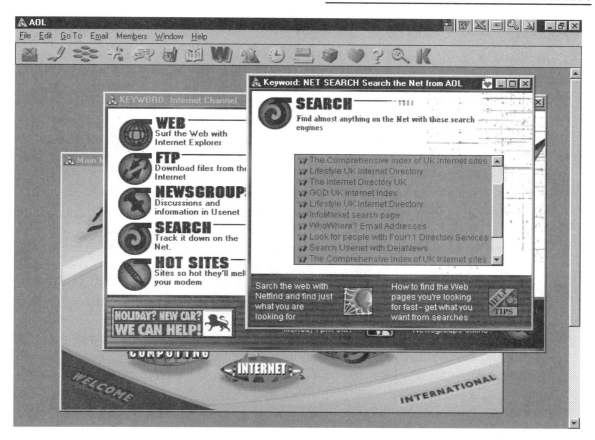

## 4    SEARCHING THE INTERNET

**Choosing a search engine**

4.1    The first thing you have to do is choose which **search engine** to use to find the information you are looking for. Your have a choice from a number of engines such as:

- Excite
- AltaVista
- WebCrawler
- Lycos
- Yahoo!
- AskJeeves

4.2    **AltaVista** is generally reckoned to find the **most** Internet pages connected with a search, but many of them will be completely irrelevant to what you are really looking for. **WebCrawler** finds far **fewer** pages, but all of them have been **checked** by WebCrawler's reviewers to see whether they are worthwhile and valid. Other search engines fall somewhere in between these two extremes.

4.3    There is **no limitation** on which search engine you can use: they are all freely available. (Most will display advertising material – this is how they make a large part of their money - but you are under no obligation to look at the adverts.) Therefore, if you do not like the results given by, say, Alta Vista, you can simply **perform another search**, using, say, Excite or Yahoo!.

### Specifying what to search for

4.4   All search engines work in a similar way. The illustrations that follow show the opening ('home') pages of AltaVista and Excite. To perform a search, you simply click in an empty box (if the cursor isn't flashing there already), type in a word or words and click on **Search**.

4.5   In the examples below, the user is searching for the words **financial information**.

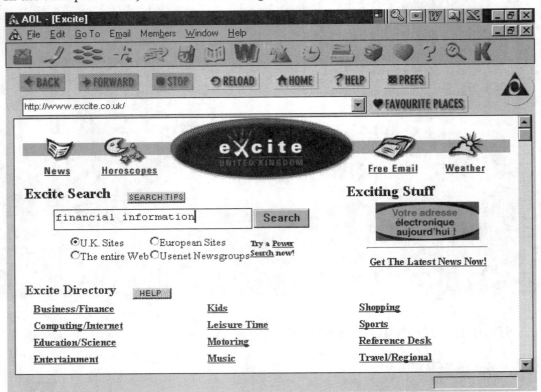

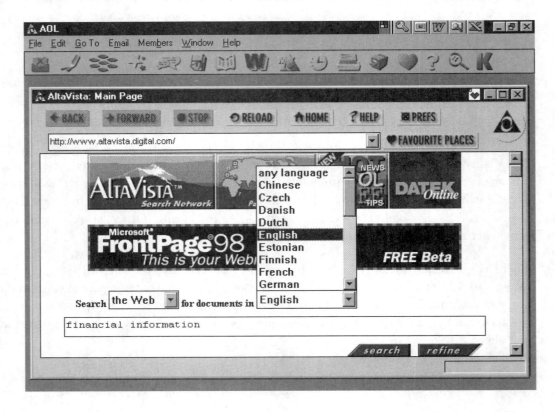

4.6 The next illustration shows what happens (with AltaVista) a few moments later when the search has been carried out.

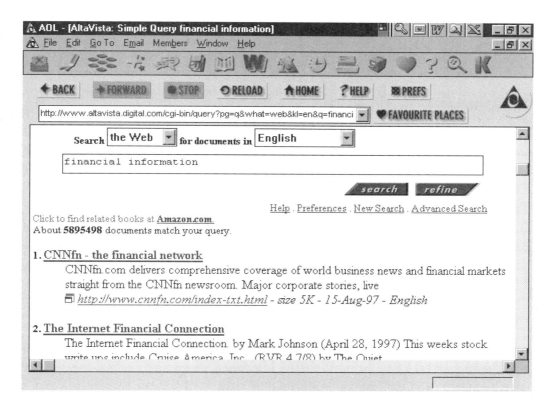

4.7 As you can see, the first line of the results tells you that AltaVista has found **nearly six million 'pages'** or documents that you could consult on your chosen subject! In a moment we shall look at ways of cutting down the number of pages that are found, but for now we shall assume that the very first item listed happens to be exactly the thing you are looking for.

4.8 To **consult** the first page found all you have to do is **click on the words underlined** next to the number 1. The browser will then connect your computer to a computer somewhere else in the world that holds the chosen information and 'download' the pages you are after. This is what will appear on your screen after a few moments if you choose the first item.

**The quality of information**

4.9 Remember, when you are looking at information on the Internet it is **not necessarily good information**, just because it is 'published'. **Anybody** can put any information they like on any subject on the Internet. If you do a search for open heart surgery, one of the pages you are directed to may be a page of tasteless jokes about heart attacks. Another may appear to be serious and reputable but actually be written by someone with no medical knowledge or training at all.

4.10 The **known reliability** of the source is the key matter. CNN, for instance is a respected worldwide news organisation. If the next page you consult is called 'Fred's Financial Advice page', you should not necessarily trust the information that it provides.

## 5 REFINING YOUR SEARCH

5.1 AltaVista came up with nearly 6 million plus pages that were relevant to a search for **financial information.** It would probably take you years to read through them all (by which time a further 6 million or so new pages may be available!). The search has clearly not been as discriminating as you might have liked.

5.2 The main reason why it found so many pages is because it searched for and found **all** pages that contain the word **financial** and all pages that contain the word **information,** not just pages with the specific phrase 'financial information'. As well as pages containing both words together, in the order you specified, the search engine will have found pages that include phrases such as 'financial considerations are irrelevant when this matter is considered from the point of view of morality', or 'information for cat owners'; or 'this page does **not** contain any information for people who are having financial difficulties'.

5.3 To be fair, pages are listed in **batches** of ten or twenty, which makes the results more manageable, and the results are sorted by **relevance,** so the first few results will have 100% matches for both 'financial' and 'information', and are likely to contain a lot of material relevant to your enquiry. Even so, three quarters of a million pages is overwhelming, and you could easily waste a lot of time looking through documents that are not quite what you were after.

5.4 There are a number of things you can do to avoid this and limit the number of pages you have to look through.

### Be specific

5.5 Firstly you should try to **be as specific as you possibly can** about what it is you are looking for. In the search we have just illustrated, if you were interested in small businesses it would have been more sensible to type 'small business' than 'financial information'. Better still, you could include all four words in your search, if that were what you wanted.

### Activity 3.2

Which of these search entries do you think would produce the fewest number of pages?

(a)  'financial' or 'banks'
(b)  'banana' or 'fruit'
(c)  'accounts' or 'money'

### Restrict the search area

5.6 Search engines generally have options to restrict the number of sites searched, for instance to **UK sites** only, or to **English language** sites only.

## More Like This

5.7 Some search engines display the words <u>More Like This</u> next to each entry. If you happened to spot a title that said <u>Financial information for small businesses</u> you could get a new list of sites specifically on that subject simply by clicking on More Like This.

## Links within websites

5.8 Many organisations provide **links** to other people's websites within their own web pages. A link is simply an underlined word or phrase that you can click on to navigate your way around the Internet. For example, the CNNfn small business page might conclude with a link such as <u>UK Govt small business support agencies</u>. Just clicking on this would take you directly to the relevant page of a UK government site.

5.9 Some people actually publish pages full of useful links. For instance if you search for 'Spice Girls' one of the first entries you see will be this:

**Spice Girls Links** [<u>More Like This</u>]
***URL***: http://www.flevel.co.uk/pasty/burgess/spice/links.html
***Summary:*** Email me with more links (This doesn`t go to Emma! ): Email Burgess, Note: This doesn`t go to Emma!

## 'Advanced' search techniques

5.10 In many (though **not all**) search engines you can use **symbols** and/or what are known as **Boolean operators** to help the search engine to understand what it should and should not look for. These so-called 'advanced' searching techniques aren't actually particularly advanced, and they are **extremely useful**.

(a) *Plus signs (+)*

If you put a plus sign (+) directly in front of a word (with no space) this tells the search engine that the word **must** be present in all the pages that are found. So if you type **+financial+information**, you will only get pages that contain both words (though not necessarily together or in this order). You can use as many pluses and words as you like.

Instead of + you can use the word AND (in capitals, with spaces) if you prefer: **financial AND information**

(b) *Minus signs (-)*

As you might expect, the - sign works in the opposite way to +. If you put a minus sign directly in front of a word the search engine will **ignore** any documents that contain that word. So, if you type **+financial+information-bank** you will avoid all the pages that have references to banking issues.

However clever you are at using the minus sign you are still likely to get some information that you are not interested in. You simply would not think of typing, say, **+financial+information-cat,** for example, because it would not occur to you that there happened to be a page of advice for penniless cat-owners.

Instead of - you can use the words AND NOT (in capitals, with spaces) if you prefer: **financial AND information AND NOT banks**

(c) *Quotation marks (")*

To find **only** pages that contain the words **financial information** together in that order, you enclose them in quotation marks: **"financial information"**. This is very useful so long as your phrase is only two or three words long (eg "spice girls").

(d) *OR*

If there is a chance that pages relevant to you will use alternative words you can use OR to make the search engine look for pages that contain at least one of the alternatives: for instance **financial OR economic**

(e) *Brackets*

Brackets can be used to devise more complicated searches. For instance **financial AND (information OR advice)** will find pages containing the word 'financial' and either the word 'information' or the word 'advice'

---

## Activity 3.3

What sort of undesirable results do you think you would get if you simply typed in:

**spice girls**

as your search criteria?

---

## Going directly to an Internet address (URLs)

5.11 You may know the precise address of an Internet site that you wish to visit, perhaps because you have seen or heard it on TV or radio or read it in a newspaper or magazine. Typically the format is something like '**http://www.bbc.co.uk**'.

5.12 The address is called a **URL** or **Uniform Resource Locator**

| URL element | Explanation |
|---|---|
| *http://* | **Hypertext Transfer Protocol**, the protocol (see Chapter 11) used on the World-Wide Web for the exchange of documents produced in what is known as 'hypertext mark-up language' (HTML). A common alternative to **http** is **ftp** (file transfer protocol) explained briefly later. The two forward slashes after the colon introduce a 'host name' such as **www**. |
| *www* | This stands for **World Wide Web**. As noted before, to put it simply the web (via its use of HTML), is what makes the Internet user-friendly |
| *bbc* | This is the **domain name** of the organisation or individual whose site is located at this URL |
| *co* | This part of the URL indicates the type of organisation concerned. The Internet actually spans many different physical networks around the world including commercial (**com** or **co**), university (**ac** or **edu**) and other research networks (**org, net**), military (**mil**) networks, and government (**gov**) networks. |
| *uk* | As you can probably guess, this indicates that the organisation is located in the UK |

5.13 If you have the URL there is **no need to do a search**: you can go straight to the page you want.

(a) If you are using **America Online** you simply click on the W symbol at the top of the screen. A dialogue box drops down with the first (http://) part of the URL already filled in for you.

You simply type in the rest of the address. For instance if you type in **www.ft.com** after the http:// you will be taken to the site of the *Financial Times*.

(b) In **CompuServe** you click on the **Go** button to get the dialogue box.

(c) If you are using **Netscape Navigator** you can use the **File** menu and then pick **Open Location**. Again you get a box to type the address into.

(d) If you are using **Microsoft Explorer**, simply use the **File** menu and then the **Open** option.

---

**Activity 3.4**

Here are some other useful URLs. Visit and explore as many of these as you can. You will need to type **http://** in front of the **www** if your browser does not do this for you.

www.microsoft.com

www.bbc.co.uk

www.amazon.com

www.streetmap.co.uk

www.dictionary.com

www.ft.com

www.the trainline.com

www.open.gov.uk

www.aat.co.uk

---

## Favourites

5.14 If you locate a site that is particularly useful to you, you do not have to do a fresh search for it every time you want to consult it again. ISPs and browers usually have an option for users to compile and save their list of '**favourites**' for future use.

## Channels

5.15 As mentioned earlier, ISPs offer lots of options besides pure Internet searching and usually offer a series of options on their main screen such as Entertainment, Computing, Business and so on.

5.16 If you choose one of these options (or channels) instead of going straight for an Internet search, you will find that a lot of very useful information has been assembled for you already in an easy to find form.

5.17 Here, for example, are the choices you get when you click on **Business** on the AOL main menu screen.

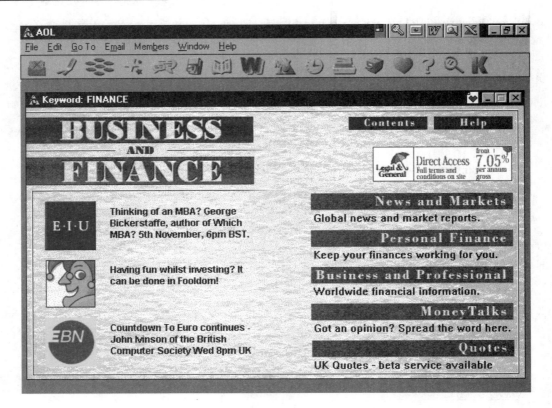

### Keywords/Go

5.18 Keywords (AOL) or Go words (CompuServe) make it possible to jump around an ISPs services quickly, without having to remember exactly how you got to a certain place. Even if you don't know that a certain word is a keyword it is worth trying it out. For instance, in AOL if you click on the K symbol and type in the word 'wine' , after a few moments AOL makes a connection and takes you to keyword FOOD with sections about cooking, eating out and drink. If you type in government you are taken to the POLITICS keyword area.

## 6 OTHER INTERNET FEATURES

### Downloading files

6.1 We have talked about downloading **pages** from the Internet in the preceding sections. This simply means that the page can be viewed via your ISP and browser while you are connected via telecommunications to that specific page. A **permanent copy is not stored** on **your** computer unless you **actively choose** to save a copy (by selecting **File** and then **Save**, just like in any other Windows program).

6.2 Downloading a **file** (or a set of files) is a different procedure. It does make a **permanent** copy of the file or files in question on your computer.

6.3 You might want to download files, for instance, if they contain **trial versions** of a new software product, or a graphic **demonstration** of a new product that will not run happily within a browser program.

### After you've downloaded a file

6.4 If you download a piece of software what you typically get is a file in a compressed form that **extracts automatically** to a **temporary directory** on your hard drive when you double-click on the file that has downloaded (which might be called something like newprog.exe.) The next step is to look at the contents of the temporary directory where there will now be a number of files. There will usually be one called **Read.Me**, which contains further instructions for installing the program, and one called **setup.exe**, which is the program that actually performs the installation process.

## Viewers

6.5    Some organisations (such as the UK Government) publish lengthy documents in a format that allows the content to be opened and viewed (after downloading it, saving it, and disconnecting from the Internet) by a **viewer** such as **Adobe Acrobat Reader..** This allows documents to be read as they were intended to be read, including all formatting such as bold headings, paragraph spacing and so on, and all diagrams. This is preferable to the HTML format of most Internet documents, which **does not preserve** all of these formatting features when pasted into word processing packages such as Microsoft Word.

### Activity 3.5

If you don't have Adobe Acrobat Reader already, find the Adobe site on the Internet and download Adobe Acrobat reader onto your computer.

## Warning

6.6    **Never** download files from the Internet unless you are sure that they are from a reliable source.

## 7    A PRACTICAL EXERCISE

7.1    This section is devoted to an **information finding exercise** that you should try out the next time you are sitting at a computer with access to the Internet.

7.2    There are **no definitive solutions** to some of these activities: it depends when you do them and what links you choose to follow up. However, we give some further hints in the answer in case you get stuck.

### Activity 3.6

These activities are likely to take at least an hour to complete satisfactorily, and probably a lot longer if it is your first real go at the Internet. You may prefer to do them, say, two at a time over a series of sessions.

On this occasion feel free to look at any other information that interests once you have reached the site suggested, since you are learning how to use the Internet as well as finding specific information. You will quickly realise that on other occasions you need to be more disciplined, otherwise you will waste a lot of time.

(a)    Using a BPP advertisement to get the address, find and visit the site of BPP Publishing Ltd on the Internet. When did BPP start publishing?

If you like, while you are visiting our site send us an e-mail giving us your constructive comments on this book, as well as filling in the prize draw review form at the end of the book.

(b)    Find and visit the site of a firm of certified accountants in the UK (other than your own firm, if your firm has a site). Note down the information provided there and any other features of interest.

(c)    Visit the site of the Inland Revenue and find out the tax allowances for 2000/2001.

(d) Buy (and read) a newspaper such as the *Times*, the *Telegraph* or the *Financial Times* and visit their Internet site, using the address shown on the front page of the newspaper. What is the top news story of the day?

(e) Find and list 3 items of business-related software that could currently be downloaded free from the site of *PC Magazine*.

(f) Find and visit the site of Sage. What other products do Sage produce besides the Sage 'Line 50' accounting package?

(g) What is the URL of The Stationery Office?

(h) You need to buy some floppy disks and a new printer cartridge. Can you find a supplier on the Internet?

(i) You have come across the phrase 'data warehousing' in a newspaper article about IT in business. What does it mean?

(j) When was the UK Prime Minister Tony Blair born?

(k) Via its 'Information Society Initiative', the Department of Trade and Industry have a number of useful documents available on the Internet. Find, and if possible save and print out, its guide to the Internet and the World Wide Web.

## Key learning points

- The Internet is accessed, simply by clicking on a icon and supplying a password, via an Internet Service Provider and a browser. Searches are done using a search engine.

- Different search engines give different results, so it is worth trying out the same search using several search engines.

- Searches can be refined by being as specific as possible, by restricting the search area, by following links, by using 'advanced' techniques (=, - etc) or Boolean operators, by typing in the URL directly, by saving favourites, and by using channels.

- Besides looking for information on the Internet you may also want to use FTP for downloading files, or follow or take part in a Usenet newsgroup.

## Quick quiz

1    How is search engine software acquired?

2    How do you move from one page to another on a website?

3    What is the effect of putting a minus sign in front of a search word?

4    What does URL stand for? What does it mean, in simple language?

5    What does http:// mean? Must it always be placed at the beginning of an Internet address?

6    How can you make pages download more quickly?

7    How do you print out a copy of a page on the Internet?

8    What should you never, ever do when you are on the Internet?

## Answers to quick quiz

1    It is not acquired, it is available free via a browser or ISP.

2    You click on buttons or graphics that say 'Click here' or on words that are underlined and in a different colour (hypertext links). You can also use the browsers Back and Forward buttons.

3    The search engine searches ignores any pages that contain that word.

4    Uniform Resource Locator, or more simply, an Internet address

5    Hypertext Transfer Protocol, used on the www to exchange documents produced in HTML. It is usually used, but another common alternative is ftp.

6     By turning off the graphics.

7     Just like in any other Windows program, by clicking on File and then Print. Alternatively you can save it and print it out later, but you will probably lose the graphics if you do this.

8     Download a file if you are not confident that it comes from a reputable source.

# Answers to activities

## Answer 3.1

The **hardware** you need is a PC, a modem and a conventional telephone line. Access is likely to be pretty slow if you have a PC less powerful than a Pentium PC and a modem slower than 28.8 kbps. Ideally you would have a more powerful PC (eg a 300MHz Pentium II) and a faster modem (say 56.6 kbps). Better still you would have an ISDN phone line (in which case you would not need a modem), but this is very expensive for individuals.

If these terms mean nothing to you have a glance through the **index** and do some reading ahead from **Part C** of this book.

Although the Internet is used for entertainment, business use is already extensive and is growing, day by day. Uses include **obtaining** information, **marketing**, **distributing** digital products, and **internal communications**.

## Answer 3.2

(a)    Banks is more specific than financial, you might think, but remember that there are other sorts of banks besides the ones that deal with money. Even so we would expect banks to give fewer pages

(b)    Banana is definitely more specific than fruit, and it is not much used outside the 'fruit' context (except perhaps in the not very common expression 'banana republic'), so we would expect it to give fewer pages.

(c)    Your first thought might be that 'accounts' is a lot more specific than 'money', but remember that 'accounts' is also a verb that is often used in a totally non-financial sense (eg 'United cannot claim that the absence of Giggs accounts for their pitiful performance ..'). Nevertheless we would still expect accounts to give fewer pages.

You might like to see whether our guesses are correct by performing each of these searches.

## Answer 3.3

You would get pages about spices (eg cloves, pepper) and some undesirable content, as well as pages specifically on the Spice Girls.

## Answer 3.6

(a)    At the date of publication BPP's site can be found at www.bpp.com. We started publishing in 1976, as you can see from the About BPP section. Have a look round the other sections while you are visiting.

(b)    The site we found had a sections on: Mergers and Acquisitions (with links to other mergers and acquisitions related sites), Audit & Accounting Services, Corporate Finance, Raising Venture Capital or Development Capital, Employee Rewards, Taxation, Trusts and Estates, Financial Services including pensions and investments, Forensic Accounting & Litigation Support, Information Technology (including a job vacancy), Industry Specific Services & Information (Agriculture, Care Homes, Construction, Dentists, Entertainment & Sport, GP's, Medical, Motor Industry, Legal, Vets ), Career Opportunities, Recruitment & Training, Trainee Vacancies 1999, and Training & Standards.

(c)    You can find the Inland Revenue site via www.open.gov.uk. Once you get there click on FAQs (Frequently Asked Questions) to find the answer. Can you think of any other Internet source you could have consulted to find this information?

(d)    Obviously we do not know what the top news story is on the day you are reading this. You probably had to register to get access to your chosen newspaper. Will you be able to remember the password you chose, for future reference?

(e)    ISPs such as AOL have a keyword link to Ziff Davis, publishers of PC Magazine. There is lots of downloadable software to be found. For instance we found a package that helps to create business forms, one that organises vehicle expense records, and one that creates barcodes.

(f)    Sage products are: Instant Accounting 2000, Sage Line 50, Sage Line 100, Sage Audit 2000, Contact Manager, Timeslips, Instant Payroll, Sage Payroll and Sage P11D Software.

(g)    www.the-stationery-office.co.uk. Although this has been privatised you can still find a link to it via open.gov.uk, and it has links back to various government departments.

(h)    We found this a surprisingly difficult search. Try related words such as 'computer consumables' if you have no luck with floppy disks and cartridges. You could always use the electronic yellow pages (www.yell.co.uk) to find an address and phone number of a supplier near you.

(i)    You should have found lots of pages on data warehousing. The term is used to describe a database that brings together a number of other databases.

This activity was meant to give you some practise at looking swiftly through a number of different sources of data until you found one that was particularly suitable.

(j)    He was born in 1953 and went to school at Durham Cathedral School. You can find this quite quickly by entering +Tony+Blair+biography. Alternatively you could go to the Labour Party's site (www.labour.org.uk).

(k)    Try www.open.gov.uk if you don't know where to start.

# Chapter 4 Presenting information

---

## Chapter topic list

1    Presenting information

2    Letters and memos

3    Reports

4    Tables and diagrams

---

## Learning objectives

On completion of this chapter you will be able to:

|  | Performance criteria | Range statement |
|---|---|---|
| • Appreciate the cost of obtaining information and the time taken | 21.1.6 | 21.1.3 |
| • *Understand some of the purposes and applications of MIS* | n/a | n/a |
| • *Organise, interpret and present information* | n/a | n/a |

Italicised objectives are areas of knowledge and understanding underlying the elements of competence for Unit 21.

BPP PUBLISHING

# 1 PRESENTING INFORMATION

1.1 In this chapter we give you a reminder of the factors that have to be considered when selecting an appropriate **method** of presenting the information you have obtained. This is followed by some reminders about the proper **formats** and **contents** of letters, memos, and reports.

> ## DEVOLVED ASSESSMENT ALERT
>
> You may be required to use any or all of these formats in your Devolved Assessment. The AAT sample Devolved Assessment, for instance, asks students to write a 'brief informal report', to 'write a note' and to 'write a brief formal report'.
>
> You will learn more about writing reports and so on in Unit 7.

## Presentation methods

1.2 Broadly speaking you can present the information that you want to communicate in three ways.

(a) **Visually**, for example by gesture, picture, or diagram.

(b) In **writing**, for example by letter or memo.

(c) **Orally**, for example speaking face to face or over the telephone.

All three of these media may be used to convey the different parts of a message. The television news is a good example.

## Choice of medium

1.3 The choice of medium will depend upon numerous factors, including the following.

(a) **Time**

How long will be needed to prepare the message, and how long will it take to transmit it in the chosen form? This must be weighed against the **urgency** with which the message must be sent.

Time of day must be considered when trying to communicate with overseas countries in different times zones.

(b) **Complexity**

What medium will enable the message to be most readily understood? If detailed or highly technical information is to be exchanged or where a message has many interdependent parts, oral communication is not appropriate.

(c) **Distance**

How far is the message required to travel? Must it be transmitted to an office on a different floor of the building, or across town, or to the other end of the country ?

(d) **Written record**

A written record may be needed as proof, confirming a transaction, or for legal purposes, or as an aid to memory. It can be duplicated and sent to many recipients. It can be stored and later retrieved for reference and analysis as required.

(e) **Interaction**

Sometimes instant feedback is needed for effective communication, for example when you are questioning a customer to find out his precise requirements ('small, medium or large?', 'green, red or blue?').

(f) **Degree of confidentiality**

Telephone calls may be overheard; faxed messages can be read by whoever is standing by the fax machine; internal memos may be read by colleagues or by internal mail staff; highly personal letters may be read by the recipient's secretary.

On the other hand a message may need to be spread widely and quickly to all staff: the notice-board, or a public announcement or the company newsletter may be more appropriate.

(g) The **recipient**

It may be necessary to be reserved and tactful, warm and friendly, or impersonal, depending upon the desired effect on the recipient. If you are trying to impress him, a high quality document may be needed .

(h) **Cost**

Cost must be considered in relation to all of the above factors. The aim is to achieve the best possible result at the least possible expense.

---

**Activity 4.1**

How many of these factors, if any, do you think are relevant to producing answers to devolved assessment tasks?

---

## Presentation of spreadsheets

1.4 Presentation of **spreadsheets** is covered at appropriate points throughout **Part B** of this book, especially in Chapter 6.

## 2 LETTERS AND MEMOS

### Letters

2.1 The modern **business letter** contains various standard elements, and if you are asked to produce a letter you will need to remember what these are and where they are located on the page.

- Letterhead
- Reference
- Date
- Recipient name and address
- Greeting/salutation
- Subject
- Substance
- Complimentary close
- Signature
- Author name and designation
- Enclosure/copy reference

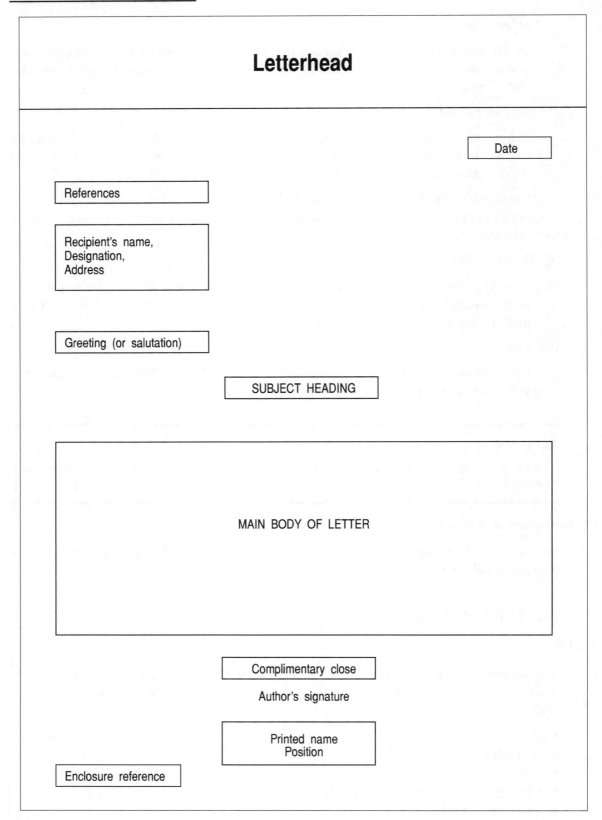

## Salutation

2.2 The opening **greeting** ('Dear ...') is conventionally paired with an appropriate **complimentary close** (your polite 'signing off'), to mark the end of the letter in similar tone and degree of formality.

| Greeting | Close | Context |
|---|---|---|
| Dear Sir/Madam/Sirs (Name not used) | Yours faithfully | Formal situations. Recipient not personally known Recipient senior in years, position |
| Dear Dr/Mr/Mrs/Miss Bloggs, Dear Sir Keith/Lady Diana, Dear Lord Nelson, (Name used) | Yours sincerely | Friendly (or would-be friendly, eg for selling or conciliatory letters). Established relationships |
| Dear Joe/Josephine My dear Joe/Josephine Etc. | Yours sincerely Kind regards Best wishes Affectionately | Close, informal relationships. More various, because more personal. |

2.3 If you are writing to a **woman** and not using her name say 'Dear Madam' whether or not she is married. If you **do not know** the sex of your correspondent you can say 'Dear Sir' (just as you often see 'he' written in books or articles rather than the clumsier 'he or she'). Some people frown upon 'Dear Sir or Madam', although it is difficult to see how it could cause offence unless the recipient knows that you already know what sex he/she is. **Never** use the form 'Dear Jane Smith', even if she signed her letter as 'Jane Smith': say 'Dear Ms Smith' or 'Dear Madam'.

## Memos and notes

2.4 The memorandum or 'memo' is used **within an organisation** for communication at all levels and for many different reasons. Internally it performs the same function as a letter does in external communication by an organisation, but it can be used for reports, brief messages or 'notes' and **any kind of internal communication** that is more easily or clearly conveyed **in writing** (rather than face-to-face or on the telephone).

Note that a memorandum may be sent 'upwards', 'downwards' or 'sideways' in the organisation's hierarchy. It may be sent from one individual to another, from one department to another, from one individual to a department or larger body of staff.

2.5 There are two standard memorandum **sizes**.

(a) **A4** (the size of this page). This is used for **long or complex messages**, with continuation sheets if necessary.

(b) **A5** (the size of the upper/lower half of this page). This is used for **short, one-idea messages**.

## Memo format

2.6 Memorandum format will vary slightly according to the **degree of formality** required and the organisation's policy on matters like filing and authorisation of memoranda by their writer. Follow the conventions of '**house style**' in your own organisation. A typical format, including all the required elements, is illustrated below.

---

**Organisation's name (optional)**

### MEMORANDUM

**To:** (recipients name or designation)     **Ref:** (for filing)

**From:** (authors name or designation)     **Date:** (in full)

**Subject:** (main theme of message)

The message of the memorandum is set out like that of a letter: good English in spaced paragraphs. Note that no inside address, salutation or complimentary close are required.

**Signed:** (optional) author signs/initials

**Copies to:** (recipient(s) of copies)

**Enc.:** to indicate accompanying material

---

## 3    REPORTS

### Types of report

3.1    There is a variety of formats and styles for reports.

(a)    **Formal or informal.** You may think of reports as huge documents with sections, subsections, paragraphs, subparagraphs, indexes, appendixes and so on. There *are* extensive, complex reports like this, but a single-sheet ordinary memorandum may be sufficient in many contexts.

(b)    Special reports may be commissioned for **one-off** planning and decision-making, such as a market research report, or reports on a proposed project or particular issue.

(c)    **Routine** reports are produced at regular intervals. Examples of routine reports are **budgetary control** reports, **sales reports** or progress reports.

### Purpose

3.2    The information contained in a business report might be used in several ways.

(a)    **To assist management**. Higher levels of management rarely have time to carry out their own detailed investigations into the matters on which they make decisions; their time, moreover, is extremely expensive. If all (and only) the information relevant to their needs can be gathered and 'packaged' by report writers, managerial time and money will be saved.

(b)    As a **permanent record and source of reference**, should details need to be confirmed or recalled in the future.

(c)    **To provide information to interested parties**, such as through an article in a newspaper or journal. This may also involve persuasion, if it is related to an issue, product or topic that is relevant to your organisation or department.

(d)    **To make your own views known**; perhaps to make suggestions, recommendations, a protest or appeal to others, based on your knowledge and experience.

3.3    There are **different types of information** that might be given in a report.

| Information type | Description |
| --- | --- |
| Factual | These are the facts. |
| Dialectical | This is what the facts seem to suggest is happening, has happened or will happen. |
| Instructive | This is what should be done about matters to sort out the situation. |

**DEVOLVED ASSESSMENT ALERT**

Be sensitive to the words that are used in the tasks you are given, because these indicate what sort of information you are required to produce: for instance 'describe', 'analyse', and 'recommend' have different meanings and require different sorts of information.

3.4 The purpose of a report must be clear to both its writers and its users.

(a) In the case of **routine reports,** the purpose of each and how it should be used ought to be specified in a procedures manual.

(b) **One-off** reports will require *terms of reference*, explaining the purpose of the report and any restrictions on its scope. For example, the terms of reference of a sales report might be to investigate the viability of the discounts offered to small customers, with a view to recommending either the withdrawal of the discount or its continuation. These terms of reference would exclude considerations of discounts to larger customers, and so place a limitation on the scope and purpose of the report.

**DEVOLVED ASSESSMENT ALERT**

It may be left up to you to use your judgement as to what should be included in a report, perhaps based on your interpretation of data elsewhere in the Assessment. You need to think about whether the information you provide can be put to good use, whether it will help solve a problem, whether it is suitable for the person who will read it - in other words about the qualities of good information. There is more on some of these issues below.

**Activity 4.2**

One of your friends, who works for another company, has just got a brand new top of the range computer for work, whereas the computer that you use at work is several years old, and not very powerful, compared with your friend's machine.

What sort of report should you write to persuade your boss to buy you a brand new computer?

## Audience

3.5 A report writer knows more about the subject matter of the report than the report user (otherwise there would be no need for the report in the first place). It is important that this information should be communicated **impartially,** so that the report user can make his own judgements.

(a) Any **assumptions, evaluations** and **recommendations** by the report writer should be clearly **labelled** as such.

(b) Facts and findings should be **balanced** against each other.

    (c)    A **firm conclusion** should, if possible, be reached. It should be clear how and **why it was reached**.

3.6    A report writer must also - as ever - recognise the needs and abilities of the report user.

    (a)    Beware of '**jargon**', overly technical terms and specialist knowledge the user may not share.

    (b)    Keep your vocabulary, sentence and paragraph structures as **simple** as possible, for clarity (without patronising an intelligent user).

    (c)    Bear in mind the type and **level of detail** that will interest the user and be relevant to his/her purpose.

    (d)    In a business context, the user may range from senior manager to junior supervisor, to non-managerial employee to complete layman (customer, press etc.). Your vocabulary, syntax and presentation, the amount of detail you can go into, the technical matter you can include and the formality of your report structure should all be influenced by such concerns.

## DEVOLVED ASSESSEMENT ALERT

You will be told in the Devolved Assessment data what role you are supposed to be playing and what position in the organisational hierarchy you occupy relative to the person or people you are writing for.

## Structure

3.7    When a **formal request** is made by a superior for a report to be prepared, such as in a formally worded memorandum or letter, the format and style of the report will obviously have to be formal as well: in particular it will have a formal structure and it will avoid colloquial expressions.

An **informal request** for a report - 'Can you jot down a few ideas for me about...' or 'Let me know what happens, will you?' - will result in an informal report, in which the structure will be less rigid, and the style slightly more personal (depending on the relationship perceived to exist between the writer and user).

**If in doubt,** it is better (more courteous and effective) to **be too formal** than over familiar.

3.8    **Large-scale formal reports** may run to hundreds of pages, and will therefore require:

    (a)    A list of **contents** and **index**.

    (b)    **Summary of findings** (to give the reader an initial idea).

    (c)    Strict **divisions into sections** with **cross-referencing** (to help the reader to 'dip in' to particular points as necessary).

    (d)    Supporting **appendices** and **list of sources** (carrying subsidiary material, in order to keep the body of the report as brief as possible) etc.

3.9    Although you would not have time and would not be asked to prepare such a report in your Devolved Assessment, you may still choose to separate supporting information (a lengthy print out of sales figures, for instance) into an **Appendix**.

## Formal reports

3.10 A formal report should be **laid out** according to certain basic guidelines. It will be split into logical **sections**, each headed appropriately.

*Ask yourself*

TITLE

I    TERMS OF REFERENCE
     (or INTRODUCTION)              *What have I been asked to do?*

II   PROCEDURE (or METHOD)          *How do I go about it?*

III  FINDINGS                       *What do I discover?*

    1   Section heading
    2   Section heading
        (a)  sub heading
            (i)  sub point

IV   CONCLUSIONS                    *What is the* general *'thrust' of the result?*

V    RECOMMENDATIONS               *What* particular *recommendations do I wish to make?*

---

### EXAMPLE OF A FORMAL REPORT

TITLE    At the top of every report (or on a title page, for lengthy ones) should be the *title* of the report (its subject), *who* has prepared it, for *whom* it is intended, the *date* of completion, and the *status* of the report ('Confidential' or 'Urgent').

I    TERMS OF REFERENCE

Here is laid out the scope and purpose of the report: what is to be investigated, what kind of information is required, whether recommendations are to be made etc. This section may more simply be called '*Introduction*', and may include the details set above under '*Title*'. The title itself would then give only the subject of the report.

II   PROCEDURE or METHOD

This outlines the steps taken to make an investigation, collect data, put events in motion etc. Telephone calls or visits made, documents or computer files consulted, computations or analyses made etc. should be briefly described, with the names of other people involved.

III  FINDINGS

In this section, if it is required, the information itself is set out, with appropriate headings and sub-headings, if the report covers more than one topic. The content should be complete, but concise, and clearly structured in chronological order, order of importance, or any other *logical* relationship.

IV   CONCLUSIONS

This section allows for a summary of main findings (if the report is complex and lengthy). For a simpler report it may include *action taken* or decisions reached (if any) as a result of the investigation, or an expression of the overall 'message' of the report.

V    RECOMMENDATIONS

Here, if asked to do so in the terms of reference, the writer of the report may suggest the solution to the problem investigated so that the recipient will be able to make a decision if necessary.

---

**BPP** PUBLISHING

## Example: a formal report

---

**REPORT ON FLOPPY DISK STORAGE SAFETY AND SECURITY**

To:      Mr M Ployer, Personnel Department Manager
From:    M Ployee, Supervisor
Date:    3 October 200X

I   INTRODUCTION

This report details the findings of an investigation into methods of computer disk storage currently employed at the Head Office of the bank. The report includes recommendations for the improvement of current procedure

II   METHOD

In order to evaluate the present procedures and to identify specific shortcomings, the following investigative procedures were adopted:

1      interview of all staff using floppy disks
2      storage and indexing system inspected
3      computer accessory firm consulted by telephone and catalogues obtained (see Appendix I)

III   FINDINGS
1      *Current system*

    (a)    Floppy disks are 'backed up' or duplicated irregularly and infrequently.

    (b)    Back-up disks if they exist are stored in plastic containers in the personnel office, the same room as the disks currently in use.

    (c)    Disks are frequently left on desk tops during the day and even overnight.

2      *Safety and security risks*

    (a)    There is no systematic provision for making copies, in the event of loss or damage of disks in use.

    (b)    There is no provision for separate storage of copies in the event of fire in the personnel office, and no adequate security against fire or damage in the containers used.

    (c)    There appears to be no awareness of the confidential nature of information on disk, nor of the ease with which disks may be damaged by handling, the spilling of beverages, dust etc.

IV   CONCLUSIONS

The principal conclusions drawn from the investigation were that there was insufficient awareness of safety and security among non-specialist staff, that there was insufficient formal provision for safety and security procedure, and that there was serious cause for concern.

V   RECOMMENDATIONS

In order to rectify the unsatisfactory situation summarised above, the author of the report recommends that consideration be given as a matter of urgency to the following measures.

1      Immediate backing up of all existing disks;
2      Drafting of procedures for backing up disks at the end of each day.
3      Acquisition of a fire-proof safe to be kept in separate office accommodation.
4      Communication to all staff of the serious risk of loss, theft and damage arising from careless handling of computer disks.

---

## Informal reports

3.11    Informal reports are used for **less complex** and **lower-level** information.

The structure of the informal report is less developed: it will be shorter and less complex in any case, so will not require elaborate referencing and layout. There will be **three main sections,** each of which may be **headed in any way appropriate** to the context in which the report is written.

---

**EXAMPLE OF AN INFORMAL REPORT**

TITLE   Again, the subject title, 'to', 'from', 'date' and 'reference' (if necessary) should be provided, perhaps in the same style as memorandum headings.

1   *Background* or *Introduction* or *Situation*
This sets the context of the report. Include anything that will help the reader to understand the rest of the report: the reason why it was requested, the current situation, and any other background information on people and things that will be mentioned in the following detailed section. This section may also contain the equivalent of 'terms of reference' and 'procedure'/'method'.

2   *Findings* or *Analysis of the situation* or *Information*
Here is set out the detailed information gathered, narrative of events or other substance of the report as required by the user. This section may or may not require subheadings: concise prose paragraphs may be sufficient.

3   *Action* or *Solution* or *Conclusion* or *Recommendations*
The main thrust of the findings may be summarised in this section and conclusions drawn, together with a note of the outcome of events, or action required, or recommendations as to how a problem might be solved.

---

## Example: an informal report

---

**REPORT ON CUSTOMER COMPLAINT BY F R VESSENT**

*Confidential*

To:       M Ployer, Sales Manager                                          Date: 13 June 200X
From:    M Ployee, Sales Assistant

---

1   *Background*

The substance of Mr Vessent's complaint was that he had paid in an amount of £1,306.70 to the Dibbin & Dobbs account on April 4. On receiving his statement, he noted that the payment had not appeared. Mr Vessent is Accounts Clerk for Dibbin & Dobbs Ltd. who have had an account with us since June 19--: account number _____.

I have questioned our Junior Sales Assistant concerning the Dibbin & Dobbs account, and we have together consulted the records. In addition I looked at the recent transactions of our client Doobey & Sons to check for possible misallocation of the payments.

2   *Findings*

Our records show no credit in April to the Dibbin & Dobbs account. However, an amount of £1,306.70 was credited to the account of Doobey & Sons on April 4. Doobey & Sons when consulted admitted to having been puzzled by the inclusion on their statement of this amount.

The Junior Sales Assistant was absent through illness that week, and a temporary Assistant employed.

It would appear that the temp credited the payment to the wrong account.

3   *Action and recommendations*

The entries have been duly corrected.

I am writing appropriate letters of apology and explanation to Mr Vessent and to Doobey & Sons.

Obviously this is a matter of some concern in terms of customer relations. I suggest that all sales assistants be reminded of the need for due care and attention, and that temporary staff in particular be briefed on this matter in the future.

---

BPP PUBLISHING

## Memorandum reports

3.12 In informal reporting situations within an organisation, the 'short informal report' may well be presented in **memorandum format**, which incorporates title headings and can thereafter be laid out at the writer's discretion. An ordinary memorandum may be used for flexible, informal reports: aside from the convenient title headings, there are no particular requirements for structure, headings or layout.

## Accounting reports

3.13 Your study of financial accounting and cost accounting for other Intermediate subjects and of cash and credit transactions at Foundation level should have made you aware of a **wide variety of formats** for accounting reports.

3.14 Common accounting reports include the following.

- Trial balance
- Aged debtors or creditors report
- Sales Day Book
- Purchases Day Book
- Fixed assets schedule
- Budget
- Cash flow statement
- Stock listing
- Sales reports, perhaps analysed by product or by region

### DEVOLVED ASSESSMENT ALERT

Your devolved assessment could ask you to analyse data extracted via a report such as the above from an accounting system into a spreadsheet package. It is therefore very important that you keep up your study of accounting subjects, and realise that your IT skills will be assessed in the context of your accounting knowledge.

### Activity 4.3

What information would you expect to see in a stock listing?

## 4 TABLES AND DIAGRAMS

4.1 The visual element can be used to add **interest** and immediate **appeal** to written communication by using **layout, colour, spacing**, different **typefaces** and so on.

**Statistical information** presents a challenge: numbers may be presented with, or independently of, text and with varying degrees of visual impact and simplicity in tables, charts or graphs.

4.2 Remember that a simple visual presentation of data has more **impact and immediacy** than a mere block of text or figures that is hard to take in at a glance and may contain superfluous elements.

4.3 Here is a brief reminder of the **most common visual methods** of presenting data. We will look at ways of creating impressive examples of many of these with a **computer** in **Part B**.

- Tables
- Line graphs
- Bar charts
- Pie charts
- Pictograms
- Drawings and graphics
- Maps
- Flow charts and family trees

## Key learning points

- Factors to consider when deciding on a method of presentation are: time, complexity, distance to travel, whether a written record is needed, whether feedback is needed, degree of confidentiality, the recipient(s) themselves, and the cost.

- If you are asked to write a letter don't forget standard elements such as the letterhead, references, date and enclosure/copy references. Make sure you get the salutation and complimentary close correct.

- Memos are for internal communication and they may be at various levels of formality. They generally follow an organisational house style. Key elements to remember are: To, From, Subject and Date.

- Reports may be formal or informal, routine or one-off. Bear in minds the needs of the reader of the report (eg avoid technical jargon if necessary). Think about whether you have been asked for facts, analysis, or recommendations (or a combination of these).

- A formal report usually includes a title, an introduction (terms of reference), procedure followed, findings, conclusions and recommendations. An informal report may have some or all of these elements, as necessary, and is more loosely structured.

- You should also make sure that you have in mind a clear structure for common accounting reports such as stock listings and aged debtor listings.

- Information can often usefully be summarised by the use of a table or diagram.

## Quick quiz

1    If it will cost a great deal to send a message by one means it should be sent by a cheaper means. True or False?

2    Why is it a bad idea to read out a set of accounts to a client over the telephone?

3    You have received a letter from a customer called Deirdre Boulding. In your reply what would be an acceptable salutation and complimentary close?

4    You have just found the answer to a query from your boss, having performed a series of spot checks on the formulae used in a spreadsheet devised by your predecessor and discovered an error. In what part of your report on this matter would you explain 'spot checks'?

5    When might you use a diagram or chart to present information.

## Answers to quick quiz_____

1    True as a rule, unless time is a factor. Sometimes the urgency of a message may make cost less important than speed (for instance an organisation may lose even more money if the message does not arrive on time).

2    Because the information is too complex to be understood orally, and because of confidentiality.

3    'Dear Ms Boulding .... Yours sincerely ....' would be the best solution.

4    In the 'method or procedure' part if it is a formal report; in the introductory section if it is informal.

5    When you have to present a mass of text of figures in a way that brings out the key point or points without overloading the reader with information.

## Answers to activities_____

## Answer 4.1

**Time** is certainly an issue: you have a limited time to complete all the tasks you are given.

**Complexity** is also relevant. You might use a spreadsheet package to prepare an Appendix containing detailed figures and a word processor to type up a summary report.

**Distance** could be an issue if your work has to be sent off somewhere to be assessed. You may need to ensure that it has some protective packaging.

There needs to be a **record** (printed out, or on disk) of your efforts, even if you feel that you have not got the 'right answers': you may have spent 4 hours beavering away on the figures, but if there is no evidence at the end to show for it you may as well not have bothered. (If there is evidence you will get a good deal of credit for your work, even if it is wrong, as long as you used a sensible approach.)

You may also have mentioned that the needs of the **recipient** (both your actual assessor, and the fictional person to whom you are supposed to be reporting in the Devolved Assessment tasks) should be considered.

**Cost** is always relevant, not least in this case because you will have put a considerable personal investment of time into studying for your Devolved Assessment and you owe it to yourself to do as well as possible.

## Answer 4.2_____

Your report would have to make out a good case for you to have a new computer, not taking into account your own bias or your jealousy of your friend, but considering the needs of the business, the cost of the new PC, the benefits it would bring in terms of time savings and/or greater productivity. This is what is meant by balance. In fact, as you were researching the report you may well come to the conclusion that there is not a good enough case for you to have a new PC.

## Answer 4.3_____

The illustration below indicates the main headings you would expect to see. You will be looking at this spreadsheet in more detail in Chapter 8.

|   | A | B | C | D | E | F | G | H | I |
|---|---|---|---|---|---|---|---|---|---|
| 1 | Component | Product | Quantity | In stock | Re-order level | Free stock | Reorder quantity | On order | Supplier |
| 2 | A001 | A | 1 | 371 | 160 | 211 | 400 | – | P750 |
| 3 | A002 | B | 5 | 33 | 40 | – | 100 | 100 | P036 |
| 4 | A003 | A | 5 | 206 | 60 | 146 | 150 | – | P888 |
| 5 | A004 | D | 3 | 176 | 90 | 86 | 225 | – | P036 |
| 6 | A005 | E | 9 | 172 | 120 | 52 | 300 | – | P750 |
| 7 | A006 | C | 7 | 328 | 150 | 178 | 375 | – | P684 |
| 8 | A007 | C | 2 | 13 | 10 | 3 | 25 | – | P227 |
| 9 | A008 | C | 6 | 253 | 60 | 193 | 150 | – | P036 |
| 10 | A009 | E | 9 | 284 | 90 | 194 | 225 | – | P888 |
| 11 | A010 | B | 3 | 435 | 100 | 335 | 250 | – | P720 |
| 12 | A011 | B | 2 | 295 | 110 | 185 | 275 | – | P036 |
| 13 | A012 | A | 3 | 40 | 190 | – | 475 | 475 | P036 |
| 14 | A013 | A | 7 | 23 | 120 | – | 300 | 300 | P227 |
| 15 | A014 | C | 4 | 296 | 110 | 186 | 275 | – | P750 |
| 16 | A015 | D | 7 | 432 | 40 | 392 | 100 | – | P684 |
| 17 | A016 | D | 4 | 416 | 100 | 316 | 250 | – | P141 |
| 18 | A017 | A | 3 | 463 | 150 | 313 | 375 | – | P888 |

See if you can do a similar exercise for some of the other reports noted. Look at the type of reports that appear in your BPP Interactive Texts for cost accounting and financial accounting topics if necessary.

# *Part B*
## *Producing spreadsheets*

# Chapter 5    Creating spreadsheets

---

## Chapter topic list

1    Introduction to spreadsheets

2    Some basic 'hands-on' skills

3    Building a model

---

## Learning objectives

On completion of this chapter you will be able to:

| | Performance criteria | Range statement |
|---|---|---|
| • Produce spreadsheets by creation and modification | | 21.2.1, 21.2.3 |
| • Title spreadsheets in a way which clearly defines their use and purpose | 21.2.1 | |
| • Arrange spreadsheets in a way consistent with organisational conventions | 21.2.2 | |
| • Use spreadsheets to carry out data modifications and for entry of related formulas | 21.2.5 | 21.2.4 |
| • Format each cell clearly and accurately | 21.2.6 | |
| • *Describe and operate a range of spreadsheet products* | n/a | n/a |
| • *Understand some of the purposes and applications of spreadsheets* | n/a | n/a |

Italicised objectives are areas of knowledge and understanding underlying the elements of competence for Unit 21.

# 1    INTRODUCTION TO SPREADSHEETS

1.1    A spreadsheet is essentially an **electronic piece of paper** divided into **rows and columns** with a built in pencil, eraser and calculator. It provides an easy way of performing numerical calculations.

1.2    Below is a spreadsheet processing budgeted sales figures for three geographical areas for the first quarter of the year.

|    | A | B | C | D | E | F | G | H |
|----|---|---|---|---|---|---|---|---|
| 1  | BUDGETED SALES FIGURES | | | | | | | |
| 2  | | *Jan* | *Feb* | *Mar* | *Total* | | | |
| 3  | | £'000 | £'000 | £'000 | £'000 | | | |
| 4  | North | 2,431 | 3,001 | 2,189 | 7,621 | | | |
| 5  | South | 6,532 | 5,826 | 6,124 | 18,482 | | | |
| 6  | West | 895 | 432 | 596 | 1,923 | | | |
| 7  | Total | 9,858 | 9,259 | 8,909 | 28,026 | | | |
| 8  | | | | | | | | |
| 9  | | | | | | | | |
| 10 | | | | | | | | |
| 11 | | | | | | | | |
| 12 | | | | | | | | |
| 13 | | | | | | | | |
| 14 | | | | | | | | |
| 15 | | | | | | | | |
| 16 | | | | | | | | |
| 17 | | | | | | | | |
| 18 | | | | | | | | |
| 19 | | | | | | | | |
| 20 | | | | | | | | |

1.3    All the totals are **calculated automatically** by the spreadsheet program. If you changed your estimate of sales in February for the North region to £3,296, you need simply input this information and the totals would change accordingly.

1.4    The main examples of spreadsheet packages are Lotus 1-2-3 and Microsoft Excel. We will be referring to Microsoft Excel, as this is the most widely-used spreadsheet.

## Uses of spreadsheets

1.5    Since spreadsheets can be used to build a wide variety of models, spreadsheet packages are **'general purpose'** software packages, as distinct from software packages which are designed for specific applications (for example a sales ledger package).

1.6    Some of the more **common applications** of spreadsheets are:

- Balance sheets
- Cash flow analysis and forecasting

- General ledger
- Stock records
- Job cost estimates
- Market share analysis and planning
- Profit projections
- Sales projections and records

1.7 What all these have in common is that they all involve data processing with:

- **Numerical** data
- **Repetitive**, time-consuming calculations
- A **logical** processing structure

## The appearance of a spreadsheet

1.8 When a 'blank' spreadsheet is loaded into a computer, the VDU monitor will show lines of empty rows and columns. **Rows** are always **horizontal** and **columns vertical**. The **rows** are **numbered** 1, 2, 3 . . . etc and the **columns lettered** A, B C . . . etc. Typically, it will look like this.

|    | A | B | C | D | E | F | G | H |
|----|---|---|---|---|---|---|---|---|
| 1  |   |   |   |   |   |   |   |   |
| 2  |   |   |   |   |   |   |   |   |
| 3  |   |   |   |   |   |   |   |   |
| 4  |   |   |   |   |   |   |   |   |
| 5  |   |   |   |   |   |   |   |   |
| 6  |   |   |   |   |   |   |   |   |
| 7  |   |   |   |   |   |   |   |   |
| 8  |   |   |   |   |   |   |   |   |
| 9  |   |   |   |   |   |   |   |   |
| 10 |   |   |   |   |   |   |   |   |
| 11 |   |   |   |   |   |   |   |   |
| 12 |   |   |   |   |   |   |   |   |
| 13 |   |   |   |   |   |   |   |   |
| 14 |   |   |   |   |   |   |   |   |
| 15 |   |   |   |   |   |   |   |   |
| 16 |   |   |   |   |   |   |   |   |
| 17 |   |   |   |   |   |   |   |   |
| 18 |   |   |   |   |   |   |   |   |
| 19 |   |   |   |   |   |   |   |   |
| 20 |   |   |   |   |   |   |   |   |

1.9 Each square is called a '**cell**'. A cell is identified by its reference according to the row or column it is in, as shown below.

|   | A  | B  | C  | D  | E  | F  | G  | H  |
|---|----|----|----|----|----|----|----|----|
| 1 | A1 | B1 | C1 | D1 | E1 | F1 | G1 | H1 |
| 2 | A2 | B2 |    |    |    |    |    |    |
| 3 | A3 |    | C3 |    |    |    |    |    |
| 4 | A4 |    |    | D4 |    |    |    |    |
| 5 | A5 |    |    |    | E5 |    |    |    |
| 6 | A6 |    |    |    |    | F6 |    |    |
| 7 | A7 |    |    |    |    |    | G7 |    |
| 8 | A8 |    |    |    |    |    |    | H8 |

1.10 The screen **cursor** will highlight any particular cell - in the example above, it is placed over cell C6.

1.11 At the top or bottom of the screen, the spreadsheet program will display such information as:

(a) the reference of the cell where the cursor lies;

(b) the width of the column where the cursor lies (you can alter column widths to suit yourself, without changing the total number of columns available on the spreadsheet);

(c) the contents of the cell where the cursor lies, if there is anything there.

1.12 The contents of any cell can be one of the following.

(a) **Text**. A cell so designated contains **words** or numerical data (eg a date) that will not be used in computations. On newer versions of all popular spreadsheets, text can be formatted in a similar way to what is possible using a WP package. Different fonts can be selected, text can be emboldened or italicised, and the point size of the lettering can be changed.

(b) **Values**. A value is a **number** that can be used in a calculation.

(c) **Formulae**. A formula **refers to other cells** in the spreadsheet, and performs some sort of computation with them. For example, if cell C1 contains the formula =A1-B1 this means that the contents of cell B1 should be subtracted from the contents of cell A1 and the result displayed in cell C1. Note that a formula starts with a specific command or choice or symbols in most packages to distinguish it from text.

(i) In Excel, a formula always begins with an equals sign: =

(ii) Where a long row or column of cells (referred to as a range) is to be added together, a '**sum**' **function** can be used. In Excel this would be entered as =SUM(B7:B18)

---

**Activity 5.1**

This activity tests some basic ideas about spreadsheets.

(a) What is a spreadsheet?

(b) Give five uses of a spreadsheet.

(c) In the spreadsheet over the page, what is the reference for the cell over which the cursor is positioned?

| | A | B | C | D | E | F | G |
|---|---|---|---|---|---|---|---|
| 1 | | | | | | | |
| 2 | | | | | | | |
| 3 | | | | | | | |
| 4 | | | | | | | |
| 5 | | | | | | | |
| 6 | | | | | | | |
| 7 | | | | | | | |
| 8 | | | | | | | |
| 9 | | | | | | | |
| 10 | | | | | | | |
| 11 | | | | | | | |
| 12 | | | | | | | |
| 13 | | | | | | | |
| 14 | | | | | | | |
| 15 | | | | | | | |
| 16 | | | | | | | |
| 17 | | | | | | | |
| 18 | | | | | | | |
| 19 | | | | | | | |
| 20 | | | | | | | |

(d) What is meant by the term 'the active cell'?

(e) A cell in a spreadsheet can contain one of three things: text, values or formulae. Briefly explain the purpose of each of these.

## 1.13 EXAMPLE: FORMULAE

Reproduced below is the simple spreadsheet encountered earlier which processes sales figures.

(a) Which of the cells require a value to be typed in? Which cells would perform calculations, ie which cells contain a formula?

(b) What formula would you put in each of the following cells?

  (i) Cell B7.
  (ii) Cell E6.
  (iii) Cell E7.

(c) If the February sales figure for the South changed from £5,826 to £5,731, what other figures would change as a result? Give cell references.

|  | A | B | C | D | E | F | G | H |
|---|---|---|---|---|---|---|---|---|
| 1 | BUDGETED SALES FIGURES | | | | | | | |
| 2 | | Jan | Feb | Mar | Total | | | |
| 3 | | £'000 | £'000 | £'000 | £'000 | | | |
| 4 | North | 2,431 | 3,001 | 2,189 | 7,621 | | | |
| 5 | South | 6,532 | 5,826 | 6,124 | 18,482 | | | |
| 6 | West | 895 | 432 | 596 | 1,923 | | | |
| 7 | Total | 9,858 | 9,259 | 8,909 | 28,026 | | | |
| 8 | | | | | | | | |
| 9 | | | | | | | | |
| 10 | | | | | | | | |
| 11 | | | | | | | | |
| 12 | | | | | | | | |
| 13 | | | | | | | | |
| 14 | | | | | | | | |
| 15 | | | | | | | | |
| 16 | | | | | | | | |
| 17 | | | | | | | | |
| 18 | | | | | | | | |
| 19 | | | | | | | | |
| 20 | | | | | | | | |
| 21 | | | | | | | | |

## 1.14  SOLUTION

You will notice in these solutions that we introduce the quick way, noted above, of adding up ('casting') a row or column of cells. This is not essential where only three cells are involved, but obviously useful for longer series of numbers.

(a)  Cells into which you would need to enter a value are: B4, B5, B6, C4, C5, C6, D4, D5 and D6. Cells which would perform calculations are B7, C7, D7, E4, E5, E6 and E7.

(b)  (i)  =B4+B5+B6 *or better* =SUM(B4:B6)

   (ii)  =B6+C6+D6 *or better* =SUM(B6:D6)

   (iii)  =E4+E5+E6 *or better* =SUM(E4:E6) Alternatively, the three monthly totals could be added across the spreadsheet: = SUM (B7: D7)

(c)  The figures which would change, besides the amount in cell C5, would be those in cells C7, E5 and E7. (The contents of E7 would change if *any* of the sales figures changed.)

### Activity 5.2

The spreadsheet below shows sales of two products, the Ego and the Id, for the period July to September.

|  | A | B | C | D | E | F | G |
|---|---|---|---|---|---|---|---|
| 1 | **Sigmund Ltd** | | | | | | |
| 2 | *Sales analysis - Q3 200X* | | | | | | |
| 3 | | M7 | M8 | M9 | Total | | |
| 4 | | £ | £ | £ | £ | | |
| 5 | Ego | 3000 | 4000 | 2000 | 9000 | | |
| 6 | Id | 2000 | 1500 | 4000 | 7500 | | |
| 7 | Total | 5000 | 5500 | 6000 | 16500 | | |
| 8 | | | | | | | |
| 9 | | | | | | | |
| 10 | | | | | | | |

Devise a suitable formula for each of the following cells.

(a)   Cell B7.
(b)   CellE6.
(c)   Cell E7.

## Activity 5.3

The following spreadsheet shows sales, exclusive of VAT, in row 6.

|  | A | B | C | D | E | F | G | H |
|---|---|---|---|---|---|---|---|---|
| 1 | **Taxable Supplies plc** | | | | | | | |
| 2 | *Sales analysis - Branch C* | | | | | | | |
| 3 | *Six months ended 30 June 200X* | | | | | | | |
| 4 | | Jan | Feb | Mar | Apr | May | Jun | Total |
| 5 | | £ | £ | £ | £ | £ | £ | £ |
| 6 | Net sales | 2,491.54 | 5,876.75 | 3,485.01 | 5,927.70 | 6,744.52 | 3,021.28 | 27,546.80 |
| 7 | VAT | | | | | | | |
| 8 | Total | | | | | | | |
| 9 | | | | | | | | |
| 10 | | | | | | | | |

Your manager has asked you to insert formulae to calculate VAT at 17½% in row 7 and also to produce totals.

(a)   Devise a suitable formula for each of the following cells.

    (i)   Cell B7.
    (ii)  Cell E8.

(b)   How could the spreadsheet be better designed?

## Activity 5.4

The following balances have been taken from the books of Ed Sheet, a sole trader, at 31 December 200X.

| | Dr £ | Cr £ |
|---|---|---|
| Plant and machinery (NBV) | 20,000 | |
| Motor vehicles (NBV) | 10,000 | |
| | | |
| Stock | 2,000 | |
| Debtors | 1,000 | |
| Cash | 1,500 | |
| | | |
| Creditors | | 2,500 |
| Overdraft | | 1,500 |
| | | |
| Drawings | 1,000 | |
| Capital (1 Jan 20XX) | | 28,000 |
| Profit for year | 3,500 | |

Your manager has tried to use a spreadsheet to produce a balance sheet. He has set up the basic structure and input the numbers, but he cannot remember how to do formulae. He has therefore highlighted with a border the cells which require a formula to be inserted and left the rest up to you.

|  | A | B | C | D | E | F |
|---|---|---|---|---|---|---|
| 1 | **Ed Sheet** | | | | | |
| 2 | *Balance sheet as at 31 Dec 200X* | | | | | |
| 3 | | £ | £ | | | |
| 4 | *Fixed assets* | | | | | |
| 5 | Plant | 20000 | | | | |
| 6 | Vehicles | 10000 | | | | |
| 7 | | | | | | |
| 8 | *Current assets* | | | | | |
| 9 | Stock | 2000 | | | | |
| 10 | Debtors | 1000 | | | | |
| 11 | Cash | 1500 | | | | |
| 12 | | | | | | |
| 13 | *Current liabilities* | | | | | |
| 14 | Creditors | 2500 | | | | |
| 15 | Overdraft | 1500 | | | | |
| 16 | | | | | | |
| 17 | Net current assets | | | | | |
| 18 | Net assets | | | | | |
| 19 | | | | | | |
| 20 | *Represented by:* | | | | | |
| 21 | Opening capital | | 28000 | | | |
| 22 | Profit for year | | 3500 | | | |
| 23 | Drawings | | 1000 | | | |
| 24 | Closing capital | | | | | |
| 25 | | | | | | |
| 26 | | | | | | |

(a)   Devise and list the formulae required to go in the cells highlighted.

(b)   Using the diagram above, show how the spreadsheet would appear when the correct formulae have been entered.

*Note*. This tests your accounting knowledge as well as your understanding of spreadsheets.

## 2   SOME BASIC 'HANDS-ON' SKILLS

2.1   In this section we are going to teach you some of the **basic skills** that will be useful **whenever** you are using a spreadsheet package. We give instructions for Microsoft Excel, the most widely used package.

2.2   There is no point in reading this section at all if you are not sitting at a computer and trying out the skills we describe, **'hands-on'**. Come back to this section later if you cannot do this right now.

### DEVOLVED ASSESSMENT ALERT

Section 2 of this chapter goes from first principles, and you may not need to study it in depth if you are used to spreadsheets already. Skim read it even so, because the intention is to get you into **good habits** and give you tips that will **speed up your work** both in practice and in your Devolved Assessment.

Section 3 is fundamental to good spreadsheet building: you will never be able to take full advantage of the power of spreadsheets unless you learn the principles we describe there.

Even if you are a very experienced spreadsheet user, therefore, we recommend that you try all the activities in this chapter.

## Which version?

2.3 We describe **Excel 97**. Later versions of Excel also work in the way described here, although they contain extra features.

## Windows skills

2.4 If you have never used Windows or a **mouse** before, however, you need to spend a bit of time getting familiar with these first. There is an Appendix on basic skills such as **clicking, double-clicking, selecting** and **dragging and dropping** at the end of this book.

## Getting started

2.5 Load up your spreadsheet by finding and double-clicking on the Excel **icon** or button (it will look like an X), or by choosing Excel from somewhere in the **Start** menus (maybe from within the **Microsoft Office** option).

## Moving about (F5)

2.6 Press the function key labelled **F5** at the top of the keyboard. A **Go To** dialogue box will appear with the 'cursor' (a flashing line or lit up section) in a box. Delete anything that is in the box with the Delete key and then type C5 (or c5 – case does not matter) and press Enter. The 'cursor' will now be over cell C5. This is the **active cell** and it will have a thick black line all round it.

2.7 Press **Ctrl** + ↑ and then **Ctrl** + ←. (This means that you hold down one of the keys marked Ctrl and, keeping it held down, press the other key.)

2.8 The cursor will move back to cell A1. Try holding down Ctrl and pressing each of the direction arrow keys in turn to see where you end up. Try using the **Page Up** and **Page Down** keys and also try **Home** and **End** and Ctrl + these keys. Try **Tab** and **Shift + Tab**, too. These are all useful shortcuts for moving quickly from one place to another in a large spreadsheet.

> **TIP OF THE DAY**
>
> The F5 key is not needed for small spreadsheets, but it is a very handy way of getting around larger ones.

## Entering data and the active cell

2.9 Get your cursor back to cell A1. Then type in 123. Then press the ↓ key. Note that the cell below (A2) now becomes the **active cell**.

2.10 Type 456 in cell A2 and then press the → key. The cell to the left (B2) is now the active cell.

2.11 Get back to cell A1. Above cell A1 you should be able to see a rectangle at the top left *telling* you that you are in cell A1 and, to the right of this a line containing the numbers 123. In other words this line at the top of the screen shows you the **cell reference** and the **contents** of the currently **active cell**.

## Editing data (F2)

2.12 Assuming you have now made cell A1 the active cell, type 45. Note what happens both in the cell and in the line above. The previous entry (123) is replaced by the number 45. Press ↓. The active cell is now A2 (check in the line at the top of the screen).

2.13 Suppose you wanted to **change the entry** in cell A2 from 456 to 123456. You have four options. Option (d) is the best.

    (a)  **Type** 123456 and press **Enter**.

        To undo this and try the next option press **Ctrl + Z**: this will always undo what you have just done.

    (b)  **Double-click** in cell A2. The cell will keep its thick outline but you will now be able to see a vertical line flashing in the cell. You can move this line by using the direction arrow keys or the Home and the End keys. Move it to before the 4 and type 123. Then press Enter.

        When you have tried this press Ctrl + Z to undo it.

    (c)  **Click** *once* on the number 456 in the line that shows the active cell reference and cell contents at the top of the screen. Again you will get the vertical line and you can type in 123 before the 4. Then press Enter, then Ctrl + Z.

    (d)  Press the **function key F2**. The vertical line cursor will be flashing in cell A2 at the *end* of the figures entered there (after the 6). Press Home to get to a position before the 4 and then type in 123 and press Enter, as before.

> **TIP OF THE DAY**
>
> **Option (d)** - F2 - may not seem much better than the other options at the moment, but after a bit of experience you will soon find that it is usually **quicker and more convenient** than the other methods.

2.14 Now make cell A3 the active cell. Type **1 2** (a 1, a space, and then a 2) in this cell and press Enter. Note that because the software finds a space it thinks you want **text** in this cell. It **aligns it to the left,** not the right. If you ever need to enter a number to be treated as text, you should enter an **apostrophe** before it. eg '1.

## Deleting

2.15 Get to cell A3 if you have not already done so and press **Delete**. The contents of this cell will disappear.

2.16 Move the cursor up to cell A2. Now hold down the **Shift** key (the one above the Ctrl key) and keeping it held down press the ↑ arrow. Cell A2 will stay white but cell A1 will go black. What you have done here is **selected** the range A1 and A2. **Anything you do next will be done to both cells A1 and A2.**

2.17 Press Delete. The contents of cells A1 and A2 will disappear.

## Activity 5.5

(a) What is the purpose of the F5 key?

(b) What are four ways of editing the data in a cell?

(c) What happens in a Windows program if you press Ctrl + Z?

(d) How do you select a cell or a range of cells using:

    (i) the mouse;
    (ii) the keyboard?

## Filling cells automatically

2.18 If you are not used to using a mouse you may find this bit quite difficult at first.

2.19 You should now have a blank spreadsheet. Type the number 1 in cell A1 and the number 2 in cell A2. Now *select* cells A1: A2, this time by positioning the mouse pointer over cell A1, holding down the left mouse button and moving the pointer down to cell A2. When cell A2 goes black you can release the mouse button.

2.20 Now position the mouse pointer at the **bottom right hand corner** of cell A2. (You should be able to see a little black lump in this corner: this is called the '**fill handle**'.) When you have the mouse pointer in the right place it will turn into a black cross.

**Hold down** the left mouse button again and move the pointer down to cell A10. You will see an outline surrounding the cells you are trying to 'fill'.

**Release** the mouse button when you have the pointer over cell A10. You will find that the software **automatically** fills in the numbers 3 to 10 below 1 and 2.

2.21 There are a number of variations on this technique that you can now experiment with.

(a) Delete what you have just done and type in **Jan** in cell A1. See what happens if you select cell A1 and fill down to cell A12: you get the months **Feb, Mar, Apr** and so on.

(b) Type the number 2 in cell A1. Select A1 and fill down to cell A10. What happens? The cells should fill up with 2's.

(c) Type the number 2 in cell A1 and 4 in cell A2. Then select A1: A2 and fill down to cell A10. What happens? You should get 2, 4, 6, 8, and so on.

(d) Can you **fill across** as well as down? You should be able to.

(e) What happens if you click on the bottom right hand corner using the **right mouse button,** drag down to another cell and then release the button? You should get a menu giving you a variety of different options for how you want the cells to be filled in.

(f) In Excel you can fill in any direction.

**TIP OF THE DAY**

We suggest you spend some time playing with your package's fill facility: it is **a useful skill to acquire.**

## A glorified calculator?

2.22 You need a clean spreadsheet for the next bit. Click on the button in the top left hand corner (above row number 1 and to the right of column letter A) and the **whole spreadsheet** will be selected: it will all go black. Press **Delete** to clear away any figures you may have entered in the last exercise. Then press ↑ or ← to clear away the highlighting.

2.23 Now enter the following figures in cells A1:B5. Make sure the **Num Lock light** on your keyboard is lit up (press the Num Lock key if not) and **use the numeric keypad** exactly as you would a calculator keypad.

|   | A | B |
|---|---|---|
| 1 | 400 | 582 |
| 2 | 250 | 478 |
| 3 | 359 | 264 |
| 4 | 476 | 16 |
| 5 | 97 | 125 |

2.24 To check that you have entered the figures correctly make cell A6 the active cell and *double-click* on the button labelled with a '**sum**' sign at the top of the screen. (The button has a Σ symbol, the mathematical sign for 'the sum of'.)

The number 1582 should shortly appear in cell A6.

2.25 Now select cell B6 and click *once* on the sum button. A formula will appear in the cell saying =SUM(B1:B5). Above cell B6 you will see a flashing dotted line encircling cells B1:B5. Click **anywhere within** the encircled area, hold down the left mouse button and move the mouse about a little from cell to cell. Watch the **formula** in cell B6 and the **boundary** of the dotted line change as you redefine the cells that are to be summed. To finish up, click on cell B5, hold down the left mouse button and move the pointer up to cell B1. Then click on the Σ button. The formula =SUM(B1:B5) will be entered and the number 1465 will be appear in cell B6.

2.26 Next select cell C1. Type in an = sign then click on cell A1. Now type in an **asterisk \*** (which serves as a **multiplication sign** in spreadsheets) and click on cell B1. Watch how the formula in cell C1 changes as you do this. (Alternatively you can enter the cell references by moving the direction arrow keys.) Finally press Enter. Cell C1 will show the result (232,800) of multiplying the figure in Cell A1 by the one in cell B1.

2.27 Your next task is to select cell C1 and **fill in** cells C2 to C5 automatically using the **dragging technique** described above. If you then click on each cell in column C and look above at the line showing what the cell contains you will find that the software has automatically filled in the correct cell references for you: A2\*B2 in cell C2, A3\*B3 in cell C3 and so on.

2.28 Spreadsheets are **not** just glorified calculators, but what you have just seen is a very useful function for carrying out **large numbers of simple but time consuming calculations** quickly and without errors, and you should certainly not be shy of using spreadsheets for this purpose.

---

**Activity 5.6**

(a) What do 'fill across' and 'fill down' mean?

(b) Use the sum *button* in your spreadsheet package to sum the following figures, laid out as shown here. Cell D5 should show the total of cells A5 to C5, cell E6 the total of cells E1 to E3 and cell C11 the sum of cells B8 to B10.

*Do not* type the formulae directly instead of using the sum button.

| | A | B | C | D | E | F |
|---|---|---|---|---|---|---|
| 1 | | | | | 1 | |
| 2 | | | | | 2 | |
| 3 | | | | | 3 | |
| 4 | | | | | | |
| 5 | 4 | 6 | 5 | | | |
| 6 | | | | | | |
| 7 | | | | | | |
| 8 | | 10 | | | | |
| 9 | | 20 | | | | |
| 10 | | 70 | | | | |
| 11 | | | | | | |
| 12 | | | | | | |
| 13 | | | | | | |

## Inserting columns and rows

2.29 Suppose we wanted to know the sum of the numbers in columns A and B as well as their product? You can probably work out that we would use the 'sum' button, but where shall we put the figures? The best place is in **column C**. To do this we have three options.

(a) Highlight cells C1 to C5 and position the mouse pointer on one of the **edges**. (It will change to an arrow shape.) Hold down the **left** mouse button and drag cells C1 to C5 into column D. There is now space in column C for our next set of sums. Any **formulae** that need to be changed as a result of moving cells about like this will be changed **automatically**.

(b) The second option is to highlight cells C1 to C5 as before, position the mouse pointer anywhere **within** column C and click on the **right** mouse button. A menu will appear offering you an option **Insert...** . If you click on this you will be asked where you want to shift the cells that are being moved. In this case you want to move them to the *right* so choose this option and click on OK.

(c) The third option is to **insert a whole new column**. You do this by clicking on the letter at the top of the column (here C) to highlight the whole of it then proceeding as in (b). The new column will always be inserted to the left of the one you highlight.

You can now use the sum button to add across cells A1 and B1, A2 and B2 and so on, and show the results in column C.

2.30 You can also insert a **new row** in a similar way (or stretch rows).

(a) To insert *one* row – for headings say – click on the row number to highlight it, click with the right mouse button and choose insert. One row will be inserted **above** the one you highlighted. Try putting some headings above the figures in columns A to C.

(b) To insert **several** rows click on the row number **immediately below** the point where you want the new rows to appear and, holding down the left mouse button select the number of extra rows you want – rows 1, 2 and 3, say, to insert three rows above the current row 1. Click on the highlighted area with the right mouse button and choose insert.

BPP PUBLISHING

## Layout

2.31 Clear the contents of your spreadsheet, as described in paragraph 2.22. Then type the following text in cell A1: **This is far too wide to fit in the column.** Press Enter. The text **will** be too wide to fit in the column, but it will overlap into columns B, C, and possibly D so you will still be able to see what you typed.

Now click on where cell B1 should be (it will be covered up with words, but you can still work out where it should be: look at the box at the top left-hand corner if you are not sure you have clicked in the right place. Now type the number 1,234,567,890. Press Enter.

2.32 The result is likely to be something like the following.

|   | A | B | C | D | E |
|---|---|---|---|---|---|
| 1 | This is far | ######### | | | |
| 2 | | | | | |
| 3 | | | | | |
| 4 | | | | | |
| 5 | | | | | |

What a disaster! You cannot see much of the text that you so carefully typed in cell A1 and you cannot see *any* of the figures that you typed in cell B1!

2.33 They are both still there, though, so don't worry. It is just that the **columns are not wide enough**. To solve this there are two options.

(a) One is to **decide for yourself** how wide you want the columns to be. Position the mouse pointer at the head of column A directly over the little line dividing the letter A from the letter B. The mouse **pointer** will change to a sort of **cross**. Hold down the left mouse button and, by moving your mouse, stretch Column A to the right, to about the middle of column D, until the words you typed fit. You can do the same for column B. Then make your columns too narrow again so you can try option (b).

(b) Often it is easier to **let the software decide for you**. Position the mouse pointer over the little dividing line as before and get the cross symbol. Then double-click with the left mouse button. The column automatically adjusts to an appropriate width to fit the widest cell in that column.

**TIP OF THE DAY**

You can either adjust the width of each column individually or you can do them all in one go. To do the latter click on the button in the top left hand corner to **select the whole sheet** and then **double-click** on just one of the dividing lines: all the columns will adjust to the 'best fit' width.

**Activity 5.7**

(a) Enter the following data in a spreadsheet.

|   | A | B | C | D | E | F |
|---|---|---|---|---|---|---|
| 1 | 1 | 2 | 3 |   |   |   |
| 2 | 2 |   |   |   |   |   |
| 3 | 3 |   |   |   |   |   |
| 4 |   |   |   |   |   |   |
| 5 |   |   |   |   |   |   |
| 6 |   |   |   |   |   |   |
| 7 |   |   |   |   |   |   |

Without typing any data and without dragging and dropping data use the mouse to make the spreadsheet look like this.

|   | A | B | C | D | E | F |
|---|---|---|---|---|---|---|
| 1 | 1 |   | 2 |   | 3 |   |
| 2 |   |   |   |   |   |   |
| 3 | 2 |   |   |   |   |   |
| 4 |   |   |   |   |   |   |
| 5 | 3 |   |   |   |   |   |
| 6 |   |   |   |   |   |   |
| 7 |   |   |   |   |   |   |

(b) Enter the text 'Profit and loss account' in cell A1 of a spreadsheet and the number 6,427,983.24 in cell B1.

Widen columns A and B so that the entries you have made can be clearly seen. Use the mouse to do this.

(c) Drag the data you have just entered in cells A1 and B1 into cells E12 and F12. Widen columns E and F so that the data fits properly.

## More keyboard shortcuts and buttons

2.34 Finally a few tricks to improve the **appearance** of your spreadsheets and speed up your work. To do any of the following to a cell or range of cells, first **select** the cell or cells and then:

(a) Press Ctrl + B to make the cell contents **bold.**

(b) Press Ctrl + I to make the cell contents *italic.*

(c) Press **Ctrl + C** to **copy** the contents of the cells.

(d) Move the cursor and press **Ctrl + V** to **paste** the cell you just copied into the new active cell or cells.

(When you copy cells the highlighted area will have a **moving dotted border** until you paste them somewhere or else press the **Esc** key.)

2.35 There are also **buttons** at the top of the screen that carry out these and other functions. Enter some numbers and text into a spreadsheet and try out the above keyboard shortcuts and any buttons you fancy to see what effect they have. You cannot break the spreadsheet by using its facilities and you do not have to save what you do unless you want to.

## Activity 5.8

(a) Look at the illustration below. Explain the purpose of each of the buttons shown.

(b) What keyboard shortcuts can be used to do the following?

(i) Copy and paste the contents of a cell or cells.

(ii) Make the contents of a cell bold.

## 3    BUILDING A MODEL

**TIP OF THE DAY**

All spreadsheets should **ideally** be constructed in **three sections** as follows.

(a) There should be in **inputs** section containing the **variables,** for example the amount of a loan and the interest rate.

(b) There should be a **calculations** section containing **formulae,** for example the loan times the interest rate.

(c) There should be a **results** section showing the outcome of performing the calculations on the input variables.

3.1    Here is a **very** simple example, arranged in this way.

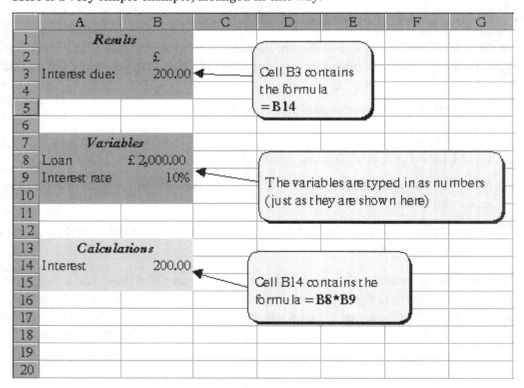

3.2 In practice many spreadsheets are fairly **small** and it is often **more convenient** to combine the results and calculations areas as follows.

| | A | B | C | D | E | F | G |
|---|---|---|---|---|---|---|---|
| 1 | *Results* | | | | | | |
| 2 | | £ | | | | | |
| 3 | Interest due: | 200.00 | | Cell B3 contains the formula =B8*B9 | | | |
| 4 | | | | | | | |
| 5 | | | | | | | |
| 6 | | | | | | | |
| 7 | *Variables* | | | | | | |
| 8 | Loan | £ 2,000.00 | | | | | |
| 9 | Interest rate | 10.00% | | The variables are typed in as numbers (just as they are shown here) | | | |
| 10 | | | | | | | |
| 11 | | | | | | | |
| 12 | | | | | | | |
| 13 | | | | | | | |
| 14 | | | | | | | |
| 15 | | | | | | | |

3.3 The reasons for building a spreadsheet in this way is that it makes it **easier to change** and **use again**, without having to build a completely new spreadsheet every time.

3.4 In this example, if we took out another loan of £4,789 at an interest rate of 7.25% we would simply need to **overwrite the figures in the variable section** with the new figures to find out how much interest was due.

3.5 We shall now look at a more complicated example. Ideally you should work through *all* the examples in this book yourself, hands-on.

3.6 **EXAMPLE: CONSTRUCTING A CASH FLOW PROJECTION**

Suppose you wanted to set up a simple six-month cash flow projection, in such a way that you could use it to estimate how the **projected cash balance** figures will **change** in total when any **individual item** in the projection is **altered**. You have the following information.

(a) Sales were £45,000 per month in 20X5, falling to £42,000 in January 20X6. Thereafter they are expected to increase by 3% per month (ie February will be 3% higher than January, and so on).

(b) Debts are collected as follows.

 (i) 60% in month following sale.
 (ii) 30% in second month after sale.
 (iii) 7% in third month after sale.
 (iv) 3% remains uncollected.

(c) Purchases are equal to cost of sales, set at 65% of sales.

(d) Overheads were £6,000 per month in 20X5, rising by 5% in 20X6.

(e) Opening cash is an overdraft of £7,500.

(f) Dividends: £10,000 final dividend on 20X5 profits payable in May.

(g) Capital purchases: plant costing £18,000 will be ordered in January. 20% is payable with order, 70% on delivery in February and the final 10% in May.

*Headings and layout*

3.7   The first job is to put in the various **headings** that you want on the cash flow projection. At this stage, your screen might look as follows.

| | A | B | C | D | E | F | G |
|---|---|---|---|---|---|---|---|
| 1 | EXCELLENT PLC | | | | | | |
| 2 | *Cash flow projection – six months ending 30 June* 20X6 | | | | | | |
| 3 | | *Jan* | *Feb* | *Mar* | *Apr* | *May* | *Jun* |
| 4 | | £ | £ | £ | £ | £ | £ |
| 5 | Sales | | | | | | |
| 6 | *Cash receipts* | | | | | | |
| 7 | 1 month in arrears | | | | | | |
| 8 | 2 months in arrears | | | | | | |
| 9 | 3 months in arrears | | | | | | |
| 10 | Total operating receipts | | | | | | |
| 11 | | | | | | | |
| 12 | Cash payments | | | | | | |
| 13 | Purchases | | | | | | |
| 14 | Overheads | | | | | | |
| 15 | Total operating payments | | | | | | |
| 16 | | | | | | | |
| 17 | Dividends | | | | | | |
| 18 | Capital purchases | | | | | | |
| 19 | Total other payments | | | | | | |
| 20 | | | | | | | |
| 21 | Net cash flow | | | | | | |
| 22 | Cash balance b/f | | | | | | |
| 23 | Cash balance c/f | | | | | | |
| 24 | | | | | | | |

3.8   A couple of points to note at this stage.

(a)   We have **increased the width** of column A to allow longer pieces of text to be inserted. Had we not done so, only the first part of each caption would have been displayed (and printed). If you skipped Section 2 of this chapter but you don't know how to widen a column, you had better go back and read it now.

(b)   We have developed a **simple style for headings**. Headings are essential, so that users can identify what a spreadsheet does. We have **emboldened** the company name and *italicised* other headings.

(c)   When **text** is entered into a cell it is usually **left-aligned** (as for example in column A). We have **centred** the headings above each column by highlighting the cells and using the relevant buttons at the top of the screen.

(d)   **Numbers** should be **right-aligned** in cells.

(e)   We have left **spaces** in certain rows (after blocks of related items) to make the spreadsheet **easier to use and read**.

*Inserting formulae*

3.9   The next stage is to put in the **calculations** you want the computer to carry out, expressed as **formulae**. For example, in cell B10 you want total operating receipts, so you move to cell B10 and put in the formula =SUM(B7:B9).

3.10   Look for a moment at cell C7. We are told that sales in January were £42,000 and that 60% of customers settle their accounts one month in arrears. We could insert the formula

=B5*0.6 in the cell and fill in the other cells along the row so that it is replicated in each month. However, consider the effect of a change in payment patterns to a situation where, say, 55% of customer debts are settled after one month. This would necessitate a **change to each and every cell** in which the 0.6 ratio appears.

3.11 An alternative approach, which makes **future changes much simpler** to execute, is to put the relevant ratio (here, 60% or 0.6) in a cell **outside** the main table and cross-refer each cell in the main table to that cell.

3.12 This means that, if the percentage changes, the change need only be reflected in **one cell**, following which all cells which are dependent on that cell will **automatically use the new percentage**.

3.13 We will therefore input such values in separate parts of the spreadsheet, as follows. Look at the other assumptions which we have inserted into this part of the spreadsheet.

> **TIP OF THE DAY**
>
> Note that **percentages** can either be input in the form 6% or as decimal 0.06. Note especially that **negative** cash flows must have a **minus sign**.

| | A | B | C | D | E | F | G |
|---|---|---|---|---|---|---|---|
| 24 | | | | | | | |
| 25 | | | | | | | |
| 26 | *This table contains the key variables for the 20X6 cash flow projections* | | | | | | |
| 27 | | | | | | | |
| 28 | Sales growth factor per month | | 1.03 | | | | |
| 29 | Purchases as % of sales | | -0.65 | | | | |
| 30 | | | | | | | |
| 31 | Debts paid within 1 month | | 0.6 | | | | |
| 32 | Debts paid within 2 months | | 0.3 | | | | |
| 33 | Debts paid within 3 months | | 0.07 | | | | |
| 34 | Bad debts | | 0.03 | | | | |
| 35 | | | | | | | |
| 36 | Increase in overheads | | 1.05 | | | | |
| 37 | | | | | | | |
| 38 | Dividends (May) | | -10000 | | | | |
| 39 | | | | | | | |
| 40 | Capital purchases | | -18000 | | | | |
| 41 | January | | 0.2 | | | | |
| 42 | February | | 0.7 | | | | |
| 43 | May | | 0.1 | | | | |
| 44 | | | | | | | |
| 45 | | | | | | | |
| 46 | *This table contains relevant opening balance data as at Jan 20X6* | | | | | | |
| 47 | | | | | | | |
| 48 | Monthly sales 19X5 | | 45000 | | | | |
| 49 | January 1996 sales | | 42000 | | | | |
| 50 | Monthly overheads 19X5 | | -6000 | | | | |
| 51 | Opening cash | | -7500 | | | | |
| 52 | | | | | | | |

3.14 Now we can go back to cell C7 and input =B5*C31 and then fill this in across the '1 month in arrears' row. (Note that, as we have no December sales figure, we will have to deal with cell B7 separately.) If you don't know what 'filling in' means, you had better go back to section 2 of this chapter. If we assume for the moment that we are copying to cells D7 through to G7 and follow this procedure, the contents of cell D7 would be shown as =C5*D31, and so on, as shown below.

| | A | B | C | D | E | F | G |
|---|---|---|---|---|---|---|---|
| | | *Jan* | *Feb* | *Mar* | *Apr* | *May* | *Jun* |
| 3 | | | | | | | |
| 4 | | £ | £ | £ | £ | £ | £ |
| 5 | Sales | | | | | | |
| 6 | *Cash receipts* | | | | | | |
| 7 | 1 month in arrears | | =B5*C31 | =C5*D31 | =D5*E31 | =E5*F31 | =F5*G31 |
| 8 | 2 months in arrears | | | | | | |
| 9 | 3 months in arrears | | | | | | |
| 10 | Total operating receipts | | | | | | |

3.15 You may notice a **problem** if you look at this closely. While the formula in cell C7 is fine - it multiplies January sales by 0.6 (the 1 month ratio stored in cell C31) - the remaining formulae are useless, as they **refer to empty cells** in row 31. This is what the spreadsheet would look like (assuming, for now, constant sales of £42,000 per month)

| | A | B | C | D | E | F | G |
|---|---|---|---|---|---|---|---|
| | | *Jan* | *Feb* | *Mar* | *Apr* | *May* | *Jun* |
| 3 | | | | | | | |
| 4 | | £ | £ | £ | £ | £ | £ |
| 5 | Sales | 42000 | 42000 | 42000 | 42000 | 42000 | 42000 |
| 6 | *Cash receipts* | | | | | | |
| 7 | 1 month in arrears | | 25200 | 0 | 0 | 0 | 0 |
| 8 | 2 months in arrears | | | | | | |
| 9 | 3 months in arrears | | | | | | |
| 10 | Total operating receipts | | | | | | |

## Activity 5.9

Below is a spreadsheet with some values in it.

| | A | B | C | D | E |
|---|---|---|---|---|---|
| 1 | **Boilermakers Ltd** | | | | |
| 2 | *Department B* | | | | |
| 3 | | | | | |
| 4 | *Production data* | Machine A | Machine B | Machine C | |
| 5 | Shift 1 | 245.84 | 237.49 | 231.79 | |
| 6 | Shift 2 | 241.14 | 237.62 | 261.31 | |
| 7 | Shift 3 | 244.77 | 201.64 | 242.71 | |
| 8 | Shift 4 | 240.96 | 238.18 | 234.50 | |
| 9 | | | | | |
| 10 | | | | | |
| 11 | *Usage data* | Machine A | Machine B | Machine C | |
| 12 | Maintenance | 35 | 71 | 6 | |
| **13** | Operational | 8.47 | 7.98 | 9.31 | |
| 14 | Idle | 1.42 | 2.4 | 0.87 | |
| 15 | Recovery | 0 | 15 | 4 | |
| 16 | | | | | |
| 17 | | | | | |
| 18 | | | | | |
| 19 | | | | | |
| 20 | | | | | |

(a) Cell B9 needs to contain an average of all the preceding numbers in column B. Suggest a formula which would achieve this.

(b) Cell C16 contains the formula

=C12+C13/C14-C15

What would the result be, displayed in cell C16?

## Relative and absolute references (F4)

3.16 There is a very important distinction between **relative** cell references and **absolute** cell references.

Usually, cell references are **relative**. A formula of =SUM(B7:B9) in cell B10 is relative. It does not really mean 'add up the numbers in cells B7 to B9'; it actually means '**add up the numbers in the three cells above this one**'. If the formula were copied to cell C10 (as we will do later), it would become =SUM(C7:C9).

3.17 This is what is causing the problem encountered above. The spreadsheet thinks we are asking it to 'multiply the number two up and one to the left by the number twenty-four cells down', and that is indeed the effect of the instruction we have given. But we are actually intending to ask it to 'multiply the number two up and one to the left by the number in cell C31'. This means that we need to create an **absolute** (unchanging) **reference** to cell C31. This is done by adding a pair of **dollar signs** ($) to the relevant formula, one before the column letter and one before the row number.

---

**TIP OF THE DAY**

**Never** type the dollar signs. In this case, add them as follows.

(a) Make cell C7 the active cell and **press F2** to edit it.

(b) Note where the **cursor** is flashing: it should be after the 1. If it is not move it with the direction arrow keys so that it is positioned somewhere **next to or within the cell reference C31.**

(c) **Press F4**

---

3.18 Like magic, the **function key F4** adds dollar signs to the cell reference: it becomes $C$31. Press F4 again: the reference becomes C$31. Press it again: the reference becomes $C31. Press it once more, and the simple relative reference is restored: C31.

(a) A dollar sign **before a letter** means that the **column** reference stays the same when you copy the formula to another cell.

(b) A dollar sign **before a number** means that the **row** reference stays the same when you copy the formula to another cell.

3.19 The spreadsheet below shows all the possibilities and the results of filling in each type of reference across columns and down rows.

| | A | B | C |
|---|---|---|---|
| 1 | | Formulae | |
| 2 | | | |
| 3 | | *Variables* | |
| 4 | Dog | Pussycat | Mouse |
| 5 | Rabbit | | |
| 6 | Goldfish | | |
| 7 | | | |
| 8 | | *A4 style* | |
| 9 | =A4 | =B4 | =C4 |
| 10 | =A5 | | |
| 11 | =A6 | | |
| 12 | | | |
| 13 | | *$ A$ 4 style* | |
| 14 | =$A$4 | =$A$4 | =$A$4 |
| 15 | =$A$4 | | |
| 16 | =$A$4 | | |
| 17 | | | |
| 18 | | *A$ 4 style* | |
| 19 | =A$4 | =B$4 | =C$4 |
| 20 | =A$4 | | |
| 21 | =A$4 | | |
| 22 | | | |
| 23 | | *$ A4 style* | |
| 24 | =$A4 | =$A4 | =$A4 |
| 25 | =$A5 | | |
| 26 | =$A6 | | |
| 27 | | | |

| | A | B | C |
|---|---|---|---|
| 1 | | What happens ... | |
| 2 | | | |
| 3 | | *Variables* | |
| 4 | Dog | Pussycat | Mouse |
| 5 | Rabbit | | |
| 6 | Goldfish | | |
| 7 | | | |
| 8 | | *A4 style* | |
| 9 | Dog | Pussycat | Mouse |
| 10 | Rabbit | | |
| 11 | Goldfish | | |
| 12 | | | |
| 13 | | *$ A$ 4 style* | |
| 14 | Dog | Dog | Dog |
| 15 | Dog | | |
| 16 | Dog | | |
| 17 | | | |
| 18 | | *A$ 4 style* | |
| 19 | Dog | Pussycat | Mouse |
| 20 | Dog | | |
| 21 | Dog | | |
| 22 | | | ' |
| 23 | | *$ A4 style* | |
| 24 | Dog | Dog | Dog |
| 25 | Rabbit | | |
| 26 | Goldfish | | |
| 27 | | | |

## 3.20 BACK TO THE EXAMPLE

In our example we have now altered the reference in cell C7 and filled in across to cell G7, overwriting what was there previously. This is the result.

(a) Formulae

| | A | B | C | D | E | F | G |
|---|---|---|---|---|---|---|---|
| 3 | | *Jan* | *Feb* | *Mar* | *Apr* | *May* | *Jun* |
| 4 | | £ | £ | £ | £ | £ | £ |
| 5 | Sales | 42000 | 42000 | 42000 | 42000 | 42000 | 42000 |
| 6 | *Cash receipts* | | | | | | |
| 7 | 1 month in arrears | | =B5*$C$31 | =C5*$C$31 | =D5*$C$31 | =E5*$C$31 | =F5*$C$31 |
| 8 | 2 months in arrears | | | | | | |
| 9 | 3 months in arrears | | | | | | |
| 10 | Total operating receipts | | | | | | |

(b) Numbers

| | A | B | C | D | E | F | G |
|---|---|---|---|---|---|---|---|
| 3 | | *Jan* | *Feb* | *Mar* | *Apr* | *May* | *Jun* |
| 4 | | £ | £ | £ | £ | £ | £ |
| 5 | Sales | 42000 | 42000 | 42000 | 42000 | 42000 | 42000 |
| 6 | *Cash receipts* | | | | | | |
| 7 | 1 month in arrears | | 25200 | 25200 | 25200 | 25200 | 25200 |
| 8 | 2 months in arrears | | | | | | |
| 9 | 3 months in arrears | | | | | | |
| 10 | Total operating receipts | | | | | | |

3.21 Other formulae required for this projection are as follows.

(a) **Cell B5** refers directly to the information we are given - **sales of £42,000** in January. We have input this variable in cell C49. The other formulae in row 5 (sales) reflect the predicted sales growth of 3% per month, as entered in cell C28.

(b) Similar formulae to the one already described for row 7 are required in rows 8 and 9.

(c) **Row 10** (total operating receipts) will display simple **subtotals**, in the form =SUM(B7:B9).

(d) **Row 13 (purchases)** requires a formula based on the data in row 5 **(sales)** and the value in cell C29 **(purchases** as a % of sales). This model assumes no changes in stock levels from month to month, and that stocks are sufficiently high to enable this. The formula is B5 * $C$29. Note that C29 is negative.

(e) **Row 15** (total operating payments), like row 10, requires **formulae** to create **subtotals**.

(f) **Rows 17 and 18** refer to the **dividends and capital purchase data** input in cells C38 and C40 to 43.

(g) **Row 21** (net cash flow) requires a **total** in the form =B10 + B15 + B21.

(h) **Row 22** (balance b/f) requires the contents of the **previous month's closing cash** figure.

(i) **Row 23** (balance b/f) requires the **total** of the **opening cash** figure and the **net cash flow** for the month.

3.22 Once the formulae have been inserted, this is what the spreadsheet would contain. (Remember, it does not normally look like this on screen, as formulae are not usually displayed in cells.)

| | A | B | C | D | E | F | G |
|---|---|---|---|---|---|---|---|
| 1 | EXCELLENT PLC | | | | | | |
| 2 | Cash flow projection - six months | | | | | | |
| 3 | | Jan | Feb | Mar | Apr | May | Jun |
| 4 | | £ | £ | £ | £ | £ | £ |
| 5 | Sales | =C49 | =B5*$C$28 | =C5*$C$28 | =D5*$C$28 | =E5*$C$28 | =F5*$C$28 |
| 6 | Cash receipts | | | | | | |
| 7 | 1 month in arrears | =$C$48*$C$31 | =B5*$C$31 | =C5*$C$31 | =D5*$C$31 | =E5*$C$31 | =F5*$C$31 |
| 8 | 2 months in arrears | =$C$48*$C$32 | =$C$48*$C$32 | =B5*$C$32 | =C5*$C$32 | =D5*$C$32 | =E5*$C$32 |
| 9 | 3 months in arrears | =$C$48*$C$33 | =$C$48*$C$33 | =$C$48*$C$33 | =B5*$C$33 | =C5*$C$33 | =D5*$C$33 |
| 10 | Total operating receipts | =SUM(B7:B9) | =SUM(C7:C9) | =SUM(D7:D9) | =SUM(E7:E9) | =SUM(F7:F9) | =SUM(G7:G9) |
| 11 | | | | | | | |
| 12 | Cash payments | | | | | | |
| 13 | Purchases | =B5*$C$29 | =C5*$C$29 | =D5*$C$29 | =E5*$C$29 | =F5*$C$29 | =G5*$C$29 |
| 14 | Overheads | =$C$50*$C$36 | =$C$50*$C$36 | =$C$50*$C$36 | =$C$50*$C$36 | =$C$50*$C$36 | =$C$50*$C$36 |
| 15 | Total operating payments | =SUM(B13:B14) | =SUM(C13:C14) | =SUM(D13:D14) | =SUM(E13:E14) | =SUM(F13:F14) | =SUM(G13:G14) |
| 16 | | | | | | | |
| 17 | Dividends | 0 | 0 | 0 | 0 | =C38 | 0 |
| 18 | Capital purchases | =C40*C41 | =C40*C42 | 0 | 0 | =C40*C43 | 0 |
| 19 | Total other payments | =SUM(B17:B18) | =SUM(C17:C18) | =SUM(D17:D18) | =SUM(E17:E18) | =SUM(F17:F18) | =SUM(G17:G18) |
| 20 | | | | | | | |
| 21 | Net cash flow | =B10+B15+B19 | =C10+C15+C19 | =D10+D15+D19 | =E10+E15+E19 | =F10+F15+F19 | =G10+G15+G19 |
| 22 | Cash balance b/f | =C51 | =B23 | =C23 | =D23 | =E23 | =F23 |
| 23 | Cash balance c/f | =SUM(B21:B22) | =SUM(C21:C22) | =SUM(D21:D22) | =SUM(E21:E22) | =SUM(F21:F22) | =SUM(G21:G22) |
| 24 | | | | | | | |

## Negative numbers

3.23 In a spreadsheet, you must be very careful to sort out the approach which you wish to take when manipulating negative numbers. For example, if total operating payments in row 15 are shown as **positive**, you would need to **subtract** them from total operating receipts in the formulae in row 23. However if you have chosen to make them **negative**, to represent outflows, then you will need to **add** them to total operating receipts. This becomes even more important when you are dealing with accounts or balances which may be sometimes positive and sometimes negative, for example the cash balances rows.

> ## TIP OF THE DAY
>
> A spreadsheet is very logical, but it will only do what you tell it to do. It does not 'know' that overheads, for example, are always cash outflows. It is up to you to adopt the same logical approach. If you want to display cash outflows (or, for example, debits in a profit and loss account) with brackets round them or a minus sign in front of them, you need to remember the effect that this will have on resulting subtotals and totals.

*Opening balances*

3.24 It is important, in an exercise like this, to get the opening balances right. However good your budgeting of income and expenses is, if you have made a **poor estimate** of the opening cash balance, this will be **reflected right through the forecast**.

*Integration*

3.25 In practice, you might well **integrate** a cash flow projection like this with a forecast profit and loss account and balance sheet. This would give a high degree of **re-assurance** that the numbers 'stacked up' and would enable you to present a 'cleaner' projection: for example, sales would appear on the profit and loss account, and the cash receipts formulae could refer direct to that part of the spreadsheet (or even to a separate spreadsheet in some packages). Similarly, cash not collected could be taken straight back into the profit and loss account as **bad debt expense**.

3.26 Here is the spreadsheet in its normal 'numbers' form.

| | A | B | C | D | E | F | G |
|---|---|---|---|---|---|---|---|
| 1 | EXCELLENT PLC | | | | | | |
| 2 | *Cash flow projection - six months ending 30 June 20X6* | | | | | | |
| 3 | | Jan | Feb | Mar | Apr | May | Jun |
| 4 | | £ | £ | £ | £ | £ | £ |
| 5 | Sales | 42000 | 43260 | 44558 | 45895 | 47271 | 48690 |
| 6 | *Cash receipts* | | | | | | |
| 7 | 1 month in arrears | 27000 | 25200 | 25956 | 26735 | 27537 | 28363 |
| 8 | 2 months in arrears | 13500 | 13500 | 12600 | 12978 | 13367 | 13768 |
| 9 | 3 months in arrears | 3150 | 3150 | 3150 | 2940 | 3028 | 3119 |
| 10 | Total operating receipts | 43650 | 41850 | 41706 | 42653 | 43932 | 45250 |
| 11 | | | | | | | |
| 12 | *Cash payments* | | | | | | |
| 13 | Purchases | -27300 | -28119 | -28963 | -29831 | -30726 | -31648 |
| 14 | Overheads | -6300 | -6300 | -6300 | -6300 | -6300 | -6300 |
| 15 | Total operating payments | -33600 | -34419 | -35263 | -36131 | -37026 | -37948 |
| 16 | | | | | | | |
| 17 | Dividends | | | | | -10000 | |
| 18 | Capital purchases | -3600 | -12600 | | | -1800 | |
| 19 | Total other payments | -3600 | -12600 | | | -11800 | |
| 20 | | | | | | | |
| 21 | Net cash flow | 6450 | -5169 | 6443 | 6521 | -4894 | 7302 |
| 22 | Cash balance b/f | -7500 | -1050 | -6219 | 224 | 6746 | 1852 |
| 23 | Cash balance c/f | -1050 | -6219 | 224 | 6746 | 1852 | 9154 |
| 24 | | | | | | | |

3.27 This needs a little **tidying up**. We will do the following.

(a) Add in **commas** to denote thousands of pounds.

(b) Put **zeros** in the cells with no entry in them.

(c) Change **negative numbers** from being displayed with a **minus sign** to being displayed in **brackets**.

| | A | B | C | D | E | F | G |
|---|---|---|---|---|---|---|---|
| 1 | EXCELLENT PLC | | | | | | |
| 2 | *Cash flow projection – six months ending 30 June* 20X6 | | | | | | |
| 3 | | Jan | Feb | Mar | Apr | May | Jun |
| 4 | | £ | £ | £ | £ | £ | £ |
| 5 | Sales | 42,000 | 43,260 | 44,558 | 45,895 | 47,271 | 48,690 |
| 6 | *Cash receipts* | | | | | | |
| 7 | 1 month in arrears | 27,000 | 25,200 | 25,956 | 26,735 | 27,537 | 28,363 |
| 8 | 2 months in arrears | 13,500 | 13,500 | 12,600 | 12,978 | 13,367 | 13,768 |
| 9 | 3 months in arrears | 3,150 | 3,150 | 3,150 | 2,940 | 3,028 | 3,119 |
| 10 | Total operating receipts | 43,650 | 41,850 | 41,706 | 42,653 | 43,932 | 45,250 |
| 11 | | | | | | | |
| 12 | *Cash payments* | | | | | | |
| 13 | Purchases | (27,300) | (28,119) | (28,963) | (29,831) | (30,726) | (31,648) |
| 14 | Overheads | (6,300) | (6,300) | (6,300) | (6,300) | (6,300) | (6,300) |
| 15 | Total operating payments | (33,600) | (34,419) | (35,263) | (36,131) | (37,026) | (37,948) |
| 16 | | | | | | | |
| 17 | Dividends | 0 | 0 | 0 | 0 | (10,000) | 0 |
| 18 | Capital purchases | (3,600) | (12,600) | 0 | 0 | (1,800) | 0 |
| 19 | Total other payments | (3,600) | (12,600) | 0 | 0 | (11,800) | 0 |
| 20 | | | | | | | |
| 21 | Net cash flow | 6,450 | (5,169) | 6,443 | 6,521 | (4,894) | 7,302 |
| 22 | Cash balance b/f | (7,500) | (1,050) | (6,219) | 224 | 6,746 | 1,852 |
| 23 | Cash balance c/f | (1,050) | (6,219) | 224 | 6,746 | 1,852 | 9,154 |
| 24 | | | | | | | |

## Activity 5.10

The following spreadsheet is designed to process monthly payroll deductions for four employees. Under a new government they pay income tax at 25% and National Insurance at 9% on gross pay. The necessary formulae have not yet been input. (These figures are not 'true' – this is only an example!)

| | A | B | C | D | E | F | G |
|---|---|---|---|---|---|---|---|
| 1 | Diamond Enterprises Ltd | | | | | | |
| 2 | Division: | *Submarines* | | | | | |
| 3 | Month: | *April* | | | | | |
| 4 | | | Johnson,J | Paul,P | George,G | Richards,R | |
| 5 | | | £ | £ | £ | £ | |
| 6 | Gross pay | | 2,166.67 | 2,200.00 | 1,900.00 | 1,779.17 | |
| 7 | | | | | | | |
| 8 | Income tax | | | | | | |
| 9 | NI | | | | | | |
| 10 | Total deductions | | | | | | |
| 11 | | | | | | | |
| 12 | Net pay | | | | | | |
| 13 | | | | | | | |
| 14 | | | | | | | |
| 15 | | | | | | | |
| 16 | | | | | | | |
| 17 | | | | | | | |
| 18 | | | | | | | |
| 19 | | | | | | | |
| 20 | | | | | | | |

*BPP* PUBLISHING

(a)  Devise a suitable formulae for each of the following cells.

   (i)    Cell C8.
   (ii)   Cell D9.
   (iii)  Cell E10.
   (iv)   Cell F12.

(b)  Show how the spreadsheet would appear when the formulae had been input. Ideally try this out in practice using a spreadsheet package.

## Changes in assumptions (what if? analysis)

3.28  We referred to earlier to the need to design a spreadsheet so that **changes in assumptions** do **not** result in **major changes** to vast ranges of cells. This is why we set up two separate areas of the spreadsheet for 20X6 assumptions and opening balances respectively. Consider each of the following.

(a)  Negotiations with suppliers and gains in productivity have resulted in cost of sales being reduced to 62% of sales.

(b)  The effects of a recession have changed the cash collection profile so that receipts in any month are 50% of prior month sales, 35% of the previous month and 10% of the month before that, with bad debt experience rising to 5%.

(c)  An insurance claim made in 20X5 and successfully settled in December has resulted in the opening cash balance being an overdraft of £3,500.

(d)  Sales growth will only be 2% per month.

3.29  Each of these can be accommodated with **no input into the main body of the spreadsheet** being necessary at all. The two reference tables are revised as follows.

| | A | B | C | D | E | F | G |
|---|---|---|---|---|---|---|---|
| 25 | | | | | | | |
| 26 | *This table contains the key variables for the* 20X6 *cash flow projections* | | | | | | |
| 27 | | | | | | | |
| 28 | Sales growth factor per month | | 1.02 | | | | |
| 29 | Purchases as % of sales | | -0.62 | | | | |
| 30 | | | | | | | |
| 31 | Debts paid within 1 month | | 0.5 | | | | |
| 32 | Debts paid within 2 months | | 0.35 | | | | |
| 33 | Debts paid within 3 months | | 0.1 | | | | |
| 34 | Bad debts | | 0.05 | | | | |
| 35 | | | | | | | |
| 36 | Increase in overheads | | 1.05 | | | | |
| 37 | | | | | | | |
| 38 | Dividends (May) | | -10000 | | | | |
| 39 | | | | | | | |
| 40 | Capital purchases | | -18000 | | | | |
| 41 | January | | 0.2 | | | | |
| 42 | February | | 0.7 | | | | |
| 43 | May | | 0.1 | | | | |
| 44 | | | | | | | |
| 45 | | | | | | | |
| 46 | *This table contains relevant opening balance data as at Jan 20X6* | | | | | | |
| 47 | | | | | | | |
| 48 | Monthly sales 19X5 | | 45000 | | | | |
| 49 | January 1996 sales | | 42000 | | | | |
| 50 | Monthly overheads 19X5 | | -6000 | | | | |
| 51 | Opening cash | | -3500 | | | | |
| 52 | | | | | | | |

3.30    The resulting (recalculated) spreadsheet would look like this.

|    | A | B | C | D | E | F | G |
|----|---|---|---|---|---|---|---|
| 1  | EXCELLENT PLC | | | | | | |
| 2  | *Cash flow projection - six months ending 30 June* 20X6 | | | | | | |
| 3  | | *Jan* | *Feb* | *Mar* | *Apr* | *May* | *Jun* |
| 4  | | £ | £ | £ | £ | £ | £ |
| 5  | Sales | 42,000 | 42,840 | 43,697 | 44,571 | 45,462 | 46,371 |
| 6  | *Cash receipts* | | | | | | |
| 7  | 1 month in arrears | 22,500 | 21,000 | 21,420 | 21,848 | 22,285 | 22,731 |
| 8  | 2 months in arrears | 15,750 | 15,750 | 14,700 | 14,994 | 15,294 | 15,600 |
| 9  | 3 months in arrears | 4,500 | 4,500 | 4,500 | 4,200 | 4,284 | 4,370 |
| 10 | Total operating receipts | 42,750 | 41,250 | 40,620 | 41,042 | 41,863 | 42,701 |
| 11 | | | | | | | |
| 12 | *Cash payments* | | | | | | |
| 13 | Purchases | -26,040 | -26,561 | -27,092 | -27,634 | -28,187 | -28,750 |
| 14 | Overheads | -6,300 | -6,300 | -6,300 | -6,300 | -6,300 | -6,300 |
| 15 | Total operating payments | -32,340 | -32,861 | -33,392 | -33,934 | -34,487 | -35,050 |
| 16 | | | | | | | |
| 17 | Dividends | 0 | 0 | 0 | 0 | -10,000 | 0 |
| 18 | Capital purchases | -3,600 | -12,600 | 0 | 0 | -1,800 | 0 |
| 19 | Total other payments | -3,600 | -12,600 | 0 | 0 | -11,800 | 0 |
| 20 | | | | | | | |
| 21 | Net cash flow | 6,810 | -4,211 | 7,228 | 7,109 | -4,423 | 7,650 |
| 22 | Cash balance b/f | -3,500 | 3,310 | -901 | 6,327 | 13,436 | 9,012 |
| 23 | Cash balance c/f | 3,310 | -901 | 6,327 | 13,436 | 9,012 | 16,663 |
| 24 | | | | | | | |

## Activity 5.11

The following data relates to the period January to March in the years 20X8 and 20X9.

|  | 20X8<br>£ | 20X9<br>£ |
|---|---|---|
| January sales | 20,000 | 22,000 |
| February sales | 18,000 | 21,000 |
| March sales | 21,000 | 23,000 |

You are required to produce a spreadsheet showing the percentage change for January, February and March 20X9 compared with 20X8. You also need to show total first quarter sales for both years and the percentage increase in total sales.

## Key learning points

- A spreadsheet is basically an electronic piece of paper divided into **rows** and **columns** with a built in pencil, eraser and calculator.

- Once the spreadsheet has been set up, when one value is changed it will **automatically recalculate** all the others.

- A spreadsheet is divided into **cells** which may contain **text**, **values** or **formulae**.

- The basics you must know are how to move the cursor about and make cells active, how to enter and edit data (**F2**), how to **fill cells automatically** with the mouse, how to **insert and delete columns and rows** and how to improve the basic **layout** and **appearance** of a spreadsheet.

- Unless they are very small spreadsheet models should **always** have **three sections**: an **input** (variables) section, a **calculations** (formulae) section, and an **output** section for the final results.

- **Relative** cell references (B3) change when you add in extra rows or columns of more data from one place to another. Absolute cell references ($B$3) stay the same. Use **F4** to 'toggle' between relative and absolute references.

## Quick quiz

1   List five common uses of spreadsheets.

2   What type of contents can a cell contain?

3   What does the F5 key do?

4   What does the F2 key do?

5   What technique can you use to insert a logical series of data such as 1, 2 …. 10, or Jan, Feb, March etc?

6   What symbol is used for multiplication in a spreadsheet? Can the letter x be used as an alternative?

7   What does paste mean? What is a keyboard shortcut for pasting?

8   What is an absolute cell reference and how do you enter one in a cell?

9   How are negative numbers entered in a spreadsheet?

## Answers to quick quiz_____

1   Balance sheets, cash flow analysis, job-costing, profit projections, stock records. Any sensible answers would do. Try to list five more!

2   Text, values or formulae.

3   It opens a GoTo dialogue box which is useful for navigating around large spreadsheets.

4   It puts the active cell into edit mode.

5   You can (and should) use the technique of 'filling' - selecting the first few items of a series and dragging the lower right corner of the selection in the appropriate direction.

6   The asterisk * is used. The letter x cannot be.

7   Pasting means reproducing something that has been copied in another location. Ctrl + V is the shortcut.

8   A reference is absolute if it stays the same when using the fill function. An absolute column reference has a dollar sign before the letter. An absolute row reference has a dollar sign before the number. Dollar signs are entered using the F4 key.

9      Type the minus sign then the number - in other words exactly as they are written by hand.

## Answers to activities

## Answer 5.1

(a)   A spreadsheet is an electronic piece of paper divided into rows and columns. It provides an easy way of performing numerical calculations. The principal feature of a spreadsheet is that, once it is set up, a change in any one of the values means that the others change automatically.

(b)   Any five of the following (although you might have thought of other valid uses).

   (i)     Cash flow projections.
   (ii)    Balance sheets.
   (iii)   Profit forecasts.
   (iv)   Sales forecasts.
   (v)    General ledger.
   (vi)   Inventory records.
   (vii)  Job cost estimates.

(c)   Cell D5.

(d)   The cell (or range of cells) that will be changed by keyboard or mouse input.

(e)   (i)     'Text' means words or numerical data, such as a date, that cannot be used in computations.

   (ii)    A value is a number that can be used in a calculation.

   (iii)   A formula operates on other cells in the spreadsheet and performs calculations with them. For example, if cell B4 has to contain the total of the values in cells B2 and B3, a formula that could be entered in B4 is =B2+B3.

## Answer 5.2

(a)   =SUM(B5:B6)

(b)   =SUM(B6:D6)

(c)   =SUM (E5:E6) *or* =SUM(B7:D7)

   *or* (best of all) =IF(SUM(E5:E6) =SUM(B7:D7),SUM(B7:D7),"ERROR")

## Answer 5.3

(a)   (i)     =B6*0.175
   (ii)    =SUM(E6:E7)

(b)   There should be a separate 'variables' section including (at least) the VAT rate and preferably also for input of six month sales.

| | A | B | C | D | E | F | G | H |
|---|---|---|---|---|---|---|---|---|
| 1 | **Taxable Supplies plc** | | | | | | | |
| 2 | *Sales analysis - Branch C* | | | | | | | |
| 3 | *Six months ended 30 June 200X* | | | | | | | |
| 4 | | Jan | Feb | Mar | Apr | May | Jun | Total |
| 5 | | £ | £ | £ | £ | £ | £ | £ |
| 6 | Net sales | =B12 | =C12 | =D12 | =E12 | =F12 | =G12 | =SUM(B6:G6) |
| 7 | VAT | =B6*$B$13 | =C6*$B$13 | =D6*$B$13 | =E6*$B$13 | =F6*$B$13 | =G6*$B$13 | =SUM(B7:G7) |
| 8 | Total | =SUM(B6:B7) | =SUM(C6:C7) | =SUM(D6:D7) | =SUM(E6:E7) | =SUM(F6:F7) | =SUM(G6:G7) | =SUM(H6:H7) |
| 9 | | | | | | | | |
| 10 | | | | | | | | |
| 11 | *Variables* | | | | | | | |
| 12 | Sales | 2491.54 | 5876.75 | 3485.01 | 5927.7 | 6744.52 | 3021.28 | |
| 13 | VAT rate | 0.175 | | | | | | |
| 14 | | | | | | | | |

## Answer 5.4

(a)
| Cell | Formulae |
|---|---|
| C7 | =SUM(B5:B6) |
| B12 | =SUM(B9:B11) |
| B16 | =SUM(B14:B15) |
| C17 | =B12-B16 |
| C18 | =SUM (C4:C17) |
| C24 | = C21+C22–C23 |

(b) The finished spreadsheet appears below. We have removed the manager's 'prompts'. It is not particularly well set up in any case. How could it be improved (eg by using column D, by using negative entries and by setting up error messages?)

| | A | B | C | D | E | F |
|---|---|---|---|---|---|---|
| 1 | **Ed Sheet** | | | | | |
| 2 | *Balance sheet as at 31 Dec 200X* | | | | | |
| 3 | | £ | £ | | | |
| 4 | *Fixed assets* | | | | | |
| 5 | Plant | 20000 | | | | |
| 6 | Vehicles | 10000 | | | | |
| 7 | | | 30000 | | | |
| 8 | *Current assets* | | | | | |
| 9 | Stock | 2000 | | | | |
| 10 | Debtors | 1000 | | | | |
| 11 | Cash | 1500 | | | | |
| 12 | | 4500 | | | | |
| 13 | *Current liabilities* | | | | | |
| 14 | Creditors | 2500 | | | | |
| 15 | Overdraft | 1500 | | | | |
| 16 | | 4000 | | | | |
| 17 | Net current assets | | 500 | | | |
| 18 | Net assets | | 30500 | | | |
| 19 | | | | | | |
| 20 | *Represented by* | | | | | |
| 21 | Opening capital | | 28000 | | | |
| 22 | Profit for year | | 3500 | | | |
| 23 | Drawings | | 1000 | | | |
| 24 | Closing capital | | 30500 | | | |
| 25 | | | | | | |

## Answer 5.5

(a) It can be used to call up a Go To window, to move quickly to a different part of a spreadsheet.

(b) Select the cell and:

(i) Overtype the existing data, or
(ii) Click in the cell until a cursor appears and add, delete and retype as necessary, or
(iii) Click on the editing line at the top of the screen and add, delete and retype as necessary.
(iv) Press function key F2 and change the cell as necessary. Function key F2 is the best option.

(c) The action just done is undone.

(d) (i) Position the mouse pointer over the first cell in the range to be selected, hold down the left mouse button, move the pointer to the last cell in the range and release the mouse button. Every cell in the range except the one where you started will be highlighted. (*All* of these cells, including the first, are *selected*.)

(ii) Position the cursor in the first cell in the range to be selected, hold down the *shift* key and use the direction arrow keys to get to the last cell in the range. Release the shift key. Every cell in the range except the one where you started will be highlighted. (The starting cell is also *selected*, even though it is not highlighted.)

## Answer 5.6

(a) *Fill across* (or 'fill right') means that you select, say, cell A1, move the mouse pointer to the bottom right hand corner of A1 until it changes appearance and, by holding down the left mouse button, drag across into, say, cells B1, C1 and D1.

Fill down is like filling across except that the mouse pointer is dragged down rather than across.

If cell A1 contained the cell reference =B5 and this was filled across, cells B1, C1 and D1 would contain the references C5, D5 and E5. If it was filled down cells A2, A3 and A4 would contain the references B6, B7 and B8.

(b) Click on cell D5 and then click the Σ button. Check that the 'moving' dotted line is circling cells A5 to C5 (if not, select this range of cells). Then click again on the Σ button. The number 15 will appear. Then make E5 the active cell and repeat the procedure. The number 6 will appear. Do likewise with cell C11 to get the sum of B8 to B10: you will have to select the range yourself after clicking on Σ. The answer is 100.

## Answer 5.7

(a) To do this you need to insert new rows and columns. Select the row *below* which, or the column to the *left* of which, you want the new row or column, click in the selected row or column with your *right* mouse button and choose Insert from the menu that appears.

(b) To do this position the mouse pointer on the line between the column headings A and B until it changes shape. Then double-click with your left mouse button.

(c) To do this select cells A1 and B1, then put the mouse pointer somewhere within the selected range, hold down the left mouse button and drag the selection to cells E12 and F12. Then release the left mouse button. Widen the columns as before.

## Answer 5.8

(a) From left to right the buttons do the following.

(i) Displays the active document in Print Preview mode (ie how it will look when printed out).

(ii) Inserts the SUM function and proposes the cell range to be summed.

(iii) Applies percent style to cells (eg displays '0.1' as 10%).

(iv) Applies comma style to cells (eg 8,456 rather than 8456).

(v) Adds one decimal place to the number format whenever it is clicked.

(vi) Removes one decimal place from the number format.

(vii) Adds or removes a double border below cells.

(viii) Adds a border around the outer edge of the cell(s) selected.

(ix) Applies bold formatting to selected text or numbers.

(x) Applies italic formatting to selected text or numbers.

(xi) Left aligns text or numbers.

(xii) Centres text or numbers in cells.

(xiii) Right aligns text or numbers.

(xiv) Justifies text (spaces it evenly).

(xv) Centres text across selected columns.

(xvi) Rotates text sideways reading bottom to top.

(xvii) Sorts data in ascending order.

(xviii) Starts the spell checker.

(xix) Applies formatting of one cell to other cells.

(xx) A button to which a user-defined function can be assigned.

(b) (i) Ctrl + C then Ctrl + V
    (ii) Ctrl + B

## Answer 5.9_____

*Tutorial note.* This activity tests whether you can evaluate formulae in the correct order. In part (a) you must remember to put brackets around the numbers required to be added, otherwise the formula will automatically divide cell B8 by 4 first and add the result to the other numbers. Similarly, in part (b), the formula performs the multiplication before the addition and subtraction.

*Solution*

(a)  (i)   =SUM(B5:B8)/4
     (ii)  An alternative, if you are clever, is = AVERAGE(B5:B8).

(b)  59.325

## Answer 5.10_____

(a)  We have started by setting up a reference area for variable data, in case of rate changes, using cells B16 and B17.

     (i)    =C6*$B$16
     (ii)   =D6*$B$17
     (iii)  =SUM(E8:E9)
     (iv)   =F6-F10

(b)  See the diagram below.

| | A | B | C | D | E | F | G |
|---|---|---|---|---|---|---|---|
| 1 | Diamond Enterprises Ltd | | | | | | |
| 2 | Division: | Submarines | | | | | |
| 3 | Month: | April | | | | | |
| 4 | | | Johnson,J | Paul,P | George,G | Richards,R | |
| 5 | | | £ | £ | £ | £ | |
| 6 | Gross pay | | 2,166.67 | 2,200.00 | 1,900.00 | 1,779.17 | |
| 7 | | | | | | | |
| 8 | Income tax | | 541.67 | 550.00 | 475.00 | 444.79 | |
| 9 | NI | | 195.00 | 198.00 | 171.00 | 160.13 | |
| 10 | Total deductions | | 736.67 | 748.00 | 646.00 | 604.92 | |
| 11 | | | | | | | |
| 12 | Net pay | | 1,430.00 | 1,452.00 | 1,254.00 | 1,174.25 | |
| 13 | | | | | | | |
| 14 | Deductions – current rates | | | | | | |
| 15 | | | | | | | |
| 16 | Income tax | 0.25 | | | | | |
| 17 | NI | 0.09 | | | | | |
| 18 | | | | | | | |
| 19 | | | | | | | |
| 20 | | | | | | | |

# Answer 5.11_____

*Tutorial note.* The spreadsheet and formulae shown here may not correspond exactly to the one you have devised, but they should be similar. Most importantly, the spreadsheet should work! This is a relatively simple problem and one which it would perhaps be quicker to solve without a spreadsheet. Suppose, however, there were several years' data. In that case, using a spreadsheet really would save a great deal of time.

*Solution*

| | A | B | C | D | E | F |
|---|---|---|---|---|---|---|
| 1 | **Exponential Components Ltd** | | | | | |
| 2 | *Sales summary - Q1* | | | | | |
| 3 | | 20X8 | 20X9 | | % change | |
| 4 | | £ | £ | | | |
| 5 | January | 20,000 | 22,000 | | 10.00 | |
| 6 | February | 18,000 | 21,000 | | 16.67 | |
| 7 | March | 21,000 | 23,000 | | 9.52 | |
| 8 | Total | 59,000 | 66,000 | | 11.86 | |
| 9 | | | | | | |
| 10 | | | | | | |

The formulae you need will be as follows. Note that the cell references, and the formulae for calculating percentage changes, may be different in your spreadsheet. *(We have given a variety of ways of setting out the formulae, for the purpose of illustration, rather than copying one version all the way down the E column. In practice you would use only one way, consistently.)* If you have a percentage format facility you can use this and replace 100 in the formulae with 1 (eg (C6–B6)/B6.

*Note.* Do not make the mistake of adding together the monthly percentage changes to get the total percentage change in cell E8. This is not logical and will not give the correct result.

| | A | B | C | D | E | F |
|---|---|---|---|---|---|---|
| 1 | ECL | | | | | |
| 2 | *Sales summary - Q1* | | | | | |
| 3 | | 20X8 | 20X9 | | % change | |
| 4 | | £ | £ | | | |
| 5 | January | 20000 | 22000 | | =(C5/B5*100)-100 | |
| 6 | February | 18000 | 21000 | | =(C6-B6)/B6*100 | |
| 7 | March | 21000 | 23000 | | =(C7-B7)*100/B7 | |
| 8 | Total | =SUM(B5:B7) | =SUM(C5:C7) | | =(C8/B8*100)-100 | |
| 9 | | | | | | |
| 10 | | | | | | |

BPP PUBLISHING

# Chapter 6    Spreadsheet facilities

---

## Chapter topic list

1    Formulae

2    Graphics facilities

3    Spreadsheets for decision making

4    Presentation of spreadsheets

---

## Learning objectives

On completion of this chapter you will be able to:

| | Performance criteria | Range statement |
|---|---|---|
| • Produce spreadsheets by creation and modification | | 21.2.1, 21.2.3 |
| • Title spreadsheets in a way which clearly defines their use and purpose | 21.2.1 | |
| • Arrange spreadsheets in a way consistent with organisational conventions | 21.2.2 | |
| • State all rates and other numeric inputs and assumptions to the correct number of decimal places | 21.2.3 | 21.2.4 |
| • Check calculated values for correctness when changes are made to the inputs | 21.2.4 | 21.2.4 |
| • Use spreadsheets to carry out data modifications and for entry of related formulas | 21.2.5 | 21.2.4 |
| • Format each cell clearly and accurately | 21.2.6 | |
| • Select a method to eliminate rounding errors which is suitable for the purpose of the spreadsheet | 21.2.7 | 21.2.2 |
| • Keep confidential information secure from unauthorised people | 21.2.8 | |
| • *Organise, interpret and present information* | n/a | n/a |
| • *Describe and operate a range of spreadsheet products* | n/a | n/a |
| • *Take advantage of interfaces between software packages* | n/a | n/a |
| • *Understand some of the purposes and applications of spreadsheets* | n/a | n/a |

Italicised objectives are areas of knowledge and understanding underlying the elements of competence for Unit 21.

# 1 FORMULAE

1.1 Now that you are familiar with the basics of spreadsheeting, we are ready to move on and look at some additional **functions and facilities** found on a typical spreadsheet, including **conditions**. First some words in general about formulae.

## Formulae

1.2 So far we have used a formula to add, subtract and multiply. Formulae can be used to perform a variety of calculations. Here are some examples.

(a) =C4*5. This formula **multiplies** the value in C4 by 5. The result will appear in the cell holding the formula.

(b) =C4*B10. This **multiplies** the value in C4 by the value in B10. In general this is better than option (a).

(c) =C4/E5. This **divides** the value in C4 by the value in E5. (Note that * means multiply and / means divide by.)

(d) =C4*B10-D1. This **multiplies** the value in C4 by that in B10 and then subtracts the value in D1 from the result. Note that generally the computer will perform multiplication and division before addition or subtraction. If in any doubt, use brackets (parentheses): =(C4*B10)–D1.

(e) =C4*117.5%. This **adds** 17.5% to the value in C4. It could be used to calculate a price including 17.5% VAT. When you enter 17.5%, it may be displayed on screen as 0.175, depending on how the spreadsheet is set up.

(f) =(C4+C5+C6)/3. This, in effect, calculates the **average** of the values in C4, C5 and C6. Note that the brackets tell the computer to perform the addition first. Without the brackets the computer would first divide the value in C6 by 3 and then add the result to the total of the values in C4 and C5.

(g) = 2^2 gives you 2 **to the power** of 2, in other words $2^2$. Likewise = 2^3 gives you 2 cubed and so on.

(h) = 4^(1/2) gives you the **square root** of 4. Likewise 27^(1/3) gives you the cube root of 27 and so on. Do not forget the brackets.

## Switching between numbers and formulae

**TIP OF THE DAY**

To **display all the underlying formulae** in your spreadsheet instead of the numbers proceed as follows.

(a) You can 'toggle' between the two types of display by pressing **Ctrl +`** (the latter is the key above the Tab key). Press **Ctrl +`** again to get the previous display back.

(b) You can also click on Tools, then on Options, then on View and put an X in the box next to Formulas to display them, or remove it to display numbers.

## 1.3 EXAMPLE: COMMISSION CALCULATIONS

The following four insurance salesmen each earn a basic salary of £14,000 pa. They also earn a commission of 2% of sales. The following spreadsheet has been created to process their commission and total earnings.

Give an appropriate formula for each of the following cells.

(a) Cell D4.
(b) Cell E6.
(c) Cell D9.
(d) Cell E9.

| | A | B | C | D | E |
|---|---|---|---|---|---|
| 1 | *Sales team salaries and commissions - 200X* | | | | |
| 2 | Name | Sales | Salary | Commission | Total earnings |
| 3 | | £ | £ | £ | £ |
| 4 | Northington | 284,000 | 14,000 | 5,680 | 19,680 |
| 5 | Souther | 193,000 | 14,000 | 3,860 | 17,860 |
| 6 | Weston | 12,000 | 14,000 | 240 | 14,240 |
| 7 | Easterman | 152,000 | 14,000 | 3,040 | 17,040 |
| 8 | | | | | |
| 9 | Total | 641,000 | 56,000 | 12,820 | 68,820 |
| 10 | | | | | |
| 11 | | | | | |
| 12 | *Variables* | | | | |
| 13 | Basic Salary | 14,000 | | | |
| 14 | Commission rate | 0.02 | | | |
| 15 | | | | | |
| 16 | | | | | |
| 17 | | | | | |
| 18 | | | | | |
| 19 | | | | | |
| 20 | | | | | |

## 1.4 SOLUTION

Possible formulae are as follows.

(a) =B4*$B$14.

(b) =C6+D6.

(c) =SUM(D4:D7).

(d) As we have already seen, there is a **variety of possibilities** here, depending on whether you set the cell as the total of the earnings of each salesman (cells E4 to E7) or as the total of the different elements of remuneration (cells C9 and D9). Of course, it would be nice to **know that the calculation works in both directions.** This would give added assurance that there are no errors. A suitable formulae for this purpose would be:

=IF(SUM(E4:E7)=SUM(C9:D9),SUM(E4:E7),"ERROR")

We will explain this formula in more detail after the next example.

## 1.5 EXAMPLE: ACTUAL SALES COMPARED WITH BUDGET SALES

A business will often need to compare its results with budgets or targets to see how far it has exceeded, or fallen short of, its expectations. It is useful to express **variations as a percentage of the original budget**, for example sales may be 10% higher than predicted.

Continuing the example of the insurance salesmen, a spreadsheet could be set up as follows showing differences between actual sales and target sales, and expressing the difference as a percentage of target sales.

| | A | B | C | D | E | F |
|---|---|---|---|---|---|---|
| 1 | *Sales team comparison of actual against budget sales* | | | | | |
| 2 | Name | Sales (Budget) | Sales (Actual) | Difference | % of budget | |
| 3 | | £ | £ | £ | £ | |
| 4 | Northington | 275,000 | 284,000 | 9,000 | 3.27 | |
| 5 | Souther | 200,000 | 193,000 | (7,000) | (3.50) | |
| 6 | Weston | 10,000 | 12,000 | 2,000 | 20.00 | |
| 7 | Easterman | 153,000 | 152,000 | (1,000) | (0.65) | |
| 8 | | | | | | |
| 9 | Total | 638,000 | 641,000 | 3,000 | 0.47 | |
| 10 | | | | | | |

Give a suitable formula for each of the following cells.

(a) Cell D4.

(b) Cell E6.

(c) Cell E9.

Try this for yourself, before looking at the solution.

## 1.6 SOLUTION

(a) =C4-B4.

(b) =(D6/B6)*100.

(c) =(D9/B9)*100. Note that in (c) you **cannot simply add up the individual percentage differences**. This is because the percentages are based on very different quantities. For example, Weston has exceeded his target by 20%, but this is only £2,000, while Northington's 3.27% difference is actually £9,000. You should **always use common sense** in thinking about any formula you choose to put in.

### Conditions in formulae

1.7 Suppose the company employing the salesmen in the above example awards a bonus (in addition to the commission) to those salesmen who exceed their target by more than £1,000. It is possible to **get the spreadsheet to work out who is entitled to the bonus**. (In our example you can see this for yourself easily enough, but if there were 100 salesmen it would be tedious to have to look down a long list.)

1.8 Look at the first section of the spreadsheet. We are trying to determine whether Ken would be shown as entitled to a bonus. The formula used may vary slightly from one spreadsheet program to the next. We will enter the following:

=IF(D4>1000,"BONUS"," ").

The formula could be entered in column F.

1.9 This formula has three parts inside the brackets:

IF (condition, result if true, result if **false**).

The **inverted commas** (") mean that **text** is to appear in the cell. Here the text will either be the word '**bonus**' or, if the target was not exceeded, a **blank space**. The contents of the cell could equally well be a number ( as in paragraph 1.4(d)).

---

**TIP OF THE DAY**

Note the following symbols which can be used in formulae with conditions:

|  |  |
|---|---|
| < | less than (like L (for 'less') on its side) |
| <= | less than or equal to |
| = | equal to |
| >= | greater than or equal to |
| > | greater than |
| <> | not equal to |

---

1.10 There is nothing very difficult about conditions in formulae, but great care must be taken to put **brackets** and **commas** in the right places. The program can only do exactly what you tell it, not what it 'thinks' you are trying to do! If, when you try out this kind of formula, you get an error message, you should not panic; it may well be a simple mistake such as leaving a comma out.

## Examples of formulae with conditions

*Discounts*

1.11 A company offers a discount of 5% to customers who order more than £1,000 worth of goods. A spreadsheet showing what customers will pay might look like this.

|  | A | B | C | D | E | F |
|---|---|---|---|---|---|---|
| 1 | **Discount Traders Ltd** |  |  |  |  |  |
| 2 | *Sales analysis - April 200X* |  |  |  |  |  |
| 3 | Customer | Sales | 5% discount | Sales (net) |  |  |
| 4 |  | £ | £ | £ |  |  |
| 5 | Arthur | 956.00 | 0.00 | 956.00 |  |  |
| 6 | Dent | 1423.00 | 71.15 | 1351.85 |  |  |
| 7 | Ford | 2894.00 | 144.70 | 2749.30 |  |  |
| 8 | Prefect | 842.00 | 0.00 | 842.00 |  |  |
| 9 |  |  |  |  |  |  |
| 10 |  |  |  |  |  |  |

1.12 The formula in cell C5 is: =IF(B5>1,000,(0.05*B5),0). This means, if the value in B5 is greater than £1,000 multiply it by 0.05, otherwise the discount will be zero. Cell D5 will calculate the amount net of discount, using the formula: =B5-C5. The same conditional formula with the cell references changed will be found in cells C6, C7 and C8. **Strictly**, the variables £1,000 and 5% should be entered in a **different part** of the spreadsheet.

*Delivery charges*

1.13 A company charges £10 for delivery on all orders of less than £200. The following spreadsheet shows the amounts payable by three customers.

| | A | B | C | D | E |
|---|---|---|---|---|---|
| 1 | **Boxes plc** | | | | |
| 2 | *Delivery charges – week ended 23 June* 200X | | | | |
| 3 | | | | | |
| 4 | Customer | Sales | Delivery charge | Invoice amount | |
| 5 | | £ | £ | £ | |
| 6 | Grouchman | 156 | 10 | 166 | |
| 7 | Harpendale | 247 | 0 | 247 | |
| 8 | Ciccolini | 201 | 0 | 201 | |
| 9 | | | | | |
| 10 | | | | | |

1.14 Cell C6 will contain a formula: =IF(B6<200,10,0). Cell D6 will add together the contents of cells B6 and C6. Again, **strictly** the variables (£200, £10) should be entered in a **separate part** of the spreadsheet.

Note that in this spreadsheet we have reduced the font size in the column headings to **improve presentation**. The alternatives would have been to have even wider columns or to have tables almost running into one another. As noted above, we will look at presentational aspects of spreadsheets later.

*Examination results*

1.15 Suppose the pass mark for an examination is 50% and you want to see easily from a long list who has passed and who has failed. If a candidate's score is in cell B2, an appropriate formula for cell C2 would be: =IF(B2<50,"FAILED","PASSED").

As you may have noticed from an earlier example, the placing of text in inverted commas in a conditional function will cause the text to be printed out or displayed as appropriate.

## Activity 6.1

A company offers a 4% discount to all customers who order more than £5,000 worth of goods. The discount only applies to the element of the order in excess of £5,000, not to the whole order. Schleiermacher, Strauss and Schweitzer each order goods to the following value in January.

| *Schleiermacher* | *Strauss* | *Schweitzer* |
|---|---|---|
| £ | £ | £ |
| 4,900 | 6,000 | 7,000 |

Set up a spreadsheet which will show sales value for all three customers, the amount of any discount taken and the amount of cash the company can expect to receive, ie sales amount net of discount. The spreadsheet should also show totals for all three customers.

## Activity 6.2

The following candidates have taken an accountancy exam for which the pass mark is 55%. They have obtained the following scores.

| | |
|---|---|
| Montesquieu | 55% |
| Rousseau | 78% |
| Smith | 90% |
| Burke | 97% |
| Paine | 9% |
| Jefferson | 26% |

The authorities of Cool Cats College where they took the exam believe that letting the candidates know their real marks will give some an inferiority complex while making others unduly complacent. It has been decided to publish a list which says either 'Pass' or 'Fail' against a candidate's name.

(a) Devise a spreadsheet which will do this.

(b)   Find out how to re-sort the names and results into alphabetical order using your spreadsheet package. This may require some investigation!

## 2   GRAPHICS FACILITIES

2.1   It is usually possible to convert tabulated data in a spreadsheet into a variety of bar chart or graphical formats. We will look again at the Discount Traders Ltd example, reproduced below.

|    | A | B | C | D | E |
|----|---|---|---|---|---|
| 1  | **Discount Traders Ltd** | | | | |
| 2  | *Sales analysis - April 200X* | | | | |
| 3  | Customer | Sales | 5% discount | Sales (net) | |
| 4  | | £ | £ | £ | |
| 5  | Arthur | 956.00 | 0.00 | 956.00 | |
| 6  | Dent | 1423.00 | 71.15 | 1351.85 | |
| 7  | Ford | 2894.00 | 144.70 | 2749.30 | |
| 8  | Prefect | 842.00 | 0.00 | 842.00 | |
| 9  | | | | | |
| 10 | | | | | |

This could be used to generate any of the charts shown below.

(As you look at them, think about how these charts could be **further improved**, based on what you have learned about best practice in chart drawing from Intermediate Unit 6 *Reports and Returns*.)

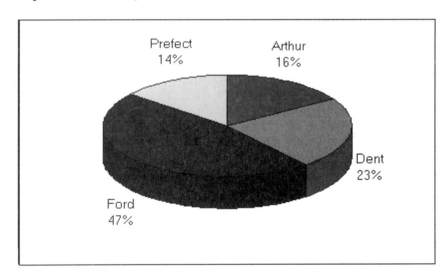

*BPP* PUBLISHING

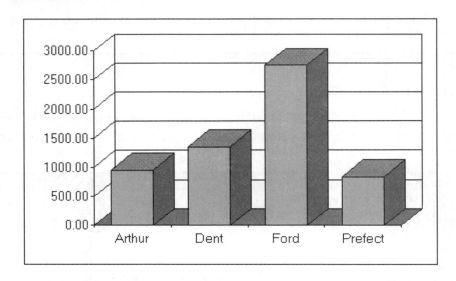

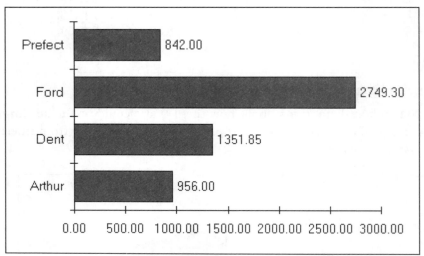

2.2 Very impressive looking-graphics can be generated simply by **selecting the range** of figures to turn into a chart and then clicking on a **chart icon** and following the step-by-step instructions on screen.

2.3 In this case we are trying to draw charts showing **net sales** to different **customers** and the relevant data to select is in cells A5 to A8 and D5 to D8. Don't worry about the fact that the data is not in **adjacent** columns. Select cells A5:A8 in the normal way, then move your pointer to cell D5, hold down **Ctrl** and drag to select cells D5:D8.

2.4 Next look at the **toolbars** at the top of the screen until you see an **icon** that looks like a little bar chart. Click on this. A 'Chart Wizard' appears. This is explained below.

## Step by step graphics

2.5 We shall describe the Excel 97 Chart Wizard, since this illustrates the steps that you need to follow (whichever package you have) particularly clearly.

*Step 1* Pick the type of chart you want. To create a chart similar (but better than) the second of the charts shown above we need to choose chart type **Column** and then select the sub-type we think will be most effective, as shown below.

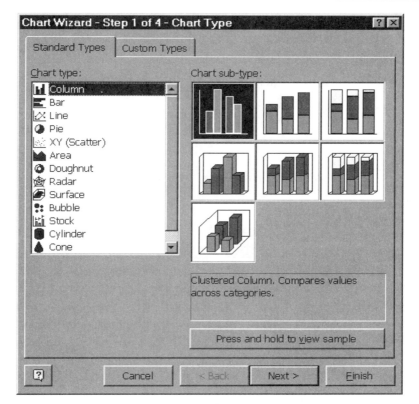

***Step 2***     This gives us the opportunity to confirm that the data we selected earlier was correct and to decide on how the **data series** should be shown: in other words whether the chart should be based on **columns** (eg Customer, Sales, Discount etc) or **rows** (Arthur, Dent etc). In this case, because there is only one series - net sales - it makes no difference, but you will see the effect of the different options when you try the next Activity.

## KEY TERM

A **data series** is a group of related data points plotted in a chart that originate from rows or columns on a single worksheet. Each data series in a chart has a unique colour or pattern. You can plot one or more data series in a chart. Pie charts have only one data series.

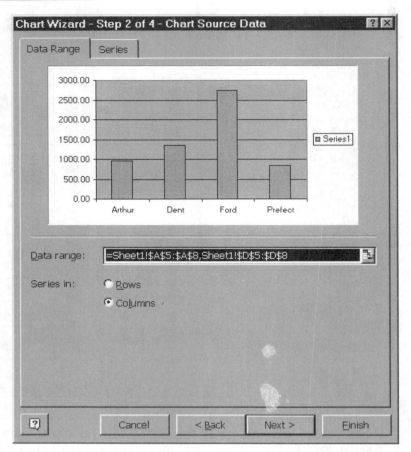

**Step 3** The next step is the one where you do all the things you usually forget to do when you are drawing charts and graphs by hand: giving your chart a **title**, **labelling** the axes and so on.

## DEVOLVED ASSESSMENT ALERT

The lack of **labels and titles** is the main fault of the charts shown earlier. If you are required or decide to produce graphics in your devolved assessment (the choice may be yours) make sure that everything is as clear as possible.

(Incidentally, one way of remembering which is the **X axis** and which is the **Y axis** is to look at the letter Y: it is the only letter that has a vertical part pointing straight up, so it must be the vertical axis!)

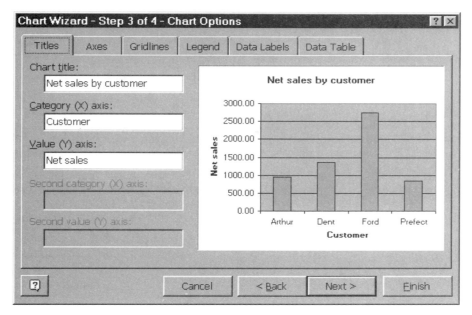

As you can see from the illustration there are lots of **other options** to look at on other index tabs. You can see the effect of selecting or deselecting each one in **preview**, so you can experiment with as many options as you like.

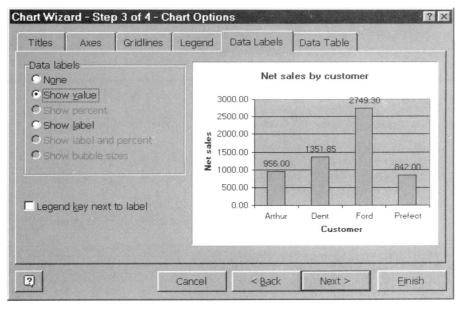

***Step 4*** The final step in Excel 97 is to choose whether you want the chart to appear on the same worksheet as the data or on a separate sheet of its own.

2.6 The final chart is shown below. Note that even now you can change it.

(a) You can **resize it** simply by selecting it and dragging out its borders.

(b) You can change **each element** by **double clicking** on them and choosing from a variety of further options. In the illustration below the user has double-clicked on the Y axis because they have decided to change the scale shown.

(c) You could also select any item of **text** and alter the wording, size or font, or change the **colours** used, or **delete elements** you did not want.

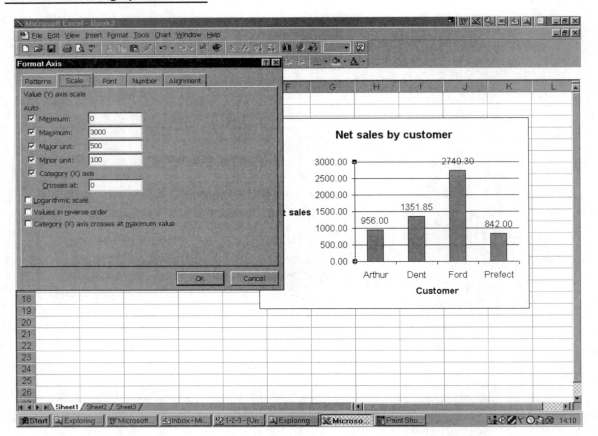

## Activity 6.3

Using the data for the Discount Traders Ltd create charts that look like the ones shown on the next page.

(a)   With **rows** shown on the Y axis.

(b)   With **columns** shown on the Y axis.

(a)

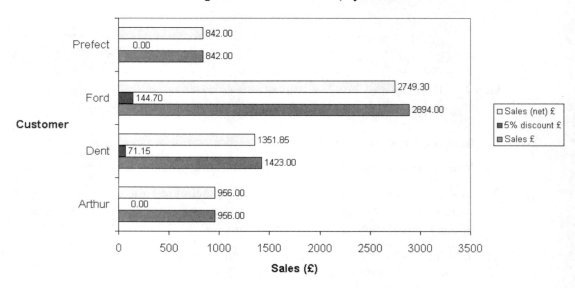

(b)

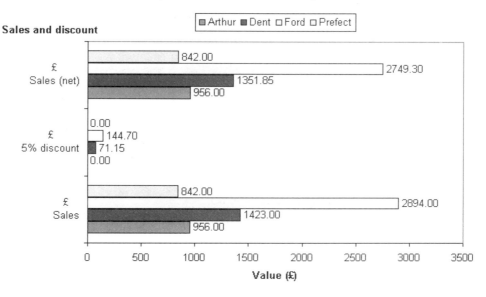

**Gross and net sales and discount by customer**

3 **SPREADSHEETS FOR DECISION MAKING**

3.1 We are now ready to build a more complicated spreadsheet incorporating some of the features discussed above.

3.2 **EXAMPLE: SOUNDS LTD**

The Northern division of Sounds Ltd makes a personal stereo called the Jogger. The following information is available.

(a) The Jogger costs £10 to make and at the moment sells for £20. If the divisional manager makes a profit of more than £18,000 for the period July to September 200X he will be entitled to a bonus of 5% of the profit.

(b) Sales of the Jogger in the three months are expected to be as follows:

| | |
|---|---|
| July: | 500 |
| August: | 600 |
| September: | 700 |

(c) The divisional manager is considering whether to raise the price of a Jogger to £21. He expects that if he increases the price above £20, there will be a reduction in sales volume as follows:

| | |
|---|---|
| July: | 490 |
| August: | 580 |
| September: | 680 |

(d) Administration expenses are £100 in July and are expected to increase by 10% in each of the following two months.

The manager is wondering whether he will get his bonus with the Jogger priced at £20, and, if not, whether it is worth increasing the price to £21. He has asked you to produce a '**what if ...?**' spreadsheet, which will set out the relevant data and enable him to try out the alternatives.

## 3.3 SOLUTION

The problem may seem complex, but it can be made straightforward by a step-by-step approach. The first step is to label the principal rows and columns, for example as follows.

3.4 The **variables** are entered as follows. Initially the data for the first 'scenarios' envisaged is entered.

| | A | B |
|---|---|---|
| 19 | *Assumptions for Q3* | |
| 20 | Unit cost | -10 |
| 21 | Unit selling price | 20 |
| 22 | Admin mthly % | 1.1 |
| 23 | Admin expense | -100 |
| 24 | Target profit | 18000 |
| 25 | Bonus % | -0.05 |
| 26 | *Forecast sales* | |
| 27 | July | 500 |
| 28 | August | 600 |
| 29 | September | 700 |
| 30 | | |

3.5 We must now consider the **formulae** required to make the spreadsheet do what we want it to do. One possible approach is to start off with the most straightforward formulae, as follows.

(a) **Sales** in value are simply sales in units multiplied by the selling price. The formula for July sales will therefore be =B6*$B$21. Similarly, August sales will =C6*$B$21.

(b) **Cost of sales** will be cost price multiplied by the number of units sold. The formula for July will be =B6*$B$20 with similar formulae for August and September.

(c) The formula for **gross profit** in July will be =SUM(B9:B10) again with similar formulae for the other months. The total column will obviously add all the contents of the row, for example in cell E9: =SUM(B9:D9).

(d) The formula for August and September **administration expenses** will be: +B12*$B$22 *and* +C12*$B$22. This will make them 'grow' at 10% per month. (Once you have typed in the contents of cell C12, you can of course copy this to cell D12, as the absolute addressing will ensure that cell B19 is brought into both calculations.)

(e) The formulae for the **net profit** will be, in cell B13, =SUM(B11:B12), and so on. Cells E11 and E13 can add either across or down: we will use an IF function to cross-check it.

3.6 The spreadsheet now looks like this.

| | A | B | C | D | E |
|---|---|---|---|---|---|
| 1 | **Sounds Ltd** | | | | |
| 2 | **Northern Division** | | | | |
| 3 | *Jogger budget - Q3 20XX* | | | | |
| 4 | | July | August | September | Total |
| 5 | | Units | Units | Units | Units |
| 6 | Sales | =B27 | =B28 | =B29 | =SUM(B6:D6) |
| 7 | | | | | |
| 8 | | £ | £ | £ | £ |
| 9 | Sales | =B6*$B$21 | =C6*$B$21 | =D6*$B$21 | =SUM(B9:D9) |
| 10 | Cost of sales | =B6*$B$20 | =C6*$B$20 | =D6*$B$20 | =SUM(B10:D10) |
| 11 | Gross profit | =SUM(B9:B10) | =SUM(C9:C10) | =SUM(D9:D10) | =IF(SUM(B11:D11)=SUM(E9:E10),SUM(E9:E10),"ERROR") |
| 12 | Admin expenses | =$B$23 | =B12*$B$22 | =C12*$B$22 | =SUM(B12:D12) |
| 13 | Net profit | =SUM(B11:B12) | =SUM(C11:C12) | =SUM(D11:D12) | =IF(SUM(B13:D13)=SUM(E11:E12),SUM(E11:E12),"ERROR") |

3.7 Once these formulae have been entered, the spreadsheet will **calculate all the other values automatically** to arrive at the total net profit for the three month period. The bonus is based on this figure, and is conditional on it. We therefore need a formula in, say, cell E14 to reflect this. For example, =IF(E13>B24,(B25*E13),0). This formula states that the bonus will be 5% (B25) of the net profit provided that the net profit exceeds £18,000 (B24), otherwise there will be no bonus.

| | A | B | C | D | E |
|---|---|---|---|---|---|
| | Sounds Ltd | | | | |
| | **Northern Division** | | | | |
| | *Jogger budget – Q3 20XX* | | | | |
| | | July | August | September | Total |
| | | Units | Units | Units | Units |
| | Sales | =B27 | =B28 | =B29 | =SUM(B6:D6) |
| | | | | | |
| | | £ | £ | £ | £ |
| | Sales | =B6*$B$21 | =C6*$B$21 | =D6*$B$21 | =SUM(B9:D9) |
| | Cost of sales | =B6*$B$20 | =C6*$B$20 | =D6*$B$20 | =SUM(B10:D10) |
| | Gross profit | =SUM(B9:B10) | =SUM(C9:C10) | =SUM(D9:D10) | =IF(SUM(B11:D11)=SUM(E9:E10),SUM(E9:E10),"ERROR") |
| | Admin expenses | =$B$23 | =B12*$B$22 | =C12*$B$22 | =SUM(B12:D12) |
| | Net profit | =SUM(B11:B12) | =SUM(C11:C12) | =SUM(D11:D12) | =IF(SUM(B13:D13)=SUM(E11:E12),SUM(E11:E12),"ERROR") |
| | Bonus | | | | =IF(E13>B24,(B25*E13),0) |
| | Profit after bonus | | | | =SUM(E13:E14) |

3.8 The spreadsheet we have constructed enables us to determine **whether the divisional manager will get a bonus** if he prices the Jogger at £20 or £21 and, if so, what this bonus will be.

3.9 This is the position if the Jogger were priced at £20.

| | A | B | C | D | E |
|---|---|---|---|---|---|
| 1 | **Sounds Ltd** | | | | |
| 2 | **Northern Division** | | | | |
| 3 | *Jogger budget – Q3 20XX* | | | | |
| 4 | | July | August | September | Total |
| 5 | | Units | Units | Units | Units |
| 6 | Sales | 500 | 600 | 700 | 1800 |
| 7 | | | | | |
| 8 | | £ | £ | £ | £ |
| 9 | Sales | 10000 | 12000 | 14000 | 36000 |
| 10 | Cost of sales | -5000 | -6000 | -7000 | -18000 |
| 11 | Gross profit | 5000 | 6000 | 7000 | 18000 |
| 12 | Admin expens | -100 | -110 | -121 | -331 |
| 13 | Net profit | 4900 | 5890 | 6879 | 17669 |
| 14 | Bonus | | | | 0 |
| 15 | Profit after bonus | | | | 17669 |
| 16 | | | | | |
| 17 | | | | | |
| 18 | | | | | |
| 19 | *Assumptions for Q3* | | | | |
| 20 | Unit cost | -10 | | | |
| 21 | Unit selling pri | 20 | | | |
| 22 | Admin mthly % | 1.1 | | | |
| 23 | Admin expens | -100 | | | |
| 24 | Target profit | 18000 | | | |
| 25 | Bonus % | -0.05 | | | |
| 26 | *Forecast sales* | | | | |
| 27 | July | 500 | | | |
| 28 | August | 600 | | | |
| 29 | September | 700 | | | |

3.10 It can be seen that if the Jogger is priced at £20 there will be no bonus, as the resulting total net profit is less than £18,000.

## What if ...?

3.11 To see the effect of increasing the selling price to £21, and a reduction in forecast sales, the values in cells B21 and B27 to B29 can be changed. The spreadsheet does the rest of the work, and will appear as follows.

|    | A | B | C | D | E |
|----|---|---|---|---|---|
| 1 | **Sounds Ltd** | | | | |
| 2 | **Northern Division** | | | | |
| 3 | *Jogger budget – Q3 20XX* | | | | |
| 4 | | July | August | September | Total |
| 5 | | Units | Units | Units | Units |
| 6 | Sales | 490 | 580 | 680 | 1750 |
| 7 | | | | | |
| 8 | | £ | £ | £ | £ |
| 9 | Sales | 10290 | 12180 | 14280 | 36750 |
| 10 | Cost of sales | -4900 | -5800 | -6800 | -17500 |
| 11 | Gross profit | 5390 | 6380 | 7480 | 19250 |
| 12 | Admin expens | -100 | -110 | -121 | -331 |
| 13 | Net profit | 5290 | 6270 | 7359 | 18919 |
| 14 | Bonus | | | | -945.95 |
| 15 | Profit after bonus | | | | 17973.05 |
| 16 | | | | | |
| 17 | | | | | |
| 18 | | | | | |
| 19 | *Assumptions for Q3* | | | | |
| 20 | Unit cost | -10 | | | |
| 21 | Unit selling pric | 21 | | | |
| 22 | Admin mthly % | 1.1 | | | |
| 23 | Admin expens | -100 | | | |
| 24 | Target profit | 18000 | | | |
| 25 | Bonus % | -0.05 | | | |
| 26 | *Forecast sales* | | | | |
| 27 | July | 490 | | | |
| 28 | August | 580 | | | |
| 29 | September | 680 | | | |

3.12 With the Jogger priced at £21, the net profit is over £18,000, and the divisional manager will receive a bonus of £946.

3.13 Clearly, in making his pricing decision, the manager will need to consider **other factors**, not least the **accuracy of his forecasts**. However, the above example serves to illustrate the usefulness of spreadsheets in decision making, and how to go about constructing one.

## Activity 6.4

The Wigan branch of Chocco Ltd makes one product only, the Trufflebox. This costs £1 to make and sells for £3. The following information is also relevant.

(a) Sales of the Trufflebox were 20,000 in January. Sales are expected to increase by 5% in each of the months February, March and April.

(b) Administration costs were £5,000 in January and are expected to increase by 4% in each of the months February, March and April.

(c) Pete, the manager of the Wigan branch, is entitled to a bonus if the branch profits exceed a certain target. Specifically, if the profit exceeds £120,000 he will get 20% of the amount by which the target has been exceeded, ie 20% of anything over £120,000.

(d) Pete is wondering whether he could increase his profit and therefore his bonus by lowering the price of a Trufflebox, at the end of January, to £2.50 to boost sales. If he did so the sales would grow more rapidly, that is by 8% per month.

*Task*

You are Pete's assistant. He has asked you to prepare a spreadsheet which will set out the relevant data and enable him to come to a decision.

*Note.* You should try to set up the spreadsheet so that minimum effort is involved in changing the data when trying out different possibilities.

## 4    PRESENTATION OF SPREADSHEETS

4.1    Generally a spreadsheet will be used to produce a **report**, usually printed. It is important, therefore, that this report is **clearly presented** so that it is easy to understand. This section deals with presentation matters.

### Titles and labels

4.2    Like any other report, a spreadsheet should be given a title which **clearly defines its use and purpose**. This presents no problems since, as you know, text can be entered in any cell. Examples of titles are follows.

(a)    Trading, profit and loss account for the year ended 30 June 200X.

(b)    (i)      Area A: Sales forecast for the three months to 31 March 200X.
         (ii)     Area B: Sales forecast for the three months to 31 March 200X.
         (iii)    Combined sales forecast for the three months to 31 March 200X.

(c)    Salesmen: Analysis of earnings and commission for the six months ended 30 June 200X.

Equally all **rows** and **columns** should be clearly **labelled** to show what the figures signify.

### Rates and assumptions

4.3    The spreadsheet should tell the user how the figures are derived. If is therefore important to **state explicitly** any rates used, for example in foreign currency transactions, and any assumptions made.

### Formatting

4.4    Formatting is done through **menus** with names like **Format, Style, Tools** (and then **Options**) or **Range** (and then **Range Properties**) or with the **buttons** at the top of the screen. They should enable you to do most, if not all, of the following tasks.

(a)    **Remove the 'gridlines'**. Most spreadsheets appear on the screen as a set of squares like the ones shown in this chapter. This is easier to work with when setting up the spreadsheet or when inputting data. However, when the report is ready to print out, you can remove the gridlines. The report will then appear more professional and less like a worksheet. Some spreadsheet programs have a **'print preview'** facility. This shows on the screen what the page will look like before it is printed out, so that you can see whether the printed version will look better and clearer with or without the gridlines.

(b)    Add **shading** or **borders** to cells. Borders can serve as 'underlinings'.

(c)    Use **different sizes of text** and different **fonts**.

(d)    Present a number as a **percentage** (eg 0.05 as 5%), and choose from a range of options for presenting values, for example, **whole numbers**, number of **decimal places** etc.

4.5    How much use need be made of the above facilities depends partly on the **purpose** for which the report is prepared. If it is for your **own use** only, or for the use of a few people in your department who are familiar with its operations, attractiveness of presentation will not be quite as important as in situations where the report is to be prepared for **outsiders** or for your **managing director**. That said, clarity and ease of reference are always important.

4.6　To reinforce this point, you may wish to compare the following two versions of the same spreadsheet.

| | A | B | C | D | E | F |
|---|---|---|---|---|---|---|
| 1 | Sales team salaries and commissions - 200X | | | | | |
| 2 | Name | Sales | Salary | Commi: | Total earnings | |
| 3 | | £ | £ | £ | £ | |
| 4 | Northingto | 284000 | 14000 | 5680 | 19680 | |
| 5 | Souther | 193000 | 14000 | 3860 | 17860 | |
| 6 | Weston | 12000 | 14000 | 240 | 14240 | |
| 7 | Eastermar | 152000 | 14000 | 3040 | 17040 | |
| 8 | | | | | | |
| 9 | Total | 641000 | 56000 | 12820 | 68820 | |
| 10 | | | | | | |

**Sales team salaries and commissions** – *200X*

| Name | Sales | Salary | Commission | Total earnings |
|---|---|---|---|---|
| | £ | £ | £ | £ |
| Northington | 284,000 | 14,000 | 5,680 | 19,680 |
| Souther | 193,000 | 14,000 | 3,860 | 17,860 |
| Weston | 12,000 | 14,000 | 240 | 14,240 |
| Easterman | 152,000 | 14,000 | 3,040 | 17,040 |
| Total | 641,000 | 56,000 | 12,820 | 68,820 |

### Activity 6.5

You have been asked to prepare a report using a spreadsheet suitable for the sales director to present to the board at their next meeting.

List three ways in which presentation of the spreadsheets could be improved.

## Formatting numbers

4.7　Most spreadsheet programs contain facilities for presenting numbers in a particular way. The following are the most important formats found in Excel, Lotus 1-2-3 and most other programs. In Excel you simply click on **Format** and then **Cells ...** to reach these options.

(a) **Fixed format** displays the number in the cell rounded off to the number of decimal places you select.

(b) **Currency format** displays the number with a '£' in front, with commas and not more than two decimal places, eg £10,540.23.

(c) **Comma format** is the same as currency format except that the numbers are displayed without the '£'.

(d) **General format** *is* the format assumed unless another format is specified. In general format the number is displayed with no commas and with as many decimal places as entered or calculated that fit in the cell.

(e) **Percent format** multiplies the number in the display by 100 and follows it with a percentage sign. For example the number 0.548 in a cell would be displayed as 54.8%.

(f) **Hidden format** is a facility by which values can be entered into cells and used in calculations but are not actually displayed on the spreadsheet. The format is useful for hiding sensitive information. For example, you might have a budget spreadsheet that includes the directors' salaries. You want to use the salaries in the calculations but you do not want them on display. You can format the column of salaries as 'hidden' so they do not show.

---

### Activity 6.6

The following number has been entered into a spreadsheet in 'general format'.

10598.3624

Re-write the number on paper as it would appear in each of the following formats. Then enter it into a spreadsheet cell and format it in each of these ways.

(a) Currency format
(b) Comma format
(c) Hidden format
(d) Fixed format rounded to one decimal place
(e) Fixed format with no decimal places

---

## Checking

4.8 Clearly one of the best ways to ensure that data in a spreadsheet is correct is to **check** it on input. The following guidelines should be observed.

(a) When the data has been input it should be **checked against the documents from which it came**. It is possible to check the data on the screen. However, it is easier and safer to print the spreadsheet out and check it from the printout.

(b) **Spot checks** should be carried out on some cells which contain **formulae**. The total should be calculated manually. If there is an error in the formula for which the user is not responsible, it should be reported to the supervisor. If, on the other hand, this particular user has devised the formula, he or she will have to amend it to achieve the desired result.

(c) It will not be practical to check all the cells that have formulae. However, those not covered by the spot checks should be scanned for **reasonableness**. For example, if a column of ten two digit numbers adds up to £1,000,000, it is clear that something has gone wrong somewhere!

## Rounding errors

4.9 The variety of formats available means that the number displayed may be different from the one actually in the cell. This can cause **apparent errors**. If you check the arithmetic in a spreadsheet by hand or with a calculator, you may not obtain exactly the same numbers as appear in the spreadsheet.

## 4.10 EXAMPLE: ROUNDING ERRORS

The following spreadsheet shows how apparent rounding errors can arise.

| | A | B | C | D |
|---|---|---|---|---|
| 1 | *Petty cash* | | | |
| 2 | *Week ended 16 August 200X* | | | |
| 3 | | £ | | |
| 4 | Opening balance | 231 | | |
| 5 | Receipts | 33 | | |
| 6 | Payments | -105 | | |
| 7 | Closing balance | 160 | | |
| 8 | | | | |

4.11 Cell B7 contains the formula =SUM(B4:B6). It appears that 231 + 33 - 105 is equal to 160, which is not true (check it). The **reason for the discrepancy** is that the cells actually contain the following values.

| | A | B | C | D |
|---|---|---|---|---|
| 1 | *Petty cash* | | | |
| 2 | *Week ended 16 August 200X* | | | |
| 3 | | £ | | |
| 4 | Opening balance | 231.34 | | |
| 5 | Receipts | 32.99 | | |
| 6 | Payments | (104.67) | | |
| 7 | Closing balance | 159.66 | | |
| 8 | | | | |

4.12 The spreadsheet has been formatted as **fixed with no decimal places**. Thus the numbers would be rounded up or down to the nearest whole number.

4.13 A report produced by a **spreadsheet** should be no more prone to such discrepancies than a report produced **by hand** or using a calculator. It would of course be possible to go through the spreadsheet manually correcting such errors, but this would defeat the object of using a spreadsheet, which is to **save time**.

## 4.14 SOLUTION

One possible solution to this difficulty is to use the **ROUND function.** The ROUND function has the following structure: ROUND (value, places)

4.15 'Value' is the value to be rounded. 'Places' is the number of places to which the value is to be rounded. In the above example, to round 231.34 to zero decimal places the formula would be =ROUND(231.34,0).

4.16 The difference between using the ROUND function and formatting a value to some number of decimal places is that using the ROUND function actually changes the **value itself,** while formatting the value only changes the **appearance** of the value. Thus, in our example, the values to be added would actually **become** 231, etc, and the total would therefore be 159.

4.17 If the ROUND function is selected to eliminate decimal places for presentation purposes, the result of the calculation will be inaccurate due to the rounding. A possible strategy for dealing with this would be to calculate, on a separate spreadsheet or part of the spreadsheet, the 'real' result. You would then find the difference between this and the rounded result and present it separately as '**Rounding ' difference**.

## Up or down?

4.18 A value of 1.5 would be rounded *up* to 2 using the ROUND function. Suppose you wanted it rounded down?

4.19 Excel also has functions called **ROUNDUP** and **ROUNDDOWN**. Thus =ROUNDUP(1.4, 0) would return the value 2, and =ROUNDDOWN(1.6, 0) would give you 1.

### Activity 6.7

The spreadsheet below shows the following calculation.

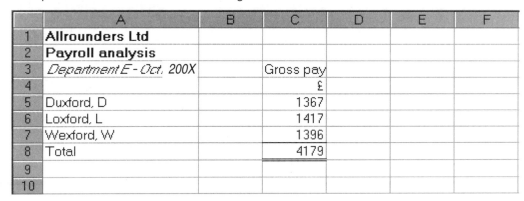

| | A | B | C | D | E | F |
|---|---|---|---|---|---|---|
| 1 | **Allrounders Ltd** | | | | | |
| 2 | **Payroll analysis** | | | | | |
| 3 | *Department E - Oct, 200X* | | Gross pay | | | |
| 4 | | | £ | | | |
| 5 | Duxford, D | | 1367 | | | |
| 6 | Loxford, L | | 1417 | | | |
| 7 | Wexford, W | | 1396 | | | |
| 8 | Total | | 4179 | | | |
| 9 | | | | | | |
| 10 | | | | | | |

Cell C8 contains the formula =SUM(C5:C7).

(a) Suggest a reason why the sum does not appear to add up.
(b) Suggest a strategy for dealing with this problem.

## Printing spreadsheets

4.20 You should be able to print the contents of the spreadsheet in total or in part, with or without the spreadsheet row and column labels. Print options are achieved by selecting **File** and then **Print**. You will then need to specify the range to be printed, check the paper orientation and choose from any other options, for example what **header** you want on the spreadsheet, and **which printer** to send the output to.

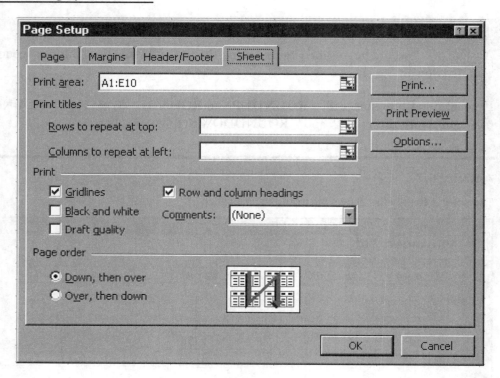

## Activity 6.8

Using the formatting and print facilities of your spreadsheet package prepare a spreadsheet that looks exactly like the following in print preview (but with *your* name and today's date).

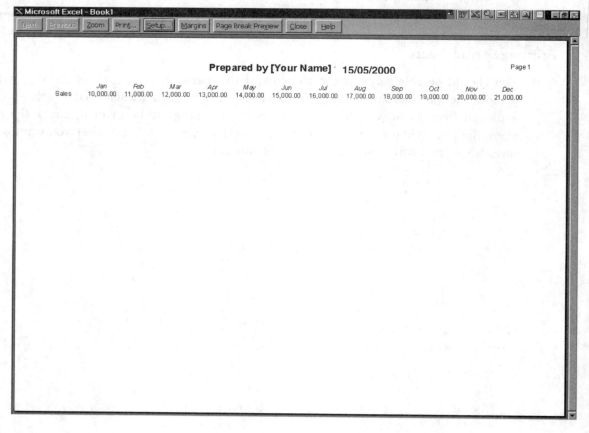

### Activity 6.9

Fill in the range A1 to F15 with headings and **random numbers** as shown below (obviously your numbers will not be the same as ours). Simply type the formula = RAND() in cell A2 and then fill across and down automatically.

|    | A | B | C | D | E | F |
|----|----------|----------|----------|----------|----------|----------|
| 1  | *Type 1* | *Type 2* | *Type 3* | *Type 4* | *Type 5* | *Type 6* |
| 2  | 0.212826 | 0.690312 | 0.767521 | 0.030618 | 0.913726 | 0.919017 |
| 3  | 0.703313 | 0.877003 | 0.26024  | 0.025492 | 0.569759 | 0.81889  |
| 4  | 0.449655 | 0.52585  | 0.581973 | 0.766266 | 0.712859 | 0.200744 |
| 5  | 0.275578 | 0.721662 | 0.651308 | 0.702936 | 0.749772 | 0.722748 |
| 6  | 0.666719 | 0.322191 | 0.451449 | 0.889475 | 0.747103 | 0.506107 |
| 7  | 0.061925 | 0.689278 | 0.611104 | 0.863325 | 0.922269 | 0.81046  |
| 8  | 0.379215 | 0.738459 | 0.613396 | 0.375213 | 0.178088 | 0.21824  |
| 9  | 0.47743  | 0.543545 | 0.368351 | 0.783415 | 0.125345 | 0.225719 |
| 10 | 0.05272  | 0.000442 | 0.549978 | 0.544684 | 0.553346 | 0.627103 |
| 11 | 0.974082 | 0.985179 | 0.657689 | 0.379094 | 0.295284 | 0.194685 |
| 12 | 0.674015 | 0.213648 | 0.449583 | 0.563053 | 0.956188 | 0.938007 |
| 13 | 0.715729 | 0.38034  | 0.531167 | 0.805179 | 0.877465 | 0.79061  |
| 14 | 0.381325 | 0.791251 | 0.091422 | 0.0623   | 0.063629 | 0.113983 |
| 15 | 0.200896 | 0.641742 | 0.759251 | 0.818738 | 0.034163 | 0.724111 |

## Spreadsheets and word processors

4.21 You may well find that you want to incorporate the results of your spreadsheet calculations into a **word processed report** to a manager. There are a number of options.

(a) The simplest option, of course, is simply to **print out** the spreadsheet and interleave the page or pages at the appropriate point in your word processed document.

(b) A neater option if you are just including a small table is to select and **copy** the relevant cells in the spreadsheet, switch to the word processing document, and **paste** them in at the appropriate point.

This also works the other way round. If you are presented with a table of figures in a **word processing** document you can select them and copy them directly into a **spreadsheet**, and then manipulate them (eg check the adding up, change the number of decimal places, etc) using all the facilities of the spreadsheet package.

(c) Office packages, such as Microsoft Office or Lotus Smartsuite, allow you to **link** spreadsheets and word processing files **dynamically**. The spreadsheet can be 'embedded' in the document.

## Controls

4.22 Finally, having made your spreadsheet look beautiful, you don't want to lose it! There are three important facilities available in spreadsheet packages which can be used as controls.

(a) **Saving and back-up**. There must be few things more frustrating than losing an hour's work by accidentally switching off the computer or pressing the wrong key. Work should be saved regularly, as often as every ten minutes. It takes only a few seconds. If work is lost and has to be done again, the user is likely to be too hasty the second time round, allowing errors to creep in.

(b) **Cell protection**. This prevents the user from inadvertently changing or erasing cells in the spreadsheet. Usually it is necessary to select first of all the cells to be 'unprotected'. These will be cells in which data needs to be changed. Then the cell protection would be turned on.

(c) **Passwords.** You can set a password for any spreadsheet that you create. In Excel, simply click on **Tools,** then on **Protection,** then on **Protect Sheet** or **Protect Workbook,** as appropriate.

## DEVOLVED ASSESSMENT ALERT

Unless you are told otherwise, do not lock up your Devolved Assessment answers!

### Key learning points

- A useful kind of formula is one which contains a **condition**. This can be used for example, in deciding whether a discount, delivery charge or bonus is applicable and the amount to be paid or charged.

- Modern spreadsheets offer facilities for producing a whole variety of **charts and graphs**. You can either accept the default formats or tailor each element of a graphic to suit your own requirements

- A spreadsheet should be given a **title** which clearly defines its purpose and columns and rows should be **labelled**. It should be formatted so it is easy to read.

- **Rounding differences** should be eliminated.

- **Numbers** can be **formatted** in several ways, for instance with commas, as percentages, as currency or with a certain number of decimal places.

- Your inputs, formulae and outputs should always be **checked** carefully. Spot checks and reasonableness checks should usually reveal errors in formulae and outputs, if there are any. Don't forget to check the inputs against the original document.

- Spreadsheets can easily **exchange data** with word processors and **vice versa**.

- **Backing-up** is a key security measure. You can also use **cell protection** and **passwords** to prevent unauthorised access.

### Quick quiz

1 How do you display formulae instead of the results of formulae in a spreadsheet?

2 List ten symbols that can be used in formulae.

3 How are graphs produced in Excel?

4 What formula would be used in a worksheet named Calculations to refer to cell A5 in a sheet named Variables?

5 List five formatting changes that you might want to make to a spreadsheet.

### Answers to quick quiz

1 Select Tools, Options and tick the Formulas box

2 *, \, +, -, ∧, <, >, =, <=, =>, <>

3 By selecting a range of figures and then clicking on a chart icon and following the instructions on screen.

4 Variables!A5

5 Removing gridlines, adding shading, adding borders, using different fonts and font sizes, presenting numbers as percentages or currency or to a certain number of decimal places.

## Answers to activities

### Answer 6.1

*Tutorial note.* Be careful with conditional formulae to get the brackets and commas in the right place.

*Solution*

|    | A | B | C | D | E | F | G |
|----|---|---|---|---|---|---|---|
| 1 | **Good Books PLC** | | | | | | |
| 2 | *Order analysis - 23 Jan* 200X | | | | | | |
| 3 | | | | | | | |
| 4 | Customer | Order | Discount | Sales value | | | |
| 5 | | £ | £ | £ | | | |
| 6 | Schleiermacher | 4,900 | 0 | 4,900 | | | |
| 7 | Strauss | 6,000 | 40 | 5,960 | | | |
| 8 | Schweitzer | 7,000 | 80 | 6,920 | | | |
| 9 | Total | 17,900 | 120 | 17,780 | | | |
| 10 | | | | | | | |

The fact that the whole of an order over £5,000 does not attract a discount complicates this one a little. We have again put a cross-check into the grand totals cell.

|    | A | B | C | D |
|----|---|---|---|---|
| 1 | Good Books PLC | | | |
| 2 | *Order analysis - 23 Jan* 200X | | | |
| 3 | | | | |
| 4 | Customer | Order | Discount | Sales value |
| 5 | | £ | £ | £ |
| 6 | Schleiermacher | 4900 | =IF(B6>5000,(B6-5000)*0.04,0) | =B6-C6 |
| 7 | Strauss | 6000 | =IF(B7>5000,(B7-5000)*0.04,0) | =B7-C7 |
| 8 | Schweitzer | 7000 | =IF(B8>5000,(B8-5000)*0.04,0) | =B8-C8 |
| 9 | Total | =SUM(B6:B8) | =SUM(C6:C8) | =IF(SUM(D6:D8)=B9-C9,B9-C9,"Error") |

An alternative (better) answer would show 5,000 and 4% as separate variables, a negative value in the discount column and a SUM function in all cells in the Sales Value column.

### Answer 6.2

(a)

|    | A | B | C | D | E | F |
|----|---|---|---|---|---|---|
| 1 | **Cool Cats College** | | | | | |
| 2 | *Accountancy exam results* | | | | | |
| 3 | | | | | | |
| 4 | Name | Result | | | | |
| 5 | | | | | | |
| 6 | Montesquieu | Pass | | | 55 | |
| 7 | Rousseau | Pass | | | 78 | |
| 8 | Smith | Pass | | | 90 | |
| 9 | Burke | Pass | | | 97 | |
| 10 | Paine | Fail | | | 9 | |
| 11 | Jefferson | Fail | | | 26 | |
| 12 | | | | | | |
| 13 | | | | | | |
| 14 | | | | | | |
| 15 | | | | | | |

A suitable formula for cell B6 would be

=IF(E6>=55,"Pass","Fail")

This formula could be filled down into the other cells in column B.

Note that you need a column to contain the candidates' scores, so that the formulae in column B have something to refer to. Since the candidates are not to see their score, this column must not be shown when the spreadsheet is printed out. It would also be possible to use the 'hidden format', discussed earlier in this Combined Text.

It is important that you do not try to get the formulae in column B to refer to the cells into which they are to be entered, for example: =IF(B6<55,"FAIL","PASS")

If you tried this, it would not work and the program would tell you it was a 'circular reference'. A formula must refer to another cell.

(b) This can be done by selecting the range A6 to E11 and clicking on the AZ button on the toolbar. You need to highlight rows 6 to 11 as far across as column E, otherwise the wrong marks would be set against the wrong students and the wrong results given.

    (i) *Right*

| | A | B | C | D | E | F |
|---|---|---|---|---|---|---|
| 6 | Burke | Pass | | | 97 | |
| 7 | Jefferson | Fail | | | 26 | |
| 8 | Montesquieu | Pass | | | 55 | |
| 9 | Paine | Fail | | | 9 | |
| 10 | Rousseau | Pass | | | 78 | |
| 11 | Smith | Pass | | | 90 | |

    (ii) *Wrong*

| | A | B | C | D | E | F |
|---|---|---|---|---|---|---|
| 6 | Burke | Pass | | | 55 | |
| 7 | Jefferson | Pass | | | 78 | |
| 8 | Montesquieu | Pass | | | 90 | |
| 9 | Paine | Pass | | | 97 | |
| 10 | Rousseau | Fail | | | 9 | |
| 11 | Smith | Fail | | | 26 | |

## Answer 6.3

Effectively, the 'answer' is shown in the question. You should compare your attempt element by element against ours. You can practice producing graphics with any spreadsheet you create on this course, and we strongly encourage you to experiment for yourself.

## Answer 6.4

*Tutorial note.* Your solution is unlikely to match the suggested one exactly. In particular, some of the cell references in the formulae may be different. However, the following should give you some idea whether you have the right approach.

*Solution*

The first step is to think what rows and columns you require. Then enter the variables in a separate input section. Include both possible prices and sales growth factors but enter the initial data (£3 and 5%) in both at first.

|    | A | B | C | D | E | F |
|----|---|---|---|---|---|---|
| 1  | Chocco Ltd | | | | | |
| 2  | Vigan Branch | | | | | |
| 3  | | | *Trufflebox - forecast for 4 months ending 30 April 200X* | | | |
| 4  | | | | | | |
| 5  | | Jan | Feb | Mar | Apr | Total |
| 6  | Unit sales | | | | | |
| 7  | | | | | | |
| 8  | | Jan | Feb | Mar | Apr | Total |
| 9  | | £ | £ | £ | £ | £ |
| 10 | Sales | | | | | |
| 11 | Cost of sales | | | | | |
| 12 | Admin costs | | | | | |
| 13 | Profit before bonus | | | | | |
| 14 | Bonus | | | | | |
| 15 | Net profit | | | | | |
| 16 | | | | | | |
| 17 | Variables | | | | | |
| 18 | Cost of sales | -1.00 | | | | |
| 19 | Selling price (1) | 3.00 | | | | |
| 20 | Selling price (2) | 3.00 | | | | |
| 21 | January sales | 20,000 | | | | |
| 22 | Sales growth factor (1) | 1.05 | | | | |
| 23 | Sales growth factor (2) | 1.05 | | | | |
| 24 | Admin costs (January) | -5,000 | | | | |
| 25 | Amincosts growth factor | 1.04 | | | | |
| 26 | Profit target | 120,000 | | | | |
| 27 | Bonus % | 20 | | | | |
| 28 | | | | | | |

The next step is to devise the formulae, which are shown below. Note the differences between the January and February columns, to accommodate Pete's experiment.

|    | A | B | C | D | E | F |
|----|---|---|---|---|---|---|
| 1  | Chocco Ltd | | | | | |
| 2  | Vigan Branch | | | | | |
| 3  | *Trufflebox - foreca* | | | | | |
| 4  | | | | | | |
| 5  | | Jan | Feb | Mar | Apr | Total |
| 6  | Unit sales | =B21 | =B6*$B$23 | =C6*$B$23 | =D6*$B$23 | |
| 7  | | | | | | |
| 8  | | Jan | Feb | Mar | Apr | Total |
| 9  | | £ | £ | £ | £ | £ |
| 10 | Sales | =B6*$B$19 | =C6*$B$20 | =D6*$B$20 | =E6*$B$20 | =SUM(B10:E10) |
| 11 | Cost of sales | =B6*$B$18 | =C6*$B$18 | =D6*$B$18 | =E6*$B$18 | =SUM(B11:E11) |
| 12 | Admin costs | =B24 | =B12*$B$25 | =C12*$B$25 | =D12*$B$25 | =SUM(B12:E12) |
| 13 | Profit before bonus | =SUM(B10:B12) | =SUM(C10:C12) | =SUM(D10:D12) | =SUM(E10:E12) | =SUM(F10:F12) |
| 14 | Bonus | | | | | =IF(F13>B26,(F13-B26)*B27,0) |
| 15 | Net profit | | | | | =SUM(F13:F14) |
| 16 | | | | | | |
| 17 | Variables | | | | | |
| 18 | Cost of sales | -1 | | | | |
| 19 | Selling price (1) | 3 | | | | |
| 20 | Selling price (2) | 3 | | | | |
| 21 | January sales | 20000 | | | | |
| 22 | Sales growth factor | 1.05 | | | | |
| 23 | Sales growth factor | 1.05 | | | | |
| 24 | Admin costs (Janua | -5000 | | | | |
| 25 | Amincosts growth f | 1.04 | | | | |
| 26 | Profit target | 120000 | | | | |
| 27 | Bonus % | -0.2 | | | | |
| 28 | | | | | | |

Once all the formulae have been input, the spreadsheet will automatically calculate the appropriate values and will appear as follows.

## Part B: Producing spreadsheets

| | A | B | C | D | E | F |
|---|---|---|---|---|---|---|
| 1 | **Chocco Ltd** | | | | | |
| 2 | **Wigan Branch** | | | | | |
| 3 | | *Trufflebox - forecast for 4 months ending 30 April, 200X* | | | | |
| 4 | | | | | | |
| 5 | | Jan | Feb | Mar | Apr | Total |
| 6 | Unit sales | 20,000 | 21,000 | 22,050 | 23,153 | |
| 7 | | | | | | |
| 8 | | Jan | Feb | Mar | Apr | Total |
| 9 | | £ | £ | £ | £ | £ |
| 10 | Sales | 60,000.00 | 63,000.00 | 66,150.00 | 69,457.50 | 258,608 |
| 11 | Cost of sales | -20,000.00 | -21,000.00 | -22,050.00 | -23,152.50 | -86,203 |
| 12 | Admin costs | -5,000.00 | -5,200.00 | -5,408.00 | -5,624.32 | -21,232 |
| 13 | Profit before bonus | 35,000.00 | 36,800.00 | 38,692.00 | 40,680.68 | 151,172.68 |
| 14 | Bonus | | | | | -6,234.54 |
| 15 | Net profit | | | | | 144,938.14 |
| 16 | | | | | | |
| 17 | | | | | | |

To test out what would happen if Pete were to lower the selling price to £2.50, all you need to do is to change cell B20 which contains the new selling price to 2.5, and cell B23 (the new sales growth factor) to 108%. All the other values will then change and the spreadsheet will appear as follows.

| | A | B | C | D | E | F |
|---|---|---|---|---|---|---|
| 1 | **Chocco Ltd** | | | | | |
| 2 | **Wigan Branch** | | | | | |
| 3 | | *Trufflebox - forecast for 4 months ending 30 April 200X* | | | | |
| 4 | | | | | | |
| 5 | | Jan | Feb | Mar | Apr | Total |
| 6 | Unit sales | 20,000 | 21,600 | 23,328 | 25,194 | |
| 7 | | | | | | |
| 8 | | Jan | Feb | Mar | Apr | Total |
| 9 | | £ | £ | £ | £ | £ |
| 10 | Sales | 60,000.00 | 54,000.00 | 58,320.00 | 62,985.60 | 235,306 |
| 11 | Cost of sales | -20,000.00 | -21,600.00 | -23,328.00 | -25,194.24 | -90,122 |
| 12 | Admin costs | -5,000.00 | -5,200.00 | -5,408.00 | -5,624.32 | -21,232 |
| 13 | Profit before bonus | 35,000.00 | 27,200.00 | 29,584.00 | 32,167.04 | 123,951.04 |
| 14 | Bonus | | | | | -790.21 |
| 15 | Net profit | | | | | 123,160.83 |
| 16 | | | | | | |
| 17 | **Variables** | | | | | |
| 18 | Cost of sales | -1.00 | | | | |
| 19 | Selling price (1) | 3.00 | | | | |
| 20 | Selling price (2) | 2.50 | | | | |
| 21 | January sales | 20,000 | | | | |
| 22 | Sales growth factor (1) | 1.05 | | | | |
| 23 | Sales growth factor (2) | 1.08 | | | | |
| 24 | Admin costs (January) | -5,000 | | | | |
| 25 | Amincosts growth factor | 1.04 | | | | |
| 26 | Profit target | 120,000 | | | | |
| 27 | Bonus % | -0.20 | | | | |
| 28 | | | | | | |

It is clear from this that Pete should not lower the price. If he does, total profits for the period will fall and he will receive a much smaller bonus.

## Answer 6.5

Any *three* of the following.

(a) The spreadsheet should have a title which clearly defines its purpose.

(b) Any rates and assumptions used should be stated explicitly.

(c) Text and values should be formatted where appropriate. This may include:

   (i) Removing the gridlines.
   (ii) Using bold or italic type.
   (iii) Adding shading or borders to cells.
   (iv) Altering column widths, particularly when a cell contains more than one word.
   (v) Using different sizes or styles of text.

# Answer 6.6

(a) £10,598.36 *or* £10,598, depending on what option is specified.

(b) 10,598.36

(c) The number will not appear at all, although it will still be contained in the cell and the spreadsheet will be able to perform calculations on it.

(d) 10,598.4

(e) 10,598

# Answer 6.7

(a) It is likely that the spreadsheet has been formatted so as to round the numbers to nil decimal places. The actual *contents* of the cells, as opposed to their display, are as follows.

| | A | B | C | D | E | F |
|---|---|---|---|---|---|---|
| 1 | **Allrounders Ltd** | | | | | |
| 2 | **Payroll analysis** | | | | | |
| 3 | *Department E - Oct. 200X* | | Gross pay | | | |
| 4 | | | £ | | | |
| 5 | Duxford, D | | =16400/12 | | | |
| 6 | Loxford, L | | =17000/12 | | | |
| 7 | Wexford, W | | =16750/12 | | | |
| 8 | Total | | =SUM(C5:C7) | | | |
| 9 | | | | | | |
| 10 | | | | | | |

(b) The way to deal with this problem depends on how concerned we are about accuracy. As the spreadsheet is formatted to round to whole numbers it is possible that we are not concerned about being spot on. If this is the case, it would be in order to use the ROUND function. This rounds the value itself rather than simply changing the appearance of the value. The formula required for, say, cell C5 would be = ROUND(16400/12,0). The spreadsheet would then appear as follows.

| | A | B | C | D | E | F |
|---|---|---|---|---|---|---|
| 1 | **Allrounders Ltd** | | | | | |
| 2 | **Payroll analysis** | | | | | |
| 3 | *Department E - Oct. 200X* | | Gross pay | | | |
| 4 | | | £ | | | |
| 5 | Duxford, D | | 1367 | | | |
| 6 | Loxford, L | | 1417 | | | |
| 7 | Wexford, W | | 1396 | | | |
| 8 | Total | | 4180 | | | |
| 9 | | | | | | |
| 10 | | | | | | |

If we are rounding to whole numbers, it is likely that we would be happy with this degree of accuracy. If the calculations were longer, involving a long list of numbers, such differences would probably be cancelled out to a large extent as some numbers were rounded up and others rounded down.

If we want the spreadsheet to be accurate, as is most likely the case here, where a sensitive area like payroll is involved, but still display only whole numbers, the strategy will have to be more complicated. One possible approach is to calculate the 'real' total manually or in another part of the spreadsheet using the 'hidden' format. We would then find the difference between this and the rounded total and display the difference as 'rounding'. The spreadsheet would then look like this.

|   | A | B | C | D | E | F |
|---|---|---|---|---|---|---|
| 1 | **Allrounders Ltd** | | | | | |
| 2 | **Payroll analysis** | | | | | |
| 3 | *Department E - Oct. 200X* | | Gross pay | | Gross pay | |
| 4 | | | £ | | £ | |
| 5 | Duxford, D | | 1367 | | 1366.67 | |
| 6 | Loxford, L | | 1417 | | 1416.67 | |
| 7 | Wexford, W | | 1396 | | 1395.83 | |
| 8 | Subtotal | | 4180 | | 4179.17 | |
| 9 | Rounding | | -1 | | | |
| 10 | Total | | 4179 | | | |
| 11 | | | | | | |
| 12 | | | | | | |

## Answer 6.8

You can enter the data quickly by using the autofill facility. Note that our version is in landscape, and watch out for the bold, italic and font sizes. Your version should contain *your* name and today's date.

## Answer 6.9

The trick here is to ensure that Row A is designated as a 'row to repeat'.

# Chapter 7    Spreadsheets and accounting

---

## Chapter topic list

1    Three dimensional spreadsheets

2    An extended trial balance (ETB)

3    Spreadsheets and cost apportionment

---

## Learning objectives

On completion of this chapter you will be able to:

| | Performance criteria | Range statement |
|---|---|---|
| • Produce spreadsheets by creation and modification | | 21.2.1, 21.2.3 |
| • Title spreadsheets in a way which clearly defines their use and purpose | 21.2.1 | |
| • Arrange spreadsheets in a way consistent with organisational conventions | 21.2.2 | |
| • State all rates and other numeric inputs and assumptions to the correct number of decimal places | 21.2.3 | 21.2.4 |
| • Check calculated values for correctness when changes are made to the inputs | 21.2.4 | 21.2.4 |
| • Use spreadsheets to carry out data modifications and for entry of related formulas | 21.2.5 | 21.2.4 |
| • Format each cell clearly and accurately | 21.2.6 | |
| • Select a method to eliminate rounding errors which is suitable for the purpose of the spreadsheet | 21.2.7 | 21.2.2 |
| • *Describe and operate a range of spreadsheet products* | n/a | n/a |
| • *Understand some of the purposes and applications of spreadsheets* | n/a | n/a |

Italicised objectives are areas of knowledge and understanding underlying the elements of competence for Unit 21.

BPP PUBLISHING

# 1 THREE DIMENSIONAL SPREADSHEETS

## What is a three dimensional spreadsheet?

1.1 Suppose you wanted to produce a profit forecast for two regions of the UK and a combined forecast for the whole of the UK. In the **two dimensional spreadsheets** that we have looked at so far, you would have, say, the months across the top as columns and the income and expenditure information down the side as rows. If there is more than one area involved, you would have to repeat this two dimensional design **separately** for each company.

1.2 In Microsoft **Excel** you can work with **workbooks**, each of which can contain a series of related sheets. This permits working in **three dimensions**. The user can flip between different sheets stacked in front or behind each other. Cells in one sheet **refer** to cells in another sheet. So, in our example, the top sheet would be the total combined results, and the lower sheets the two regions. The formulae in the cells in the top sheet could refer to the cells in the other sheets behind it.

1.3 Excel has a series of 'tabs', one for each worksheet.

Here is how Excel appears. The tabs are at the **foot** of the screen.

| | A | B | C | D | E |
|---|---|---|---|---|---|
| 1 | | | Dimension plc: UK | | |
| 2 | | | | | |
| 3 | | Jan | Feb | Mar | Total |
| 4 | | £ | £ | £ | £ |
| 5 | Sales | =Variables!B4 | =Variables!C4 | =Variables!D4 | =SUM(B5:D5) |
| 6 | Expenses | =Variables!B5 | =Variables!C5 | =Variables!D5 | =SUM(B6:D6) |
| 7 | Commission | =B5*Variables!$B$11 | =C5*Variables!$B$11 | =D5*Variables!$B$11 | =SUM(B7:D7) |
| 8 | Profit | =SUM(B5:B7) | =SUM(C5:C7) | =SUM(D5:D7) | =SUM(E5:E7) |
| 9 | | | | | |
| 10 | Bonus | | | | =IF(E8>Variables!B16,E8*Variables!C16,0) |

Tabs: Variables \ UK \ France (FFr) \ France (£) \ Europe

## Inserting extra sheets

1.4 **Excel** can be set up so that it always opens a fresh file with a certain number of worksheets ready and waiting for you. Click on **Tools … Options** … and then the **General** tab and set the *Sheets in new workbook* option to the number you want.

1.5 If you subsequently want to insert more sheets you just **right click** on the index tab after which you want the new sheet to be inserted and choose **Insert** … and then **Worksheet** (don't worry about the other types of sheet you an insert).

1.6 By default sheets are called **Sheet 1, Sheet** 2 etc. However, they can have almost **any name you like** (except that certain characters are not permitted: you will get a warning message if you use a character that is not allowed). To **rename** a sheet in **Excel, right click** on its index tab and choose the rename option. It is best to keep sheet names fairly short.

## Pasting from one sheet to another

1.7 The simplest use of multiple worksheets is to copy data on one sheet in the normal way, select the next sheet and paste. This gives you a **fresh copy** of the data: the two sheets are **not dependent** on each other in any way.

## Inserting references

1.8 Making one sheet refer to (ie collect data from) another sheet is also simple.

*Step 1* In the cell that you want to refer to a cell from another sheet, type =.

*Step 2* Click on the index tab for the sheet containing the cell you want to refer to and select the cell in question.

*Step 3* Press Enter or Return.

---

### Activity 7.1

Try this out. Open a new file and ensure that it contains at least two sheets, as described above.

Type the number 1,746, 243 in cell A1 of the first sheet. Then select the tab for the next sheet and select A1 in that sheet (step 1 above). Type =. Follow the remaining steps above through and you should end up with the same number in cell A1 of both sheets.

However, what is actually contained in cell A1 of the second sheet? See if you can find out before reading on.

---

1.9 After completing these three steps the cell with the reference will contain the formula **=Sheet1!A1**

1.10 If you wish you can **type in** Sheet1! (or whatever your new name for the sheet is) yourself. This is sometimes quicker if the name of the sheet is short and you know the cell reference you want, but it is **easy to make a mistake** so we do not recommend this.

1.11 The two cells **do not have to be in the same place** in their respective sheets. For instance cell Z658 of one sheet could refer to cell P24 of another. If you **move cells** or insert **extra rows** or columns on the sheet with the original numbers the cell references on the other sheet will **change automatically**.

**TIP OF THE DAY**

However, beware! In older spreadsheets if you insert 3D references and then **rename** the sheet that you are referring to, the spreadsheet may **no longer recognise the reference.**

## Uses for 3D spreadsheets

1.12 Here are a variety of possible uses for the extra dimension.

*BPP* PUBLISHING

(a) You can be even more disciplined about **constructing models,** having one sheet for variables, a second for calculations, and a third for outputs.

(b) You can keep better track of the **stages in development** of a model. Once you have got so far in building a model you should save the worksheet, name it something like 'Stage 1' and then copy it into a fresh sheet named 'Stage 2'. If the changes you make in stage 2 go disastrously wrong, you have not lost all the hard work you did for stage 1. You can simply abandon the stage 2 work and start stage 2 again (you could, of course, also do this by saving files with different names periodically).

(c) You can easily **consolidate** similar sets of data from different sources, for example the financial results of two subsidiaries or the budgets of two departments.

(d) You can have **different views** of the same data. For instance you could have one sheet of data sorted in product code order and another sorted in product name order. (If you do this with linked sheets remember that you should only make **changes** to the sheet with the **original data,** not the one with the references.)

### Activity 7.2

Company X has two divisions, A and B. The divisions have the following results for a period.

|  | Division A (UK) £ | Division B (France) £ FF |
|---|---|---|
| Sales | 1,458,742 | 26,924,713 |
| Expenses | 572,866 | 9,147,922 |

There are 10 French francs to the pound.

Using a three dimensional spreadsheet, calculate the total Sales, Expenses and net profit of Company X for the period in pounds.

## 2    AN EXTENDED TRIAL BALANCE

2.1    Now that you understand how spreadsheets work, applying them in accounting contexts is largely a matter of common sense.

### Spreadsheets and the extended trial balance

2.2    Spreadsheets lend themselves very well to one particular aspect of financial accounting familiar to you from your other studies: the **extended trial balance**. Setting up the spreadsheet requires care and attention, but once it is set up it can be **used again and again**. If last minute changes are made there is **no need to recalculate everything** with the risk of error that this entails. Moreover, the same model can be used from year to year with different data; if a new account is opened you need only insert a line.

2.3    It should be emphasised that, while a spreadsheet can be a useful tool in financial and management accounting, it **cannot do the thinking for you**. If you do not understand how the extended trial balance works and what you are trying to achieve, the spreadsheet will not be able to help you!

## 2.4    EXAMPLE: SPREADSHEETS AND THE EXTENDED TRIAL BALANCE

Throughout this example it will be assumed that you understand the principles of the extended trial balance. We will concentrate on the spreadsheet aspects. If you are unsure of any aspects of the extended trial balance, you should look at your Financial Accounting study material.

2.5 The ledger accounts of Leigh, a trader, as at 31 December 20X0 before any adjustments have been made to them, are as follows.

|  | £ |
|---|---|
| Shop fittings at cost | 6,000 |
| Depreciation provision at 1 January 20X0 | 300 |
| Leasehold premises at cost | 37,500 |
| Depreciation provision at 1 January 20X0 | 1,875 |
| Stock in trade at 1 January 20X0 | 78,000 |
| Debtors | 159,000 |
| Provision for doubtful debts at 1 January 20X0 | 2,880 |
| Cash in hand | 150 |
| Cash at bank | 12,150 |
| Creditors for supplies | 195,000 |
| Share capital | 60,000 |
| Profit and loss account at 1 January 20X0 | 18,345 |
| Purchases | 306,000 |
| Sales | 387,000 |
| Wages | 54,600 |
| Advertising | 6,900 |
| Rates for 15 months to 31 March 20X1 | 4,500 |
| Bank charges | 600 |

The adjustments Leigh needs to make to his accounts are:

(a) Depreciation of shop fittings £300.

(b) Depreciation of leasehold premises £1,875.

(c) A debt of £1,500 is irrecoverable and is to be written off and the doubtful debts provision is to be increased to 2% of the present debtors figure.

(d) The stock in trade at 31 December 20X0 is valued at £90,000.

(e) On 31 December 20X0, £360 was owed for advertising expenses but an invoice has not yet been received.

2.6 You are required to give effect to these adjustments on an extended trial balance using a spreadsheet.

## 2.7 SOLUTION

It is vital that you work through this solution **hands-on**, following the text as you prepare the spreadsheet.

*Setting up the spreadsheet*

2.8 The first step is to set up the spreadsheet, **label your rows and columns** and enter the trial balance. This stage is shown on the next page. Note that you should enter (in column B) a P beside a P&L account and a B beside a Balance sheet account. The reason for this will become clear later.

2.9 Remember to **save your work** every few minutes.

2.10 At this early stage you can deal with **points of style.**

(a) Your spreadsheet package's 'formatting' facilities can present all numbers so that the commas appear in the right place. You can format the cells even before you enter the data. You can also adjust the column width: the 'description' column will need to be wider than the others.

(b) You can change some of the fonts for emphasis. We have the column headings in bold.

All these stylistic features give the spreadsheet ETB a professional appearance.

## Part B: Producing spreadsheets

2.11 When entering the data in the columns, you have to know which side they go on. The spreadsheet does not know if you don't tell it! Enter **Debits** as **positive** figures and **Credits** as **negative** ones. (There is a neater way of doing this that makes minus signs unnecessary, but it is quite complex and, in any case, it is good discipline for you to think about pluses and minuses.)

2.12 As a check use the **Autosum button** to do the totals at the foot of the Debit and Credit columns. The totals should be the same if you have entered all the figures in the right place.

2.13 However, **beware!** It is quite likely that you will need to insert extra rows as your work proceeds and it is all too easy to forget that your SUM formula only covers some of the rows (here SUM (B3:B20)). If you **inserted a line 21** at a later stage it would **not be included in the total** because it is not within the range 3-20. Here are three ways of dealing with this.

(a) Leave plenty of **blank rows** at the bottom of your TB (at least 10) and include those rows in your SUM function from the beginning. For as long as there is nothing in them they will count as 0 in the sum.

(b) Use **total formulae** to check your work as you go along but, as a double check, delete them and do them again when you think you have finished making entries.

(c) Only **insert rows between existing rows**. If you do this, though, any formulae that you filled down earlier would not appear in the new row.

|    | A | B | C | D | E | F |
|----|---|---|---|---|---|---|
| 1 | **Account** | | **Trial balance** | | | |
| 2 | | | £ | £ | | |
| 3 | Shop fittings | B | 6,000 | | | |
| 4 | Depreciation | B | | (300) | | |
| 5 | Leasehold | B | 37,500 | | | |
| 6 | Depreciation | B | | (1,875) | | |
| 7 | Stock 1.1.19X0 | P | 78,000 | | | |
| 8 | Debtors | B | 159,000 | | | |
| 9 | Debtors provision | B | | (2,880) | | |
| 10 | Cash | B | 150 | | | |
| 11 | Bank | B | 12,150 | | | |
| 12 | Creditors | B | | (195,000) | | |
| 13 | Share capital | B | | (60,000) | | |
| 14 | Profit and loss account | B | | (18,345) | | |
| 15 | Purchases | P | 306,000 | | | |
| 16 | Sales | P | | (387,000) | | |
| 17 | Wages | P | 54,600 | | | |
| 18 | Advertising | P | 6,900 | | | |
| 19 | Rates | P | 4,500 | | | |
| 20 | Bank charges | P | 600 | | | |
| 21 | | | | | | |
| 22 | SUB-TOTAL | | 665,400 | (665,400) | | |
| 23 | | | | | | |
| 24 | TOTAL | | 665,400 | (665,400) | | |
| 25 | | | | | | |
| 26 | | | | | | |

*Entering the adjustments, accruals and prepayments*

2.14 The results of entering the adjustments, accruals and prepayments into the spreadsheet can be seen in the next diagram. Some of the cells contain formulae, which will be explained below.

2.15 We suggest that the best practice is to do any calculations that need to be done on a **separate part** of the spreadsheet (or on a different worksheet).

(a) If you have any practical experience of preparing accounts you will know that, in reality, lots of adjustments are put through **after** the first attempt at drawing up an ETB. If a single cell contains numerous consecutive adjustments your spreadsheet will be very difficult to follow and to adjust safely.

(b) As we have seen throughout this book it is good practice to have separate **input, calculation** and **output** areas.

2.16 Although this is quite a simple example we therefore recommend that you have a separate area on your spreadsheet such as the following. Follow through the calculations by reference to paragraph 2.5 to make sure you understand them before reading on.

| | A | B | C | D | E |
|---|---|---|---|---|---|
| 33 | | | | | |
| 34 | **Adjustments** | | | | |
| 35 | *Depreciation* | | | | |
| 36 | Shop fittings | | 300 | | |
| 37 | Leasehold premises | | 1875 | | |
| 38 | Depreciation expense | | | 2175 | |
| 39 | | | | | |
| 40 | *Bad debts* | | | | |
| 41 | Debtors | | 159,000 | | |
| 42 | Provision % | | 2% | | |
| 43 | New provision | | 3180 | | |
| 44 | Current provision | | -2,880 | | |
| 45 | Increase | | | 300 | |
| 46 | Bad Debts | | 1500 | | |
| 47 | | | | 1500 | |
| 48 | | | | 1800 | |
| 49 | | | | | |
| 50 | *Stock* | | | | |
| 51 | Closing stock | | 90000 | | |
| 52 | | | | | |
| 53 | **Accruals** | | | | |
| 54 | Advertising | | 360 | | |
| 55 | | | | 360 | |
| 56 | | | | | |
| 57 | **Prepayments** | | | | |
| 58 | Rates | | 900 | | |
| 59 | | | | 900 | |
| 60 | | | | | |

2.17 Now you can enter cell references in your Adjustment, Accrued and Prepaid columns. Remember to **keep the double entry going.** You will need to enter new rows for Depreciation, Bad debts, Stock (2 rows, as shown below), Accruals and Prepayments.

2.18 Here are the entries you should make assuming you have set up a separate section for calculations as illustrated above. Don't forget the minus signs in the 'Credit' columns. The results are shown in the next diagram.

| Account | Cell | DR | CR | Amount |
|---|---|---|---|---|
| Depreciation (B) | F4 | | = –C36 | (300) |
| Depreciation (B) | F6 | | = –C37 | (1,875) |
| Depreciation (P) | E21 | = D38 | | 2,175 |
| Debtors (B) | F8 | | = – D47 | (1,500) |
| Debtors provision (B) | F9 | | = –D45 | (300) |
| Bad debts (P) | E22 | = D48 | | 1,800 |
| Stock c/f (P) | F23 | | = – C51 | (90,000) |
| Stock c/f (B) | E24 | = C51 | | 90,000 |
| Advertising (P) | G18 | =C54 | | 360 |
| Accounts (B) | H25 | | = –D55 | (360) |
| Rates (P) | H19 | | = – C58 | (900) |
| Prepayments (B) | G26 | = D59 | | 900 |

Note that you can avoid lots of scrolling to and fro when making these entries by using the **split screen** facility, which divides the screen into two halves which can scroll independently. In Excel select row 33, click on **Window** and click on **Split**.

2.19 Your ETB will now look like this.

| | A | B | C | D | E | F | G | H |
|---|---|---|---|---|---|---|---|---|
| 1 | Account | | Trial balance | | Adjustments | | Accrued | Prepaid |
| 2 | | | £ | £ | £ | £ | £ | £ |
| 3 | Shop fittings | B | 6000 | | | | | |
| 4 | Depreciation | B | | -300 | | -300 | | |
| 5 | Leasehold | B | 37500 | | | | | |
| 6 | Depreciation | B | | -1,875 | | -1875 | | |
| 7 | Stock 1.1.19X0 | P | 78000 | | | | | |
| 8 | Debtors | B | 159000 | | | -1500 | | |
| 9 | Debtors provision | B | | -2,880 | | -300 | | |
| 10 | Cash | B | 150 | | | | | |
| 11 | Bank | B | 12150 | | | | | |
| 12 | Creditors | B | | -195,000 | | | | |
| 13 | Share capital | B | | -60,000 | | | | |
| 14 | Profit and loss account | B | | -18,345 | | | | |
| 15 | Purchases | P | 306000 | | | | | |
| 16 | Sales | P | | -387,000 | | | | |
| 17 | Wages | P | 54600 | | | | | |
| 18 | Advertising | P | 6900 | | | | 360 | |
| 19 | Rates | P | 4500 | | | | | -900 |
| 20 | Bank charges | P | 600 | | | | | |
| 21 | Depreciation | P | | | 2,175 | | | |
| 22 | Bad debts | P | | | 1,800 | | | |
| 23 | Stock 31.12.19X0 | P | | | | -90,000 | | |
| 24 | Stock 31.12.19X0 | B | | | 90,000 | | | |
| 25 | Accruals | B | | | | | | -360 |
| 26 | Prepayments | B | | | | | 900 | |
| 27 | | | | | | | | |
| 28 | | | | | | | | |
| 29 | SUB-TOTAL | | 665,400 | -665,400 | 93,975 | -93,975 | 1,260 | -1,260 |
| 30 | | | | | | | | |
| 31 | **TOTAL** | | 665,400 | -665,400 | 93,975 | -93,975 | 1,260 | -1,260 |
| 32 | | | | | | | | |

## Totalling and extending the trial balance

2.20 If you were preparing a **manual** trial balance your next step would be to work across each row in turn (from C to H) with your calculator and put the result in the appropriate P&L or Balance Sheet column.

  (a) *IF* the result is positive it will go in the debit column of the P&L or Balance sheet.
  (b) *IF* it is negative it will go in the credit column of the P&L or Balance sheet.

2.21 This is where **manual** ETBs become such **agony**: it is so easy to press the wrong key on your calculator that you can spend hours trying to get it all to balance. You may have personal experience of this.

2.22 As you know very well by now, however, spreadsheets are much better than you are at adding up long lists of numbers. They can also take IFs, such as those described above, in their stride.

  (a) IF the result is >0 (ie positive) it is a debit.
  (b) IF the result is <0 (ie negative) it is a credit.
  (c) IF the account has a B beside its name it is a Balance Sheet account.
  (d) IF the account has a P, it is a P&L account.

*Constructing the formula*

2.23 We will need **two IFs in the same formula**, which is not something you have encountered before. You might like to have a go at constructing the formula yourself though: it will certainly help you to understand the correct approach.

2.24 What you should have done is as follows.

  (a) Click on cell I3, the first cell in the debit column of the P & L. We want a figure to be shown here **IF** the account is a P& L one and **IF** the sum of C3 to H3 is positive (>0). Otherwise it will have a 0.

  (b) Type the following in cell I3. Take great care with brackets and $ signs. When we copy this formula we want the row number to change but not the column letter, so the correct style is $B3.

   **=IF($B3="P",IF(SUM($C3:$H3)>0,SUM($C3:$H3),0),0)**

  (c) Copy this cell into cells J3, K3 and L3, by filling across.

  (d) Alter cell J3 as follows. The changes from the formula in Cell I3 are shown enlarged in **bold** so you know what to alter.

   **=IF($B3="P",IF(SUM($C3:$H3)<0,SUM($C3:$H3),0),0)**

   In other words, all you need to do is alter the > to a <, because you are looking for negative figures.

  (e) Alter cell K3 as follows.

   **=IF($B3="B",IF(SUM($C3:$H3)>0,SUM($C3:$H3),0),0)**

   All you need alter here is the P to a B. When you do this and press Enter the number 6000 should appear in this cell.

  (f) Alter cell L3 as follows.

   **=IF($B3="B",IF(SUM($C3:$H3)<0,SUM($C3:$H3),0),0)**

   You alter the P to a B and the > to a <.

143

| | I | J |
|---|---|---|
| 1 | Profit and loss | |
| 2 | £ | £ |
| 3 | =IF($B3="P",IF(SUM($C3:$H3)>0,SUM($C3:$H3),0),0) | =IF($B3="P",IF(SUM($C3:$H3)<0,SUM($C3:$H3),0),0) |
| 4 | =IF($B4="P",IF(SUM($C4:$H4)>0,SUM($C4:$H4),0),0) | =IF($B4="P",IF(SUM($C4:$H4)<0,SUM($C4:$H4),0),0) |
| 5 | =IF($B5="P",IF(SUM($C5:$H5)>0,SUM($C5:$H5),0),0) | =IF($B5="P",IF(SUM($C5:$H5)<0,SUM($C5:$H5),0),0) |

| | K | L |
|---|---|---|
| 1 | Balance sheet | |
| 2 | £ | £ |
| 3 | =IF($B3="B",IF(SUM($C3:$H3)>0,SUM($C3:$H3),0),0) | =IF($B3="B",IF(SUM($C3:$H3)<0,SUM($C3:$H3),0),0) |
| 4 | =IF($B4="B",IF(SUM($C4:$H4)>0,SUM($C4:$H4),0),0) | =IF($B4="B",IF(SUM($C4:$H4)<0,SUM($C4:$H4),0),0) |
| 5 | =IF($B5="B",IF(SUM($C5:$H5)>0,SUM($C5:$H5),0),0) | =IF($B5="B",IF(SUM($C5:$H5)<0,SUM($C5:$H5),0),0) |

2.25 This is all the difficult stuff over. Now you just fill down. Highlight cells I3 to L3 and drag down to row 28. Like magic:

(a) All the remaining formulae will be filled in for you.

(b) The P&L and Balance Sheet columns will fill themselves in with the correct balances.

This is what you should see now. If not, you have got a sign wrong somewhere (in which case your columns won't balance), or something in the wrong column or you have typed in the formulae wrongly.

| | A | B | C | D | E | F | G | H | I | J | K | L |
|---|---|---|---|---|---|---|---|---|---|---|---|---|
| 1 | Account | | Trial balance | | Adjustments | | Accrued | Prepaid | Profit and loss | | Balance sheet | |
| 2 | | | £ | £ | £ | £ | £ | £ | £ | £ | £ | £ |
| 3 | Shop fittings | B | 6000 | | | | | | 0 | 0 | 6000 | 0 |
| 4 | Depreciation | B | | -300 | | -300 | | | 0 | 0 | 0 | -600 |
| 5 | Leasehold | B | 37500 | | | | | | 0 | 0 | 37500 | 0 |
| 6 | Depreciation | B | | -1,875 | | -1875 | | | 0 | 0 | 0 | -3750 |
| 7 | Stock 1.1.19X0 | P | 78000 | | | | | | 78000 | 0 | 0 | 0 |
| 8 | Debtors | B | 159000 | | | -1500 | | | 0 | 0 | 157500 | 0 |
| 9 | Debtors provision | B | | -2,880 | | -300 | | | 0 | 0 | 0 | -3180 |
| 10 | Cash | B | 150 | | | | | | 0 | 0 | 150 | 0 |
| 11 | Bank | B | 12150 | | | | | | 0 | 0 | 12150 | 0 |
| 12 | Creditors | B | | -195,000 | | | | | 0 | 0 | 0 | -195000 |
| 13 | Share capital | B | | -60,000 | | | | | 0 | 0 | 0 | -60000 |
| 14 | Profit and loss account | B | | -18,345 | | | | | 0 | 0 | 0 | -18345 |
| 15 | Purchases | P | 306000 | | | | | | 306000 | 0 | 0 | 0 |
| 16 | Sales | P | | -387,000 | | | | | 0 | -387000 | 0 | 0 |
| 17 | Wages | P | 54600 | | | | | | 54600 | 0 | 0 | 0 |
| 18 | Advertising | P | 6900 | | | | 360 | | 7260 | 0 | 0 | 0 |
| 19 | Rates | P | 4500 | | | | | -900 | 3600 | 0 | 0 | 0 |
| 20 | Bank charges | P | 600 | | | | | | 600 | 0 | 0 | 0 |
| 21 | Depreciation | P | | | 2,175 | | | | 2175 | 0 | 0 | 0 |
| 22 | Bad debts | P | | | 1,800 | | | | 1800 | 0 | 0 | 0 |
| 23 | Stock 31.12.19X0 | P | | | | -90,000 | | | 0 | -90000 | 0 | 0 |
| 24 | Stock 31.12.19X0 | B | | | 90,000 | | | | 0 | 0 | 90000 | 0 |
| 25 | Accruals | B | | | | | | -360 | 0 | 0 | 0 | -360 |
| 26 | Prepayments | B | | | | | 900 | | 0 | 0 | 900 | 0 |
| 27 | | | | | | | | | 0 | 0 | 0 | 0 |
| 28 | | | | | | | | | 0 | 0 | 0 | 0 |
| 29 | SUB-TOTAL | | 665,400 | -665,400 | 93,975 | -93,975 | 1,260 | -1,260 | 454,035 | -477,000 | 304,200 | -281,235 |
| 30 | | | | | | | | | | | | |
| 31 | TOTAL | | 665,400 | -665,400 | 93,975 | -93,975 | 1,260 | -1,260 | 454,035 | -477,000 | 304,200 | -281,235 |

## Profit for the year

2.26 The P & L and Balance Sheet don't balance yet because we have not calculated the profit for the year. This is simply the difference between the sub-totals of the P & L account: 477,000 – 454,035 = 22,965. This is a debit in the P&L (to make it balance) and so it must be a credit in the Balance Sheet - a profit!

2.27 Type Profit for the Year in cell A30, between the labels Sub-total and Total.

2.28 You can work out the profit by hand if you like. You should put a debit entry of 22,965 in cell I30 and an equivalent credit in cell L30. This will make everything balance.

2.29 If you are not exhausted, you might like a formula that will automate the profit calculation too. Again it is just a matter of typing the basic formula in cell I30, then filling across, then making tiny changes, this time to the < or > and the minus sign or lack of one.

144

| (a) | I30 | =IF($I$29+$J$29 < 0,−($I$29+$J$29),0) | |
| --- | --- | --- | --- |
| (b) | J30 | =IF($I$29+$J$29 > 0,−($I$29+$J$29),0) | (Alter < to >) |
| (c) | K30 | =IF($I$29+$J$29 > 0,($I$29+$J$29),0) | (Alter < to > and delete the minus sign) |
| (d) | L30 | =IF($I$29+$J$29 < 0,($I$29+$J$29),0) | (Delete the minus sign) |

2.30 If you find this last bit difficult to follow, don't worry: just work out the profit by hand. But do try to understand how to do the formulae for the P & L and the Balance Sheet because they will save you huge amounts of time and effort once you have the knack.

## Further adjustments

2.31 The spreadsheet has taken quite a long time to set up but if you change any of the figures it will become clear how easy it is to use.

2.32 Suppose, for example, another **bad debt** of £500 is written off and there are also **accrued bank charges** of £140. Make the appropriate additions in your adjustments section (taking care over **inserting extra lines** and **keeping the double entry going**) and watch the spreadsheet do the rest. The spreadsheet should appear as below.

| | A | B | C | D | E | F | G | H | I | J | K | L |
|---|---|---|---|---|---|---|---|---|---|---|---|---|
| | | | Trial balance | | Adjustments | | Accrued | Prepaid | Profit and loss | | Balance sheet | |
| 1 | Account | | £ | £ | £ | £ | £ | £ | £ | £ | £ | £ |
| 2 | | | | | | | | | | | | |
| 3 | Shop fittings | B | 6000 | | | | | | | 0 | 0 | 6000 | 0 |
| 4 | Depreciation | B | | -300 | | -300 | | | 0 | 0 | 0 | -600 |
| 5 | Leasehold | B | 37500 | | | | | | 0 | 0 | 37500 | 0 |
| 6 | Depreciation | B | | -1,875 | | -1875 | | | 0 | 0 | 0 | -3750 |
| 7 | Stock 1.1.19X0 | P | 78000 | | | | | | 78000 | 0 | 0 | 0 |
| 8 | Debtors | B | 159000 | | | -2000 | | | 0 | 0 | 157000 | 0 |
| 9 | Debtors provision | B | | -2,880 | | -300 | | | 0 | 0 | 0 | -3180 |
| 10 | Cash | B | 150 | | | | | | 0 | 0 | 150 | 0 |
| 11 | Bank | B | 12150 | | | | | | 0 | 0 | 12150 | 0 |
| 12 | Creditors | B | | -195,000 | | | | | 0 | 0 | 0 | -195000 |
| 13 | Share capital | B | | -60,000 | | | | | 0 | 0 | 0 | -60000 |
| 14 | Profit and loss account | B | | -18,345 | | | | | 0 | 0 | 0 | -18345 |
| 15 | Purchases | P | 306000 | | | | | | 306000 | 0 | 0 | 0 |
| 16 | Sales | P | | -387,000 | | | | | 0 | -387000 | 0 | 0 |
| 17 | Wages | P | 54600 | | | | | | 54600 | 0 | 0 | 0 |
| 18 | Advertising | P | 6900 | | | | 360 | | 7260 | 0 | 0 | 0 |
| 19 | Rates | P | 4500 | | | | | -900 | 3600 | 0 | 0 | 0 |
| 20 | Bank charges | P | 600 | | | | 140 | | 740 | 0 | 0 | 0 |
| 21 | Depreciation | P | | | 2,175 | | | | 2175 | 0 | 0 | 0 |
| 22 | Bad debts | P | | | 2,300 | | | | 2300 | 0 | 0 | 0 |
| 23 | Stock 31.12.19X0 | P | | | | -90,000 | | | 0 | -90000 | 0 | 0 |
| 24 | Stock 31.12.19X0 | B | | | 90,000 | | | | 0 | 90000 | | |
| 25 | Accruals | B | | | | | -500 | | 0 | 0 | 0 | -500 |
| 26 | Prepayments | B | | | | | | 900 | 0 | 0 | 900 | 0 |
| 27 | | | | | | | | | | | | |
| 28 | | | | | | | | | | | | |
| 29 | SUB-TOTAL | | 665,400 | -665,400 | 94,475 | -94,475 | 1,400 | -1,400 | 454,675 | -477,000 | 303,700 | -281,375 |
| 30 | Profit for the year | | | | | | | | 22325 | 0 | 0 | -22325 |
| 31 | **TOTAL** | | 665,400 | -665,400 | 94,475 | -94,475 | 1,400 | -1,400 | 477,000 | -477,000 | 303,700 | -303,700 |

## Points to remember

2.33 Building up a spreadsheet for an ETB is a logical, commonsense based exercise. The above approach is not the only which may be followed. There are other ways of arriving at the same result. None of the formulae involved are really very complicated or difficult to understand; the challenge lies in **applying the principles of financial accounting in a computerised context**.

**BPP** PUBLISHING

2.34 You can nearly always distinguish between debits, credits P&L accounts and Balance Sheet accounts because you **know** at least one of the entries through common sense. For example, you **know** closing stock is a debit in the balance sheet, so it *must* be a credit in the P&L.

|  | P&L | | Balance sheet | |
|---|---|---|---|---|
|  | Dr | Cr | Dr | Cr |
| Opening stock | ✓ |  |  |  |
| Closing stock |  | ✓ | ✓ |  |
| Accruals |  |  |  | ✓ |
| Prepayments |  |  | ✓ |  |
| Provisions |  |  |  | ✓ |
| Expenses | ✓ |  |  |  |

## Activity 7.3

Bettabikkis is a sole trader, making and selling biscuits for retail and wholesale customers in the Bradford area. You are Richard Tee, the bookkeeper, faced with the task of producing the trial balance at the end of the year to 30 June 20X5. You decide to use a spreadsheet, building it up from scratch this year, in order to save time in future years. The following balances have been extracted from the ledgers.

|  | £ |
|---|---|
| Sales | 276,156 |
| Purchases | 169,122 |
| Carriage | 5,866 |
| Drawings | 15,600 |
| Rent and rates | 13,244 |
| Postage and stationery | 6,002 |
| Advertising | 2,660 |
| Salaries and wages | 52,840 |
| Bad debt expense | 1,754 |
| Provision for bad debts | 260 |
| Debtors | 24,240 |
| Creditors | 12,942 |
| Cash in hand | 354 |
| Cash at bank | 2,004 |
| Stock as at 1 July 20X4 | 23,854 |
| Equipment:      at cost | 116,000 |
| accumulated depreciation | 38,000 |
| Capital | 106,182 |

Your enquiries reveal the following additional information which needs to be taken into account.

(a)   Rates are payable 6 months in advance. A payment of £1,760 made on 30 June 20X5 represents rates for July to December 20X5.

(b)   A rent demand for £420 for the three months ended 30 June 20X5 was not received until 1 July 20X5.

(c)   Equipment is to be depreciated at 15% per annum using the straight line method.

(d)   The provision for bad debts is to be increased by £80.

(e)   Stock at the close of business was valued at £27,102.

*Task*

Prepare an extended trial balance using a spreadsheet package. If you saved the ETB you prepared when following through this section you can just delete the contents of columns A to H rows 1-29 and input the new data. Also head up the spreadsheet with the name of the company and the date Year Ended 30/06/X5.

## Activity 7.4

(a) Having prepared the extended trial balance in Activity 7.3, you now discover that, following a re-assessment of net realisable values, closing stock was £15,605. In addition, the provision for doubtful debts is to be increased by £65 rather than £80.

*Task*

Amend your spreadsheet ETB to reflect these discoveries.

*Note.* If you have done Activity 7.3 correctly, this should only take a few seconds. That is the whole point of spreadsheets.

(b) Without looking at your spreadsheet note down the formulae that would appear in the following cells.

    (i)    I5
    (ii)   J5
    (iii)  K5
    (iv)  L5
    (v)   J32
    (vi)  K32

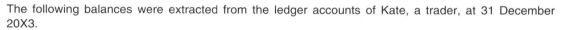

## Activity 7.5

The following balances were extracted from the ledger accounts of Kate, a trader, at 31 December 20X3.

|  | £ |
| --- | --- |
| Capital | 38,728 |
| Freehold land and buildings | 25,000 |
| Furniture & fittings: cost | 3,360 |
| accumulated depreciation | 1,680 |
| Motor car: cost | 1,900 |
| accumulated depreciation | 600 |
| Purchases | 93,964 |
| Sales | 133,298 |
| Rent received | 720 |
| Drawings | 6,460 |
| Car expenses | 792 |
| Stock at 1.1.20X3 | 9,976 |
| Bad debt expense | 844 |
| Provision for doubtful debts at 1.1.20X3 | 452 |
| General expenses | 1,654 |
| Rent and rates | 2,324 |
| Trade debtors | 15,842 |
| Trade creditors | 13,866 |
| Wages and salaries | 17,966 |
| Discounts allowed | 4,328 |
| Bank | 4,934 |

Investigation reveals the following.

(a) Stock at 31 December 20X3 was £10,858.

(b) Wages and salaries accrued at 31 December 20X3 were £396.

(c) Rates paid in advance at 31 December 20X3 were £96.

(d) The provision for doubtful debts at 31 December 20X3 is to be £516.

(e) The tenant owes £240 in rent at 31 December 20X3.

(f) Depreciation is to be provided:

    (i)   on the motor car at 20% pa on cost;
    (ii)  on the furniture and fittings at 10% pa on cost.

(g) Kate rents a postal franking machine. Unused stamps at 31 December 20X3 were worth £94.

*Task*

Prepare an extended trial balance as at 31 December 20X3 to reflect the above information. Try to build a new ETB model from scratch this time.

---

**Activity 7.6**

Having prepared the ETB as in Activity 7.5 you then decide that the provision for doubtful debts is inadequate, and that it would be better to have a provision of 5% of debtors as at 31.12.20X3.

*Task*

Amend your spreadsheet accordingly.

*Note.* You should only need to change one cell.

---

## 3     SPREADSHEETS AND COST APPORTIONMENT

3.1    From your studies of other units at intermediate level you have probably realised that many management accounting techniques involve **setting up tables of data** and performing simple calculations. If so, you should now appreciate the usefulness of spreadsheets in these circumstances.

3.2    The following example uses your knowledge of **absorption costing**, specifically **cost apportionment**. (Familiarity with this technique is assumed here. Consult your other Intermediate Units if you need to.)

### 3.3    EXAMPLE: SPREADSHEET FOR COST APPORTIONMENT

Tradco Ltd is a manufacturing business with four factories. It wants to develop a spreadsheet model for the absorption of overheads. Sample data for East Factory has been collected and input into a spreadsheet.

(a)   The following **overhead costs** are allocated to East Factory.

|  | £ |
|---|---|
| Factory rent | 5,000 |
| Machine depreciation | 10,000 |
| Heat and light | 6,450 |

(b)   The factory has **three departments,** further details of which are as follows.

|  | *Dept 1* | *Dept 2* | *Dept 3* |
|---|---|---|---|
| Floor area (ms) | 500 | 300 | 200 |
| Cubic capacity (md) | 2,500 | 1,200 | 600 |
| Value of machinery (£) | 100,000 | 20,000 | 80,000 |
| Labour hours | 3,000 | 2,150 | 11,800 |

(c)   East Factory produces **two products,** x and y, and overheads are absorbed on a labour hour basis. The labour hours required in each department to produce one unit of each product are shown below.

|  | *Dept 1* | *Dept 2* | *Dept 3* |
|---|---|---|---|
| Product x (hours) | 3 | 1 | 2 |
| Product y (hours) | 2 | 0.5 | 3 |

(d)   The **direct costs** of product x are £7 per unit and those of product y, £5 per unit. The spreadsheet is to be designed so as to calculate the full cost of one unit of each product after the absorption of departmental overheads.

148

## SOLUTION

3.4 To keep matters simple we shall concentrate on the **formulae** that must be entered for **Department 1** and then those to calculate the unit cost of **product x**.

3.5 Take your time with our solution to make sure you follow it. First of all, though, a look at the spreadsheet once the **variable data** has been entered.

| | A | B | C | D | E |
|---|---|---|---|---|---|
| 1 | Tradco Ltd | | | | |
| 2 | Cost apportionment | | | | |
| 3 | | | | | |
| 4 | *Overhead costs* | | | | |
| 5 | | | | | £ |
| 6 | Factory rent | | | | 5,000 |
| 7 | Machine depreciation | | | | 10,000 |
| 8 | Heat and light | | | | 6,450 |
| 9 | | | | | 21,450 |
| 10 | *Departmental statistics* | | | | |
| 11 | | *Dept 1* | *Dept 2* | *Dept 3* | |
| 12 | | | | | |
| 13 | Floor area (sq. m) | 500 | 300 | 200 | |
| 14 | Cubic capacity (cbc. m) | 2,500 | 1,200 | 600 | |
| 15 | Value of machinery (£) | 100,000 | 20,000 | 80,000 | |
| 16 | Labour hours | 3,000 | 2,150 | 11,800 | |
| 17 | | | | | |
| 18 | *Labour hours* | | | | |
| 19 | | *Dept 1* | *Dept 2* | *Dept 3* | |
| 20 | Product x | 3 | 1 | 2 | |
| 21 | Product y | 2 | 0.5 | 3 | |
| 22 | | | | | |
| 23 | *Direct costs* | | | | |
| 24 | | | | | £ |
| 25 | Product x | | | | 7.00 |
| 26 | Product y | | | | 5.00 |
| 27 | | | | | |
| 28 | | | | | |

3.6 Spreadsheet packages offer so much capacity that there is little point in bunching everything up in the top left corner, so we have designed **plenty of 'space'** around each subgroup of data.

3.7 Now look at the **calculation section** of the spreadsheet.

| | A | B |
|---|---|---|
| 27 | | |
| 28 | **Apportionment of overheads** | |
| 29 | | |
| 30 | *Overheads apportioned* | |
| 31 | | *Dept 1* |
| 32 | Factory rent | =$E$6*B13/SUM($B13:$D13) |
| 33 | Machine depreciation | =$E$7*B15/SUM($B15:$D15) |
| 34 | Heat and light | =$E$8*B14/SUM($B14:$D14) |
| 35 | | =SUM(B32:B34) |
| 36 | | |
| 37 | **Calculation of absorption rate** | |
| 38 | | |
| 39 | | *Dept 1* |
| 40 | *Absorption rate* | =B35/B16 |
| 41 | | |
| 42 | **Allocation of overheads to products** | |
| 43 | | |
| 44 | | *Product x* |
| 45 | Direct costs | =E25 |
| 46 | Dept 1 overheads | =B20*B40 |
| 47 | Dept 2 overheads | =C20*C40 |
| 48 | Dept 3 overheads | =D20*D40 |
| 49 | | =SUM(B45:B48) |

3.8 In cells B32 to B34 the allocated overheads listed in rows 6 to 8 are first **apportioned** to the different departments using the **bases** shown in rows 13 to 16.

3.9 The absorption basis is **labour hours** and so in cell B40 the **absorption rate per labour hour** is calculated by dividing the total Department 1 overhead by the total labour hours.

3.10 The same procedure would be followed to calculate absorption rates for departments 2 and 3. Finally, in rows 46 to 48, the **rates would be applied to the hours spent** by each product in each department.

3.11 Try this for yourself using a spreadsheet package. Enter any additional formulae you may need and calculate absorption rates for departments 2 and 3.

3.12 Now study our spreadsheet below. Yours should look fairly similar. You should find that the total cost of product x is £21.25 and that of product y £15.

| | A | B | C | D | E | F |
|---|---|---|---|---|---|---|
| 1 | Tradco Ltd | | | | | |
| 2 | Cost apportionment | | | | | |
| 3 | | | | | | |
| 4 | *Overhead costs* | | | | | |
| 5 | | | | | £ | |
| 6 | Factory rent | | | | 5,000 | |
| 7 | Machine depreciation | | | | 10,000 | |
| 8 | Heat and light | | | | 6,450 | |
| 9 | | | | | 21,450 | |
| 10 | *Departmental statistics* | | | | | |
| 11 | | *Dept 1* | *Dept 2* | *Dept 3* | | |
| 12 | | | | | | |
| 13 | Floor area (sq. m) | 500 | 300 | 200 | | |
| 14 | Cubic capacity (cbc. m) | 2,500 | 1,200 | 600 | | |
| 15 | Value of machinery (£) | 100,000 | 20,000 | 80,000 | | |
| 16 | Labour hours | 3,000 | 2,150 | 11,800 | | |
| 17 | | | | | | |
| 18 | *Labour hours* | | | | | |
| 19 | | *Dept 1* | *Dept 2* | *Dept 3* | | |
| 20 | Product x | 3 | 1 | 2 | | |
| 21 | Product y | 2 | 0.5 | 3 | | |
| 22 | | | | | | |
| 23 | *Direct costs* | | | | | |
| 24 | | | | | £ | |
| 25 | Product x | | | | 7.00 | |
| 26 | Product y | | | | 5.00 | |
| 27 | | | | | | |
| 28 | **Apportionment of overheads** | | | | | |
| 29 | | | | | | |
| 30 | *Overheads apportioned* | | | | | |
| 31 | | *Dept 1* | *Dept 2* | *Dept 3* | | |
| 32 | Factory rent | 2500 | 1500 | 1000 | | |
| 33 | Machine depreciation | 5000 | 1000 | 4000 | | |
| 34 | Heat and light | 3750 | 1800 | 900 | | |
| 35 | | 11250 | 4300 | 5900 | | |
| 36 | | | | | | |
| 37 | **Calculation of absorption rate** | | | | | |
| 38 | | | | | | |
| 39 | | *Dept 1* | *Dept 2* | *Dept 3* | | |
| 40 | *Absorption rate* | 3.75 | 2 | 0.5 | | |
| 41 | | | | | | |
| 42 | **Allocation of overheads to products** | | | | | |
| 43 | | | | | | |
| 44 | | *Product x* | *Product y* | | | |
| 45 | Direct costs | 7.00 | 5.00 | | | |
| 46 | Dept 1 overheads | 11.25 | 7.50 | | | |
| 47 | Dept 2 overheads | 2.00 | 1.00 | | | |
| 48 | Dept 3 overheads | 1.00 | 1.50 | | | |
| 49 | | 21.25 | 15.00 | | | |
| 50 | | | | | | |

3.13 **Additional formulae** you will have needed are as follows. Yours may not be exactly the same as these; we have used absolute cell addresses where we were expecting to copy cell contents.

| | A | B | C | D |
|---|---|---|---|---|
| 28 | **Apportionment of overheads** | | | |
| 29 | | | | |
| 30 | *Overheads apportioned* | | | |
| 31 | | *Dept 1* | *Dept 2* | *Dept 3* |
| 32 | Factory rent | =$E$6*B13/SUM($B13:$D13) | =$E$6*C13/SUM($B13:$D13) | =$E$6*D13/SUM($B13:$D13) |
| 33 | Machine depreciation | =$E$7*B15/SUM($B15:$D15) | =$E$7*C15/SUM($B15:$D15) | =$E$7*D15/SUM($B15:$D15) |
| 34 | Heat and light | =$E$8*B14/SUM($B14:$D14) | =$E$8*C14/SUM($B14:$D14) | =$E$8*D14/SUM($B14:$D14) |
| 35 | | =SUM(B32:B34) | =SUM(C32:C34) | =SUM(D32:D34) |
| 36 | | | | |
| 37 | **Calculation of absorption rate** | | | |
| 38 | | | | |
| 39 | | *Dept 1* | *Dept 2* | *Dept 3* |
| 40 | *Absorption rate* | =B35/B16 | =C35/C16 | =D35/D16 |
| 41 | | | | |
| 42 | **Allocation of overheads to products** | | | |
| 43 | | | | |
| 44 | | Product x | Product y | |
| 45 | Direct costs | =E25 | =E26 | |
| 46 | Dept 1 overheads | =B20*B40 | =B21*B40 | |
| 47 | Dept 2 overheads | =C20*C40 | =C21*C40 | |
| 48 | Dept 3 overheads | =D20*D40 | =D21*D40 | |
| 49 | | =SUM(B45:B48) | =SUM(C45:C48) | |

3.14 Having built this basic model it can be **expanded and adapted** as appropriate for the other three factories, **used again** for subsequent periods, and could also be used to perform 'what **if**' analysis. If you imagine that in reality there may be many more different overheads, several more departments, and lots of different products you should appreciate the **time saved** in the long run by investing a little time at the outset to construct the model.

## DEVOLVED ASSESSMENT ALERT

Any of the topics you have learned for other accounting subjects (such as calculating financial **ratios**, calculating **variances** etc) are fair game for Devolved Assessments in Unit 21.

## Key learning points

- Spreadsheet packages permit the user to work in **three dimensions**. Although this requires careful planning it is a very useful facility.

- Spreadsheets can be used in a variety of **accounting** contexts. You should practise using spreadsheets for these purposes until it becomes as easy as using a calculator.

## Quick quiz

1 What formula would be used in a worksheet named Calculations to refer to cell A5 in a sheet named Variables?

2 What is the danger of inserting extra rows in an extended trial balance set up on a spreadsheet?

3 What are four ways of using 3D spreadsheets?

4 How can a spreadsheet-based ETB know whether an account is a P & L account or a balance sheet account?

5 Can spreadsheets be used for variance analysis?

## Answers to quick quiz_____

1 Variables! A5

2 The SUM formulae at the foot of the ETB may only cover the original rows, not the ones newly inserted.

3 They can help discipline the construction of models. They can be used to record the stages of model building. They can help consolidate data from different sources. They can offer different views of the same data.

4 Each account has to be predesignated as a P & L (eg P) or a balance sheet (eg B) account. When it is 'extended' it can recognise which is which by means of an IF function.

5 Yes, of course they can. You can use any numerical question in any of the BPP Interactive Texts to practise your spreadsheet building skills - and revise the accounting techniques you have learned at the same time!

## Answers to activities_____

## Answer 7.1

The answer is in paragraph 1.9

## Answer 7.2

We named three sheets Div A, Div B and Company X and inserted the data as follows.

| | A | B |
|---|---|---|
| 1 | | Div A |
| 2 | | (UK) |
| 3 | | £ |
| 4 | Sales | 1,458,742 |
| 5 | Expenses | -572,866 |
| 6 | | 885,876 |

| | A | B |
|---|---|---|
| 1 | | Div B |
| 2 | | |
| 3 | | FFr |
| 4 | Sales | 26,924,713 |
| 5 | Expenses | -9,157,992 |
| 6 | | 17,766,721 |

| | A | B |
|---|---|---|
| 1 | | Co. X |
| 2 | | |
| 3 | | £ |
| 4 | Sales | 4,151,213 |
| 5 | Expenses | -1,488,665 |
| 6 | | 2,662,548 |

The formulae in the Company X sheet are as follows.

| | A | B |
|---|---|---|
| 1 | | Co. X |
| 2 | | |
| 3 | | £ |
| 4 | Sales | ='Div A'!B4+('Div B'!B4/10) |
| 5 | Expenses | ='Div A'!B5+('Div B'!B5/10) |
| 6 | | ='Div A'!B6+('Div B'!B6/10) |

Better would be to set up a separate variable for the exchange rate and include that, instead of the figure 10, in the Company X formulae.

## Answer 7.3

The solution (after the amendments required in Activity 7.4) is shown under Answer 7.4 below.

The formulae required for the P&L and Balance Sheet columns are as described in section 1 of this Chapter. For adjustments, accruals and prepayments you could either have a separate variables section or enter the amounts and calculations directly into columns E to H.

## Answer 7.4

(a)

| | A | B | C | D | E | F | G | H | I | J | K | L |
|---|---|---|---|---|---|---|---|---|---|---|---|---|
| 1 | Bettabikkis | | | | | | | | | | | |
| 2 | ETB Year Ended 30/06/X5 | | | | | | | | | | | |
| 3 | Account | | Trial balance | | Adjustments | | Accrued | Prepaid | Profit and loss | | Balance sheet | |
| 4 | | | £ | £ | £ | £ | £ | £ | £ | £ | £ | £ |
| 5 | Sales | P | | (276,156) | | | | | | (276,156) | | |
| 6 | Purchases | P | 169,122 | | | | | | 169,122 | | | |
| 7 | Carriage | P | 5,866 | | | | | | 5,866 | | | |
| 8 | Drawings | B | 15,600 | | | | | | | | 15,600 | |
| 9 | Rent and rates | P | 13,244 | | | | 420 | (1,760) | 11,904 | | | |
| 10 | Postage and stationery | P | 6,002 | | | | | | 6,002 | | | |
| 11 | Advertising | P | 2,660 | | | | | | 2,660 | | | |
| 12 | Salaries and wages | P | 52,840 | | | | | | 52,840 | | | |
| 13 | Bad debt expense | P | 1,754 | | 65 | | | | 1,819 | | | |
| 14 | Provision for Bad Debts | B | | (260) | | (65) | | | | | | (325) |
| 15 | Debtors | B | 24,240 | | | | | | | | 24,240 | |
| 16 | Creditors | B | | (12,942) | | | | | | | | (12,942) |
| 17 | Cash in hand | B | 354 | | | | | | | | 354 | |
| 18 | Cash at bank | B | 2,004 | | | | | | | | 2,004 | |
| 19 | Stock as at 1 July 19X4 | P | 23,854 | | | | | | 23,854 | | | |
| 20 | Equipment | B | 116,000 | | | | | | | | 116,000 | |
| 21 | Depreciation | B | | (38,000) | | (17,400) | | | | | | (55,400) |
| 22 | Capital | B | | (106,182) | | | | | | | | (106,182) |
| 23 | Prepaymets | B | | | | | | 1,760 | | | 1,760 | |
| 24 | Accruals | B | | | | | (420) | | | | | (420) |
| 25 | Depreciation expense | P | | | 17,400 | | | | 17,400 | | | |
| 26 | Closing stock | B | | | 15,605 | | | | | | 15,605 | |
| 27 | Closing stock | P | | | | (15,605) | | | | (15,605) | | |
| 28 | | | | | | | | | | | | |
| 29 | | | | | | | | | | | | |
| 30 | | | | | | | | | | | | |
| 31 | SUB-TOTAL | | 433,540 | (433,540) | 33,070 | (33,070) | 2,180 | (2,180) | 291,467 | (291,761) | 175,563 | (175,269) |
| 32 | Profit for the year | | | | | | | | 294 | | | (294) |
| 33 | TOTAL | | 433,540 | (433,540) | 33,070 | (33,070) | 2,180 | (2,180) | 291,761 | (291,761) | 175,563 | (175,563) |
| 34 | | | | | | | | | | | | |

## Part B: Producing spreadsheets

(b) Check your answer very carefully against the following.

(i)   I5     =IF($B5="P",IF(SUM($C5:$H5)>0,SUM($C5:$H5),0),0)

(ii)   J5    =IF($B5="P",IF(SUM($C5:$H5)<0,SUM($C5:$H5),0),0)

(iii)  K5   =IF($B5="B",IF(SUM($C5:$H5)>0,SUM($C5:$H5),0),0)

(iv)  L5    =IF($B5="B",IF(SUM($C5:$H5)<0,SUM($C5:$H5),0),0)

(v)   J32  =IF($I$31+$J$31>0,-($I$31+$J$31),0)

(vi)  K32 =IF($I$31+$J$31>0,($I$31+$J$31),0)

## Answer 7.5

| | A | B | C | D | E | F | G | H | I | J | K | L |
|---|---|---|---|---|---|---|---|---|---|---|---|---|
| 1 | Kate | | | | | | | | | | | |
| 2 | ETB Year Ended 31/12/X3 | | | | | | | | | | | |
| 3 | Account | | Trial balance | | Adjustments | | Accrued | Prepaid | Profit and loss | | Balance sheet | |
| 4 | | | £ | £ | £ | £ | £ | £ | £ | £ | £ | £ |
| 5 | | | | | | | | | | | | |
| 6 | Capital | B | | (38,728) | | | | | | | | (38,728) |
| 7 | Freehold L & B | B | 25,000 | | | | | | | | 25,000 | |
| 8 | F & F cost | B | 3,360 | | | | | | | | 3,360 | |
| 9 | F & F depn | B | | (1,680) | | (336) | | | | | | (2,016) |
| 10 | MV cost | B | 1,900 | | | | | | | | 1,900 | |
| 11 | MV depn | B | | (600) | | (380) | | | | | | (980) |
| 12 | Purchases | P | 93,964 | | | | | | 93,964 | | | |
| 13 | Sales | P | | (133,298) | | | | | | (133,298) | | |
| 14 | Rent received | P | | (720) | | (240) | | | | (960) | | |
| 15 | Drawings | B | 6,460 | | | | | | | | 6,460 | |
| 16 | Car expenses | P | 792 | | | | | | 792 | | | |
| 17 | Stock at 01 Jan 19X3 | P | 9,976 | | | | | | 9,976 | | | |
| 18 | Bad debt expense | P | 844 | | 64 | | | | 908 | | | |
| 19 | Doubtful debt provision | B | | (452) | | (64) | | | | | | (516) |
| 20 | General expenses | P | 1,654 | | | | | (94) | 1,560 | | | |
| 21 | Rent and rates | P | 2,324 | | | | | (96) | 2,228 | | | |
| 22 | Trade debtors | B | 15,842 | | | | | | | | 15,842 | |
| 23 | Trade creditors | B | | (13,866) | | | | | | | | (13,866) |
| 24 | Wages and salaries | P | 17,966 | | | | 396 | | 18,362 | | | |
| 25 | Discounts allowed | P | 4,328 | | | | | | 4,328 | | | |
| 26 | Bank | B | 4,934 | | | | | | | | 4,934 | |
| 27 | Stock at 31 Dec 19X3 | P | | | | (10,858) | | | | (10,858) | | |
| 28 | Stock at 31 Dec 19X3 | B | | | 10,858 | | | | | | 10,858 | |
| 29 | Accruals | B | | | | | | (396) | | | | (396) |
| 30 | Prepayments | B | | | | | 190 | | | | 190 | |
| 31 | Depreciation expense | P | | | 716 | | | | 716 | | | |
| 32 | Sundry debtors | B | | | 240 | | | | | | 240 | |
| 33 | | | | | | | | | | | | |
| 34 | | | | | | | | | | | | |
| 35 | | | | | | | | | | | | |
| 36 | SUB-TOTAL | | 189,344 | (189,344) | 11,878 | (11,878) | 586 | (586) | 132,834 | (145,116) | 68,784 | (56,502) |
| 37 | Profit for the year | | | | | | | | 12,282 | | | (12,282) |
| 38 | TOTAL | | 189,344 | (189,344) | 11,878 | (11,878) | 586 | (586) | 145,116 | (145,116) | 68,784 | (68,784) |

154

# Answer 7.6

| | A | B | C | D | E | F | G | H | I | J | K | L |
|---|---|---|---|---|---|---|---|---|---|---|---|---|
| 1 | Kate | | | | | | | | | | | |
| 2 | *ETB Year Ended 31/12X3* | | | | | | | | | | | |
| 3 | Account | | Trial balance | | Adjustments | | Accrued | Prepaid | Profit and loss | | Balance sheet | |
| 4 | | | £ | £ | £ | £ | £ | £ | £ | £ | £ | £ |
| 5 | | | | | | | | | | | | |
| 6 | Capital | B | | (38,728) | | | | | | | | (38,728) |
| 7 | Freehold L & B | B | 25,000 | | | | | | | | 25,000 | |
| 8 | F & F cost | B | 3,360 | | | | | | | | 3,360 | |
| 9 | F & F depn | B | | (1,680) | | (336) | | | | | | (2,016) |
| 10 | MV cost | B | 1,900 | | | | | | | | 1,900 | |
| 11 | MV depn | B | | (600) | | (380) | | | | | | (980) |
| 12 | Purchases | P | 93,964 | | | | | | 93,964 | | | |
| 13 | Sales | P | | (133,298) | | | | | | (133,298) | | |
| 14 | Rent received | P | | (720) | | (240) | | | | (960) | | |
| 15 | Drawings | B | 6,460 | | | | | | | | 6,460 | |
| 16 | Car expenses | P | 792 | | | | | | 792 | | | |
| 17 | Stock at 01 Jan 19X3 | P | 9,976 | | | | | | 9,976 | | | |
| 18 | Bad debt expense | P | 844 | | 340 | | | | 1,184 | | | |
| 19 | Doubtful debt provision | B | | (452) | | (340) | | | | | | (792) |
| 20 | General expenses | P | 1,654 | | | | | (94) | 1,560 | | | |
| 21 | Rent and rates | P | 2,324 | | | | | (96) | 2,228 | | | |
| 22 | Trade debtors | B | 15,842 | | | | | | | | 15,842 | |
| 23 | Trade creditors | B | | (13,866) | | | | | | | | (13,866) |
| 24 | Wages and salaries | P | 17,966 | | | | 396 | | 18,362 | | | |
| 25 | Discounts allowed | P | 4,328 | | | | | | 4,328 | | | |
| 26 | Bank | B | 4,934 | | | | | | | | 4,934 | |
| 27 | Stock at 31 Dec 19X3 | P | | | | (10,858) | | | | (10,858) | | |
| 28 | Stock at 31 Dec 19X3 | B | | | 10,858 | | | | | | 10,858 | |
| 29 | Accruals | B | | | | | | (396) | | | | (396) |
| 30 | Prepayments | B | | | | | 190 | | | | 190 | |
| 31 | Depreciation expense | P | | | 716 | | | | 716 | | | |
| 32 | Sundry debtors | B | | | 240 | | | | | | 240 | |
| 33 | | | | | | | | | | | | |
| 34 | | | | | | | | | | | | |
| 35 | | | | | | | | | | | | |
| 36 | SUB-TOTAL | | 189,344 | (189,344) | 12,154 | (12,154) | 586 | (586) | 133,110 | (145,116) | 68,784 | (56,778) |
| 37 | Profit for the year | | | | | | | | 12,006 | | | (12,006) |
| 38 | TOTAL | | 189,344 | (189,344) | 12,154 | (12,154) | 586 | (586) | 145,116 | (145,116) | 68,784 | (68,784) |

You may have noticed that the recalculated contents of cells E18 and D19 are £340.10. You will need to decide how best to deal with this!

# Chapter 8    Macros and databases

---

## Chapter topic list

1    Macros

2    Spreadsheets as databases

3    Other useful formulae and functions

4    Pivot tables

5    Databases

---

## Learning objectives

On completion of this chapter you will be able to:

| | Performance criteria | Range statement |
|---|---|---|
| • Produce spreadsheets by creation and modification | | 21.2.1, 21.2.3 |
| • Title spreadsheets in a way which clearly defines their use and purpose | 21.2.1 | |
| • Arrange spreadsheets in a way consistent with organisational conventions | 21.2.2 | |
| • State all rates and other numeric inputs and assumptions to the correct number of decimal places | 21.2.3 | 21.2.4 |
| • Check calculated values for correctness when changes are made to the inputs | 21.2.4 | 21.2.4 |
| • Use spreadsheets to carry out data modifications and for entry of related formulas | 21.2.5 | 21.2.4 |
| • Format each cell clearly and accurately | 21.2.6 | |
| • *Understand the purposes and applications of spreadsheets* | n/a | n/a |
| • *Describe and operate a range of spreadsheet products* | n/a | n/a |
| • *Take advantage of interfaces between software packages* | n/a | n/a |
| • *Organise, interpret and present information* | n/a | n/a |

Italicised objectives are areas of knowledge and understanding underlying the elements of competence for Unit 21.

# 1    MACROS

1.1    A macro is a sort of mini-program that you write by **recording** your key-strokes and mouse clicks. You do not need any programming knowledge at all to do this.

1.2    Macros can get **very complex** indeed – in fact you **can** build whole Windows-like applications using them, if you are so inclined. (Doing so is a very good introduction to programming proper.) However, for complex tasks they are not nearly as efficient as proper programs, not least because they take up a good deal of RAM once they get beyond a certain level of detail.

1.3    We are **not** going to be demonstrating anything very elaborate, here. We are just going to show you how macros can be used to **eliminate a few key-strokes and mouse clicks** for tasks that you have to **perform frequently** enough to warrant writing a macro in the first place.

1.4    We are going to explain the basic principles of macros by reference to Microsoft **Excel.**

## 1.5    EXAMPLE: A SIMPLE MACRO

Suppose you decided that **every spreadsheet you created** should have your **first name and surname** in the bottom right corner of the footer in **Arial 8pt font.** You could write a macro and do all of this just by pressing two keys.

To write this macro you would proceed as follows. As always, follow this example through **hands-on** if possible.

*Step 1*    **Excel:** Open a fresh file. Click on the **Tools** menu and then on the option **Macro**

*Step2*    This gives a sub-menu including the option **Record New Macro.** Select this.

*Step 3*    **A** dialogue box like the following will appear.

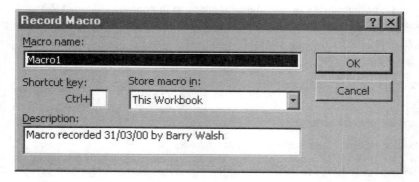

*Step 4*    Give the macro a name such as InsertName and press **Tab.** Excel will not allow spaces within macro names.

*Step 5*    Choose a shortcut key. This must be a **letter,** and it should be one that you don't frequently use for other purposes such as Ctrl + C or Ctrl + B. We will choose **Ctrl + m**

    (Note that we use lower case **m;** if we had used **M** we would subsequently have to type Ctrl +**Shift** +m to start the macro).

*Step 6*    Accept the option to store the macro in **This Workbook** and **click on OK**

*Step 7*    Take care now because you are being watched! **Everything you do is being recorded.** (A little window will have appeared on the screen with a dark square

**158**

inside it. You click on the dark square when you have finished recording your macro.)

*Step 8*     From the menu select **View, Header and Footer.**

*Step 9*     Click on **Custom Footer** and click into the **Right section**.

*Step 10*    Type your name and highlight the text by clicking and dragging the cursor over it.

*Step11*     Click on the **A** button to activate the font menu, and select Arial 8pt.

*Step 12*    Close the menus by clicking on **OK**. (Three **OK** boxes require clicking.)

*Step13*     Click on the stop recording button.

---

**TIP OF THE DAY**

**Always start** a macro by **returning the cursor to cell A1** (by pressing Ctrl + Home), even if it is already there. You may well not want to make your first entry in cell A1, but if you select your first real cell (B4 say) **before** you start recording, the macro will always begin at the currently active cell, whether it is B4 or Z256.

**Always finish** a macro by **selecting the cell** where the user of your spreadsheet will make his or her **next entry**. This means that the user can get straight on with their work once the macro has run, without having to scroll back to the right position.

---

1.6     That's all there is to it. Test your macro now by **selecting a fresh sheet** in this workbook then pressing Ctrl + m together. Then type 'Test' in cell A1 (as Excel will not Print Preview a blank sheet), and select **File, Print Preview.** You will see your name has been inserted into the footer.

1.7     Now save your file with a suitable name and **close down** your spreadsheet package completely. Then open it up again and open a completely **new file**. Press Ctrl + m. Regrettably, nothing will happen. This does not mean that your macro is lost forever, just that it is not currently in the computer's memory (because you closed down the package).

1.8     However, if you **open up the file you just saved**, your macro will work again, because it is actually **stored** in that file. If you want your macro to be **available to you whenever** you want it you have the following choices.

(a)     Keep this file, with no contents other than your 'name' macro (and any others you may write) and always use it as the basis for any new spreadsheets you create, which will subsequently be saved with new file names.

(b)     You can add the macro to your **Personal Macro Workbook.** You do this at the point when you are naming your workbook and choosing a shortcut key, by changing the option in the **Store macro in:** box from This Workbook to Personal Macro Workbook. The macro will then be loaded into memory whenever you start up Excel and be available in any spreadsheet you create.

## TIP OF THE DAY

If you forget to assign a keyboard shortcut to a macro (or do not want to do so), you can still run your macros by clicking on **Tools ...Macro ... Macros.** This gives you a list of all the macros currently available. Select the one you want then click on **Run.**

**Do not accept** the **default names** offered by Excel of Macro1, Macro2 etc. You will soon forget what these macros do, unless you give them a meaningful name.

### Activity 8.1

Try recording some more macros that simplify tasks that you often do and that involve four or five separate key-strokes and/or mouse clicks. Examples might include adding double and single underlining to totals and making them bold, or centring headings and making them italic.

If you make a mistake just click on stop and start again from the beginning.

Also experiment with saving macros in the current workbook and making them available in the Personal Macro Workbook.

When you feel you have mastered the art of being watched while you work try Activity 8.2.

### Activity 8.2

You have been given a large pile of files and print-outs relating to a variety of your firm's clients and you have been asked to extract from these the following summary information for each client. Sample data is given for a company called Little Ltd.

| A | B | C | D | E |
|---|---|---|---|---|
| 1 | Company name: | **Little Ltd** | | |
| 2 | | | | |
| 3 | | | | |
| 4 | | *1998* | *1997* | *% difference* |
| 5 | Sales | 145,789 | 157,582 | -7% |
| 6 | Cost of Sales | (53,246) | (62,143) | -14% |
| 7 | Gross profit | 92,543 | 95,439 | -3% |
| 8 | Operating expenses | (22,411) | (14,567) | 54% |
| 9 | Net profit | 70,132 | 80,872 | -13% |

Each set of summary information is to be saved to a separate file.

The first thing you do (obviously) is count up how may different clients you have to deal with, so that you can work out an average time and give your boss some idea of how long this task will take you and get deadlines agreed. You discover that there are 200 clients to deal with.

The next thing you do is **write a macro** including headings and formulae that will automatically give you a formatted template for each client and minimise the data entry that you have to do.

Write the macro.

## 2 SPREADSHEETS AS DATABASES

## KEY TERMS

A database is a collection of **structured data.** Any item of data within the database can be used as a subject of enquiry.

2.1 More loosely speaking, a database is a **collection of data** which is integrated and organised so as to provide a **single comprehensive system.** The data is governed by rules which define its structure and determine how it can be accessed.

2.2 The **purpose** of a database is to provide **convenient access** to common data for a **wide variety** of **users** and **user needs.** The point of storing all the data in a single place is to avoid the problems that arise when several similar versions of the same data exist, so that it is not clear which is the **definite version,** and also to avoid the need to have to input the same data more than once.

2.3 For instance, both the sales administration and the marketing departments of an organisation may need **customer name and address details.** If these two departments operated **separate** systems they will **both** need to input details of any change of address. If they **share a common database** for this information, it **only needs to be input once.**

## DEVOLVED ASSESSMENT ALERT

Modern database design is a very complex topic which, if done properly, requires a good understanding of a number of topics that you will not even meet until you Go on to higher studies of computing. At Accounting Technician level questions are unlikely to require anything more than a very basic understanding of what a database is.

## Sorting facilities

2.4 In the illustration below data has been sorted by highlighting columns A to C and then clicking on **Data** and then **Sort.** It has been sorted into **ascending** product name order and **descending** order of number of parts used in that product. Then the data has been copied into columns E to G where it can be **re-sorted** according to part number and product name.

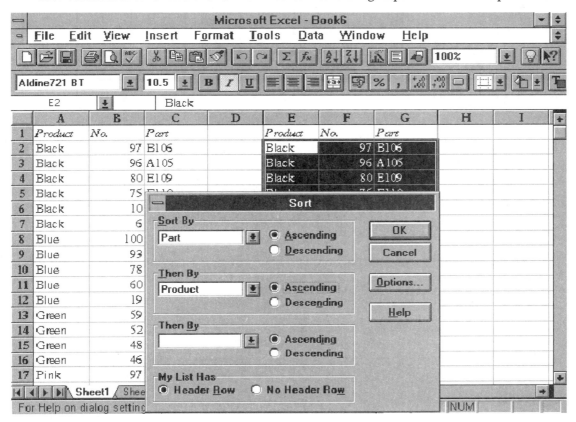

## Spreadsheets and databases

2.5 Spreadsheet packages are **not true databases,** but they often have database-like facilities for manipulating tables of data, if only to a limited extent compared with a true database.

### Activity 8.3

Can you name two examples of a true database package?

## 2.6 EXAMPLE: SPREADSHEETS AND DATABASES

Here is a spreadsheet used for **stock control**.

| | A | B | C | D | E | F | G | H | I |
|---|---|---|---|---|---|---|---|---|---|
| 1 | Component | Product | Quantity | In stock | Re-order level | Free stock | Reorder quantity | On order | Supplier |
| 2 | A001 | A | 1 | 371 | 160 | 211 | 400 | - | P750 |
| 3 | A002 | B | 5 | 33 | 40 | - | 100 | 100 | P036 |
| 4 | A003 | A | 5 | 206 | 60 | 146 | 150 | - | P888 |
| 5 | A004 | D | 3 | 176 | 90 | 86 | 225 | - | P036 |
| 6 | A005 | E | 9 | 172 | 120 | 52 | 300 | - | P750 |
| 7 | A006 | C | 7 | 328 | 150 | 178 | 375 | - | P684 |
| 8 | A007 | C | 2 | 13 | 10 | 3 | 25 | - | P227 |
| 9 | A008 | C | 6 | 253 | 60 | 193 | 150 | - | P036 |
| 10 | A009 | E | 9 | 284 | 90 | 194 | 225 | - | P888 |
| 11 | A010 | B | 3 | 435 | 100 | 335 | 250 | - | P720 |
| 12 | A011 | B | 2 | 295 | 110 | 185 | 275 | - | P036 |
| 13 | A012 | A | 3 | 40 | 190 | - | 475 | 475 | P036 |
| 14 | A013 | A | 7 | 23 | 120 | - | 300 | 300 | P227 |
| 15 | A014 | C | 4 | 296 | 110 | 186 | 275 | - | P750 |
| 16 | A015 | D | 7 | 432 | 40 | 392 | 100 | - | P684 |
| 17 | A016 | D | 4 | 416 | 100 | 316 | 250 | - | P141 |
| 18 | A017 | A | 3 | 463 | 150 | 313 | 375 | - | P888 |

2.7 If you scrutinise this table you may notice that there are certain common items. For instance both components A001 and A003 are used to make Product A. Both components A001 and A005 are bought from supplier P750.

2.8 Wouldn't it be handy if we could **manipulate** this data in some way, say, to get a full list of all components used to make product A, or a list of all components supplied by supplier P750? Of course, we **can** do this, almost at the click of a button.

2.9 In Excel you simply click in the **Data** menu and choose the option **Filter ... Auto filter.** A downward pointing arrow now appears beside each heading, and if you click on one of the arrows a list of each different item in the corresponding column drops down.

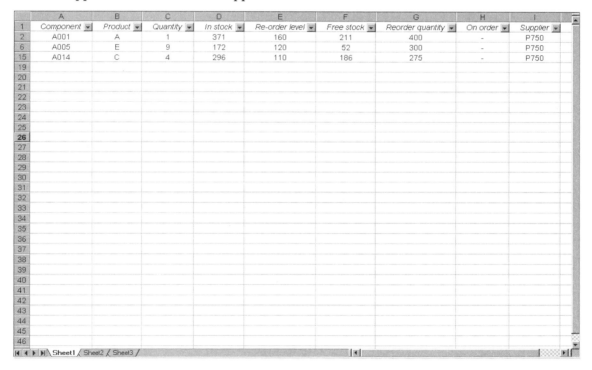

2.10 In this illustration the user has clicked on the arrow in the Supplier column and is about to select Supplier 750. This is what happens.

| | A | B | C | D | E | F | G | H | I |
|---|---|---|---|---|---|---|---|---|---|
| 1 | Component | Product | Quantity | In stock | Re-order level | Free stock | Reorder quantity | On order | Supplier |
| 2 | A001 | A | 1 | 371 | 160 | 211 | 400 | - | P750 |
| 6 | A005 | E | 9 | 172 | 120 | 52 | 300 | - | P750 |
| 15 | A014 | C | 4 | 296 | 110 | 186 | 275 | - | P750 |

2.11 This shows that supplier P750 supplies components A001, A005 and A014, that there is nothing on order from this supplier at present, that this supplier is important for products A, E and C only, and so on.

2.12 If the original data were restored (by clicking on the Supplier arrow and choosing All) and then we clicked on the arrow in the **Product** column we would be able to see at a glance all the components used for product A and all the suppliers for those components, whether any components were on order at present (possibly meaning delays in the availability of the next batch of Product A) and so on.

BPP
PUBLISHING

## Activity 8.4

Construct the spreadsheet illustrated above yourself (hopefully you won't need to look back at Chapter 5 to find out what formulae are used: you should be able to work this out for yourself by now).

Use the **Data ... Filters** option to answer the following questions.

(a)   What components does supplier P888 supply?

(b)   What components are used in product E?

(c)   Which suppliers are due to deliver fresh supplies. (*Hint:* are they Top of the Pops?)

## Spreadsheets and data tables

### KEY TERMS

The term **data table** is used by some spreadsheet packages (for example Excel) to refer to a group of cells that show the results of changing the value of variables.

2.13   **Data tables** can be most clearly explained using a simple example.

## 2.14   EXAMPLE: A ONE-INPUT DATA TABLE

Don't be put off by the terminology here. All this means is that **one** of the bits of the calculation changes and the other bits don't.

Suppose a company has production costs which it would expect to be in the region of £5m were it not for the effects of inflation. Economic forecasts for the inflation rate in the coming year range from 2% to 10%.

If this were part of a **scenario** that the company was trying to model on a spreadsheet a 'data table' could be produced showing the range of effects of these various possible levels of inflation simply by:

(a)   Entering the basic data.

(b)   Entering just one formula per item affected (production costs and profits in the example illustrated).

(c)   Using the computer's data table tool.

2.15   Here is the problem set up on Microsoft Excel.

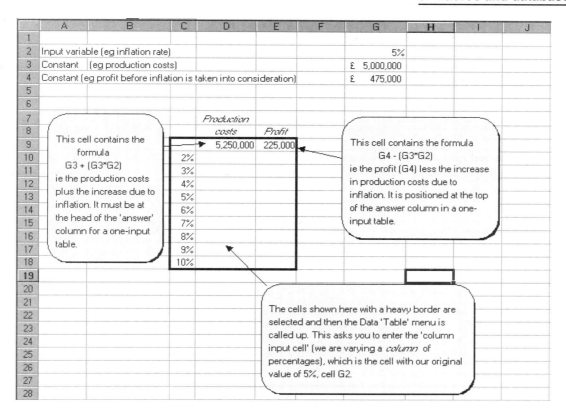

2.16 This is what happens after a single cell reference (G2) is entered, as prompted by the **data table menu**.

| | A | B | C | D | E | F | G | H | I |
|---|---|---|---|---|---|---|---|---|---|
| 1 | | | | | | | | | |
| 2 | Input variable (eg inflation rate) | | | | | | 5% | | |
| 3 | Constant (eg production costs) | | | | | | £5,000,000 | | |
| 4 | Constant (eg profit before inflation is taken into consideration) | | | | | | £ 475,000 | | |
| 5 | | | | | | | | | |
| 6 | | | | | | | | | |
| 7 | | | | Production | | | | | |
| 8 | | | | costs | Profit | | | | |
| 9 | | | | 5,250,000 | 225,000 | | | | |
| 10 | | | 2% | 5,100,000 | 375,000 | | | | |
| 11 | | | 3% | 5,150,000 | 325,000 | | | | |
| 12 | | | 4% | 5,200,000 | 275,000 | | | | |
| 13 | | | 5% | 5,250,000 | 225,000 | | | | |
| 14 | | | 6% | 5,300,000 | 175,000 | | | | |
| 15 | | | 7% | 5,350,000 | 125,000 | | | | |
| 16 | | | 8% | 5,400,000 | 75,000 | | | | |
| 17 | | | 9% | 5,450,000 | 25,000 | | | | |
| 18 | | | 10% | 5,500,000 | (25,000) | | | | |
| 19 | | | | | | | | | |
| 20 | | | | | | | | | |

The shaded cells are automatically filled by the spreadsheet package to show the impact of inflation on production costs and profits.

## Two-input data tables

2.17 It is also possible to use this facility if **two** of the numbers in the calculation are to be changed.

## 2.18 EXAMPLE: A TWO-INPUT DATA TABLE

Suppose the company is not sure that its production costs will be £5m - they could alternatively be only £4.5m or else they could be up to £5.5m. The problem is set up in a similar way on Excel. Study the diagram carefully.

| | A | B | C | D | E | F | G | H |
|---|---|---|---|---|---|---|---|---|
| 1 | | | | | | | | |
| 2 | **Column** input variable (eg inflation rate) | | | | 5% | | | |
| 3 | **Row** input variable (eg production costs) | | | | £5,000,000 | | | |
| 4 | | | | | | | | |
| 5 | | | | | | | | |
| 6 | | | | *Production* | | | | |
| 7 | | | | *costs* | | | | |
| 8 | | 5,250,000 | 4,500,000 | 5,000,000 | 5,500,000 | | | |
| 9 | | 2% | | | | | | |
| 10 | | 3% | | | | | | |
| 11 | | 4% | | | | | | |
| 12 | | 5% | | | | | | |
| 13 | | 6% | | | | | | |
| 14 | | 7% | | | | | | |
| 15 | | 8% | | | | | | |
| 16 | | 9% | | | | | | |
| 17 | | 10% | | | | | | |

This cell contains the formula G3 + (G3*G2), as in the last example, but it must be positioned here in the corner for a two-input table.

The cells shown here with a heavy border are selected and the Data 'Table' menu is called up again. This time cell reference G3 is entered as the 'row input variable' (the different levels of production costs shown in a row at the top of the table), as well as the column input variable (G2) - the inflation rate.

## 2.19 SOLUTION

Here is the solution, obtained with three or four clicks of the mouse!

| | A | B | C | D | E | F | G | H |
|---|---|---|---|---|---|---|---|---|
| 1 | | | | | | | | |
| 2 | **Column** input variable (eg inflation rate) | | | | 5% | | | |
| 3 | **Row** input variable (eg production costs) | | | | £5,000,000 | | | |
| 4 | | | | | | | | |
| 5 | | | | | | | | |
| 6 | | | | *Production* | | | | |
| 7 | | | | *costs* | | | | |
| 8 | | 5,250,000 | 4,500,000 | 5,000,000 | 5,500,000 | | | |
| 9 | | 2% | 4,590,000 | 5,100,000 | 5,610,000 | | | |
| 10 | | 3% | 4,635,000 | 5,150,000 | 5,665,000 | | | |
| 11 | | 4% | 4,680,000 | 5,200,000 | 5,720,000 | | | |
| 12 | | 5% | 4,725,000 | 5,250,000 | 5,775,000 | | | |
| 13 | | 6% | 4,770,000 | 5,300,000 | 5,830,000 | | | |
| 14 | | 7% | 4,815,000 | 5,350,000 | 5,885,000 | | | |
| 15 | | 8% | 4,860,000 | 5,400,000 | 5,940,000 | | | |
| 16 | | 9% | 4,905,000 | 5,450,000 | 5,995,000 | | | |
| 17 | | 10% | 4,950,000 | 5,500,000 | 6,050,000 | | | |
| 18 | | | | | | | | |

Once more the cells shown here with shading are filled in automatically by the spreadsheet package

## Activity 8.5

Moist, Damp and Brown is a firm of solicitors mainly engaged in conveyancing business, domestic disputes and small claims.

The partners are trying to assess their likely income from conveyancing in the next year. They charge a standard fee of £300 for conveyancing work. On average they reckon that a conveyancing job takes about 5 hours but this varies considerably from case to case due to the large number of unknown factors involved.

Years of experience enable them to assess the likely difficulty of a job (based on their knowledge of the other solicitor involved, the lending organisation, the local authority, the price of the property and so on). They have assigned weighting factors to as many of the variables as possible such that an average job has a total weighting factor of 1. They have a policy of refusing any jobs with a total weighting factor greater than 2.

The most likely scenario for the coming year has been set up on a spreadsheet as follows.

| | A | B | C | D | E | F | G | H |
|---|---|---|---|---|---|---|---|---|
| 1 | | | | | | | | |
| 2 | Standard fee (£) | 300 | | | | | | |
| 3 | Number of clients (£) | 100 | | | | | | |
| 4 | Average time (hours) | 5 | | | | | | |
| 5 | Variable costs per hour (£) | 20 | | | | | | |
| 6 | Fixed costs per annum (£) | 5,000 | | | | | | |
| 7 | | | | | | | | |
| 8 | Variability index | 1.00 | | | | | | |
| 9 | | | | | | | | |
| 10 | | £ | | | | | | |
| 11 | Fee income | 30,000.00 | | | | | | |
| 12 | Variable costs | (10,000.00) | | | | | | |
| 13 | Fixed costs | (5,000.00) | | | | | | |
| 14 | Net profit | 15,000.00 | | | | | | |
| 15 | | | | | | | | |

A data table is needed to assess the consequences of different scenarios. However the partners cannot remember how to set this up.

*Required*

Tell them what should be put in the top left hand corner and what should be the row variable and the column variable. Using a spreadsheet calculate the figures that will appear in the data table. What will be the net profit if 125 jobs are taken on with an overall average weighting factor of 1.25?

| | A | B | C | D | E | F | G | H |
|---|---|---|---|---|---|---|---|---|
| 18 | =B14 | 0.50 | 0.75 | 1.00 | 1.25 | 1.50 | 1.75 | 2.00 |
| 19 | 0 | | | | | | | |
| 20 | 25 | | | | | | | |
| 21 | 50 | | | | | | | |
| 22 | 75 | | | | | | | |
| 23 | 100 | | | | | | | |
| 24 | 125 | | | | | | | |
| 25 | 150 | | | | | | | |
| 26 | 200 | | | | | | | |
| 27 | 225 | | | | | | | |
| 28 | 250 | | | | | | | |

## 3 OTHER USEFUL FORMULAE AND FUNCTIONS

3.1 In this section we shall have a quick look at some functions that are useful when you are presented with pre-prepared data in a spreadsheet and you want to extract certain items.

## LEFT, RIGHT and MID

3.2 Sometimes you may want to extract only specific characters from the data entered in a cell. For instance, suppose a set of raw materials codes had been entered into a spreadsheet as follows.

| | A | B |
|---|---|---|
| 1 | 6589D | |
| 2 | 5589B | |
| 3 | 5074D | |
| 4 | 8921B | |
| 5 | 3827B | |
| 6 | 1666D | |
| 7 | 5062A | |
| 8 | 7121D | |
| 9 | 7457C | |
| 10 | 9817D | |
| 11 | 6390C | |
| 12 | 1148A | |
| 13 | 4103A | |
| 14 | 8988A | |
| 15 | 6547C | |
| 16 | 5390A | |
| 17 | 6189D | |
| 18 | 8331C | |
| 19 | 1992B | |
| 20 | 7587A | |

3.3 The four **digits** are, say, a number derived from the supplier's reference number, while the **letter** indicates that the material is used to make Product A, B, C or D.

3.4 If you wanted to sort this data in **alphabetical** order of **Product** you would have a problem, because it is only possible to arrange it in ascending or descending **numerical** order, using the standard Sort method.

3.5 To get round this you can extract the letter from each cell using the **RIGHT** function, as follows.

| | A | B |
|---|---|---|
| 1 | 6589D | =RIGHT(A1,1) |
| 2 | 5589B | =RIGHT(A2,1) |
| 3 | 5074D | =RIGHT(A3,1) |
| 4 | 8921B | =RIGHT(A4,1) |
| 5 | 3827B | =RIGHT(A5,1) |
| 6 | 1666D | =RIGHT(A6,1) |

3.6 The formula in cell B1 means "Extract the last (or rightmost) one character from cell A1". If we wanted to extract the last **two** characters the formula would be **=RIGHT(A1,2)**, and so on.

3.7 The formula can then be filled down and then the data can be sorted by column B, giving the following results.

| | A | B |
|---|---|---|
| 1 | 5062A | A |
| 2 | 1148A | A |
| 3 | 4103A | A |
| 4 | 8988A | A |
| 5 | 5390A | A |
| 6 | 7587A | A |
| 7 | 5589B | B |
| 8 | 8921B | B |
| 9 | 3827B | B |
| 10 | 1992B | B |
| 11 | 7457C | C |
| 12 | 6390C | C |
| 13 | 6547C | C |
| 14 | 8331C | C |
| 15 | 6589D | D |
| 16 | 5074D | D |
| 17 | 1666D | D |
| 18 | 7121D | D |
| 19 | 9817D | D |
| 20 | 6189D | D |

3.8 The function **LEFT** works in the same way, except that it extracts the **first** (or leftmost) character or characters.

3.9 The function **MID**, as you might expect, extracts a character or characters from the **middle** of the cell, starting at the **position** you specify, counting from left to right:

**=MID([Cell],[Position],[Number of characters]).**

In Excel the first character extracted is the one at the position specified, so if you want to extract the **third** character you specify position 3. In Lotus 1-2-3 it is the next character after the position specified, so if you want to extract the third character you specify position 2.

---

### Activity 8.6

Cell A1 contains the data:

**12-D-496**

(a)   What formula would you use to extract the **D** into a different cell?
(b)   What formula would you use to extract the **12** into a different cell?

---

## LOOKUP

3.10 The LOOKUP function allows you to enter data that corresponds to a value in one cell in a column and return the data in the corresponding row in a different column. A simple example will make this clearer.

|   | A | B | C | D | E | F | G |
|---|---|---|---|---|---|---|---|
| 1 | 1 | Red | | | | | |
| 2 | 2 | Green | | | | | |
| 3 | 3 | Blue | | | | | |
| 4 | 4 | Yellow | | | | | |
| 5 | | | | | | | |
| 6 | | | | | 1 | Red | |
| 7 | | | | | | | |
| 8 | | | | | | | |

3.11   Here the user enters a figure between 1 and 4 in cell E6 and the spreadsheet returns the corresponding colour from the range A1:B4. If the user had entered **3** then cell F6 would say **Blue**.

3.12   Here is the formula that is used to do this.

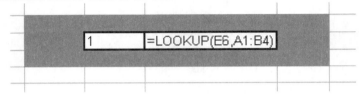

| 1 | =LOOKUP(E6,A1:B4) |

## Merging the contents of cells

3.13   The next formula that is only available in Excel 97 and above.

3.14   Suppose data had been entered into a spreadsheet as follows.

3.15   What if you wanted the data in cells A1, B1 and C1 in a single cell: 21A64? To do this in Excel 97 you can simply join the contents of individual cells together using the **&** symbol, as follows. The formula could be filled down to give the same results for the rest of the list.

|   | A | B | C | D |
|---|---|---|---|---|
| 1 | 21 | A | 64 | =A1&B1&C1 |
| 2 | 62 | P | 14 | |
| 3 | 87 | T | 26 | |
| 4 | | | | |
| 5 | | | | |

## Paste special

3.16   Sometimes you may wish to convert a formula into an absolute value, for example you may want the contents of cell D1 in the above example to be "21A64", not a formula that gives this result.

3.17   To convert a formula to an absolute value, copy the relevant cell or cells in the normal way, then highlight another cell (say, E1 in the above example) and **right click**. From the menu that appears, choose **Paste Special**. The following dialogue box will appear.

3.18   Here, if you choose **Values** then what will be pasted into cell E1 is the value "21A64", not the formula in cell D1.

## Activity 8.7

Spend some time seeing what other functions are available (click on the *fx* button and have a go at using it. Try for instance the DAY(), MONTH() and YEAR() functions to manipulate data entered as dates.

Also, see what other options are available in the **Paste Special** dialogue box.

There is no answer to this activity: we are trying to encourage you to experiment and find things out for yourself.

## 4 PIVOT TABLES

> **KEY TERM**
>
> A **pivot table** is an interactive table that summarises and analyses data from existing lists and tables. After a PivotTable has been created it is possible to reorganise the data simply by dragging the fields and items.

4.1 To understand pivot tables we first need to get a little bit more understanding of records and fields.

## Records and fields

4.2 A typical database is made up of **records** and each record is made up of a number of **fields**. Here's an example of five records, each with four fields.

| Surname | First name | Title | Age |
|---------|-----------|-------|-----|
| Foreman | Susan | Miss | 42 |
| McDonald | David | Dr | 56 |
| McDonald | Dana | Mrs | 15 |
| Sanjay | Rachana | Ms | 24 |
| Talco | Giovanni | Mr | 32 |

(a) Each **Row** is one **Record**. (Notice that both Row and Record begin with the letter R.)

(b) Each **Column** is one **Field**. (If you can remember that Rows are Records, this shouldn't be too hard to work out!)

The example above has records for five people, and each record contains fields for the person's surname, first name, title and age.

## Analysing and interpreting data

4.3 There are lots of ways of analysing this data.

(a) We could find the **total number** of occurrences of each surname to see which was the most and least common. Likewise first names.

(b) We could find the **total number** of each title, as an indication of the most and least common marital status of the people.

(c) We could find the **average** age of the people

(d) We could find the **maximum** and **minimum** ages.

4.4 These simple statistics - **totals, averages, and highest and lowest** - are the most common way of finding some meaning amongst a mass of figures. We are also often interested in **unusual** information (for instance an age of minus seven), because it tends to highlight areas where there could be errors in our information.

## Pivot tables

4.5    To extract information quickly and easily from a table in Excel we can simply highlight it and click on **Data** and then **Pivot Table Report**. This starts up a Wizard which first asks you to confirm the location of the data you want to analyse and then offers you the following options.

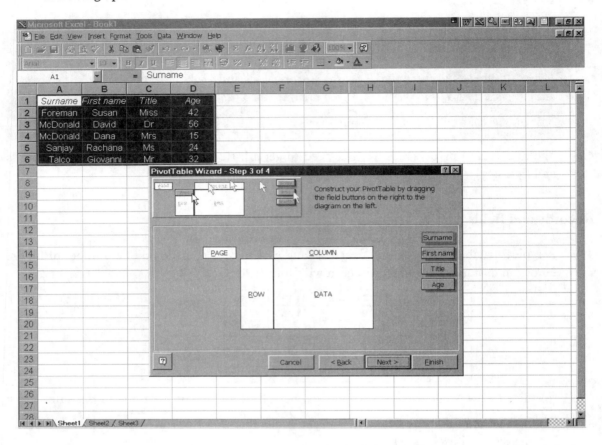

4.6    All you have to do to analyse the data is drag any of the labelled buttons on the right into the appropriate part of the white area. For instance, if we wanted to know the total number of surnames of each type we could drag the Surname label into the row area and then drag another instance of the surname label into the Data area. This is what you would see.

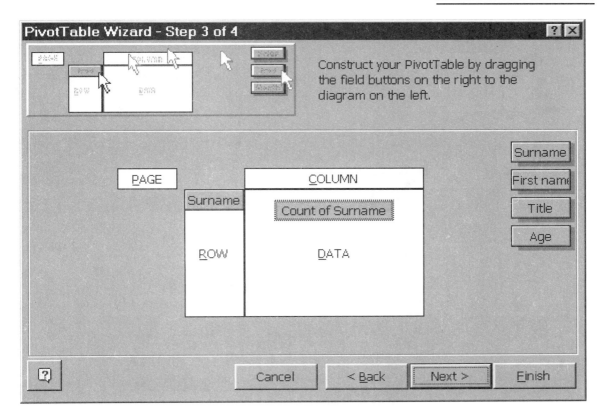

4.7 Note that in the Data area the name of the Surname label changes to Count of Surname but we do not have to accept this if it is not what we want. If we double-click on Count of Surname we are offered other options such as Sum, Average, Max, Min.

4.8 For now we will accept the Count option. Clicking on Next and Finish gives the following results.

|   | A | B |
|---|---|---|
| 1 | Count of Surname | |
| 2 | Surname | Total |
| 3 | Foreman | 1 |
| 4 | McDonald | 2 |
| 5 | Sanjay | 1 |
| 6 | Talco | 1 |
| 7 | Grand Total | 5 |

**DEVOLVED ASSESSMENT ALERT**

Because you can see what the data in our example means at a glance, just by looking at the example, the analyses we produce may not seem very useful. However, imagine that your Devolved Assessment gave you the task of analysing and interpreting 500 records (rows), each with 10 fields! You would have to organise the information before you could begin to score marks for your interpretation of it.

4.9 More elaborate analyses than this can be produced. For instance, you could try setting up a pivot table like this.

**BPP** PUBLISHING

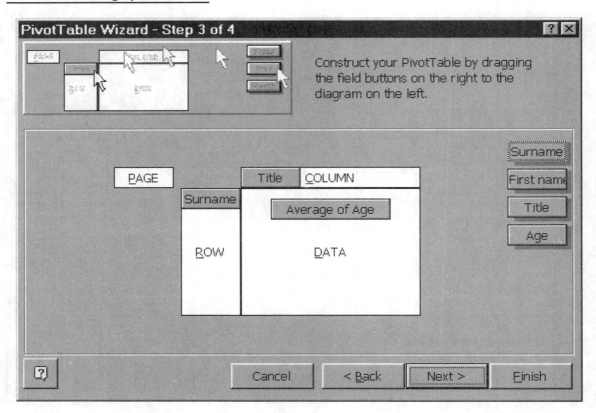

4.10 The result is as follows, showing that the average age of people called McDonald is 35.5 and the average age overall is 33.8.

| | A | B | C | D | E | F | G |
|---|---|---|---|---|---|---|---|
| 1 | Average of Age | Title | | | | | |
| 2 | Surname | Dr | Miss | Mr | Mrs | Ms | Grand Total |
| 3 | Foreman | | 42 | | | | 42 |
| 4 | McDonald | 56 | | | 15 | | 35.5 |
| 5 | Sanjay | | | | | 24 | 24 |
| 6 | Talco | | | 32 | | | 32 |
| 7 | Grand Total | 56 | 42 | 32 | 15 | 24 | 33.8 |

This arrangement of the data also draws attention to the fact that the data includes a 'Mrs' who is only 15 years old. This is not impossible, but it is quite unusual and should be checked because it could be an inputting error.

4.11 If we don't happen to like the way Excel arranges the data it can be changed in a flash, simply by dragging the labels in the results to another part of the table. For instance if Title is dragged down until it is over cell B3 the data is automatically rearranged as follows.

| | A | B | C |
|---|---|---|---|
| 1 | Average of Age | | |
| 2 | Surname | Title | Total |
| 3 | Foreman | Miss | 42 |
| 4 | Foreman Total | | 42 |
| 5 | McDonald | Dr | 56 |
| 6 | | Mrs | 15 |
| 7 | McDonald Total | | 35.5 |
| 8 | Sanjay | Ms | 24 |
| 9 | Sanjay Total | | 24 |
| 10 | Talco | Mr | 32 |
| 11 | Talco Total | | 32 |
| 12 | Grand Total | | 33.8 |

## More extensive examples

4.12 As we have said, pivot tables really come into their own when there is a great deal of data to analyse. However, to practise you would have to enter this data in the first place which would be so laborious and time consuming that you would probably not bother.

4.13 For this reason further examples of the use of Pivot Tables will be found in the BPP Using Information Technology Devolved Assessment Kit, which will be accompanied by suitable ready-prepared data.

---

### Activity 8.8

In the mean time, of course, there is no reason why you should not set up the above example for yourself (or any other example you like) and experiment with Pivot Tables for yourself.

---

## 5 DATABASES

5.1 Finally we are going to take a look at the use of a proper database package to analyse data. This is only an **introduction** to a topic that quickly becomes rather complex. We will concentrate on **Microsoft Access**. Other database packages have similar functionality, and follow the same principles. Users of other packages are encouraged to read these paragraphs on Access, and relate them to the package they are familiar with.

5.2 As explained earlier this chapter, a database is an organised collection of data.

### What distinguishes a database from a spreadsheet?

5.3 Spreadsheets do have some database capabilities such as sorting and filters. However, spreadsheets are designed more for flexibility in manipulation and presentation of information. Generally, mathematical manipulation of data is more easily achieved in a spreadsheet.

5.4 Databases are designed to store **greater volumes of data,** and they enable data required for different purposes to be stored in a single location. Databases can manipulate data using **Queries,** which are particularly useful when dealing with large data volumes. In very simple terms, a spreadsheet is the electronic equivalent of a piece of graph paper, while a database could be likened to a filing cabinet.

### Importing data

5.5 Databases store data in **tables**. Tables can be created within the database package, and data records manually added to the table. This is time consuming, as data volumes handled by database packages are often large. The more common scenario is to **import** data from **a text file** (ASCII text), downloaded from an accounting software package. Or, the situation may arise where data held on a **spreadsheet** needs to be transferred into a database, perhaps to be held alongside other related data.

5.6 The **procedure for importing data** from either a text file or spreadsheet into a Microsoft Access table is outlined below.

**Step 1** Make a note of the file name and location that contains the source data. If the data is held on a spreadsheet, also note the name of the particular sheet you want to import(eg 'Sheet 3').

**Step 2** Save and Close the spreadsheet, or, if importing from a text file ensure the file is not being accessed by another application.

**Step 3** Database packages are quite hungry for memory, so close all applications that you don't need.

**Step 4** Open up Access, choose the option to create a new blank database, and give it a suitable file name. The elements of an Access database are arranged on a series of tabs as shown in the next illustration.

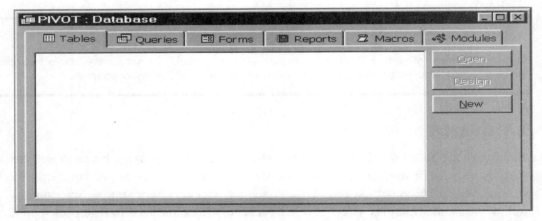

**Step 5** Ensure the Table tab is active. Select the **File** menu, choose the **Get External Data** and then the **Import** option. Clicking on this produces a dialogue box identical to the familiar **Open file** dialogue. Change the **file type** to that required. For instance, if importing from an Excel spreadsheet change to Microsoft Excel; for a text file change to Text File. Then locate the file and click on **Import**.

**Steps 6 and 7** The options Access presents you with next will vary depending on the file type you selected in Step 5. In both cases, the 'Import Wizard' steps are straightforward.

| *Importing from a spreadsheet* | *Importing from a text file* |
|---|---|
| You will get a list of all the **worksheets** in the spreadsheet file you specify. Choose the sheet that you want to import (you noted this down earlier) and click on **Next**. | You will be asked to identify how the text file is formatted to identify the positioning of column breaks. **Fixed width**, means the position of the characters within each line is consistent. **Delimited** means a character, such as a comma, identifies the division between columns. (You, or the person that created the file should know what format the file is. If in doubt, opening the file in Notepad or a similar text editor enables the contents to be viewed and the delimiter identified). Click on **Next**. |
| If the first row of your spreadsheet contains column headings, check the box that says **First Row Contains Column Headings,** then click on Next. | For fixed width files you are given the opportunity to identify the position of column breaks using the mouse. For delimited files you are asked to identify the delimiter (eg comma). |

*Step 8*    As a rule you will want to store your data in a **New Table**, so this is the next option to choose. The ability to 'Append' (add to the bottom of an existing table), exists. This is useful when importing data into the same table, but from different source files.

*Step 9*    You are given the choice of specifying **further information** about the fields (columns) that you are importing, but there is no need to do this at this basic level, so click **Next**.

*Step 10*    You then have the choice of defining your own '**Primary Key**', which is the unique field in each line, or letting Access do it for you. It is usually acceptable to **let Access do it** for you, the default selection. Click **Next**.

*Step 11*    Finally **choose a name** for your table if you do not like the one that Access suggests, and click on **Finish**. You will then see an entry for your new database table.

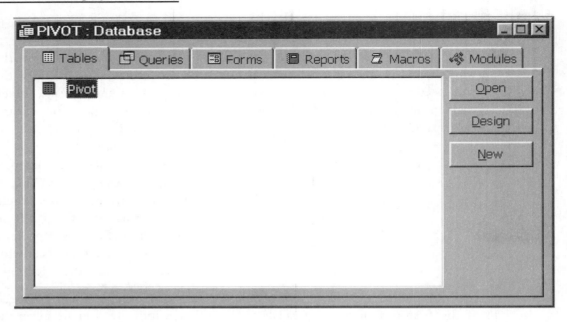

5.7 If you **select your table and click Open** you will see how data is stored within the table. This view is known as the **datasheet**.

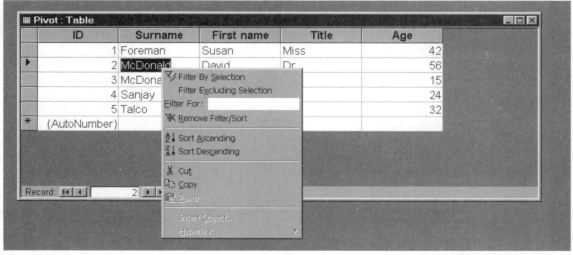

5.8 Within the datasheet you can select columns, right click then **sort** the data in them in ascending or descending order. You can apply and remove **filters** simply by right clicking on a record and including or excluding the item as you wish. In the illustration below, clicking on **Filter By Selection** would show you table including only the details for people called McDonald.

5.9 New records can be entered or existing ones edited, and there is a **Find** option in the edit menu to help locate particular items of information.

5.10 To see, or edit, the **table design** it is necessary to **open the datasheet**, then select the **Design View** icon below the File menu option. Field size and formats are then available for editing. Modifying table design should not be necessary at this level, but investigate if you wish to discover more about the workings of the database package.

## Queries

5.11 The **real power** of a database, however, lies in its ability to **analyse and manipulate** data using practically any criteria you can dream up.

5.12 If you close your table, return to the set of index tabs, select **Queries** and click on **New** you get the following options.

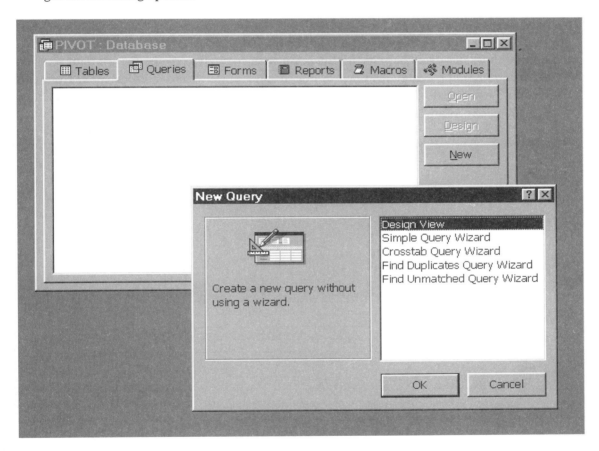

5.13 We shall not look at all of these options. The Simple Query Wizard takes you step by step through the process of building a query. The CrossTab Query Wizard performs a similar function to a Pivot Table. The functions of the other wizards speak for themselves. In this case, however, we are going to choose **Design View**.

5.14 If you click on this the first thing you are asked to do is to specify **which tables** the query will apply to. In our example we have only one table so we can simply select it and click on **Add** and then close the **Show Table** dialogue box. The screen will now look like this.

**BPP**
PUBLISHING

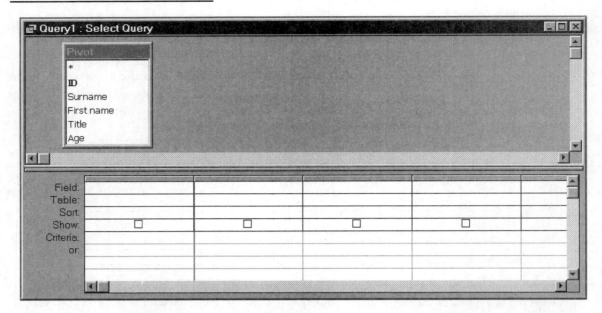

5.15 To design a query we click on the fields we wish to analyse in the list at the top to make them appear in the **design grid** below. For instance if we wish to perform an analysis of the **ages** in our table we would click on Surname (so we know which record is which) and Age to produce the following.

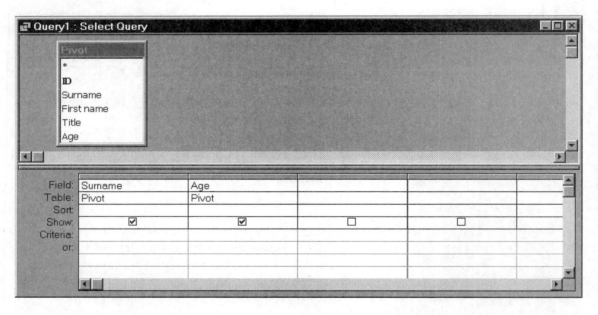

5.16 The cell entitled Criteria is the one that wants our attention. For instance, if we wanted to find the records of everyone who was over 40 or under 20 we could make the following entries for the Age field.

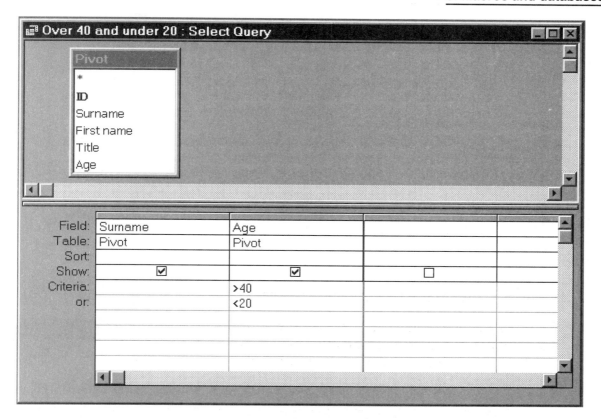

5.17 Clicking on Query and Run produces the following results.

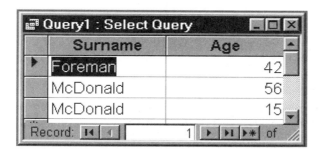

5.18 If you are satisfied that you have the information you want you can **save** the query for future use (for instance to be run again when you have entered more records). If you are not satisfied you can switch back to design view (**View ... Design**), and alter it as you wish.

## Queries using multiple tables

5.19 A query can pull together data from more than one Table.

5.20 For example we may have a Customer table containing customer codes and names, an Items table containing stock codes and descriptions, and a Transactions table. The three tables are shown below.

*BPP*
PUBLISHING

**Customers : Table**

| | Cust | Name |
|---|---|---|
| ▶ | CABD | Cable Darlington |
| | DESF | Desire Fencing |
| | FINC | Final Countdown |
| | FORF | Forfar Four Limited |
| | FULD | Fulham Drainage |
| | HANS | Hansens |
| | KRID | Krisp Demolition |
| | LIVF | Liverpool First |
| | LONC | London Cabs |
| | NOTP | Nottingham Paper |
| | PCDI | PC Direct |
| | PLUM | Plumbing World |
| | SOUH | South West Haulage |

Record: 1 of 13

**Items : Table**

| | item | desc |
|---|---|---|
| ▶ | BUCL | Bucket - large |
| | BUCS | Bucket - small |
| | HAMB | Ball Hammer |
| | HAMD | Demolition hammer |
| | PGBL | Paint - gloss blue 1000ml |
| | PGRM | Paint - gloss red 500ml |
| | PGWS | Paint - gloss white 200ml |
| | PLIE | Pliers |
| | PLUE | Electric plug |
| | PMBS | Paint - matt black 200ml |
| | SACB | Black sacks |
| | SAH1 | Hacksaw - small |
| | SAH2 | Hacksaw - medium |

Record: 1 of 19

**Transactions : Table**

| | ID | invoice | item | quantity | unitprice | Cust |
|---|---|---|---|---|---|---|
| ▶ | 1 | AK1 | HAMB | 2 | 5.49 | LONC |
| | 2 | AK2 | SAH1 | 1 | 4.99 | LIVF |
| | 3 | AK3 | HAMD | 1 | 6.99 | DESF |
| | 4 | AK4 | BUCS | 1 | 2.49 | KRID |
| | 5 | AK5 | PMBS | 3 | 5.49 | CABD |
| | 6 | AK6 | SAH2 | 1 | 6.99 | FORF |
| | 7 | AK7 | PGBL | 2 | 15.99 | HANS |
| | 8 | AK8 | PLIE | 1 | 6.49 | FULD |
| | 9 | AK9 | TINM | 2 | 3.99 | PLUM |
| | 10 | AK10 | PGRM | 2 | 10.99 | PCDI |
| | 11 | AK7 | BUCL | 2 | 3.49 | HANS |
| | 12 | AK5 | SPAC | 3 | 2.49 | CABD |
| | 13 | AK5 | SACB | 5 | 1.99 | CABD |

Record: 1 of 20

5.21 Using this data we could write a query that would combine the following details of every invoice line for a specified period:

*Customer code, Name, Invoice Number, Stock Item, Description, Quantity, Unit Price*

We could use the resulting datasheet as a basis for more detailed reporting.

5.22 To write a query that combines data from multiple tables follow the following steps.

***Step 1*** Before we are able to combine information from separate Tables, we need to tell Access how the information is related. To do this we form a **Relationship.** Ensure the Tables tab is active and select **Tools, Relationships**. Then select **Relationships, Show Table** and **Add** all three tables to the view. The window will now look like this.

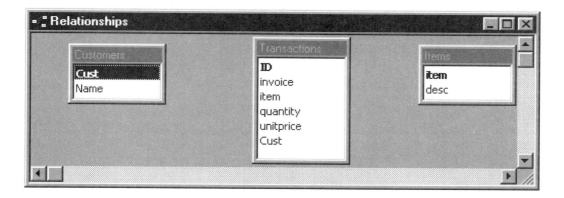

***Step 2*** Click and hold down the mouse while dragging the **common field** over to the other table. In the example above you would click over **Cust** in Customers, hold the left mouse button down, and drag over to the **Cust** in Transactions. Release the mouse button, click on **Create** and the **link** will show. The same procedure would be followed to link Item between the Transactions and Items tables.

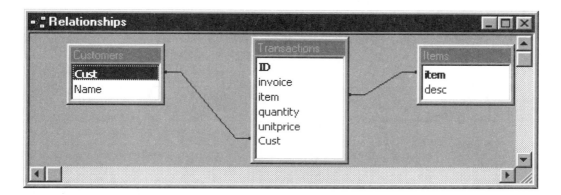

***Step 3*** Close the Relationship window, saving your changes.

***Step 4*** Activate the **Query tab** and click **New**. The options are as shown earlier under 5.12. If we chose the **Design View** option, the same principles explained in 5.13 to 5.15 can be applied to build this Query. Alternately, select the **Simple Query Wizard** option and click OK.

***Step 5*** Select each of the three tables in turn under the Tables/Queries option. For each Table select which fields you wish to appear in the Query using the **>** or **>>** buttons. After you have completed this procedure for all three tables, Click Next.

***Step 6*** Accept the default of Detail for the next option by clicking Next.

***Step 7*** Give your Query a title that will enable you to remember its purpose, and click **Finish**.

5.23 A sample of the resulting datasheet is shown overleaf.

| Cust | Name | invoice | item | desc | quantity | unitprice |
|------|------|---------|------|------|----------|-----------|
| CABD | Cable Darlington | AK5 | PLUE | Electric plug | 6 | 1.99 |
| CABD | Cable Darlington | AK5 | SACB | Black sacks | 5 | 1.99 |
| CABD | Cable Darlington | AK5 | PMBS | Paint - matt black 200ml | 3 | 5.49 |
| DESF | Desire Fencing | AK3 | BUCL | Bucket - large | 6 | 3.49 |
| DESF | Desire Fencing | AK3 | HAMD | Demolition hammer | 1 | 6.99 |
| FORF | Forfar Four Limited | AK6 | SAH2 | Hacksaw - medium | 1 | 6.99 |
| FULD | Fulham Drainage | AK8 | PLIE | Pliers | 1 | 6.49 |
| HANS | Hansens | AK7 | SPAF | Sandpaper - fine | 4 | 2.49 |

*Transactions Query : Select Query*

Record: 1 of 19

## Exporting data

5.24 The situation may arise where you wish to **extract data from a database** using a query, then export this sub-set of data into a spreadsheet, to perform further manipulations and formatting. The procedure for exporting data from Microsoft Access into a spreadsheet is explained below.

5.25 *Step 1* Design, run and save the query following the instructions above.

*Step 2* Select the Query tab, then click the name of the table or query you want to export. Select the **File** menu, and click **Save As/Export**.

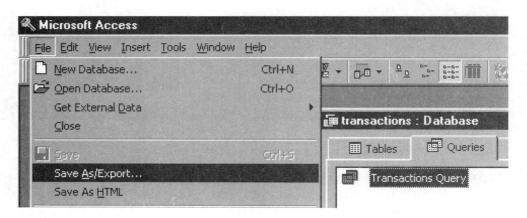

*Step 3* In the Save As box, select **To An External File Or Database**, and then click OK.

*Step 4* In the Save As Type box, change the **file type** to that required, for example Microsoft Excel.

*Step 5* Within the Save In box, change the **location** to where you wish the spreadsheet to be saved. Enter the **name** you wish to give the spreadsheet in the File Name box.

*Step 6* Click **Export**. Microsoft Access creates the spreadsheet file containing the data from your query.

*Step 7* Close Microsoft Access (to free up memory), start your spreadsheet application and open the new file from the location you specified in Step 5.

5.26 Note that the same procedure can be followed to export the contents of a complete Table. Simply select the Table itself in step 2 rather than a query.

## Expressions

5.27 When building queries a very wide variety of '**expressions**' can be used to define how the data in the table is displayed. Expressions are entered either in the **Criteria** cell or in the **Field** cell. Here are a couple of examples.

(a) **Extracting parts of fields only**. For instance you can enter the expression **Left([First name],1)** in the first Field cell and set Surname as the second field to display in the normal way, as follows.

| Field: | Expr1: Left([First name],1) | Surname |
|---|---|---|
| Table: | | Pivot |
| Sort: | | |
| Show: | ☑ | ☑ |
| Criteria: | | |
| or: | | |

(Access itself inserts the **Expr1:** part).

You will get the following results when you run the query.

| Expr1 | Surname |
|---|---|
| S | Foreman |
| D | McDonald |
| D | McDonald |
| R | Sanjay |
| G | Talco |
| * | |

(b) **Performing calculations**. For instance the following query would extract records of people who will have reached retirement age in 10 years time.

| Field: | Surname | Expr1: [Age]+10 |
|---|---|---|
| Table: | Pivot | |
| Sort: | | |
| Show: | ☑ | ☑ |
| Criteria: | | >65 |
| or: | | |

---

### Activity 8.9

What results would we get if we ran this query?

---

## Reports

5.28 Microsoft Access includes a powerful report writer. This enables professional presentation of meaningful data drawn from the database.

5.29 Report writing in databases is not as simple as formatting a spreadsheet. For this reason, always consider the possibility of exporting the data to a spreadsheet, and using the manipulation and formatting functions available within the spreadsheet to produce your report.

5.30 The steps involved in producing a report within Access are outlined below.

*Step1*    **Design a query** that will extract the data you wish the report to contain. Run and save the query following the instructions given earlier this chapter.

*Step2*    Close your query, return to the set of index tabs, select **Reports** and click on **New.** The following options are now available.

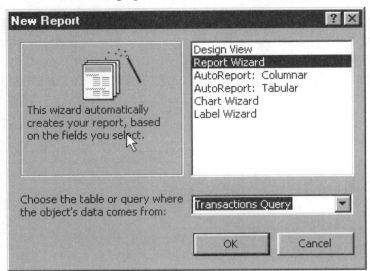

*Step 3*    For Unit 21 purposes report writing using the Report Wizard should enable all requirements to be met. Highlight Report Wizard, and in the lower box select the Query you wrote in Step 1. Click OK.

*Step 4*    You are now asked to select the fields you wish to report on. As we designed a query specifically for this report (in step1), we can simply ensure the name of this query is displayed in the Tables/Query box, and click on the double arrow (>>)box to select all fields. Click Next.

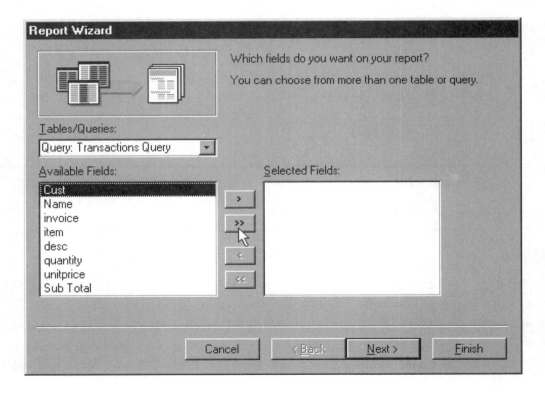

*Step 5*    You are then asked how would you like to view your data. This relates to grouping, and the criteria selected will depend on the purpose of the Report. Highlight the item you wish the report to be grouped by, such as Customers and click Next.

*Step 6*    Sorting criteria within these groupings is then requested. Up to four criteria can be selected by using the down arrows on the right of each box. (One criteria would often be sufficient.) Select your criteria and click Next.

*Step 7*    The layout options will then be presented. The options presented will vary depending on the data reported on, and the answers to the previous wizard questions. Make your layout and page orientation selections, and ensure the 'Adjust field width so all fields fit on a page' box is checked, then click Next.

*Step 8*    Select the style of the Report. Corporate is an appropriate style for business documents. Click Next.

*Step 9*    Enter a meaningful title for your report. If data relates to a particular date or time frame, be sure to disclose that in your title. Ensure the 'Preview the report' option is checked, and click Finish.

*Step 10*   The report will appear in Print Preview mode on screen. Print it out, and close the report window.

5.31    As a learning exercise, don't be afraid to **repeat the report producing process** a number of times, taking different options along the way. Unwanted reports can be deleted from the Reports index tab by highlighting the title to be deleted, right mouse clicking and selecting delete.

5.32    Reports can be **renamed** through right mouse clicking and selecting rename. To change the **heading** within the report highlight the report, click on the Design button, then double click in the Report Header text box. Overtype the title, select File save, and then File close.

5.33    As mentioned earlier, report writing in databases is not simple. **Experience** and **experimentation** will help ensure the correct choices are made at each Wizard stage for different types of reports.

5.34    This section has demonstrated some of the features of database packages. To fully appreciate the value of queries and the power of databases, consider these principles in the context of **vast stores of data** rather than the small number of records used here.

## Key learning points

- A **macro** is a mini-program that can be written by recording key-strokes and mouse clicks. This is useful for automating frequently repeated tasks.

- Spreadsheets also offer **database** facilities for manipulating and sorting tables of data.

- **Filters** can be applied at the click of a button and these allow the user to view a large spreadsheet with only selected items of data showing.

- A **data table** is a special facility that can be set up so that a group of cells show the results of changing the value of variables.

- Functions such as **LEFT** and **LOOKUP** and operators such as **&** can be helpful when manipulating data in a spreadsheet.

- A **pivot table** is an interactive table that summarises and analyses data from existing lists and tables.

- Data can be input or **imported into a database package** such as Microsoft Access, and then **analysed and manipulated using queries.**

- Selected data can be **exported from a database package** such as Microsoft Access, into a spreadsheet for further analysis, manipulation and formatting.

- Databases include report writing facilities to enable meaningful information to be presented professionally.

## Quick quiz

1   How should a macro be started?

2   How should a macro be finished?

3   If you want to make a macro available to anyone who uses a spreadsheet designed by you, where should it be saved?

4   What is a database?

5   What is the purpose of a database?

6   What are the most common ways of making sense of a mass of figures?

7   Suggest two ways in which 'expressions' can be used to manipulate data.

## Answers to quick quiz

1   By returning the cursor to cell A1

2   By selecting the cell where the user will make the next entry.

3   Within the spreadsheet itself, not in your personal macro workbook, which is only available on your own PC.

4   A collection of structured data in which any item can be the subject of enquiry.

5   To provide convenient access to common data for a wide variety of users and user needs. To avoid the problems of duplication of data.

6   Totals, averages, largest and smallest, and unusual items.

7   Expressions can be used to extract parts of fields and to perform calculations with data in fields.

# Answers to activities

## Answer 8.2

This is not a macro that you will use forever more so lose a mark if you saved it to your Personal Macro Workbook.

The template that the macro should produce, including the formulae and formatting, is shown below.

| | A | B | C | D |
|---|---|---|---|---|
| 1 | Company name: | **Little Ltd** | | |
| 2 | | | | |
| 3 | | | | |
| 4 | | *1998* | *1997* | *% difference* |
| 5 | Sales | | | =IF(B5=0,0,(B5-C5)/C5) |
| 6 | Cost of Sales | | | =IF(B6=0,0,(B6-C6)/C6) |
| 7 | Gross profit | =SUM(B5:B6) | =SUM(C5:C6) | =IF(B7=0,0,(B7-C7)/C7) |
| 8 | Operating expenses | | | =IF(B8=0,0,(B8-C8)/C8) |
| 9 | Net profit | =SUM(B7:B8) | =SUM(C7:C8) | =IF(B9=0,0,(B9-C9)/C9) |

Did your macro format the relevant parts as bold or italic? Did it format the spreadsheet not to show zero values? Did it include the conditions in column E (this avoids the irritating error message **Div0!** when the spreadsheet has no figures in the 1998 and 1997 columns). Did it format the percentage column correctly? Did it format the numbers to the comma format and negative numbers to be shown in brackets?. Did it include the underlining?

Did your macro begin by selecting cell A1 and end by selecting cell B5 (the first data entry point when the macro has finished?

Did it work at all?

Lose a mark for any point you missed.

## Answer 8.3

Probably the best known are Microsoft Access (for smallish businesses) and Oracle (for large businesses).

## Answer 8.4

Make sure you do this using the spreadsheet facilities rather than just by looking through the table. You wouldn't be able to cheat like this if you had 2,000 stock components to search through!

(a)   A003, A009 and A017.
(b)   A005 and A009.
(c)   P036 and P227.

## Answer 8.5

Cell A18 should contain the formula =B14. The row variable is B8 and the column variable is B3. The figures are as follows. Reading from the table the net profit in the circumstances described will be £16,875.

| | A | B | C | D | E | F | G | H |
|---|---|---|---|---|---|---|---|---|
| 18 | 15,000.00 | 0.50 | 0.75 | 1.00 | 1.25 | 1.50 | 1.75 | 2.00 |
| 19 | 0 | (5,000) | (5,000) | (5,000) | (5,000) | (5,000) | (5,000) | (5,000) |
| 20 | 25 | 1,250 | 625 | 0 | (625) | (1,250) | (1,875) | (2,500) |
| 21 | 50 | 7,500 | 6,250 | 5,000 | 3,750 | 2,500 | 1,250 | 0 |
| 22 | 75 | 13,750 | 11,875 | 10,000 | 8,125 | 6,250 | 4,375 | 2,500 |
| 23 | 100 | 20,000 | 17,500 | 15,000 | 12,500 | 10,000 | 7,500 | 5,000 |
| 24 | 125 | 26,250 | 23,125 | 20,000 | 16,875 | 13,750 | 10,625 | 7,500 |
| 25 | 150 | 32,500 | 28,750 | 25,000 | 21,250 | 17,500 | 13,750 | 10,000 |
| 26 | 200 | 45,000 | 40,000 | 35,000 | 30,000 | 25,000 | 20,000 | 15,000 |
| 27 | 225 | 51,250 | 45,625 | 40,000 | 34,375 | 28,750 | 23,125 | 17,500 |
| 28 | 250 | 57,500 | 51,250 | 45,000 | 38,750 | 32,500 | 26,250 | 20,000 |

## Answer 8.6

(a) =MID(A1,4,1). The starting position is position 4 because the hyphen between the 2 and the D counts as position 3.

(b) =LEFT(A1,2).

## Answer 8.9

We should find that only David McDonald will reach 65 in the next ten years. Once again, this is obvious when we only have five records to look through. A database could quickly at extract this data if there were 50,000 records to search.

# *Part C*
## *Improving the MIS*

# Chapter 9    Improving the MIS

---

## Chapter topic list

1    Improving an MIS

2    Information for decision making

3    Types of MIS

4    Costs and benefits

5    Cost-benefit analysis

---

## Learning objectives

On completion of this chapter you will be able to:

| | Performance criteria | Range statement |
|---|---|---|
| • Understand the range of computerised MIS | | 21.3.1 |
| • Identify potential improvements to the MIS and consider them for their impact on the quality of the system and any interrelated systems | 21.3.1 | |
| • Make suggestions for changes supported by a clear rationale as to how they could improve the quality of the system | 21.3.2 | |
| • Assess and clearly state whether assumptions and judgements made are reliable | 21.3.3 | |
| • Accurately describe the benefits and costs of all changes | 21.3.4 | |
| • Present suggestions clearly and in a way which helps people to understand and act on them | 21.3.5 | |
| • *Understand the purposes and applications of MIS* | n/a | n/a |
| • *Understand the relationship between MIS and other IT applications* | n/a | n/a |
| • *Describe a range of MIS used in organisations* | n/a | n/a |
| • *Apply cost benefit analysis techniques* | n/a | n/a |

Italicised objectives are areas of knowledge and understanding underlying the elements of competence for Unit 21.

BPP PUBLISHING

## 1 IMPROVING AN MIS

1.1 It is worth stressing from the outset that there is **no point in changing** a system if it works well already. A small organisation might easily get by with no computers at all, or with just a Word Processor to write letters. If a newer system would **not save** time, not make **better use** of time, not **save money**, and would **not offer new opportunities** there is no point in changing it.

1.2 Likewise, even if the objective of the organisation is not to make money (a **charity**, for instance): if a new system would **not help** it to do whatever it does more **quickly** or **effectively** or at **lower cost** then why change?

### Improvements: value for money

1.3 Very broadly, an information system is likely to need improving if the improvements will have a **positive impact** on 'value for money' (VFM). VFM is made up of the following **three E's**.

| *Economy* | Organisations should employ **suitable resources** for the lowest **cost** possible. |
| *Efficiency* | Organisations should try to produce the **maximum outputs** for the **minimum inputs** of any resource (time, people, machines, space, information etc). |
| *Effectiveness* | Organisations should **do what they aim to do as well as possible**. |

1.4 To drive the point home, think of a bottle of **Fairy Liquid.** If we believe the advertising, Fairy is good 'value for money' because it washes half as many plates again as any other washing up liquid.

Bottle for bottle it may be more expensive, but plate for plate it is cheaper. Not only this, but Fairy gets plates 'squeaky' clean.

To summarise, Fairy gives us VFM because it exhibits the following characteristics.

| More clean plates per pound | *Economy* |
| More clean plates per squirt | *Efficiency* |
| Plates as clean as they should be | *Effectiveness* |

### DEVOLVED ASSESSMENT ALERT

If you have considered the 'Fairy Liquid' aspects of an information system described in a Devolved Assessment and you have made some reasonable suggestions to enhance the **VFM** it offers, then you will probably have written a good answer.

1.5 Ideally, there should be **no conflict** between one E and another E.

(a) There is no point in achieving *low costs* (**Economy**) by using the cheapest available materials if one of your *aims* (**Effectiveness**) is to produce the *highest quality* products on the market.

(b) There is no point in employing a member of staff who demands a *lower salary* than anyone else (**Economy**) if that member of staff will produce a *poorer quality of work* than someone who costs a bit more to employ (**Efficiency**).

## Activity 9.1

Give your own example of a conflict between **effectiveness** and **efficiency**.

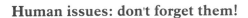

---

### KEY TERMS

Here are some formal definitions.

(a) **Economy**: attaining the appropriate quantity and quality of physical, human and financial resources (*inputs*) at lowest cost. An activity would not be economic, if, for example, there was over-staffing or failure to purchase materials of requisite quality at the lowest available price.

(b) **Efficiency**: the relationship between goods or services produced (outputs) and the resources used to produce them. An efficient operation produces the maximum **output** for any given set of resource **inputs**; or it has minimum inputs for any given quantity and quality of product or service provided.

(c) **Effectiveness**: this is concerned with how well an activity is achieving its overall objectives or other intended effects.

## Human issues: don't forget them!

1.6 Fairy Liquid is effective not only in the sense that it gets plates 'squeaky clean'. It is also **kind to hands**. In other words the **people** that use it must **like using it**. The same rule applies to information systems, and to your suggested improvements.

1.7 Always consider the **impact on the human operators**. If your suggestion will save lots of time and money, but turn an interesting and challenging job into a low-skilled and boring job then you also need to come up with some ideas for how to motivate the person whose job it is or was, or employ them in another way. It is **wasteful** to throw talented and knowledgeable people away and, unlike machines, people are capable of **learning new skills**.

## Information technology and the MIS

1.8 Many of an organisation's MIS activities can be improved through the use of **information technology**.

### KEY TERM

**Information technology** is a term used to describe the coming together of **computer** technology with **data transmission** technology, to revolutionise information systems. Cheap computer hardware, based on microchip technology with ever-increasing power and capacity, has been harnessed to an extensive telecommunications network.

1.9 There are a number of reasons why **manual** office systems are **less beneficial** than **computerised** systems.

(a) Labour **productivity** is usually lower, particularly in routine and operational applications.

(b) Processing is **slower** where large volumes of data need to be dealt with.

(c) Besides taking up more time and requiring more staff, slower processing means that **information that could be provided**, such as statistical analyses of data or lists (of customers or products or whatever) categorised in a variety of ways, **will not be provided** at all, because there is not time.

(d) The **risk of errors** is greater, especially in repetitive work like payroll calculations.

(e) Information is generally **less accessible**. Unless there is a great deal of duplication of records access to information is restricted to one user at a time. Paper files can easily be mislaid or buried in in-trays, in which case the information they contain is not available at all. This can mean inconvenience and wasted time internally and may prevent the organisation from providing its services to customers.

(f) It is difficult to make **corrections or alterations**. If a document contains errors or needs updating it is often necessary to recreate the **whole** document from scratch, rather than just a new version with the relevant details changed. If several copies of a paper record are stored in different places each of them will need to be changed: this can easily be overlooked and so some parts of the system will be using out of date or inaccurate data. Unless changes are dated, it may not be clear which is the correct version.

(g) **Quality of output** is less consistent and not as high as well-designed computer output. At worst, handwritten records may be illegible and so completely useless. Badly presented information may fail to communicate because key points will not have their intended impact.

(h) Paper based systems are generally very **bulky** both to handle and to store, and office space is expensive.

## 2 INFORMATION FOR DECISION MAKING

2.1 Information necessary to help people make decisions within an organisation can be analysed into three levels: **strategic, tactical, and operational**.

### DEVOLVED ASSESSMENT ALERT

The distinction between strategic, tactical and operational information is discussed in the AAT's own suggested solution to one of the tasks in their sample Devolved Assessment.

### Strategic information

2.2 Strategic information is used to **plan the objectives** of their organisation, and to assess whether the objectives are being met in practice. This information includes **overall profitability**, the profitability of different segments of the business, future **market prospects**, the availability and cost of raising **new funds**, total **cash needs**, total **manning levels** and **capital equipment needs**.

2.3 Strategic information is therefore:

(a) Derived from both **internal and external** sources.
(b) **Summarised** at a high level.
(c) Relevant to the **long term**.
(d) Relevant to the **whole organisation** (although it might go into some detail).
(e) Often prepared on an 'ad hoc' basis.
(f) Both **quantitative and qualitative**.
(g) **Never absolutely certain**, given that the future cannot be predicted.

## Tactical information

2.4 Tactical information is used to decide how the **resources** of the business should be employed, and to monitor how they are being and have been employed. This information includes **productivity measurements** (output per man hour or per machine hour), **budgetary control** or **variance analysis** reports, and **cash flow forecasts**, profit results within a particular **department** of the organisation, **labour turnover** statistics within a department and **short-term purchasing** requirements.

2.5 Tactical information is therefore:

(a) **Primarily generated internally**.

(b) **Summarised at a lower level** - a report might be included with summaries and raw data as backup.

(c) Relevant to the **short and medium term**.

(d) Intended to describe or analyses **activities or departments**.

(e) Prepared **routinely and regularly**.

(f) Based on **quantitative** measures.

## Operational information

2.6 Operational information is used to ensure that **specific tasks** are planned and carried out properly within a factory or office. In the payroll office, for example, operational information relating to weekly paid workers will include the **hours worked** each week by each employee, his **rate of pay** per hour, details of his **deductions**, and for the purpose of wages analysis, details of the **time** each man spent on individual jobs during the week. In this example, the information is required **weekly**, but more urgent operational information, such as the amount of raw materials being input to a production process, may be required **daily, hourly**, or in the case of automated production, **second by second**.

2.7 Operational information is:

(a) Derived **almost entirely from internal sources.**

(b) **Highly detailed**, being the processing of raw data.

(c) Related to the **immediate term.**

(d) **Task-specific.**

(e) Prepared **constantly**, or very **frequently.**

(f) Largely **quantitative.**

2.8 A table showing typical **inputs, processes and outputs** at each level of a management information system is provided below.

|  | *Inputs* | *Processes* | *Outputs* |
|---|---|---|---|
| *Strategic* | Long-term plans<br>Competitor information<br>Market information | Summarise<br>Investigate<br>Compare<br>Forecast | Key ratios<br>Ad hoc market analysis<br>Strategic plans |
| *Tactical* | Historical data<br>Budget data | Compare<br>Classify<br>Summarise | Variance analyses<br>Exception reports |
| *Operational* | Customer orders<br>Programmed stock<br>control levels | Update files<br>Output reports | Updated files<br>Listings<br>Invoices |

## 3 TYPES OF MIS

### Transaction processing systems

3.1 Transactions processing systems could be said to represent the **lowest level** in an organisation's use of information systems. They are used for **routine tasks** in which data items or **transactions** must be processed so that operations can continue. Handling sales orders, purchase orders, payroll items and stock records are typical examples.

3.2 Transactions processing systems provide the **raw material** which is often used more extensively by management information systems or office support systems. In other words, transactions processing systems might be used to produce management information, such as reports on cumulative sales figures to date, total amounts owed to suppliers or owed by debtors, total stock turnover to date, value of current stock-in-hand, and so on, but the main purpose of transaction processing systems is **operational**, as an integral part of day-to-day operations.

### Decision support systems

3.3 Decision support systems (DSS) are a form of management information system. Decision support systems are used to assist in making decisions on issues which are **poorly defined**, with high levels of uncertainty about the true nature of the problem, the various responses which management could undertake or the likely impact of those actions. These highly ambiguous environments do not allow the easy application of many of the techniques or systems developed for more well defined problems or activities. Decision support systems are intended to provide a wide range of alternative information gathering and analytical tools with a major emphasis upon flexibility and user-friendliness.

3.4 The term decision support system is usually taken to mean computer systems which are designed to produce information in such a way as to help managers to make better decisions. They are now often associated with information 'at the touch of a button' at a manager's personal computer or workstation. DSS can describe a range of systems, from fairly simple **information models based on spreadsheets** to expert systems (see later).

3.5 Decision support systems **do not make decisions**. The objective is to allow the manager to **consider a number of alternatives** and evaluate them under a variety of potential conditions. A key element in the usefulness of these systems is their ability to function interactively. This is a feature, for example, of **spreadsheets**. Managers using these systems often develop **scenarios** using earlier results to refine their understanding of the problem and their actions.

3.6 Some decision support computer systems are composed of three elements. These subsystems then combine to provide the capabilities required for an effective decision support system.

   (a) A **language subsystem** used by the manager to communicate interactively with the decision support system.

   (b) A **problem processing** subsystem which provides analytical techniques and presentation capabilities.

   (c) A **knowledge subsystem** which holds internal data and can access any needed external data.

## Executive information systems

3.7 An **executive information system (EIS)** is a type of DSS that gives the 'executive' (ie a senior manager) easy access to key internal and external data. An EIS is likely to have the following features.

(a) Provision of **summary-level data,** captured from the organisation's main systems.

(b) A facility which allows the executive to '**drill-down**' from higher levels of information to lower.

(c) **Data manipulation** facilities (for example comparison with budget or prior year data, trend analysis).

(d) **Graphics,** for user-friendly presentation of data.

(e) A **template** system. This will mean that the same type of data (eg sales figures) is presented in the same format, irrespective of changes in the volume of information required.

3.8 The basic design philosophy of executive information systems is as follows.

(a) They should be **easy to use** ('idiot-proof' not just user friendly) as an EIS may be consulted during a meeting, for example.

(b) They should make data **easy to access,** so that it describes the organisation from the executive's point of view, not just in terms of its data flows.

(c) They should provide **tools for analysis** (including ratio analysis, forecasts, what-if analysis, trends).

(d) They should provide **presentational aids** so that information can be conveyed 'without bothering the executive with too many trivial choices of scale, colour and layout.'

3.9 Executive information systems have also been more generally described as **executive support systems** (ESS). Typical examples include the following.

(a) Provision of data on the **performance** of the organisation. This would include actual, budget and forecast figures for key areas such as sales, production and profitability.

(b) Provision of **internal communications** facilities. This would include storage and retrieval of personal correspondence, minutes of meetings and financial and other reports.

(c) **Environmental scanning**. An organisation needs data on the political and economic environment. It might also collect competitor and market intelligence.

## Expert systems

3.10 Expert systems are computer programs which allow users to benefit from **expert knowledge and information,** and also advice. An expert system therefore holds a large amount of **specialised data,** for example on legal, engineering or medical information, or tax matters. The user keys in certain facts and the program uses its information on file to produce a decision about something on which an expert's decision would normally be required.

(a) A user without a legal background can obtain **guidance on the law** without having to consult a solicitor - for example, on property purchase matters, or for company law guidance.

(b) A user without much tax knowledge could consult an expert system for **taxation** for guidance on particular matters of tax.

    (c) **Doctors** can use an expert medical system to arrive at a diagnosis.

3.11   Applications of expert systems include the following.

    (a) In some **database** systems they can speed up the process of retrieving data from a database file.

    (b) Diagnostic systems can **identify causes of problems**, for example in production control systems, or in medical applications.

    (c) In some decision support systems they can **provide advice** to a decision maker.

    (d) **Tax** advice.

    (e) **Credit** scoring.

3.12   This is a diagram of an expert system.

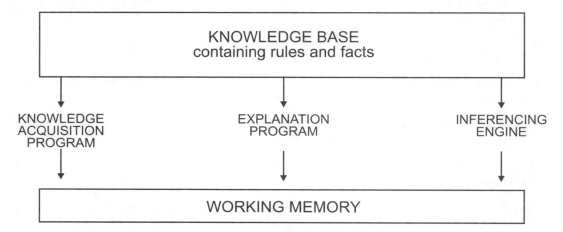

3.13   The **knowledge base** contains facts (assertions like 'a rottweiler is a dog') and rules ('if you see a rottweiler, then run away'). Some facts contradict rules, of course, or even each other ('all birds can fly' is contradicted by the existence of ostriches and kiwis). The **knowledge acquisition program** is a program which enables the expert system to acquire new knowledge and rules. The **working memory** is where the expert system stores the various facts and rules used during the current enquiry, and the current information given to it by the user. The **inferencing engine** is the software that executes the reasoning. It needs to discern which rules apply, and allocate priorities.

### Activity 9.2

At strategic levels of management the information most useful to management can be characterised as subjective, incomplete, unstructured, summary, ad-hoc and long-term. How would you characterise the information used at lower levels of the hierarchy?

### Activity 9.3

A decision support system can be described as having the following characteristics.

| | |
|---|---|
| *Objective:* | Assist management |
| *Who makes the decision:* | Manager |
| *Orientation:* | Decision-making |
| *Applications:* | Functional areas |
| *Database:* | Factual |
| | (Beaumont & Sutherland: *Information resources management*) |

Using the same five criteria, how would you describe the features of an expert system?

# 4 COSTS AND BENEFITS

## The costs of a proposed system

4.1 The costs of a new system will include costs in a number of different **categories**.

| Cost | Example |
| --- | --- |
| *Equipment costs* | • Computer and peripherals<br>• Ancillary equipment<br>• The initial system supplies (disks, tapes, paper etc) |
| *Installation costs* | • New buildings (if necessary)<br>• The computer room (wiring, air-conditioning if necessary) |
| *Development costs* | These include costs of measuring and analysing the existing system and costs of looking at the new system. They include software/consultancy work and systems analysis and programming. Changeover costs, particularly file conversion, may be very considerable. |
| *Personnel costs* | • Staff training<br>• Staff recruitment/relocation<br>• Staff salaries and pensions<br>• Redundancy payments<br>• Overheads |
| *Operating costs* | • Consumable materials (tapes, disks, stationery etc)<br>• Maintenance<br>• Accommodation costs<br>• Heating/power/insurance/telephone<br>• Standby arrangements, in case the system breaks down |

## Capital and revenue costs

4.2 The distinction between capital costs and revenue costs is important.

(a) To establish the **cash** outflows arising from the system, the costs/benefit analysis of a system ought to be based on **cash flows and DCF**.

(b) The annual charge against **profits** shown in the financial accounts is of interest to **stakeholders.**

4.3 **Capital** items will be capitalised and depreciated, and revenue items will be expensed as incurred as a regular annual cost.

4.4 Items treated as **one-off revenue costs** are costs which would usually fall to be treated as revenue which, by virtue of being incurred during the period of development only and in connection with the development are one-off.

4.5 In practice, **accounting treatment** of such items may **vary widely** between organisations depending on their accounting policies and on agreement with their auditors.

### Activity 9.4

Draw up a table with three headings: capital cost items, one-off revenue cost items and regular annual costs. Identify at least three items to be included under each heading. You may wish to refer back to the preceding paragraphs for examples of costs.

## The benefits of a proposed system

4.6 The benefits from a proposed new system must also be evaluated. These ought to consist of benefits of several types.

(a) **Savings** because the **old system** will no longer be operated. The savings should include:

(i) Savings in **staff costs**.

(ii) Savings in **other operating costs**, such as consumable materials.

(b) Extra **savings** or revenue benefits because of the improvements or enhancements that the **new system** should bring:

(i) Possibly **more sales revenue** and so additional contribution.

(ii) **Better stock control** (with a new stock control system) and so fewer stock losses from obsolescence and deterioration.

(iii) Further savings in **staff time**, resulting perhaps in reduced future staff growth.

(c) Possibly, some one-off revenue benefits from the **sale of equipment** which the existing system uses, but which will no longer be required. Second-hand computer equipment does not have a high value, however! It is also possible that the new system will use **less office space**, and so there will be benefits from selling or renting the spare accommodation.

4.7 Some benefits might be **intangible**, or impossible to give a money value to.

(a) Greater **customer satisfaction**, arising from a more prompt service (eg because of a computerised sales and delivery service).

(b) Improved **staff morale** from working with a 'better' system.

(c) **Better decision making** is hard to quantify, but may result from better MIS, DSS or EIS.

## 5 COST-BENEFIT ANALYSIS

5.1 There are three principal methods of evaluating a capital project.

| Method | Comment |
|---|---|
| *Payback period* | This method of investment appraisal calculates the length of time a project will take to recoup the initial investment; in other words how long a project will take to pay for itself. The method is based on **cash flows**. |
| *Accounting rate of return* | This method, also called **return on investment**, calculates the profits that will be earned by a project and expresses this as a percentage of the capital invested in the project. The higher the rate of return, the higher a project is ranked. This method is based on **accounting** results rather than cash flows. |

| Method | Comment |
|---|---|
| *Discounted cash flow (DCF)* | This is a method which may be sub-divided into two approaches.<br><br>(a) **Net present value (NPV)**, which considers all relevant cash flows associated with a project over the whole of its life and adjusts those occurring in future years to 'present value' by discounting at a rate called the 'cost of capital'.<br><br>(b) **Internal rate of return (IRR)**, which involves comparing the rate of return expected from the project calculated on a discounted cash flow basis with the rate used as the cost of capital. Projects with an IRR higher than the cost of capital are worth undertaking. |

## DEVOLVED ASSESSMENT ALERT

The performance criteria for Unit 21 make it clear that only a very basic understanding of cost-benefit analysis will be expected.

## Cash flow forecasting

5.2 Before looking at each of these methods in turn it is worth considering one **problem** common to all of them, that of **estimating future cash flows**. Cash flow forecasting is never easy, but in capital budgeting the problems are particularly acute. This is because the period under consideration may not be merely a year or two, but five or even ten years.

5.3 It is therefore important that decision makers should consider how **variations** in the estimates **might affect their decision**. For the time being, it is assumed that future cash flows are known with certainty.

## The payback method

### KEY TERM

The **payback period** is the length of time required before the total cash inflows received from the project is equal to the original cash outlay. In other words, it is the length of time the investment takes to pay itself back.

## 5.4 EXAMPLE: PAYBACK

The payback method has obvious disadvantages. Consider the case of two projects for which the following information is available.

|  | Project P<br>£ | Project Q<br>£ |
|---|---|---|
| Cost | 100,000 | 100,000 |
| *Cash savings* |  |  |
| Year 1 | 10,000 | 50,000 |
| 2 | 20,000 | 50,000 |
| 3 | 60,000 | 10,000 |
| 4 | 70,000 | 5,000 |
| 5 | 80,000 | 5,000 |
|  | 240,000 | 120,000 |

### 5.5 SOLUTION

Project Q pays back at the end of year two and Project P not until early in year four. Using the payback method Project Q is to be preferred, but this ignores the fact that the total profitability of Project P (£240,000) is double that of Q.

5.6 Despite the disadvantages of the payback method it is **widely used in practice**, though often only as a **supplement** to more sophisticated methods.

5.7 Besides being simple to calculate and understand, the argument in its favour is that its use will tend to **minimise** the effects of **risk** and **help liquidity**. This is because greater weight is given to **earlier cash flows** which can probably be **predicted more accurately** than distant cash flows.

## Accounting rate of return

5.8 A project may be assessed by calculating the accounting rate of return (ARR) and comparing it with a pre-determined target level. Various formulae are used, but the important thing is to be **consistent** once a method has been selected. A formula for ARR which is common in practice is:

> **KEY TERM**
>
> **Accounting rate of return** is calculated as follows
>
> $$ARR = \frac{\text{Estimated average profits}}{\text{Estimated average investment}} \times 100\%$$

### 5.9 EXAMPLE: ARR

Caddick Limited is contemplating a computerisation project and has two alternatives. Based on the ARR method which of the two projects would be recommended?

|  | Project X | Project Y |
|---|---|---|
| Hardware cost | £100,000 | £120,000 |
| Estimated residual value | 10,000 | £15,000 |
| Estimated life | 5 years | 5 years |
| Estimated future cost savings per annum before depreciation | £28,000 | £32,500 |

### 5.10 SOLUTION

It is first necessary to calculate the average profits (net savings) and average investment.

|  | Project X £ | Project Y £ |
|---|---|---|
| Total savings before depreciation | 140,000 | 162,500 |
| Total depreciation | 90,000 | 105,000 |
| Total savings after depreciation | 50,000 | 57,500 |
| | | |
| *Average savings* | 10,000 | 11,500 |
| | | |
| Value of investment initially | 100,000 | 120,000 |
| Eventual scrap value | 10,000 | 15,000 |
| | 110,000 | 135,000 |
| *Average investment* | 55,000 | 67,500 |

5.11    The accounting rates of return are as follows. Project X would therefore be chosen.

Project X =    $\dfrac{£10,000}{£55,000}$    = 18.1%

Project Y =    $\dfrac{£11,500}{£67,500}$    = 17.0%

5.12    The return on investment is a measure of (accounting) profitability and its major **advantages** that it can be obtained from **readily available accounting data** and that its meaning is **widely understood**.

5.13    Its major **shortcomings** are that it is based on accounting profits rather than cash flows and that it fails to take account of the **timing** of cash inflows and outflows. For example, in the problem above cash savings in each year were assumed to be the same, whereas management might favour higher cash inflows in the **early years**. Early cash flows are less risky and they improve liquidity. This might lead them to choose a project with a lower ARR.

> **KEY TERM**
>
> **Discounted cash flow** or DCF is a technique of evaluating capital investment projects, using **discounting arithmetic** to determine whether or not they will provide a satisfactory return.

5.14    A typical investment project involves a payment of capital for fixed assets at the **start** of the project and then there will be profits coming in from the investment over a number of years. When the system goes live, there will be **running costs** as well. The benefits of the system should exceed the running costs, to give net annual benefits.

5.15    DCF recognises that there is a **'time value'** or interest cost and **risk** cost to investing money, so that the expected benefits from a project should not only pay back the costs, but should also yield a satisfactory return. Only **relevant** costs are recognised: accounting conventions like depreciation, which is not a real cash flow, are ignored.

5.16    £1 is now worth more than £1 in a year's time, because £1 now could be used to earn interest by the end of year 1. Money has a lower and lower value, the further from 'now' that it will be earned or paid. With DCF, this time value on money is allowed for by converting cash flows in future years to a smaller, **present value**, equivalent.

## 5.17   **EXAMPLE: NPV**

A DCF evaluation, using NPV analysis, of a proposed computer project might be as follows.

*Project: new network system for administration department*

| | | |
|---|---|---|
| Development and hardware purchase costs (all incurred now) | | £150,000 |
| | | |
| Operating costs of new system (cash outflows per annum) | £55,000 | |
| Annual savings from new system (cash inflow) | £115,000 | |
| Annual net savings (net cash inflows) | | £60,000 |
| | | |
| Expected system life | 4 years | |
| Required return on investment | 15% pa | |

## 5.18 SOLUTION

The calculation of NPV can be performed **by spreadsheet** as follows. (Skip this part and make a note come back to it later if you have not studied spreadsheets in any great depth yet.)

| | A | B | C |
|---|---|---|---|
| 1 | **NPV calculation** | | |
| 2 | | | £ |
| 3 | Costs incurred now | | (150,000) |
| 4 | Benefits in year 1 | 60,000 | |
| 5 | Benefits in year 2 | 60,000 | |
| 6 | Benefits in year 3 | 60,000 | |
| 7 | Benefits in year 4 | 60,000 | |
| 8 | Discounted value | | 171,299 |
| 9 | **Net present value** | | 21,299 |
| 10 | | | |
| 11 | **Variables** | | |
| 12 | | | |
| 13 | Discount rate | 15% | |
| 14 | | | |

The underlying formula are shown below, together with the 'function wizard' entries that are needed (just click on the *fx* symbol in the toolbar to start the function wizard).

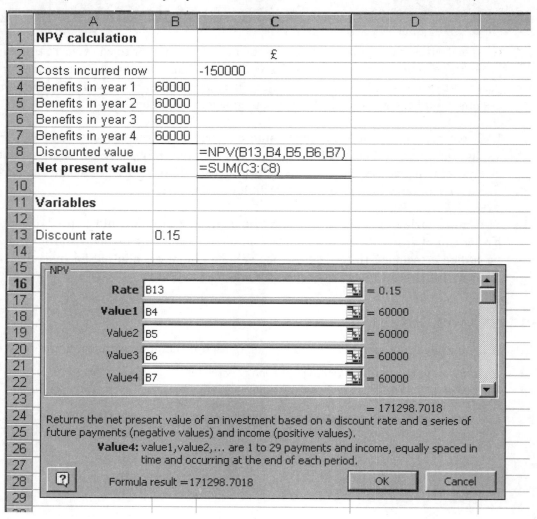

| | A | B | C | D |
|---|---|---|---|---|
| 1 | **NPV calculation** | | | |
| 2 | | | £ | |
| 3 | Costs incurred now | | -150000 | |
| 4 | Benefits in year 1 | 60000 | | |
| 5 | Benefits in year 2 | 60000 | | |
| 6 | Benefits in year 3 | 60000 | | |
| 7 | Benefits in year 4 | 60000 | | |
| 8 | Discounted value | | =NPV(B13,B4,B5,B6,B7) | |
| 9 | **Net present value** | | =SUM(C3:C8) | |
| 10 | | | | |
| 11 | **Variables** | | | |
| 12 | | | | |
| 13 | Discount rate | 0.15 | | |
| 14 | | | | |

NPV

| Rate | B13 | | = 0.15 |
| **Value1** | B4 | | = 60000 |
| Value2 | B5 | | = 60000 |
| Value3 | B6 | | = 60000 |
| Value4 | B7 | | = 60000 |

= 171298.7018

Returns the net present value of an investment based on a discount rate and a series of future payments (negative values) and income (positive values).

**Value4:** value1,value2,... are 1 to 29 payments and income, equally spaced in time and occurring at the end of each period.

Formula result =171298.7018    OK    Cancel

5.19 In this example, the present value of the expected **benefits** of the project **exceed** the present value of its **costs**, all discounted at 15% pa, and so the project is financially **justifiable** because it would be expected to earn a yield greater than the minimum target return of 15%. Payback of the development costs and hardware costs of £150,000 would occur after 2½ years.

5.20 The main **disadvantage** of the NPV method is that in practice it is very **difficult to determine the true cost of capital**. Another possible disadvantage is that it might be **difficult to understand** for some people.

## Internal rate of return

5.21 The internal rate of return(IRR) methods of DCF involves two steps.

(a) Calculating the **rate of return** which is expected from a project.
(b) **Comparing** the rate of return with the **cost of capital**.

5.22 If a project earns a **higher rate of return than the cost of capital**, it will be **worth undertaking** (and its NPV would be positive). If it earns a lower rate of return, it is not worthwhile (and its NPV would be negative). If a project earns a return which is exactly equal to the cost of capital, its NPV will be 0 and it will only just be worthwhile.

5.23 The **manual** method of calculating the rate of return is sometimes considered to be rather 'messy' and unsatisfactory because it involves some guesswork and approximation, but **spreadsheets** can do it with great speed and precision. In our example the IRR comes to **22%,** easily exceeding the cost of capital of 15%..

|   | A | B |
|---|---|---|
| 1 | **IRR calculation** | |
| 2 | | £ |
| 3 | Costs incurred now | (150,000) |
| 4 | Benefits in year 1 | 60,000 |
| 5 | Benefits in year 2 | 60,000 |
| 6 | Benefits in year 3 | 60,000 |
| 7 | Benefits in year 4 | 60,000 |
| 8 | | |
| 9 | **IRR** | 22% |
| 10 | | |

|  | A | B | C | D |
|---|---|---|---|---|
| 1 | **IRR calculation** | | | |
| 2 | | £ | | |
| 3 | Costs incurred now | -150000 | | |
| 4 | Benefits in year 1 | 60000 | | |
| 5 | Benefits in year 2 | 60000 | | |
| 6 | Benefits in year 3 | 60000 | | |
| 7 | Benefits in year 4 | 60000 | | |
| 8 | | | | |
| 9 | **IRR** | =IRR(B3:B7) | | |
| 10 | | | | |
| 11 | | | | |
| 12 | | | | |
| 13 | | | | |
| 14 | | | | |
| 15 | | | | |
| 16 | | | | |
| 17 | | | | |
| 18 | | | | |
| 19 | | | | |
| 20 | | | | |
| 21 | | | | |
| 22 | | | | |

IRR

**Values** B3:B7      = {-150000;60000;60(

Guess 15      = 15

= 0.218622696

Returns the internal rate of return for a series of cash flows.

**Guess** is a number that you guess is close to the result of IRR; 0.1 (10 percent) if omitted.

Formula result =0.218622696      OK      Cancel

## Activity 9.5

Draw up a table which identifies, for each of payback, ARR and NPV, two advantages and two disadvantages.

## Key learning points

- An information system is likely to need improving if the improvements will have a positive impact on 'value for money' (VFM). VFM is made up of three E's: economy, efficiency and effectiveness.

- Computerised systems offer advantages such as higher productivity, faster processing, greater information access, greater accuracy, ease of correction, higher quality output and less bulk.

- The information required for planning and control may be classified as strategic, tactical and operational, matching the three levels of the Anthony hierarchy. Similarly, different types of management information system can be discerned.

- Transaction processing systems are used for routine operational information processing. They provide the raw material used more extensively in management information systems.

- A management information system can be described as a system which provides information to management to assist them in decision-making in their roles of planning and controlling.

- Decision support systems are a form of management information system. They are used by management to provide assistance in decision making. A DSS does not make decisions itself. An example of a DSS is the spreadsheet. Spreadsheets are used by end-users, who can create the required model, input the data, manipulate the data and read or print the output themselves. Spreadsheets are particularly well suited to sensitivity analysis.

- Executive information systems are a form of management information system designed to give senior executives easy access to data. They typically include a 'drill-down' facility, graphics and data manipulation facilities for rapid and simple retrieval of the required data.

- Expert systems use artificial intelligence, the concept that computers can be programmed to imitate certain features of human reasoning. Expert systems can be used where problems are reasonably well defined and can be solved by reference to a set of rules.

- A highly important issue when suggesting improvements is cost-benefit analysis.

  o Costs may be analysed in different ways, but include equipment costs, installation costs, development costs, personnel costs and running costs.

  o Benefits are usually somewhat more intangible, but include cost savings, revenue benefits and qualitative benefits.

- There are three principal methods of evaluating a capital project.

  o Payback period calculates the length of time a project will take to cover the initial investment in cashflow terms.

  o Accounting rate of return calculates the profits which will be generated and expresses this return as a percentage of the capital invested.

  o DCF techniques are also cash flow based; two approaches are net present value calculations and the internal rate of return.

## Quick quiz

1    Define efficiency.

2    Define information technology.

3    What are the characteristics of strategic information?

4    What is the objective of a decision support system?

5    Give three examples of intangible benefits.

6    What is a payback period?

7    What is the accounting rate of return?

## Answers to quick quiz_____

1 Efficiency is the relationship between goods or services produced (outputs) and the resources used to produce them. An efficient operation produces the maximum **output** for any given set of resource **inputs**; or it has minimum inputs for any given quantity and quality of product or service provided.

2 **Information technology** is a term used to describe the coming together of **computer** technology with **data transmission** technology, to revolutionise information systems. Cheap computer hardware, based on microchip technology with ever-increasing power and capacity, has been harnessed to an extensive telecommunications network.

3 Derived from both internal and external sources; summarised at a high level; relevant to the long term; deals with the whole organisation; often prepared on an 'ad hoc' basis; both quantitative and qualitative; never absolutely certain.

4 The objective is to allow the manager to consider a number of alternatives and evaluate tehm under a variety of potential conditions.

5 Greater customer satisfaction, improved staff morale, and better decision making.

6 The payback period is the length of time required before the total cash inflows received from the project is equal to the original cash outlay. In other words, it is the length of time the investment takes to pay itself back.

7 Estimated average profits over estimated average investment.

## Answers to activities_____

## Answer 9.1_____

There is no point in achieving a very high quality product (effectiveness) if it takes so long to do so (inefficiency) that the customer cannot wait and goes elsewhere.

## Answer 9.2_____

Information used at lower levels of the management hierarchy could be characterised as routine, complete, structured, detailed, computational and short-term.

## Answer 9.3_____

The objective of an expert system is to replace management. The decision is actually made by the computer. The orientation of an expert system is towards the transfer of experience. They are used in specific problems. The database in an expert system is procedural as well as factual.

# Answer 9.4

| Capital cost items | 'One-off' revenue cost items | Regular annual costs |
|---|---|---|
| Hardware purchase costs | Consultancy fees | Operating staff salaries/wages |
| Software purchase costs | Systems analysts' and programmers' salaries | Data transmission costs |
| Purchase of accommodation (if needed) | Costs of testing the system (staff costs, consumables) | Consumable materials |
| Installation costs (new desks, cables, physical storage etc) | Costs of converting the files for the new system | Power |
| | | Maintenance costs |
| | Staff recruitment fees | Cost of standby arrangements |
| | | Ongoing staff training |

# Answer 9.5

| Method | Advantages | Disadvantages |
|---|---|---|
| Payback | (1) Easy to calculate<br>(2) Favours projects that offer quick returns | (1) Ignores cash flows after payback period<br>(2) Only a crude measure of timing of a project's cash flows. |
| ARR | (1) Easy to calculate<br>(2) Easy to understand | (1) Doesn't allow for timing of inflows/outflows of cash<br>(2) Subject to accounting conventions. |
| NPV | (1) Uses relevant cost approach by concentrating on cash flows<br>(2) Represents increase to company's wealth, expressed in present day terms | (1) Not easily understood by laymen.<br>(2) Cost of capital may be difficult to calculate. |

# Chapter 10  Computer hardware

---

## Chapter topic list

1     Computers

2     The processor

3     Manual input devices

4     Automatic input devices

5     Output devices

6     Storage devices

---

## Learning objectives

On completion of this chapter you will be able to:

| | Performance criteria | Range Statement |
|---|---|---|
| • Identify improvements/suggest changes to: | 21.3.1, 21.3.2 | |
|    o (micro)processor | | |
|    o memory | | |
|    o backing storage | | |
|    o visual display unit | | |
|    o printing facilities | | |
|    o computer output | | |
| • Understand the range of computerised MIS | | 21.3.1 |
| • Identify potential improvements to the MIS and consider them for their impact on the quality of the system and any interrelated systems | 21.3.1 | |
| • Make suggestions for changes supported by a clear rationale as to how they could improve the quality of the system | 21.3.2 | |
| • Assess and clearly state whether assumptions and judgements made are reliable | 21.3.3 | |
| • Present suggestions clearly and in a way which helps people to understand and act on them | 21.3.5 | |
| • *Describe an organisation's computer software, systems and networking* | n/a | n/a |

Italicised objectives are areas of knowledge and understanding underlying the elements of competence for Unit 21.

BPP
PUBLISHING

## 1 COMPUTERS

1.1 You probably think of a computer as something with a **screen** like a TV, a **box** or **tower** for the screen to sit on or next to (with some slots to put disks in), a **keyboard**, and a **mouse**.

1.2 What we describe is actually a PC, which is certainly a **type** of computer—it is the type that now most regularly sits on desks in the average office or home. However, larger computers are still common, and these days there are also 'computers' in cars and planes and even in some domestic appliances.

> **KEY TERM**
>
> A **computer** is a device which will accept input data, process it according to programmed logical and arithmetic rules, store and output data and/or calculate results. The ability to store programmed instructions and to take decisions which vary the way in which a program executes (although within the defined logic of the program) are the principal distinguishing features of a computer.
>
> (CIMA, *Computing Terminology*)

1.3 Let's look more closely at this definition.

(a) The **device** is actually a group of electronic and electromechanical devices working together to accept or retrieve **inputs** (some figures, say), **process** them and give you the **output**.

In terms of a PC, the computing device is a collection of electronic circuits, with electrons rushing to and fro along cables: perhaps **from** things like impact-sensitive keyboards **to** things like 'cathode ray tubes' (the screen) and/or **to** the magnetic surface of floppy discs (or **vice versa**, rushing from disk, via the circuits, to the screen).

(b) A computer **accepts** and then **processes** input data according to the instructions it is given.

(c) A computer's operations are performed 'according to **programmed** logical and arithmetic rules.' The **arithmetic** element might be as simple as x + y = z. The **logic** will be something along the lines of 'if x + y **does not** = z, **then** add 3 to x and try again'.

> **KEY TERM**
>
> A **program** is a set of coded instructions which tells the computer what to do.

1.4 A **computer** is therefore a mixture of physical, **tangible** things like keyboards, mice, screens, circuits and cables (**hardware**) and **intangible** arithmetic and logic (**software**). Using electrical impulses, the two are connected and communicate with each other.

1.5 The main types of **software** will be covered in later chapters.

## Hardware

**KEY TERM**

**Hardware** means the various physical components which comprise a computer system, as opposed to the non-tangible software elements.

CIMA, *Computing Terminology*

1.6 Most of these physical components are physically separate from, or **peripheral** to, the main circuitry that does the arithmetical and logical processing, but they are the most familiar bits of a computer: keyboards, screens, disks and so on. These are described at greater length later in this Chapter. Developments in **communications** devices and terminology are covered in Chapter 11.

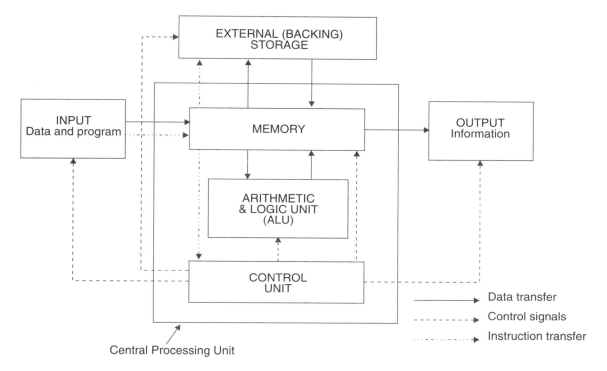

Central Processing Unit

## Types of computer

1.7 Computers can be **classified** as follows, although the differences between these categories are becoming increasingly **vague**.

- Supercomputers
- Mainframe computers, now sometimes called 'enterprise servers'
- Minicomputers, now often called 'mid-range' computers
- Microcomputers, now commonly called PCs

**Activity 10.1**

If you are studying at a college do a class survey to find out what types of computer each member uses at work. Most will probably use PCs but there may be some who have experience of larger systems, and it will be useful to share this knowledge.

## Supercomputers

1.8 A supercomputer is used to process **very large amounts of data** very quickly. They are particularly useful for occasions where high volumes of calculations need to be performed, for example in meteorological or astronomical applications. Manufacturers of supercomputers include Cray and Fujitsu. They are **not used commercially**.

## Mainframes

1.9 A mainframe computer system is one that has at its heart a **very powerful central computer**, linked by cable or telecommunications to hundreds or thousands of **terminals**, and capable of accepting simultaneous input from all of them. A mainframe has many times more processing power than a PC and offers very **extensive data storage facilities**.

### DEVOLVED ASSESSMENT ALERT

Devolved assessment data should give you an indication of what sort of computers the organisation is presently using, if improving the hardware aspects of the system is an issue. It could be important to know about the different classifications when dealing with tasks that ask whether you would recommend changing from one sort of system to another. We shall come back to this issue in **Chapter 11**.

It is pretty unlikely that you will be confronted with organisations that use mainframe computers or even minicomputers in your Devolved Assessment, but you may well work for such organisations now or in the future.

### *Minicomputers*

1.10 A minicomputer is a computer whose size, speed and capabilities lie somewhere between those of a mainframe and a PC. The term was originally used before PCs were developed, to describe computers which were cheaper but less well-equipped than mainframe computers (which had until then been the only type of computer available). The advent of more powerful components now means that some 'superminis', and even PCs linked in a network, can run more powerfully than some older mainframes.

1.11 With the advent of PCs, and with mainframes now being physically smaller than in the past, the definition of a minicomputer has become rather vague. There is really **no definition** which distinguishes adequately between a PC and a minicomputer. Price, power and number of users supported have been used to identify distinguishing features, but these differences have tended to disappear as microchip technology has progressed. Manufacturers of minicomputers include IBM with its **AS400**, ICL and DEC.

### *PCs*

1.12 The '**personal**' **computer** (or '**microcomputer**') market was first developed by companies like **Apple** Computers, but a key event was the launch of the **IBM PC** in August 1981. In the early years of the development of the PC, the Apple Macintosh (technically not a PC) became the standard for graphics-based applications, while the IBM PC and a host of IBM-compatibles, or 'clones', were chosen for text-based (business) applications. However, as microchips have become more powerful, the difference in emphasis has become less important. Apple have recently introduced the PowerPC, which **is** IBM-compatible.

1.13 PCs are now the **norm** for small to medium-sized business computing and for home computing. Often they are linked together in a **network** to enable sharing of information between users.

*File servers*

1.14 A file server is more powerful than the average desktop PC and it is dedicated to providing **additional services** for users of networked PCs. We shall discuss these in more detail in Chapter 11.

1.15 A very large network is likely to use a 'mainframe' computer as its server, and in fact mainframes are now often referred to as '**enterprise servers**'.

*Portables*

1.16 The original portable computers were heavy, weighing around five kilograms, and could only be run from the mains electricity supply. Subsequent developments allow true portability. Many portables are now the size of an A4 pad of paper.

1.17 The **laptop** (or notebook) is powered either from the electricity supply or using a rechargeable battery. It uses 3½" disks, CD-ROMs and DVDs a liquid crystal or gas plasma screen and is fully compatible with desktop PCs.

1.18 The **pocket computer,** palmtop or handheld, may or may not be compatible with true PCs. They range from machines which are little more than electronic diaries to relatively powerful processors with PC compatibility and communications features.

1.19 While portable PCs are becoming more popular (even in the office, as they save precious space on crowded desks), they have some **disadvantages**, in particular the following.

(a) Keyboard **ergonomics** (ie keys which are too small, or too close together, for easy, quick typing).

(b) **Battery power** (although manufacturers are trying to reduce power consumption).

*Workstations*

1.20 Originally, a workstation was a computer used by one person, particularly for graphics and design applications, and was used primarily in **engineering**. It had a fast and powerful central processor, a high resolution monitor, and a large memory. This enabled complex designs to be easily manipulated.

1.21 These characteristics, however, are no longer unique to workstations. High performance personal computers can offer very similar services; so the distinction is a historical one. Personal computers are now generally fitted with some kind of **graphics expansion card** — a circuit board containing the necessary electronics.

## A typical PC specification

1.22 Here is the specification for a **fairly powerful PC**, extracted from an advertisement that appeared in the Spring of 2000. This PC cost around **£1,000** (excluding VAT) at this time.

## DEVOLVED ASSESSMENT ALERT

In your devolved assessment it is most unlikely that you will be tested specifically on highly technical terms like IDE or UART shown below, so don't let them scare you. We include this information because you might well want to have such things demystified if you are buying a PC for work or personal use.

---

### PC SPECIFICATION

| | |
|---|---|
| Intel 650 MHz Pentium III Processor | 4MB 3D 64-bit SUPER Graphics Accelerator Card |
| 55.6 kpbs internal fax modem | 12GB hard disk drive |
| High performance motherboard | 3.5" (1.44MB) Floppy Disk Drive |
| 512K CPU Cache | 105 Key UK Windows 98 Keyboard |
| 128MB RAM | Logitech 2 button mouse |
| 15" SVGA Colour Monitor | Midi Tower Case 3 × 5.25"& 3 × 3.5" drive bays, 2 serial ports, 1 parallel port |
| 32 Speed CD ROM | Windows 98 pre-loaded |

---

1.24 By the end of Chapter 11 you should understand most of the terms used here.

### Activity 10.2

Look at a PC magazine or a quality newspaper (eg the *Times* on Wednesdays) and compare this specification with what is currently available for around £1,000. No doubt hard disk size and processor speed will have increased dramatically by the time you come to read this.

## 2    THE PROCESSOR

2.1    The processor is the 'brain' of the computer.

### KEY TERM

The **processor** is the collection of circuitry and registers that performs the processing in a particular computer and provides that computer with its specific characteristics. In modern computers the CPU comprises a single (albeit increasingly sophisticated) chip device but this is supported by other chips performing specialist functions.'

(CIMA, *Computing Terminology*)

2.2    The processor (sometimes referred to as the **central processing unit** (or **CPU**)) is divided into three areas:

- The **arithmetic and logic unit**
- The **control unit**
- The main store, or **memory**

The set of operations that the processor performs is known as the **instruction set**, or repertoire, and this determines in part the speed at which processing can be performed.

## Chips with everything

2.3    In modern computer systems the processing unit may have all its elements - arithmetic and logic unit, control unit, and the input/output interface-on a single 'chip'. A chip is a small piece of silicon upon which is etched an integrated circuit, which consists of transistors and their interconnecting patterns on an extremely small scale.

2.4    The chip is mounted on a carrier unit which in turn is 'plugged' on to a circuit board - called the **motherboard -** with other chips, each with their own functions, such as sound (a 'sound card') and video (a 'video card').

## Arithmetic and logic unit

2.5    The ALU is the part of the central processor where the arithmetic and logic operations are carried out. These include **arithmetic** (for example adding and multiplying) and **logical** functions such as comparison, branch operations (a branch instruction changes the order of program instructions) and movement of data. The operations are all simple but, as we shall see in a moment, the significant feature of computer operations is the very rapid speed with which computers can perform vast numbers of simple-step instructions, which combine to represent very complex processing.

## Control unit

2.6    The control unit receives program instructions, one at a time, from the main store and decodes them. It then sends out **control signals** to the peripheral devices.

### *MHz, cycles and clock speed*

2.7    The signals are co-ordinated by a **clock** which sends out a 'pulse' - a sort of tick-tock sequence called a **cycle** - at regular intervals. A clock pulse indicates to some circuits that they should **start** sending data on their wires and at the same time indicates to others when the data from the previous pulse should have **arrived**. This ensures that devices do not start the next stage of processing until all the data that is needed has arrived in the right place.

2.8    This sounds rather laborious until you realise the phenomenal speed at which computers work. The **number of cycles** produced per second is usually measured in **MegaHertz** (MHz).

1 MHz = one **million** cycles per **second**.

A typical modern business PC might have a specification of 300 MHz, but models with higher clock speeds (eg 450 or 500 MHz) are now common.

### *Catching the bus*

2.9    A signal travels along an electronic path that is called a **bus** in computer jargon. A 'local bus' is a particularly fast route.

## Intel inside

2.10 If you have been working for some time you have probably noticed the shift from '386' processors to the '**Pentium**' processors common today. This refers to the chips made by the Intel company. Each generation of Intel CPU chip has been able to perform operations in **fewer clock cycles** than the previous generation, and therefore works more quickly.

2.11 For example, suppose an accounting program were trying to add up a column of numbers.

A **386** CPU requires a minimum of 6 clock ticks to add two numbers.

A **486** CPU can generally add two numbers in 2 clock ticks.

A **Pentium** CPU can add two numbers in 1 clock tick.

A **Pentium Pro** can add **three** numbers in 1 clock tick.

And so on. The **Pentium II** and **Pentium III** processors are faster still.

2.12 **You need not remember the precise details** here: just be aware that a Pentium of any kind is much faster than a 486 or a 386.

2.13 Other manufacturers of processors include IBM, with their **6×86 chip** (similar to a Pentium) and Digital with their **Alpha** chip.

## Memory

2.14 Just as humans can work more quickly if they can **remember** the rules for doing something rather than having to look them up, a computer's processing is much faster if it has the information it needs readily to hand. The computer's **memory** is also known as main store or internal store. This is circuitry which is used to store data within the processing unit while the computer is operating.

2.15 The memory will hold the following.

(a) **Programs**. The control unit acts on program instructions that are held in the store; these program instructions include the operating system.

(b) Some **input data**. A small area of internal store is needed to take in temporarily the data that will be processed next.

(c) A **working area**. The computer will need an area of store to hold data that is currently being processed or is used for processing other data.

(d) Some **output data**. A small area of store is needed to hold temporarily the data or information that is ready for output to an output device.

*Bits and bytes*

2.16 Each individual storage element in the computer's memory consists of a simple circuit which can be switched **on** or **off**. These two states can be conveniently expressed by the numbers **1** and **0** respectively. Any piece of data or instruction must be coded in these symbols before processing can commence.

2.17 Since a byte has 8 bits, there are $2^8$, or 256, different combinations of 1s and 0s, which is sufficient to cover numeric digits, upper and lower case alphabets, punctuation marks and other symbols. Business PCs now make use of **32 bit** processors. Put simply, this means that data travels around from one place to another in groups of 16 or 32 bits, and so modern PCs operate considerably faster than the original 8 bit models introduced in the early 1980s.

2.18 The processing capacity of a computer is in part dictated by the capacity of its memory. Capacity is calculated in **kilobytes** (1 kilobyte = $2^{10}$ (1,024) bytes) and **megabytes** (1 megabyte = $2^{20}$ bytes) and **gigabytes** ($2^{30}$). These are abbreviated to Kb, Mb and Gb.

2.19 The reason for holding programs in the memory is to **speed up processing**. The transfer of data, such as program instructions, within memory is faster than the transfer of data between the processor and peripheral devices. However, a computer's memory is limited in its size, and can only hold a certain volume of data at any time. A program can be too big for some computers, because the computer's memory is not large enough to hold it.

**Activity 10.3**

For convenience a kilobyte (1,024 bytes) is generally thought of as 1,000 bytes (hence the name *kilo*).

(a) How many bytes in a megabyte?

(b) How many megabytes in a gigabyte?

(c) If an average English word has five letters and a document is 300 words long, how many Kb will it take up on a computer?

## Types of memory

2.20 A distinction can be made between two main types of memory, **RAM** and **ROM**. The term **cache** is also important.

*RAM*

2.21 RAM can be defined as memory with the ability to access any location in the memory in any order with the same speed. **Random access** is an essential requirement for the main memory of a computer. RAM in microcomputers is '**volatile**' which means that the contents of the memory are **erased** when the computer's power is switched off.

2.22 The RAM on a typical modern business PC is likely to be in the range **32 to 128 megabytes** (most usually 64Mb). The size of the RAM is **extremely** important. A computer with a 300 MHz clock speed but only 16 Mb of RAM will not be as efficient as a 200 MHz PC with 64 Mb of RAM.

### Activity 10.4

When you start up a program on a typical modern PC you generally hear a crackling noise and a little light flickers on the front of the base unit. What is happening?

*Cache*

2.23 The **cache** (or primary cache) is a small capacity but **extremely fast** memory chip which saves a second copy of the pieces of data most recently read from or written to main memory. When the cache is full, older entries are 'flushed out' to make room for new ones. Primary cache is often part of the same chip as the CPU.

2.24 The principle is that if a piece of data is accessed once it is highly likely that it will be accessed again soon afterwards, and so keeping it readily to hand will speed up processing.

2.25 **Secondary cache** is a larger, slower cache between the primary cache and the main memory. You may also see the term **pipeline burst cache** in PC ads. 'Pipeline burst' refers to an extremely efficient method of handling data in memory.

*ROM*

### KEY TERM

**ROM (read-only memory)** is a memory chip into which fixed data is written permanently at the time of its manufacture. New data cannot be written into the memory, and so the data on the memory chip is unchangeable and irremovable.

2.26 ROM is '**non-volatile**' memory, which means that its contents do not disappear when the computer's power source is switched off. A computer's **start-up program**, known as a 'bootstrap' program, is always held in a form of a ROM. 'Booting up' means running this program.

2.27 When you turn on a PC you will usually see a reference to **BIOS** (basic input/output system). This is part of the ROM chip containing all the programs needed to control the keyboard, screen, disk drives and so on.

## 3 MANUAL INPUT DEVICES

3.1 Input is a **labour-intensive** process, typically involving the keying in of data using a keyboard. In many cases, transcription, the process of inputting data by keyboard so that it can be converted into the electronic pulses on which the computer circuitry operates, is avoided by a process of **data capture**, where data is recorded in such a way as to be directly convertible into a machine-sensible form without any human intervention. In many situations, data capture or transcription occur far away from the main computer, and data has to be **transmitted** to where it is to be processed.

## The keyboard

3.2 You will already be familiar with the basic QWERTY typewriter keyboard which includes the **alphabet, numbers** 0 - 9 and some basic **punctuation**, together with other keys (for example a space bar and a shift key, which allows a second set of key features to be used, including the upper case alphabet keys). Computer keyboards are derived from this standard keyboard.

### Activity 10.5

A typical computer keyboard has 102 or 105 keys and is a development of the QWERTY design. What types of keys does it have?

## The VDU

3.3 A VDU (visual display unit) or 'monitor' displays text and graphics. The screen's **resolution** is the number of pixels that are lit up. A **pixel** is a picture element -a 'dot' on the screen, as it were. The fewer the pixels on screen, the larger they will be: the resolution of any picture will be low. More and smaller pixels enable detailed high-resolution display.

3.4 Older PCs often have a resolution of 640 × 480, the resolution offered by IBM's VGA standard. Higher resolution requires more processing power. Super VGA, or SVGA, is the standard for newer monitors and offers resolutions up to 1,280 × 1,024.

### DEVOLVED ASSESSMENT ALERT

Again, this explanation is probably more techy than anything that you would need to provide in an answer to a devolved assessment task, but may be useful if you are buying a PC. However, you may get questions on **screen design** – the way in which things are laid out on the screen. There is more on this in **Chapter 12.**

3.5 The user must 'scroll' up, down or sideways across the screen when he or she wants to view a different piece of text. Alternatively two or more bits of text which are in different places in the overall layout (or even in different documents) can be viewed on screen at the same time by making use of **'windows'**.

3.6 The screen is used in conjunction with a keyboard to display text to allow the operator to carry out a **visual check** on what he or she has keyed in, to help the operator to input data by displaying 'forms' for filling in, and to display **output**, for example answers to file enquiries.

3.7 In addition, the screen can be used to **give messages to the operator,** and the operator can respond to messages by keying in new instructions. Touch-sensitive screens have been developed but they are expensive and not widely used.

## Mouse

3.8 A mouse is usually used in conjunction with a keyboard, particularly in Windows-based systems. A mouse is a handheld device with a rubber or metal ball protruding from a small hole in its base. The **mouse is moved** over a flat surface, usually a special mouse mat which is designed to possess enough friction to prevent the ball slipping, and as it moves, internal sensors pick up the motion and convert it into electronic signals which instruct the **cursor on screen to move** in the same direction.

3.9 The mouse has two or three **buttons** which can be pressed (**clicked**) to send specific signals. For example, a 'click' on the left hand button can be used to send the cursor to a new cell in a spreadsheet and a 'double click' can select a particular application from a Windows menu. The latest variety also have a **wheel** to facilitate scrolling up and down a screen display.

3.10 Similar to the mouse is the **trackball**. This are often found on notebook computers, where there is not always space to place a mouse mat on a flat surface next to the computer. It operates in a similar way, except that the casing is fixed to the computer and a ball, which protrudes upwards, is manipulated by hand. Some mobile computers use a **touch sensitive pad** for mouse functions; others have a tiny **joystick** (called a '**nipple**') in the centre of the keys on the keyboard.

## 4 AUTOMATIC INPUT DEVICES

### Document reading methods

4.1 Copying manually-prepared data into a computer-sensible form such as disk or tape is costly in terms of manpower, time and accuracy. Document reading methods **reduce human 'intrusion'** into data capture and cut out the need to transcribe manually-prepared data on to a computer-sensible input medium. This **saves time and money** and also **reduces errors** because it cuts out all data preparation errors and also, in the case of **pre-printed documents** such as cheques, many data recording errors too.

### *Magnetic ink character recognition*

4.2 MICR is the recognition by a machine of special formatted characters printed in **magnetic ink**. Using ink which contains a metallic powder, highly stylised characters (such as those as on a **cheque**) are encoded on to documents by means of special typewriters. The document must be **passed through a magnetic field** before the characters can be detected by a suitable reading device.

4.3 The main advantage of MICR is its **accuracy**, but MICR documents are **expensive** to produce, and so MICR has only limited application in practice. A large MICR reader in the banking system can scan up to 2,000 documents per minute.

### *Optical character recognition and scanners*

4.4 OCR is a method of input involving a machine that is able to read characters by **optical detection** of the **shape** of those characters. Optical (or laser) **scanners** can read **printed documents** at up to 300 pages per hour. They recognise the characters, convert them into machine code and record them.

4.5 The advantage of OCR over MICR is that the computer can read **ordinary** typed or printed text, provided that the quality of the input document is satisfactory.

4.6 The technology now exists for computers to recognise **handwriting** and devices that allow the user to 'write' on a screen and have this writing automatically converted into computer sensible form are becoming quite widely used in applications such as police work, where fairly standard details need to be noted quickly and accurately while **on the scene** of an incident. Commercial applications include warehousing and stock control.

*Optical mark reading*

4.7 Optical mark reading is generally used for **numeric** characters. Values are denoted by a line or cross in an appropriate box, whose **position** represents a value, on the preprinted source document (or card). The card is then read by a device which senses the mark in each box using an **electric current** and translates it into machine code. A computer program written specifically for the application interprets each marks as appropriate.

4.8 Applications in which OMR is used are the recording of gas and electricity meter readings on to preprinted documents, **National Lottery** entry forms, and answer sheets for **multiple choice questions**. Once the readings are made, the documents are input to the computer using an OMR reading system.

*Turnaround documents*

4.9 OCR and OMR methods of character recognition can make use of a turnaround document. A turnaround document is a document that is initially **produced by computer**. It is then used to collect more data and then **re-input to the computer** for processing of the additional data. The main drawback to turnaround documents is their limited application. There are not many situations where an organisation can produce a document which can then be used for subsequent data input. Examples of turnround documents are as follows.

(a) Credit card companies, for example Visa and Mastercard, include a **payment counterfoil** with their computer-produced bill, which is returned with payment and then used for inputting payment data to a computer.

(b) An examining body that stores multiple choice questions on a computer file can produce **examination answer sheets** by computer. Candidates are then asked to tick the correct answer, and the position of the answer mark will be detectable by an OMR reader, and so the examination paper can be marked by computer.

*Bar coding and EPOS*

4.10 A bar code reader is a device which reads bar codes, which are groups of marks which, by their **spacing and thickness**, indicate specific codes or values. Look at the back cover of this book for an example of a bar code.

4.11 Such devices are now commonly used as an input medium for **point of sale systems** in **supermarkets** - nearly all food and drink products now carry bar coding on their labels. When a customer buys bar coded items and takes them to the checkout to pay, the shop assistant will use a bar code reader which transmits the bar coded data to a central processor in the store. The computer then provides the price of the item being purchased (from a price list held on the stock file) and this is output to the cashier's check-out point.

4.12 At the same time, the data about the purchases that have been read into the computer from the bar codes can be used to **update the stock file** and **record the sales data** for management information purposes.

4.13 Many retail stores have introduced **Electronic Point of Sale (EPOS)** devices, using bar coding, which act both as cash registers and as terminals connected to a main computer. This enables the computer to produce **useful management information** such as sales details and analysis and stock control information **very quickly**. The provision of immediate sales information (for example, which products sell quickly), perhaps analysed on a branch basis, permits great speed and flexibility in **decision-making** (certainly of a short-term nature), as consumer wishes can be responded to quickly.

## Card reading devices

*Magnetic stripe cards*

4.14 The face of the card contains the name of the **issuer**, the **payments system** the card applies to (for example VISA), and often a **hologram image** for security purposes. The customer's **name**, the card **number** and the card **expiry date** also appear.

4.15 However, none of this surface information is strictly necessary for data input to a computer system. All the machine-sensible data is contained on the back, on a **magnetic stripe**, which is a thin strip of magnetic recording tape stuck to the back of the card. The magnetic card reader converts this information into directly computer-sensible form.

4.16 The widest application of magnetic stripe cards is as bank credit or service cards, for use in **automated teller machines** (ATMs) and bank payment systems. Many retailers have now introduced systems for the **Electronic Funds Transfer at the Point Of Sale** (EFTPOS) (see the next chapter).

*Smart cards*

4.17 A smart card is a plastic card in which is embedded a **microprocessor chip**. Smart cards are much **more versatile** than magnetic stripe cards.

4.18 Besides basic account data, a smart card would typically contain a **memory** and a **processing capability**. The smart card is used in a similar way to magnetic stripe cards for money transmission. One of the principal economic advantages of smart cards over magnetic stripe cards is that they are much **harder to duplicate**, and so are more secure. On the other hand, the technology is **more expensive** to produce.

## Voice recognition

4.19 Computer software has been developed that can **convert speech** into computer sensible form: the input device needed in this case is simply a **microphone**. Speech needs to be slow and clear for best results.

## Activity 10.6

In view of the above, what are the advantages and disadvantages of *keyboard* input?

## 5 OUTPUT DEVICES

5.1 The commonest methods of computer output are **printers** and **screen display.**

### The choice of output medium

5.2 Choosing a suitable output medium depends on a number of factors.

| Factor | Comment |
| --- | --- |
| Hard copy | Is a hard copy of the output required; in other words, is a printed version of the output needed? If so, what quality must the output be? |
| Volume | The **volume** of information produced may affect the choice. For example, a VDU screen can hold a certain amount of data, but it becomes more difficult to read when information goes 'off-screen' and can only be read a 'page' at a time. |
| Speed | The **speed** at which output is required may critical. For example, to print a large volume of data, a high speed printer might be most suitable to finish the work more quickly. If a single enquiry is required, it may be quicker to make notes from a VDU display. |
| Suitability for further use | The **suitability** of the output medium to the purpose for which the output is needed. Output on to a magnetic disk or tape would be appropriate if the data is for further processing. Large volumes of reference data for human users to hold in a library might be held on microfilm or microfiche, and so output in these forms would be appropriate. |
| Cost | Some output devices would not be worth having because their advantages would not justify their **cost**, and so another output medium should be chosen as 'second best'. |

### DEVOLVED ASSESSMENT ALERT

You might be given the task of writing a memo to a colleague explaining which sort of output device was suitable for what circumstances. Alternatively you may have to describe, say, the characteristics of a laser printer to a manager who had asked for advice on what sort of printer to buy.

### Printers

5.3 A **line printer** prints a complete line in a single operation, usually printing between 600 and 1,000 lines per minute. They offer the operational speeds necessary for the **bulk printing requirements** of many systems.

5.4 **Character printers** print a single character at a time. Examples include daisy-wheel printers, dot matrix printers.

(a) Daisy wheel printers are **slow and noisy**, but produce print of a **high quality.** Companies are unlikely to buy new daisy wheel printers today because other types printers are more versatile.

(b) Dot matrix printers are quite widely used in accounting departments. Their main drawback is the **low-resolution** of their printed characters, which is unsuitable for many forms of printed output. They are also relatively **slow**.

5.5 **Inkjet** printers are small and prices start at less than £100, making them popular where a 'private' output device is required, for example in a director's office. They work by sending a jet of ink on to the paper to produce the required characters. They are fairly **quiet and fast**, but they may produce **smudged** output if the paper is not handled carefully.

5.6 **Laser printers** print a whole page at a time, rather than line by line. Unlike daisywheel and dot matrix printers, they print on to individual **sheets of paper** (in the same way as photocopiers do) and so they do not use 'tractor fed' continuous computer stationery.

5.7 The resolution of printed characters and diagrams with laser printers is **very high** and this high-quality resolution makes laser printing output good enough to be used for commercial printing.

5.8 Typically, a desk-top laser printer will print about 8 or 10 A4 pages per minute, although faster speeds are possible. **High speed** laser printers print up to 500 pages per minute. Laser printers are a microprocessor in their own right, with **RAM memory** for storing data prior to printing.

5.9 Laser printers are **more expensive** than other types (£400 or more for a sturdy model capable of a reasonable volume of output). However, it is quite possible that several users will be able to **share** a single laser printer.

5.10 There are several **advantages** of laser printers.

(a) They can be used to combine different **fonts**, for example italics or bold characters, and a wide range of characters, including mathematical symbols and Greek letters.

(b) They can be used to produce **graphics** and logos as well as characters. A firm can therefore produce letter-heads as well as the letters themselves on to blank paper using a laser printer.

(c) They are **quiet,** because unlike daisy wheel and dot matrix printers, laser printers are not impact printers which rely on the striking of hammers or pins.

## The VDU

5.11 Screens were described earlier in this chapter, as they are used together with computer keyboards for **input**. It should also be clear that they can be used as an **output** medium, primarily where the output **volume is low** (for example a single enquiry) and **no permanent output** is required (for example the current balance on an account).

### Activity 10.7

Buy a PC magazine (ideally) or else visit a shop such as Dixons that sells PCs. Name two manufacturers for each of the following items.

(a) PCs
(b) Scanners
(c) Modems
(d) Printers

## 6    STORAGE DEVICES

### Disks

6.1    Disks are the predominant form of backing storage. Disks are covered on both sides with a **magnetic** material. Data is held on a number of circular, concentric **tracks** on the surfaces of the disk, and is read or written by rotating the disk past read/write heads, which can write data from the CPU's memory on to disk, or can read data from the disk for input to the CPU's memory. The mechanism that causes the disk to rotate is called a **disk drive**.

### Hard disks

6.2    A modern business PC invariably has an **internal hard disk,** but external disks may be used too. At the time of writing the average new **PC** has a hard disk size of **6 to 8 Gigabytes** ($2^{30}$ bytes), but 10 Gb disks (or more) are common. The standard size has increased dramatically over recent years as ever more Windows-based software, which is hungry for hard disk space, is released.

6.3    A **Zip Drive** is a **removable** 100 megabyte hard disk for PCs. The drive is suitable for back-up, mass storage or for moving files between computers.

### Floppy disks

6.4    A 'floppy' disk is an **exchangeable** circular, flexible disk ($3^{1}/_{2}$ inches in diameter) which is held permanently in a plastic case. The case can bear an identification label for recognising the disk. A $3^{1}/_{2}$" disk can hold up to **1.44 Mb** of data. The floppy disk provides a **cost-effective** means of on-line storage for small business computer systems.

6.5    The data on floppy disks can be **easily corrupted**. In particular, they are subject to **physical wear,** because the read/write head actually comes into contact with the disk surface during operation.

### Tape storage

6.6    Like an audio or video cassette, data has to be recorded **along the length** of a computer tape and so it is **more difficult to access** (compare the time it takes to find your favourite record on an audiocassette compared with the time it takes with a vinyl record or CD).

6.7    In using tapes, it is not practical to read from and then write on to a single piece of tape. **Reading and writing are separate operations**, using separate heads, and so two drives are necessary for the two operations.

6.8    It follows that magnetic tape as a file storage medium is only practical when **every record** on the file will be **processed in turn**. For example a supermarket's stock records might have movements in every item of stock every day, and so tape would be a suitable for **backing up** at the end of the day.

6.9    Tape cartridges have a **larger capacity** than floppy disks and they are still widely used as a **backing storage** medium. Some are similar to but larger in size than a normal audio cassette, some are larger and some are about the size of a dictaphone mini-cassette. They are generally measured in terms of tape width and length. For instance an 8mm tape that is 112m long can store up to **5Gb** of data; a 4mm tape of 125m can store up to **12Gb**. Fast tapes which can be used to create a back-up file very quickly are known as **tape streamers**.

6.10 Tapes can only be **updated** by producing a completely new carried forward tape, and this provides an automatic means of **data security**. The brought forward tapes can be kept for two or three 'generations' to safeguard against the loss of data on a current file.

6.11 This **'grandfather-father-son' technique** allows for files to be reconstructed if a disaster should occur. Once the stipulated number of generations has passed, the former 'grandfather' tape can be purged and used again for other processing.

## CD-ROM

6.12 Optical disks, which use similar technology to the laser-based compact disc audio system, are being used increasingly for data storage. Optical disks have **very high capacity** compared with other media and they are **more difficult to damage**: these advantages suggest that they are likely to develop into the main form of removable storage in the future. PCs are now automatically supplied with a CD-ROM drive.

6.13 The initials ROM stand for **read-only memory**. This means that all data is implanted onto the disc when it is made, and subsequent users can only **retrieve** information, they cannot alter or overwrite or delete what is already on the disk. The **speed** of a CD-ROM drive is relevant to how fast data can be retrieved: an **eight speed** drive is quicker than a **four speed** drive.

6.14 CD recorders are now available for general business use with blank CDs (CD-R), but this does not alter the fact that, until recently CDs have not been reusable in the way that floppy disks are. This is why PCs invariably have floppy disk drives as well as CD-ROM drives. However, **a rewritable disk** (CD-RW) is now available. A CD can hold up to **650 Mb** of data.

## DVD

6.15 Digital Versatile Disk (DVD) technology can store almost 5 gigabytes of data on one disk. Access speeds are improved as is sound and video quality. Many commentators believe DVD will not only replace CD ROMs, but also VHS cassettes, audio CDs and laser discs. Read the case example below

---

### Case example: DVD

CD-Roms are rapidly becoming obsolete as far as new media are concerned. The replacement is Digital Versatile Disk (DVD) Rom technology which can store almost 5 gigabytes of data with excellent access speeds, and Internet-based technologies which promise three-dimensional worlds, CD-quality sound, and video.

DVD will take a couple of years to become established as a standard, and in the meantime, CD-Rom titles combining Internet links will fill the gap. Local CD-Rom or DVD-Rom disks will provide PC users with much of the graphics and audio content since sending such large files over the Internet will remain a slow process, at least for the next few years until faster communications technologies become available.

DVD has a key advantage in that it will be backward compatible with current CD-ROMs which will protect the user's current investment in CD-ROM titles while adding the superior capabilities of DVD.

*Financial Times*

---

## Document image processing

6.16 Document image processing (DIP) is an electronic form of filing. In a DIP system, a document is passed through a **scanner**, translated into **digital form** and a digitised image is then stored on a storage device (perhaps an **optical disk**). (This can then be retrieved at will and shown on a computer screen. The image of the document can include handwriting and printed text.)

6.17 The **advantages** of DIP are as follows.

- **Reduced space** needed for files
- The same file can be viewed by **different users** simultaneously
- Files **cannot be** 'lost' as the original image is on disk
- **Faster retrieval** of files than with a manual system

6.18 One optical disk could contain **60,000 pages of A4** (this could range from 60,000 single page letters to over 1,000 sets of accounts.) The main cost savings of using DIP over paper are in storage and retrieval, as the time taken to hunt for a file is eliminated. In order for these savings to be achieved, documents must be scanned as soon as they are received by the mail room, for computer usage.

6.19 Applications of DIP include **electronic data interchange, desktop publishing** (by enabling photographs, for example, or other images to be stored) and management of **accounting transactions** - all the documentation relating to an accounting transaction can be referenced to the ledger record: an entry in the sales ledger for example could be accompanied by images of all the related paperwork.

---

### Key learning points

- A computer may be defined as a device which will accept input data, process it according to programmed logical and arithmetic rules, store and output data and/or calculate results. Computers have traditionally been classified as supercomputers, mainframes, minicomputers and microcomputers, but the distinctions are vague nowadays.

- The processor is at the heart of any computer. It consists of an arithmetic and logic unit, a control unit and a memory. Important concepts are clock speed (MHz) and RAM.

- Data for input may originally be recorded manually on a keyboard. Alternatively, data for input may originally be recorded in computer-sensible form, for example via a document reading device. The ideal method of data input in a given application is one which minimises input time, cost, errors and the period before receipt of output.

- Output might be human-sensible, which means that it can be recognised and understood by humans (printed, visual or sound output) and uses a printer, the VDU or speakers, or computer-sensible, with output stored for later processing or for processing by another computer.

- The most common types of storage are magnetic disk and magnetic tape, though optical storage on CD is becoming more common. Document image processing systems allow documents to be scanned and then filed in electronic form.

---

## Quick quiz

1  How does a computer process data? (*Hint:* look at the Key Term)

2  Define hardware.

3  Why do some organisations still use mainframes?

4  What types of medium and small business computers are there?

5      What is the difference between MegaHertz and megabytes?

6      What is RAM?

7      List ten input devices.

8      What five factors affect the choice of output medium?

9      What sort of printer prints a whole page at a time?

10     Why are disks the predominant form of backing storage?

11     How much can be stored on a CD-ROM?

## Answers to quick quiz

1      According to programmed logical and arithmetic rules.

2      The various physical components which comprise a computer system.

3      Because they have to process very large volumes of data and have special security needs. (Or because they can't afford to replace an old mainframe with a completely new system.)

4      Minicomputers, PCs, file servers and portables (or laptops) are the main types.

5      MegaHertz measure the *cycles* of the computer's internal clock. Megabytes measure *bits* of data (0s and 1s).

6      Random Access Memory is directly available to the processing unit. It holds the data and programs in current use. Data can be written on to or read from RAM.

7      Keyboard, VDU, mouse, MICR reader, scanner, optical mark reader, turnaround document, bar code, magnetic stripe card, smart card, microphone.

8      Hard copy requirements, volume, speed, suitability for further use and cost.

9      A laser printer.

10     Because they offer direct (ie immediate) access to data, unlike tapes.

11     Up to 650 Mb.

## Answers to activities

## Answers 10.1 - 10.2

These are *practical* activities. Make sure you do them!

## Answer 10.3

(a)   1 million or, more accurately, $2^{20}$ = 1,048,576.

(b)   1,000 or, more accurately, 1,024.

      ($2^{30}/2^{20}$ = 1,073,741, 824/1,048,576 = 1,024)

(c)   1 letter = 1 byte, so 300 × 5 letters = 1,500 bytes or about 1.5 Kb.

      If you test this out on a computer you will find that a 300 word document takes up more than 1.5kb, because the program you use to create it (eg Microsoft Word) adds in additional data of its own such as date created, name of computer user, time spent editing and so on.

      For instance, a 300 word document created using Word 97 may take up 20kb or more. Using a simpler word processor, such as Notepad, it would take up less than 2kb.

## Answer 10.4

The program is being read from the PC's hard disk into its RAM. There will be more crackling and flickering if you open an existing document or if you wish to use a part of the program that is not automatically loaded when the program starts.

(For instance, start up Microsoft Word and then click on Format ... Paragraph, or Tools... Spelling. You will hear and see the hard drive talking to the RAM.)

# Answer 10.5

A basic keyboard includes the following.

(a)     Ordinary **typing keys** used to enter data or text.

(b)     A separate **numeric key pad** for use with the built-in calculator.

(c)     **Cursor control** keys, basically up/down/left/right **arrow** keys to move the cursor.

(d)     Additional **cursor keys**, such as Home, End, Pg Up and Pg Dn, for rapid movement through documents/files.

(e)     A number of **function keys** (usually 12) for use by the system and application software. Each represents a particular command or string of commands.

(f)     **Return** or **Enter** key. All commands direct to the system must be 'entered' with this key.

(g)     **Esc**ape key. This key can be used to exit from a procedure.

(h)     Control (**Ctrl**) key and Alternate (**Alt**) key. These tell the machine that a command is about to be entered.

(i)     A **Windows 95** keyboard has three extra keys which operate the '**Start**' button where the Windows 95 operating system is being used.

# Answer 10.6

By far the most significant **advantage** of direct input via keyboard is that a computer user can have **interactive processing** using a keyboard and VDU. Interactive processing is when data can be input to a computer, output information received quickly, and where appropriate further input keyed in and output received. The computer user gets the information he or she wants 'instantly'.

The other advantages of keyboard input are as follows.

(a)     The person keying in the data can be in a **location far away** from the computer itself, with the keyboard terminal linked to the computer by telephone link or private wire. The source document never has to leave the computer user's office and so the data is always under the user's own control.

(b)     The person keying in the data can **check it on the VDU** before inputting it to the computer. Any keying errors, or even errors in the data itself, might be identified and corrected on the spot.

(c)     Keyboard input is convenient for **small volumes** of data when the time taken up by data input is only short. Most microcomputer systems in offices use keyboard and VDU for data input.

Direct keyboard input has a number of **disadvantages**.

(a)     It is unsuitable for **large volumes** of transaction data. Keying in takes a long time (in computer terms), and when a keyboard terminal is on-line to a computer, the CPU is idle for much of the time. Input via tape or disk makes much better use of the computer's processing capabilities, and processing is much faster as a result.

(b)     Keyboard input is likely to be **error-prone** because the only data verification that can be done is a visual check of the data on the VDU screen before input.

(c)     There might be **security problems**. Keyboard terminals are less 'secure' than a computer centre, and there is a possibility that unauthorised users can gain access to a keyboard terminal in an office (or that unauthorised people can gain access from their own personal terminal to someone else's computer).

# Answer 10.7

*Major* manufacturers include the following.

(a)     PCs - Dell, Compaq, IBM, Hewlett Packard, Viglen, Elonex
(b)     Scanners - Canon, Epson, Hewlett Packard
(c)     Modems - Hayes, Motorola, US Robotics
(d)     Printers - Brother, Canon, Epson, Hewlett Packard, Lexmark

There are many others.

# Chapter 11 Computer networks and data communications

---

## Chapter topic list

1   Computer configurations

2   LANs, WANs and client-server computing

3   Data communications

---

## Learning objectives

On completion of this chapter you will be able to:

|  | Performance criteria | Range Statement |
|---|---|---|
| • Identify improvements/suggest changes to: | 21.3.1, 21.3.2 | |
|    o  different types of hardware configuration (eg PC, network, mainframe) | | |
|    o  Local Area Networks | | |
|    o  Wide Area Networks | | |
|    o  the Client/Server approach and file servers | | |
|    o  telecommunications | | |
| • Understand the range of computerised MIS | | 21.3.1 |
| • Identify potential improvements to the MIS and consider them for their impact on the quality of the system and any interrelated systems | 21.3.1 | |
| • Make suggestions for changes supported by a clear rationale as to how they could improve the quality of the system | 21.3.2 | |
| • Assess and clearly state whether assumptions and judgements made are reliable | 21.3.3 | |
| • Present suggestions clearly and in a way which helps people to understand and act on them | 21.3.5 | |
| • _Describe an organisation's computer software, systems and networking_ | n/a | n/a |

Italicised objectives are areas of knowledge and understanding underlying the elements of competence for Unit 21.

_BPP_ PUBLISHING

## 1    COMPUTER CONFIGURATIONS

1.1    The term **configuration** refers to the way in which computers are **linked together**.

(a)    At one extreme an organisation may have just a **single** 'stand-alone' computer that can only be used by one person at a time.

(b)    At the other extreme an organisation may have **hundreds or thousands** of computers, all able to be used simultaneously and to communicate with each other – a network.

### Centralised processing

1.2    Centralised processing means holding and processing data in a central place, such as a **computer centre** at head office. Data will be collected at 'remote' (ie geographically separate) offices and other locations and sent in to the central location.

1.3    At the central location there will be:

(a)    A **central computer**, either a mainframe or powerful sever PC.
(b)    **Central files**, containing all the files needed for the system.

### Decentralised processing

1.4    Decentralised processing means having the data/information processing carried out at several **different locations**, away from the 'centre' or 'head office'. Each region, department or office will have its own processing systems, and so:

(a)    There will be several different and **unconnected computers** in the various offices.
(b)    Each computer will operate with its own **programs** and its own **files.**

### Multi-user and distributed systems

1.5    In practice, information systems do not have to be entirely centralised or entirely decentralised, and a suitable **mixture of centralisation and decentralisation** is now normally used.

(a)    Local offices can have their own **local systems**, perhaps on PC, and also input some data to a centralised processing system.

(b)    Computer systems can be **networked,** and there might be:

(i)    A **multi-user system**, or
(ii)    A '**distributed**' data processing system.

---

### Activity 11.1

When would you expect a **stand-alone** computer to be used?

---

*Multi-user systems*

1.6    With a multi-user system there is a central computer with a number of terminals connected to it. The terminals are **dumb terminals,** which means that they do not include a CPU and so **cannot do independent data processing**. A dumb terminal relies on the central computer for its data processing power.

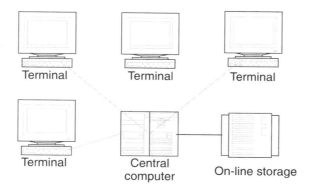

1.7 Many users, each with their own VDU and keyboard, might be connected to the same computer, with the capability for all the users to carry out processing work **simultaneously**.

1.8 The terminals in a multi-user system might be sited in the **same room** or building as the central computer, or may be **geographically distant** from the central computer, connected by an external data link.

### KEY TERM

**Remote access** describes access to a central computer installation from a terminal which is physically 'distant'.

## Distributed processing

1.9 Distributed processing links several computers together. A typical system might consist of a mainframe computer, linked to local mini-computers, linked to desktop PCs as **intelligent terminals**, and to a range of peripheral equipment.

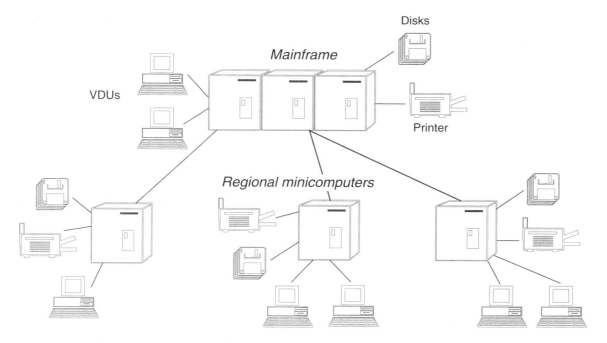

**KEY TERM**

A **distributed system** is a combination of processing hardware located at a central place, eg a mainframe computer, with other, usually smaller, computers located at various sites within the organisation. The central and dispersed computers are linked by a communications network.

(CIMA, *Computing Terminology*)

1.10 The key features of distributed processing are as follows.

(a) Computers distributed or spread over a **wide geographical area**.

(b) A computer can **access** the information files of **other computers** in the system.

(c) The ability for computers within the system to **process data 'jointly'** or **'interactively'**.

(d) **Processing** is **either** carried out centrally, or at dispersed locations.

(e) **Files** are held **either** centrally or at local sites.

(f) **Authority is decentralised** as processing can be performed autonomously by local computers.

(g) **End-users** of computing facilities are given responsibility for, and control over, their own data.

## Networks

**KEY TERM**

A **network** is an interconnected collection of **autonomous** processors, for example a number of connected PCs.

1.11 There are two main types of network, a **local area network** (LAN) and a **wide area network** (WAN).

1.12 The key idea of a network is that users need **equal access to resources** such as data, but they do not necessarily have to have equal computing power.

1.13 LANs, WANs and this **'client-server'** concept are so important in modern computing that they deserve a section to themselves.

**Activity 11.2**

See if you can draw diagrams representing:

(a) a centralised system
(b) a decentralised system
(c) a multi-user system
(d) a distributed system
(e) a network

## 2 LANS, WANS AND CLIENT-SERVER COMPUTING

### Local area networks (LANs)

2.1 A *local area network* (LAN) is a network of computers located in a single building or on a **single site**. The parts of the network are linked by **computer cable** rather than via telecommunications lines.

### *Network topologies*

2.2 Network topology means the physical arrangement of items (**nodes**) in a network. A **node** is any device connected to a network: it can be a computer, or a peripheral device such as a printer.

2.3 There are several types of LAN system configuration. For example, in a **bus structure** (shown below), messages are sent out from one point along a single communication channel, and the messages are received by other connected machines. Bus systems generally use a network standard called *Ethernet*, and this is the most popular LAN technology in use.

2.4 Each device can **communicate with every other device** and communication is quick and reliable. Nodes can be **added or unplugged** very easily. Locating cable faults is also relatively simple.

*Bus system*

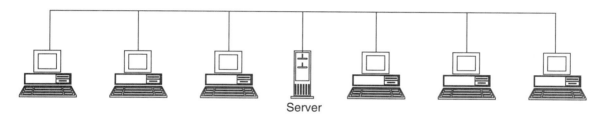

Server

2.5 Local area networks have been **successful** for a number of reasons. First of all, personal computers of sufficient **power** and related software were developed, so that network applications became possible. Networks have been made available to computer users at a fairly **low price**. Some computer users who could not afford a mainframe or minicomputer with terminal links have been able to afford a LAN with personal computers and software packages.

BPP PUBLISHING

### Activity 11.3

Look at the illustration below. A computer user who is connected to a network has clicked on the Network Neighbourhood icon and the window shown beneath it has appeared.

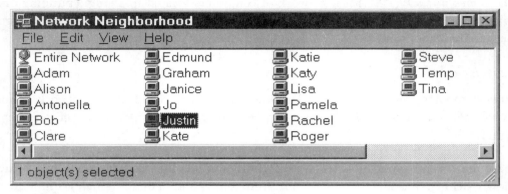

What will happen if the user does the following things?

(a) Clicks with his mouse on Entire Network once and then presses the Delete button on his keyboard.

(b) Highlights Justin and then double clicks with his mouse.

## Wide area networks (WANs)

2.6 **Wide area networks** (WANs) are networks on a number of sites, perhaps on a wide geographical scale. WANs often use minicomputers or mainframes as the 'pumps' that keep the data messages circulating, whereas shorter-distance LANs normally use PCs for this task.

2.7 A wide area network is similar to a local area network in concept, but the key differences are as follows.

(a) The **geographical area** covered by the network is greater, not being limited to a single building or site.

(b) WANs will send data over **telecommunications links.**

(c) WANs will often use a **larger computer** as a file server.

(d) WANs will often be larger than LANs, with **more terminals or computers** linked to the network.

(e) A WAN can link two or more LANs, using **gateways**.

    (i) Connections may be **leased**. This is the preferred option where there is a high volume of inter-office communication.

    (ii) Connections may be made over the **public telephone network**. Standard call charges will apply, so this is beneficial where communication levels are relatively low.

## Client-server computing

2.8 The term client-server computing has gained widespread usage. This is a way of describing the relationship between the devices in a network. With client-server computing, the tasks that need to be carried out are shared among the various machines on the network.

## KEY TERMS

A **client** is a machine which requests a service, for example a PC running a spreadsheet application which the user wishes to print out.

A **server** is a machine which is dedicated to providing a particular function or service requested by a client. Servers include file servers (see below), print servers, e-mail servers and fax servers.

2.9 A client-server system allows **computer power** to be distributed to where it is most needed. The **client**, or user, will use a powerful personal workstation with local processing capability. The **server** provides services such as shared printers, communications links, special-purpose processing and database storage.

2.10 A server computer (or file server) may be a powerful PC or a minicomputer. As its name implies, it **serves** the rest of the network offering a generally-accessible hard disk file for all the other processors in the system and sometimes offering other resources, such as a **shared printer** for the network.

2.11 Clients on a network generally have their **own hard disk** storage capability. The server's hard disk can also be **partitioned** into separate drives for use by each node, and **programs** or data (eg a database) for **common use** can be stored on the file server. Accounting packages written for small businesses are usually available in a multi-user version for this purpose.

*File servers*

2.12 File servers must be powerful enough to handle **multiple user requests** and provide **adequate storage**. File servers are typically classified as 'low end' or 'high end'.

(a) A **low end file server** might be used in a network of around six users, running 'office' type software. A low end server might be a dedicated machine or might be a highly specified standard PC. Once it is asked to support more than 10 users, it will probably need replacing and can be 'demoted' for use as a desktop PC.

(b) It might be replaced by a '**mid range server**'. A mid range server might support 20-30 users.

(c) A **high end file server** might be used in a large department network of about 50-100 users handling transaction processing and an accounting system. High end servers have now been joined by **superservers** and '**enterprise servers**' (effectively, mainframes). These are either departmental or organisation-wide, running sophisticated mission-critical systems and offering fault tolerance features. They might support upwards of 250 users.

*Network operating systems*

2.13 To carry out the administrative tasks connected with operating a network a special 'operating system' is required. This establishes the links between the nodes of the network, monitors the operation of the network and controls recovery processes when the system or part of it breaks down. The main examples are **Novell Netware** and Microsoft **Windows NT. UNIX** is also used on larger systems. There is more on operating systems in the next Chapter.

## The advantages of client/server computing

2.14 The advantages of the network approach using the client/server model are as follows.

| Advantage | Comment |
| --- | --- |
| Greater resilience | Processing is spread over several computers, so client/server systems are more resilient. If one server breaks down, other locations can carry on processing. |
| Scalability | They are highly scalable. In other words instead of having to buy computing power in large quantities you can buy just the amount of power you need to do the job. When you need more you simply add another server. |
| Shared programs and data | Program and data files held on a file server can be shared by all the PCs in the network. With stand-alone PCs, each computer would have its own data files, and there might be unnecessary duplication of data. |
| | A system where everyone uses the same data will help to improve data processing and decision making. The value of some information increases with its availability. |
| Shared work-loads | Each PC in a network can do the same work. |
| | If there were separate stand-alone PCs, A might do job 1, B might do job 2, C might do job 3 and so on. In a network, any PC, (A, B or C) could do any job (1, 2 or 3). This provides flexibility in sharing work-loads. In a peak period for job 1, say, two or more people can share the work without having to leave their own desk. |
| Shared peripherals | Peripheral equipment can be shared. For example, in a LAN, five PCs might share a single on-line printer, whereas if there were stand-alone PCs, each might be given its own separate printer. If resources are scarce (for example fast laser printers) this is a significant benefit. |
| Communication and time management | LANs can be linked up to the office communications network, thus adding to the processing capabilities in an office. Electronic mail can be used to send messages, memos and electronic letters from node to node. Electronic calendar and diary facilities can also be used. |
| Compatibility | Client/server systems are more likely than centralised systems to have Windows interfaces, making it easier to move information between applications such as spreadsheets and accounting systems. |
| Ad hoc enquiries | They enable information to be moved to a separate server, allowing managers to make ad hoc enquiries without disrupting the main system. |

## The disadvantages of client/server computing

2.15 The client/server approach has some drawbacks.

(a) **Mainframes** are better at dealing with **very large volumes** of transactions.

(b) It is easier to **control** and **maintain** a system centrally. In particular it is easier to keep data **secure**.

(c) It may be **cheaper** to 'tweak' an existing mainframe system rather than throwing it away and starting from scratch: for example it may be possible to give it a graphical user interface and to make data exchangeable between Windows and non-Windows based applications.

(d) Each location may need its own expert **network administrator** to keep things running smoothly, so there may be unnecessary duplication of **skills** and **overmanning**.

(e) Duplication of **data** may be a problem if individual users do not follow a disciplined approach.

## 3    DATA COMMUNICATIONS

3.1 Typical means of communication are oral communication, paper-based communication and electronic communication.

| Method | Comment |
|---|---|
| Oral communication | Oral communication may occur in a **face-to-face** situation or by **telephone**. The chief accountant may telephone the sales ledger department to find out when payment of an overdue debt is expected. The request and the response are both provided verbally. |
| Paper | Paper-based communication methods include the use of internal **memoranda**, computer **printouts** and monthly **accounting reports**. Thus copies of despatch notes raised might be sent to the relevant department to be physically matched with customer orders, so that invoices can be raised. This method means that there is a permanent 'hard copy' record of each transaction. This method may be **cheaper** than electronic communication, as data communications links do not need to be set up. The disadvantages are that there may be a **delay** in the delivery of information, particularly between sites, and the necessity for data transcription increases the **risk of error**. |
| Electronic or digital | Much information is exchanged by **computer**. Thus details of despatches of goods from stock might be automatically passed to the sales ledger or accounting subsystem by the warehousing/stock control subsystem, so that invoices can be raised. Digital communication is also possible for one-off messages, for example through the use of **electronic mail**. Benefits of digital communication are speed, accuracy and the elimination of much human processing. |

## Activity 11.4

What are the advantages and disadvantages of oral communication?

3.2 When all data processing is done in the **same office,** no serious problem should arise with the transmission of data between input and output devices and the central processor. The equipment will be joined together by **internal cable**.

3.3 When the input or output device is located away from the computer, so that it has to be transmitted along a **telecommunications** link (for example a telephone line) there are additional items of data transmission equipment which have to be used, and the way in which the data is to be transmitted has to be resolved.

3.4 A data link might typically connect the following.

(a) A **computer** and a **remote terminal** (keyboard and VDU). A computer may have a number of remote terminals linked to it by data transmission equipment.

(b) **Two computers** located some distance from each other (for example a mainframe and a PC, which would use the link to exchange data).

(c) Several **processors** in a **network**, with each computer in the network able to transmit data to any other.

## Data transmission terminology

3.5 Here are some terms you are likely to encounter in the context of data communications.

*Modems and digital transmission*

3.6 New technologies require transmission systems capable of delivering substantial quantities of data at great speed. For data transmission through the existing 'analogue' telephone network to be possible, there has to be a device at each end of the telephone line that can convert (MOdulate) the data from digital form to analogue form, and (DEModulate) from analogue form to digital form, depending on whether the data is being sent out or received along the telephone line. This conversion of data is done by devices called **modems**. There must be a modem at each end of the telephone line.

3.7 **Digital** means 'of digits or numbers'. Digital information is information in a coded (binary) form. Information in analogue form uses continuously variable signals. It is enough for you to appreciate that there is a distinction between the two and that digital methods are more advanced.

3.8 Modern PCs generally have a modem fitted **internally**. The current standard is a modem that can transmit or receive 56.6 megabits per second.

*Multiplexors*

3.9 In some computer systems, several PCs share the same data link. A **multiplexor** is used where it is necessary to send data from **several sources** down a **single line** at the same time. It codes the data in a special way so that it can be sorted out at its destination. Where a number of terminals are linked to the control computer, the multiplexor is an essential piece of hardware handling the input/output and reducing line charges (as only one line, rather than several, is necessary).

*Bandwidth*

3.10 The amount of data that can be sent down a telecommunications line is in part determined by the bandwidth. **Bandwidth** is the range of frequencies that the channel can carry. Frequencies are measured in cycles per second, or in **Hertz**. The wider the bandwidth, the greater the number of messages that a channel can carry at any particular time.

*Baud rate*

3.11 Baud rate is a measure of the speed of data transmission and roughly equates to number of bits per second. (**300 baud is roughly equal to 300 bits per second,** so at 300 baud the words in bold here could be transmitted in one second.)

*Interfaces*

3.12 The term **interface** is frequently used in computer communications contexts, but it has at least three different meanings.

| INTERFACE | |
|---|---|
| **What links two systems** | The point at which two applications software systems are linked. For example, the *interface* between a computerised purchase ledger and a nominal ledger will normally consist of an analysis file produced by the purchase ledger being read by an *interface program* in the nominal ledger. |
| **How you communicate with the computer** | The point of interaction between the computer and the user, principally in terms of using a display screen for input and retrieval of information. The two principal forms of interface are often described as *Graphical User Interface* (GUI) or Character-based User Interface (CUI). GUIs (eg Windows) are now generally more favoured than CUIs (eg MS-DOS). |
| **Electronic connections** | The circuitry which connects two devices. Interfaces may be: *serial*, in which case data is transmitted as a stream of individual bits through a single wire, or *parallel*, where a number of wires each carry one bit so that eight wires, for example, will enable the eight bits comprising one byte to be transferred simultaneously. |

*Ports*

3.13 In practical terms a **port** is the **socket** on a computer into which you plug a peripheral device such as a printer, although the term is sometimes used interchangeably with the term **interface**. Ports can be serial or parallel, as explained above. Data is converted from **serial** to **parallel** or vice versa by a piece of circuitry called a UART (Universal Asynchronous Receiver/Transmitter).

## ISDN

3.14 An important development is the spread of **Integrated Systems Digital Networks (ISDN)**, which in effect will make the entire telephone network **digital** – it will therefore be possible to send voice, data, video and fax communications from a single desktop computer system over the telecommunication link, **without using a modem.**

*BPP* PUBLISHING

3.15 Integrated Services Digital Network (ISDN) started in 1991 in the UK but use has **grown slowly** because installation and rental charges are perceived as being too high.

3.16 Data can be transmitted significantly **faster** over ISDN than standard communications links, such as analogue lines.

3.17 Advantages of ISDN (besides speed and cost savings on call times) are that:

(a) Computer **networks can be extended** to small branch offices.

(b) A **number of services** can be sent over the link **at one time** (eg it would be possible, for example, for architects to use one telecommunications link to view building plans on a PC, and also to discuss them on a handset).

## Protocols

3.18 One of the big problems in transmitting data down a public or private telephone wire is the possibility of **distortion or loss of the message**. There needs to be some way for a computer to:

(a) Detect whether there are **errors** in data transmission (eg loss of data, or data arriving out of sequence, ie in an order different from the sequence in which it was transmitted).

(b) take steps to **recover** the lost data, even if this is simply to notify the computer or terminal operator to telephone the sender of the message that all the data will have to be re-transmitted. However, a more 'sophisticated' system can identify the corrupted or lost data more specifically, and request re-transmission of only the lost or distorted parts.

3.19 The mechanism used to detect and usually then to correct errors is known as a **communications protocol**.

### KEY TERM

**Protocol** is defined as 'an agreed set of operational procedures governing the format of data being transferred, and the signals initiating, controlling and terminating the transfer'.

## Mobile communications

3.20 Networks for portable telephone communications, also known as 'cellular phones', started up in the late 1980s and have boomed in developed countries.

3.21 **Digital** networks are being installed and are beginning to supersede the early transmission systems. These are better able to support data transmission then the older analogue networks, with higher transmission speeds and less likelihood of data corruption. This means that a salesperson out on the road, say, can send or receive a fax simply by plugging a lap-top PC into a mobile handset. A combined **palmtop** computer and cellular phone is already on the market. **Internet access through mobile phones** will soon be a reality.

## Activity 11.5

One piece of communications hardware that is very common is the telephone? What features would you expect to be available from a telephone system in a modern office?

---

### Key learning points

- **Centralisation** of computer facilities allows the use of a single set of files and offers better security and control. Disadvantages include the extent of local office reliance on head office and the risk of delays in processing.

- A **multi-user system** is a system that appears to serve more than one user at one time. A multi-user system normally has one central computer and set of files which are accessed by a number of dumb terminals.

- **Distributed data processing** is processing done by a distributed system, a system containing a number of separate but connected processors, in which some centralised processing is possible.

- A **local area network** is a system of interconnected PCs (and other devices, such as printers and disks) which are connected by special cable. LANs can have a **server** computer holding files used by more than one computer, and providing storage capacity to the other computers in the network. In a LAN, data processing tasks can be shared between a number of PCs, and single items of peripheral equipment can be accessed by all of them.

- A **wide area network** is a network of computers which are dispersed on a wider geographical scale than LANs. They are connected over the public **telecommunications** network. A WAN will normally use minicomputers or powerful PCs.

- **Client-server** computing is a configuration in which desktop PCs are regarded as 'clients' that request access to the services available on a more powerful server PC, such as access to a file, e-mail, or printing facilities.

- Information may be communicated **orally** or on **paper** or via **electronic means** along **internal cables** or external **telecommunications** links.

- A **modem** is needed at either end of a **conventional** telecommunications link to convert digital signals into analogue signals and vice versa.

- **Digital telecommunications** networks such as ISDN do not require a modem. Digital networks for **mobile** phones also exist.

---

## Quick quiz

1   What is a dumb terminal?

2   What is a distributed system?

3   What does 'autonomous' mean?

4   What is a server?

5   What does 'scalability' mean?

6   What does 'digital' mean?

7   Give three meanings for the term 'interface'.

8   What is a protocol?

BPP
PUBLISHING

## Answers to quick quiz_____

1   A VDU and screen without a CPU and so unable to do processing independently of a central computer.

2   A combination of processing hardware located at a central place with other, usually smaller, computers located at various other sites but linked by a communications network.

3   Literally 'having the right or power of self-government'. PCs in a network are autonomous: they can use a server, but they are not controlled by it.

4   Usually a fairly powerful PC which is dedicated to providing a service requested by a 'client' PC, such as providing access to files or sharing printing facilities.

5   Instead of having to buy computing power in large quantities you can buy just the amount of power you need, and simply add more when more is needed.

6   Literally 'of digits or numbers'. Digital information is information in binary form. It is possible for computer systems to interpret digital information.

7   The interface is what links systems, for instance one program and another; it is how users communicate with computers; it is an electronic connection.

8   An agreed set of operational procedures governing the format of data transferred, and the signals initiating, controlling and terminating the transfer.

## Answers to activities_____

### Answer 11.1_____

Stand-alone computers are used in the following situations.

(a)   When the data processing requirements can be handled by one user with one computer. Very small businesses often have a stand-alone machines for use by an individual, for example for keeping accounts and writing letters.

(b)   Where very large volumes of transaction data are being handled by a mainframe.

(c)   When security or confidentiality could be compromised by the use of a multi-user system, for instance for keeping computerised payroll records.

### Answer 11.2_____

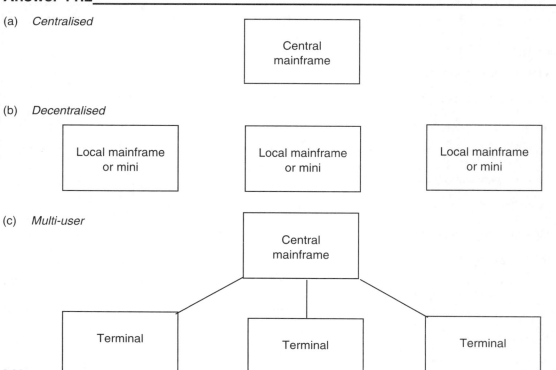

(a)   *Centralised*

Central mainframe

(b)   *Decentralised*

Local mainframe or mini    Local mainframe or mini    Local mainframe or mini

(c)   *Multi-user*

Central mainframe

Terminal    Terminal    Terminal

(d)   *Distributed*

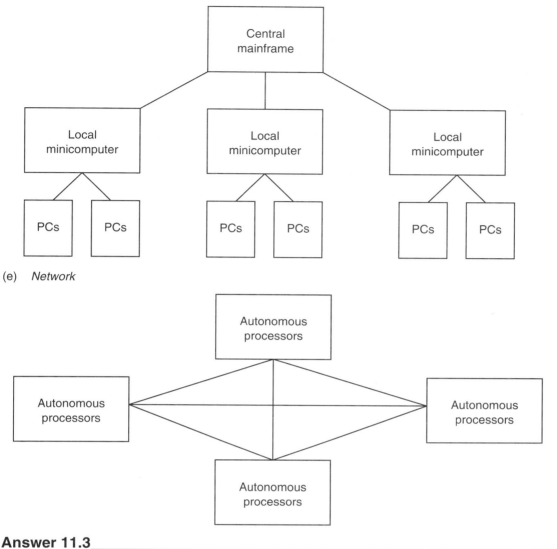

(e)   *Network*

## Answer 11.3

(a)   Hopefully *nothing* will happen except that a message will appear telling the user that he is not *allowed* to delete the entire network (ie delete all the files on everybody's computers)!

Networks can and should be set up to prevent this sort of mischief.

(b)   Double-clicking on Justin would show the resources connected to Justin's PC that are shared by other users of the network, such as Justin's hard disk drive (or part of it) or Justin's printer.

## Answer 11.4

Advantages are that only specified or requested information is provided and that information can be provided immediately. Disadvantages are that the scope for error is increased and there is no permanent record of the communication. The 'human-intensive' nature of the communication can be balanced by the benefits of increased personal contact in the organisation.

## Answer 11.5

Modern telephone systems offer many sophisticated functions. Telephones may have a small display that shows the user the name and number of the person who is ringing them. Group pick-up facilities mean that it is possible to pick up a call coming through on another telephone on the other side of the office without leaving your desk.

## Part C: Improving the MIS

Other features include the following.

(a)    Hands-free operation via a speaker

(b)    Different ringing tones for internal or external calls.

(c)    Different tones for different users (useful in working areas with a large number of telephones)

(d)    Speed dialling - frequently used numbers can be stored in memory and dialled by pressing just one or two keys.

(e)    Call diversion, for times when you know you will not be at your desk.

(f)    Call barring, preventing certain numbers (such as chat lines) from being dialled, or preventing international calls.

(g)    Conference calls allowing more than two people to listen to and take part in a conversation.

BPP PUBLISHING

# Chapter 12  Computer software

---

## Chapter topic list

1  Software

2  The operating system

3  The user interface

4  User-friendliness

5  Applications software

---

## Learning objectives

On completion of this chapter you will be able to:

|  | Performance criteria | Range Statement |
|---|---|---|
| • Identify improvements/suggest changes to: | 21.3.1, 21.3.2 | |
| ○ operating system software (eg MS DOS, Windows)<br>○ output design<br>○ VDU Screen Design<br>○ application software packages | | |
| • Understand the range of computerised MIS | 21.3.1 | 21.3.1 |
| • Identify potential improvements to the MIS and consider them for their impact on the quality of the system and any interrelated systems | 21.3.1 | |
| • Make suggestions for changes supported by a clear rationale as to how they could improve the quality of the system | 21.3.2 | |
| • Assess and clearly state whether assumptions and judgements made are reliable | 21.3.3 | |
| • Present suggestions clearly and in a way which helps people to understand and act on them | 21.3.5 | |
| • *Describe an organisation's computer software, systems and networking* | n/a | n/a |

Italicised objectives are areas of knowledge and understanding underlying the elements of competence for Unit 21.

# 1 SOFTWARE

**KEY TERM**

**Software** is the name given to programs or sets of programs that tell the computer what to do.

1.1 We can identify three separate categories of software. First, we will look at the **operating system**. This provides the link between hardware and software, and it controls the human-computer interface, or HCI.

1.2 **Programming and translation** software is the category you are least likely to come across in practice, so we won't be describing it in much detail. You may of course wish, or need, to write programs for certain applications, but packages are available to support most commercial activities and for anything major you would employ professional programmers anyway.

1.3 The third, and largest, category is **applications** software. This covers everything from specially written software to control train timetabling and signalling on the London Underground to 'pick your National Lottery numbers' programs. We introduce the topic in this chapter and we shall look at examples in more detail in the next chapter.

**Activity 12.1**

Name three examples of software.

# 2 THE OPERATING SYSTEM

2.1 An **operating system** is like a 'silent partner' for the computer user, providing the interface between the computer hardware, the user and other software.

**KEY TERM**

An **operating system** is a program that provides the 'bridge' between **applications** software (such as word processing packages, spreadsheets or accounting packages) and the **hardware**.

For example, access to data files held on disk during the processing of a business application would be managed by the operating system.

2.2 An operating system will typically perform the following tasks.

(a) Initial **set-up** of the computer once it has 'booted up' via the BIOS.

(b) Checking that the **hardware** (including peripheral devices such as printers) is functioning properly.

(c) Calling up of program files and data files from disk storage into **memory**.

(d) **Opening and closing** of files, checking of file labels etc.

(e) Maintenance of **directories** in disk storage.

(f)   Controlling **input and output** devices, including the interaction with the user.

(g)   Controlling system **security** (for example monitoring the use of passwords).

(h)   Handling of **interruptions** (for example program abnormalities or machine failure).

(i)   Managing **multitasking**.

2.3   **Multitasking** means what it says: doing a lot of tasks at once, for example printing out a document you have just finished while you get on with working on the next one.

## UNIX

2.4   The UNIX operating system was developed as a **non-proprietary** (ie not specific to one manufacturer) **multitasking** operating system that could be portable to different computer architectures.

2.5   UNIX works equally well in a PC network environment as in a mainframe system. Particular areas where UNIX has demonstrated its capabilities are **communications**, where the ability to accommodate PC operating systems in the UNIX environment supports the use of electronic mail, and **engineering**, where UNIX's capabilities are suited to driving high-resolution graphics systems.

## PC operating systems

2.6   In the PC market there is a sort of **de facto** open systems arrangement, given that there are so many 'clones' of the PC originally developed by IBM, all of which use versions of a Microsoft operating system, **Windows** .

*Windows*

2.7   Early incarnations of Windows, culminating in **Windows 3.1** and **Windows for Workgroups 3.11**, were not genuine operating systems in their own right, but were really an operating environment for an older Microsoft system called **MS-DOS**.

2.8   **Windows NT** is a complete operating system in its own right, designed for **networks**, and now providing strong competition for other network operating systems like Novell Netware.

2.9   For PCs and smaller networks there is **Windows 95**, and its upgrade Windows 98. Windows 2000 has recently been launched, but it is not yet in widespread use.

### DEVOLVED ASSESSMENT ALERT

The choice of operating system is a key consideration in any task you might be given relating to computer equipment. It also dictates, to some extent what **hardware** is chosen. For instance if you suggest that an organisation uses Windows 98, bear in mind that Windows 98 runs best with at least 32Mb of RAM.

2.10  Features of Windows 95/98 and NT include the following.

(a)   A 'desktop', from which everything in the system branches out. Disk drives, folders (directories), applications and files can all be placed on the desktop.

(b)   A 'taskbar' which includes a **Start** button and buttons representing every open application.

*BPP*
PUBLISHING

(c)  **Long file names** are supported (up to 256 characters).

(d)  There is a **Recycle Bin** for easy deletion and recovery of files.

(e)  Easy integration with widely used **networking** software is possible.

(f)  **Multitasking** is available. It is described as 'true' or pre-emptive multitasking, under which each program is allocated a time slice and tasks switch whenever the operating system dictates.

(g)  The **Microsoft Internet Explorer** browser is included.

2.11  Although it has bugs and irritations for the experienced user, Microsoft Windows provides a **comprehensive working environment**, managing programs specifically written for it. This makes it **easier for beginners** to learn how to use PCs, as most new applications tend to look and 'feel' the same as existing ones.

*Windows 98*

2.12  Other features of Windows 98 are explained in the table below.

| Area | Comments |
|---|---|
| *User-friendly* | User interface enhancements include easier navigation, such as **single-click launching** of applications, icon highlighting, forward/backward buttons, and an easy to customise Start Menu. |
| *Reliability* | (a)  Windows 98 can be set up to regularly **test** the user's hard disk, system files, and configuration information to increase the system reliability, and in many cases fix problems automatically. |
| | (b)  Enhanced **backup** and **restore** functions. |
| *Web integration* | There are a variety of features designed to enhance **Internet access** and use of Internet facilities and technologies, and integrate them with the users system. |
| *More entertaining* | Windows 98 has better **graphics** and **video capabilities** and better support for **games** hardware such as joysticks. It supports **digital video disks** (DVD) and technologies connected with **digital television**. |
| *More manageable for businesses* | Tools such as Dr. Watson and System Information Utility make it easier for IT support staff to **diagnose and correct problems**. |

*Windows 2000*

2.13  **Windows 2000** is a new version of the **Windows** operating system. Windows 2000 is expected to eventually replace Windows NT and Windows 98, but at the time of publication was yet to gain wide acceptance. It is essentially the same product, with enhancements. The overall look and feel is similar to Windows 98

*Apple Macs*

2.14  There are some computer users, particularly those working in design and graphics, who prefer the **Apple Macintosh** system. For an organisation that already has many Apple Macs and many staff familiar with them the best option may be to continue to use them.

*Other operating systems*

2.15 Other competitors to Windows exist, such as **IBM's OS/2** but, since the majority of PC manufacturers send out their products with Windows pre-loaded, this is the system that is likely to predominate.

---

### Activity 12.2

List the tasks typically performed by an operating system.

---

## Windows CE

2.16 Microsoft Windows CE is a **scaled down operating system** for small communications, entertainment and mobile-computing devices. Windows CE allows **non-PC devices** to communicate with each other, share information with Windows-based PCs, and connect to the Internet.

2.17 These include **handheld** PCs, 'wallet' PCs, wireless-communication devices such as digital information **pagers** and **cellular phones,** entertainment and multimedia consoles including **DVD players,** and purpose-built Internet access devices such as **Internet TVs**, digital set-top boxes and Internet 'Web phones.'

## 3 THE USER INTERFACE

### Dialogue design

3.1 The operating system is most obvious to the users of a computer from what they see in front of them and what they have to do to make things happen.

3.2 Most people operate computers using a keyboard and a screen. The important thing about screen and keyboard is the capacity for **'feedback'** between user and computer that they provide, allowing the system to be highly flexible, interactive and conversational.

3.3 This **dialogue** between the system and its users might be a central feature of the running of a program, and the term **conversational mode** describes a method of operation in which the operator appears to be carrying on a continual interactive dialogue with the computer, receiving immediate replies to input messages.

3.4 In modern computing, there are three principle ways of using a keyboard with VDU to input data. Any system is likely to use a combination of the three.

- By selecting options from a **menu**
- By filling in a **form**
- Using a **graphical user interface**

### Menu selection

3.5 A menu is a **list of items to choose from**. For example, a main menu for a sales ledger system might include the following items.

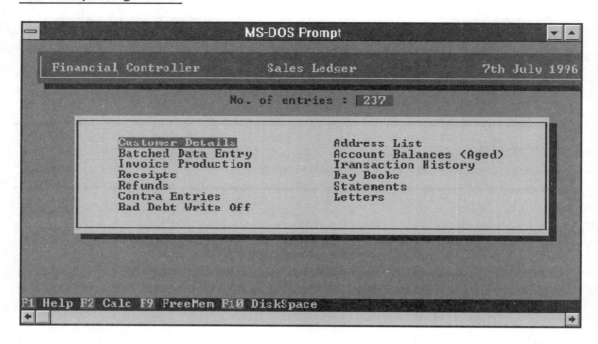

3.6 By selecting **Account Balances (Aged)**, the operator will be specifying that he or she wants to call up a list of account balances. **Another menu** may then be displayed, calling for the operator to narrow down still further the specification of what he or she wants to see, for example by specifying a particular account number or range of codes.

3.7 A menu system is thus a **hierarchical** list of options.

### Activity 12.3

Look at the screen illustration above. This type of display is common in older systems, but not much favoured today.

List two good points about the screen display and two bad points.

### Form filling

3.8 With form filling the screen is landscaped for specific user requirements. Relevant data fields may be set up within an on-screen **skeleton** form.

3.9 **Screen formatting** for this purpose usually includes several features.

- **Different colours** for different screen areas
- **Reverse video** (where colours in a selected area are the reverse of the rest of it)
- **Flashing** items
- **Larger characters** for titles
- Paging or **scrolling** depending on the volume of information

3.10 Data is entered **automatically** in some fields when codes are entered. Other entries are made by **moving the cursor** (the part of the screen that is highlighted or flashing) from one place to the next and typing in the data.

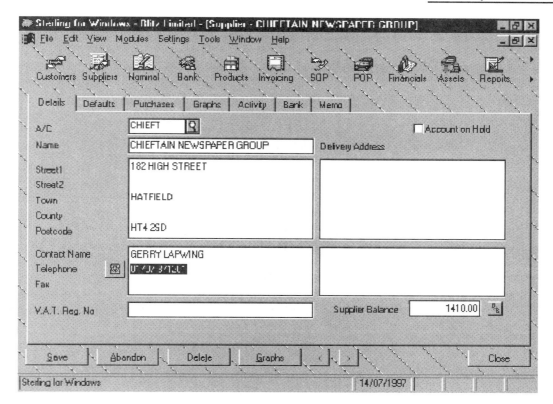

## Graphical user interfaces

3.11 Graphical user interfaces (GUIs) were designed to make computers more '**user-friendly**'.

3.12 A GUI involves the use of two design ideas and two operating methods which can be remembered by the abbreviation **WIMP**. This stands for 'Windows, Icons, Mouse, Pull-down menu' and is an environment which offers a **method of accessing the computer without using the keyboard**. Dialogue is conducted through images rather than typed text.

*Windows*

3.13 This basically means that the screen can be divided into sections, 'windows' of flexible size, which can be opened and closed. This enables **two or more documents to be viewed and edited** together, and sections of one to be inserted into another. For instance figures from an Excel spreadsheet can be pasted directly into a Word word-processing document.

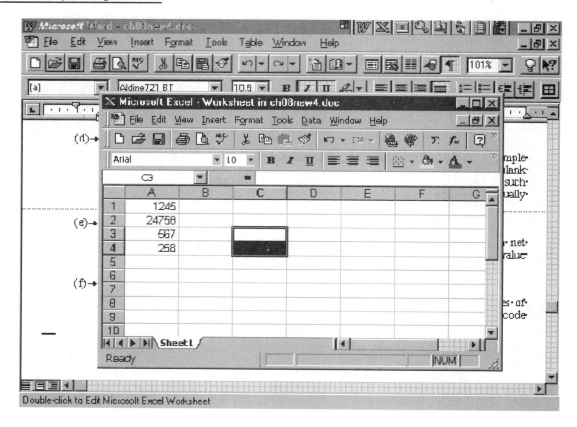

*Icons*

3.14 An icon is an image of an object used to represent a function or a file in an obvious way. For instance Windows based packages use a **picture of a printer** which is simply clicked to start the printing process.

3.15 Icons, windows and menus are shown in the illustration below, which is a Windows 98 'desktop' screen.

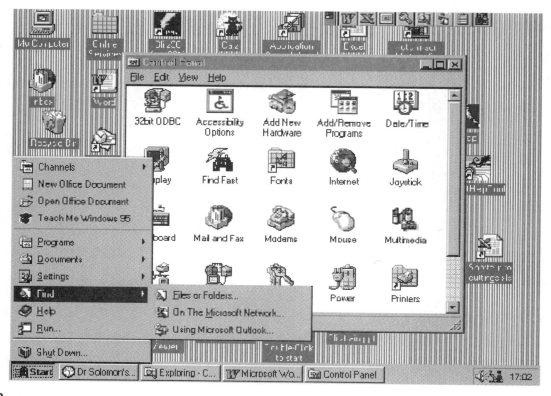

*Mouse*

3.16 As the mouse moves around on the desktop a *pointer* (cursor) on the screen mimics its movements. A mouse can be used to **pick out and activate an icon or button,** to **highlight** a block of text for deletion/insertion, or to **drag** data from one place on the screen to another. It also has buttons which are **clicked** to execute the current command.

*The cursor*

3.17 You know exactly where your next character will be if you enter data on a page by hand or typewriter, and in the same way the cursor (an arrow, line or 'blob') shows you on screen the **point in your text that will be affected** (written on, deleted, moved etc) by your keyboard entries.

3.18 The cursor is a 'marker' of where the **computer's 'attention'** is at any given moment. It is generally moved about the screen by means of direction keys on the keyboard or a mouse.

*Pull-down menu*

3.19 A '**menu-bar**' will be shown across the top of the VDU screen. Using the mouse to move the pointer to the required item in the menu, the pointer '**pulls down**' a subsidiary menu - somewhat similar to pulling down a roller blind at a window. The pointer and mouse can then be used to **select** (input) the required item (output) on the pulled-down menu, which may lead to more menus.

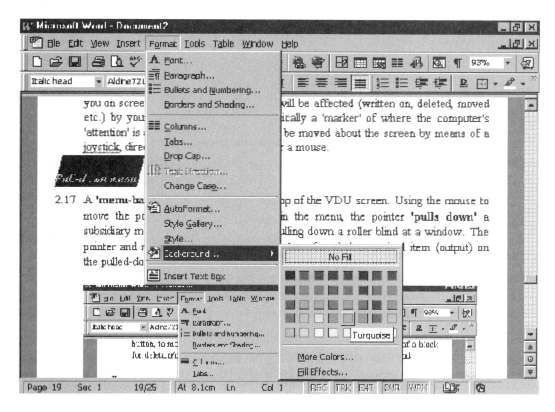

## 4    USER-FRIENDLINESS

4.1 These days most people in an organisation are likely to use a computer and most of these are not computer professionals. The modern trend, therefore, is towards user friendliness, or **ease of use**. The following features all improve the user-friendliness of a system.

## Ease of data entry

4.2     It must be easy for the user to input data into the system. This has several aspects.

(a)   The **data entry screen** should be designed in the **same logical order** as the **input form** (source document).

The user should be able to work down the form in a logical order with the screen cursor moving down the screen to the next input field in the same order. Data entry will be inefficient if the user has to search around for the item to go into the next field.

(b)   The data entry screen should be **clearly designed**, so that, for example, input fields are highlighted, perhaps by **colour, flashing** or **reverse colouring**. The position of the cursor should be clear.

**Titles** of fields should be **easy to read** and should **match** the titles used on **source** documents.

(c)   **Default entries** should be provided for items such as the date (usually today's date) or the standard VAT rate.

The defaults will then be **entered automatically** by the software unless the user wishes to change them. This can speed up data entry considerably.

## Intuitiveness

4.3     It should be possible for users to make **reasonable guesses about what they need to do**.

4.4     For example in Windows a program is started simply by double-clicking on an **icon** that represents that program in an **obvious** way ('W' for Microsoft Word; a bin for deleted items). The user does not need to know where the program is stored on disk or have to type in command words to start up the application.

## Design principles consistent with other modules/packages

4.5     Many computer users use **more than one part of a system**. Even in a non-accounting environment, an increasing number of users must be able to operate a spreadsheet and WP, and, in an accounting environment, it is useful for staff to have 'transferable' skills.

4.6     This means that the more systems can '**look and feel' the same** and operate in a similar way (eg F1 is always 'Help') the easier it will be for users to switch between packages/modules without going through a huge learning curve.

4.7     One of the advantages of the **Windows** environment is that packages specifically written for Windows are generally **similar in design**. This **reduces training time** and costs and makes **skills transferable**.

## On-screen help

4.8     It is increasingly common to find software pre-loaded onto computers without manuals being provided, or to find that, when manuals *are* provided, they are rarely referred to. This is because packages invariably include **on-screen help**.

4.9　If a user requires help, he or she requests it at the touch of a **single key** (eg **F1**) or by clicking on '**Help**' on a **menu bar**. The help screen is usually **context specific**, so that, for example, if a particular dialogue box in a package is open, the system will offer help related to relevant functions and options. Problems can be resolved more quickly and productivity improved.

4.10　Help files are usually written in **hypertext,** which provides **links** between topics. The user can click on words that are underlined and move directly to another topic.

## Use of dialogue boxes and on-screen prompts

4.11　The more critical the potential effect of a command issued by the user, the more important it is that the user is not allowed simply to **start a process by mistake**.

4.12　Thus where commands such as **delete** a file, **format** a disk or **update** a ledger are being made, user-friendly software should issue a **warning** that such an operation is about to be carried out, *after* the initial command is entered.

4.13　This gives the user a **second chance** to confirm that the command was intended and that the computer is indeed required to carry out the specified process.

4.14　In turn this means that users will spend less time attempting to reverse the effects of **unintentionally-used commands**.

## Escapability

4.15　An inexperienced user, or someone 'exploring' in a hit-or-miss way to try to find the right command, might find himself or herself faced with a command which he or she *knows* to be the wrong one.

4.16　It is important that an option is available which offers a **harmless alternative** to following the **unwanted route**. Thus in Windows there is usually a '**Cancel**' button next to the 'OK' button in each dialogue box. Selection of 'Cancel' enables the user to return to where he or she was before the wrong path was taken. An alternative is often the '**Esc**' key on the keyboard. These options are to be preferred to simply switching off the machine, which can have undesirable consequences.

## Customisation

4.17　Many users find that they perform the **same series of actions** so frequently that it becomes tedious to click their way through menus and dialogue boxes. User-friendly software will recognise this and offer **fast alternatives**.

(a)　'**Shortcut keys**' (typically pressing the Ctrl key together with one or more other keys) can be assigned to standard actions so that they are performed literally at the touch of a button.

(b)　A series of actions can be 'recorded' as they are done in the form of '**macros**', which can then be activated using a shortcut key or user-defined button.

---

**Activity 12.4**

Look at the various illustrations of screens in this chapter and elsewhere in this book. How many 'user friendly features' can you identify?

---

*BPP*
PUBLISHING

## 5    APPLICATIONS SOFTWARE

### KEY TERM

**Applications software** consists of programs which carry out a task for the user as opposed to programs which control the workings of a computer.

5.1    Whenever a computer is being used, it will be under the control of an **application program**, for example controlling stock, designing a car, dispensing cash, preparing accounts, running a computer game, word processing, economic forecasting, statistical analysis or recording sales at a cash desk.

### Application packages

5.2    Application packages are **ready-made programs** written to perform a particular job. The job will be common to many potential users, so that the package could be adopted by all of them for their data processing operations.

5.3    The suppliers of application packages include manufacturers, software houses, computer bureaux, government and other research organisations and trade associations. Originally only routine accounting applications were 'packaged' but nowadays there is a considerable range of application packages available. Provided that there are enough potential customers who might buy a package for a given application, software houses will develop them.

5.4    Application packages play an important role in the growing use of PCs by small firms because the small users would otherwise be **unable to afford** the software they need for their systems.

5.5    **Off-the-shelf application packages** are now being designed and developed for a wide range of business applications and, with any necessary tailoring, provide a tested and cheaper means of obtaining a program than would be the case writing the programs from scratch.

### General purpose packages

5.6    A distinction can be made between **application** packages and more **general purpose packages**.

### KEY TERMS

(a)  An **application package** is a program or set of programs that will carry out a **specific** processing application - for example, a **payroll** package would be specific to payroll processing.

(b)  A **general purpose package** is an off-the-shelf program that can be used for processing of a general type, but the computer user can apply the package to a variety of **uses** of his own choice. **Spreadsheet** packages and **word processing** packages are examples of general purpose packages.

5.7    **Examples** of general purpose software are described in more detail in the next chapter.

### Integrated software

5.8    Integrated software refers to programs, or packages of programs, that perform a variety of different processing operations, using **data which is compatible** with whatever operation is being carried out. The term is generally used in two different situations.

(a) **Accounts packages** often consist of program **modules** that can be integrated into a larger accounting system. There will be a module for each of the sales ledger system, the purchase ledger system, the nominal ledger, and so on. Output from one 'module' in an integrated system can be used as input to another, without the need for re-entry of data.

(b) There are some PC software packages that allow the user to carry out a **variety of processing operations,** such as word processing, using spreadsheets and creating and using a database. Examples of integrated software packages that provide these varied facilities are Lotus Smartsuite and Claris Works.

Such packages allow **data to be freely transferred** between elements of the package, for example data from a spreadsheet can be imported into a report which is being word processed.

A potential **disadvantage** of such packages is that they may not offer the range of features which a specialist user of a stand-alone element.

---

### Key learning points

- Software which supervises the running of other programs, providing a 'bridge' between applications software and the hardware, is known as operating systems software.

- The most widely used operating system is Windows, in either its Windows 95, Windows 98, Windows NT or Windows 2000 version. Other OS's include MS DOS, UNIX, the Apple Mac system and IBM's OS/2.

- Dialogue design refers to the messages that the computer system displays on screen and the ways that users can respond. Modern systems use menus, form-filling and above all graphical user interfaces.

- User friendliness is enhanced by good input screen design, intuitiveness, consistency between packages, on-screen help, dialogue boxes, escapability and customisation.

- Software which processes data for a particular purpose, or which is written for a particular data processing function, is known as applications software.

- General purpose software allows data to be handled in a particular way, for example in a spreadsheet, but its specific use in a particular situation is determined by the user.

- Software for specific applications is designed to support particular data processing tasks, for example, a payroll system or a computer aided design package.

---

## Quick quiz

1   What is 'software'?

2   List nine things that an operating system does.

3   What is Windows NT?

4   How can you have a conversation with a computer?

5   List five features of screen formatting.

6   What is an icon?

7   What is a default entry?

8   What is hypertext and where is it often used within Windows-type programs?

9   What is a shortcut key?

10   What is applications software? Give an example.

11   What is a general purpose package? Give an example.

## Answers to quick quiz

1   It is the program or sets of programs that tell the computer what to do.

2   Initial set-up (after booting up), checking hardware devices, handling data in memory, opening and closing files, maintaining directories, controlling interaction with users, controlling security, handling interruptions and managing multi-tasking.

3        It is an operating system designed to run networks.

4        Via the VDU screen. Messages from the computer appear on the screen (sometimes accompanied by a sound such as a beep) and the user replies by pressing a key on the keyboard or clicking a button on screen using a mouse.

5        Different colours, reverse video, flashing items, larger characters for tables, scrolling pages.

6        An image of an object used to represent a function or a file. The user clicks with a mouse on the  icon to start up a process (open a program, print a document etc).

7        Input that will be entered by the system automatically unless the user changes it, eg today's date.

8        It is <u>underlined text</u> that is linked to another part of a program (or another program). For instance in Windows Help files by clicking on the underlined words the user can find out more abut the topic in question.

9        It is a key (or combination of keys) that can be pressed to make the computer perform a series of frequently repeated actions at a single touch (eg Ctrl + W closes a Microsoft Word document).

10       Programs which carry out a task for the user as opposed to controlling the workings of a computer. An example is a payroll application package.

11       Software that can be used for a variety of purposes such as a spreadsheet package.

## Answers to activities

### Answer 12.1

There are probably millions of examples to choose from. Here are six.

(a)    Windows 95/98/2000/NT
(b)    Microsoft Word
(c)    Microsoft Excel
(d)    Sage Line 50
(e)    Netscape Navigator
(f)    Any computer game you care to think of

### Answer 12.2

**Learn** this list if you had to look back to the beginning of the chapter to find the answers.

(a)    Initial **set-up** of the computer once it has 'booted up' via the BIOS.
(b)    Checking that the **hardware** (including peripheral devices such as printers) is functioning properly.
(c)    Calling up of program files and data files from disk storage into **memory**.
(d)    **Opening and closing** of files, checking of file labels etc.
(e)    Maintenance of **directories** in disk storage.
(f)    Controlling **input and output** devices, including the interaction with the user.
(g)    Controlling system **security** (for example monitoring the use of passwords).
(h)    Handling of **interruptions** (for example program abnormalities or machine failure).
(i)    Managing **multitasking**.

### Answer 12.3

The screen is relatively uncomplicated. Someone familiar with the system could quickly learn to key in, say, 3, if they wanted to do a particular task.

However, the screen is very unpleasant to look at. The descriptions of options would not be at all obvious to the first-time user.

### Answer 12.4

Look at the buttons, menus, keyboard shortcut hints (eg <u>F</u>ile means press Alt + F on the keyboard to bring up the file menu), scalability of windows, system messages, Help facilities, and so on. You may have found lots of other examples.

# Chapter 13  Office automation

---

## Chapter topic list

1    Office automation

2    Spreadsheets

3    Word processing, DTP and graphics

4    Communications

5    Conferencing and data interchange

6    Groupware, workflow and intranets

---

## Learning objectives

On completion of this chapter you will be able to:

| | Performance criteria | Range Statement |
|---|---|---|
| • Identify improvements/suggest changes to: | 21.3.1, 21.3.2 | |
| ○ office technology and office automation ○ general purpose software packages such as word processors and spreadsheets ○ telecommunications facilities ○ application software packages | | |
| • Understand the range of computerised MIS | 21.3.1 | 21.3.1 |
| • Identify potential improvements to the MIS and consider them for their impact on the quality of the system and any interrelated systems | 21.3.1 | |
| • Make suggestions for changes supported by a clear rationale as to how they could improve the quality of the system | 21.3.2 | |
| • Assess and clearly state whether assumptions and judgements made are reliable | 21.3.3 | |
| • Present suggestions clearly and in a way which helps people to understand and act on them | 21.3.5 | |
| • *Describe an organisation's computer software, systems and networking* | n/a | n/a |

Italicised objectives are areas of knowledge and understanding underlying the elements of competence for Unit 21.

*BPP*
PUBLISHING

# 1    OFFICE AUTOMATION

1.1    In this chapter we shall be looking at some of the **application packages** that are widely used in offices and at some of the developments in **communications.**

1.2    As you know, if you are reading this book in order, there is more on word-processing, spreadsheets, the Internet and so on in **Parts A and B** of this book where we take a more **hands-on** approach.

# 2    SPREADSHEETS

2.1    We have, of course, looked at spreadsheets in some depth in **Part B** of this book. This section simply summarises some key points in a form that may be useful for answers to **written tasks** in devolved assessments.

## KEY TERM

A **spreadsheet** is a general purpose software package for **modelling,** 'spreadsheet' being a term loosely derived from the application's likeness to a 'spreadsheet of paper' divided into **rows** and **columns**. Modern spreadsheets have added a **third dimension** to columns and rows so that separate **sheets** can be manipulated together and linked to one another.

2.2    The spreadsheet was one of the software products which **made a success of the PC** in the business environment. While originally used as an aid to accountants or financial specialists, it is now a **ubiquitous** feature of many organisations' computer systems.

## Commands and facilities

2.3    Spreadsheets are **versatile** tools that can be used for a wide variety of tasks and calculations. The only pre-ordained structure imposed on the end user is the grid of rows and columns. The absence of imposed formats or contents gives the spreadsheet great flexibility and it is this that users find so valuable in **decision making**.

2.4    Different spreadsheets will offer different **facilities**, but some of the more basic ones which should feature in all spreadsheet programs are as follows.

| Facility | Explanation |
|---|---|
| File commands | Opening, naming, saving, printing and closing the spreadsheet file are the key tasks. |
| Editing | Data (cells rows or columns) can easily be copied or moved from one part of the spreadsheet to another using a mouse and 'cut and paste' and 'drag and drop' facilities. Data entry is facilitated by intelligent software that can guess, for example, that if you type *Jan 2001* in the first cell you are likely to want *Feb 2001*, *Mar 2001* and so on in the cells below. |
| Facilities to rearrange the spreadsheet | You can insert a column or row at a desired spot. For example, you might wish to split 'cash receipts' into 'trade' and 'other'. The insert command facilitates this, and the formulae in the spreadsheet are adjusted automatically. |
| Format | This command controls the way in which headings and data are shown, for example by altering column widths, 'justifying' text and numbers (to indent or have a right-hand justification, etc), changing the number of decimal places displayed, or the font used. You can format the whole spreadsheet, or a specified range of cells. |
| Protect facilities | A protect facility ensures that the contents of a specified range of cells (for example the text titles, or a column of base data) cannot be tampered with. |
| Sorting | Data can be sorted alphabetically or numerically. |
| Graphics facility | Most spreadsheets also contain a graphics facility which enables the presentation of tables of data as graphs or pie charts for example. |
| Macros | Many spreadsheets provide a macro facility. This allows the user to automate a sequence of actions or commands, executing them with the depression of just two pre-defined keys. |

## Potential drawbacks

2.5 Spreadsheets are immensely popular and can be used for a very wide range of modelling tasks. However, because they are essentially **single-user packages** and because each one is **designed from scratch**, there are risks in their use.

(a) Spreadsheets may be **badly designed**, increasing the risk of errors or inefficiency.

(i) For example, a user may put a second large table of data immediately below a first, rather than diagonally offset. If he or she then deletes a column of data from the first table, then data may be **unintentionally lost** from the second one as well.

(ii) Another common error is to set up data *en bloc* rather than having a **separate 'input' section, 'calculation' section and 'output' section**. This makes it very difficult to use the spreadsheet to analyse different scenarios. A fresh sheet has to be constructed whenever the variables change.

*BPP* PUBLISHING

(b) Users are unlikely to **document** the workings of their spreadsheet, as they consider it 'obvious'. This makes it difficult for other staff to understand, use or modify the model.

(c) Macros can be **difficult to understand** and are not as conducive to tight control as the use of a programming language.

(d) The **lack of a proper audit trail** can be a disadvantage. Because the user works with a spreadsheet in memory (RAM), only saving it at certain intervals, it is unlikely that a record of the intermediate stages will be maintained. When a spreadsheet is saved, the previous version is usually overwritten.

## 3 WORD PROCESSING, DTP AND GRAPHICS

> **KEY TERM**
>
> **Word processing** is the **processing of text information**. Typically, word processing software may be used for the production of standard letters and for the drafting and redrafting of documents.

3.1 Word processing enables the person preparing the text to check the input visually on the VDU as it is being keyed in, and to **correct errors immediately**. Instead of having to erase typing mistakes with a manual eraser or Tipp-Ex, the WP operator can quickly key in the corrections and print a fresh corrected version of the text.

3.2 It is a straightforward matter to **make amendments** to the original text. If the contents of the text are discussed and as a result of these discussions, changes are agreed, the changes can be made quickly and simply. For example, a company might hold its rules and procedures books, or its price lists, on a WP file and update them just before they are to be reprinted.

### Word processing hardware

3.3 Modern word processors are essentially PCs with a **word processing software** package.

3.4 **Laser printers** are widely used with word processors, as they offer the high quality required for many letters and documents.

3.5 The WYSIWYG (What You See Is What You Get) facility is another helpful feature for users who wish to see on screen exactly the **format and typeface** (italics, bold etc) they will get on paper.

3.6 The word processor screen is given **all the characteristics of a sheet of paper**. The operator is able to specify the width and length of the area (s)he wishes the text to cover on the page, taking into account desired **margins** when the text is printed on to paper. If the text area is larger than the screen can accommodate, the operator has the facility, rather like a movie cameraman, to **scroll up and down** or to **pan from side to side** in order to view and edit a page.

### Software features

3.7 Once the text in its basic form has been keyed in, the **editing** facilities of the software come into their own. The functions of **deletion, correction, insertion** that used to have to be done by hand in updating or reorganising printed material are all available on screen with the word processor. Blocks of text can be **moved or duplicated**. Text can be **justified automatically** within preset margins.

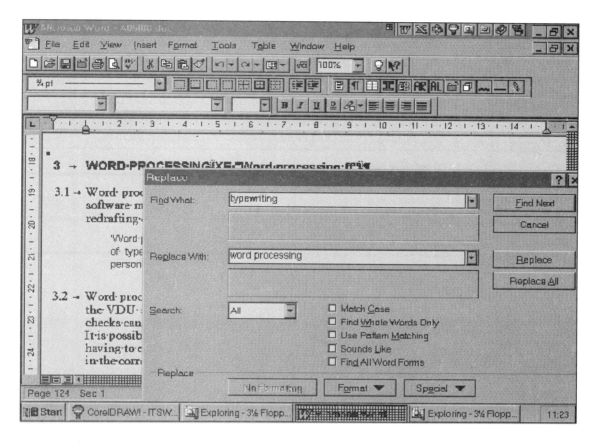

3.8 Examples of other valuable aids in producing documents include the following.

| Aid | Comment |
|---|---|
| Headers | Page headers (chapter titles) are keyed in only once, but inserted by the program at the top of each page of the chapter. |
| Page numbers | An 'input' point may be inserted so that the appropriate page number within the document will be printed automatically. |
| Spell checking | A spell-checker program which checks a specified word, page or file against its own dictionary and calls attention to any word it cannot recognise: the operator then has the choice of ignoring the word (if it is unfamiliar to the machine, but correctly spelt), adding it to the dictionary (if it is unfamiliar, correctly spelt and much used), or correcting the error (by substituting a word offered by the machine from its dictionaries, or by typing afresh). |
| Presentation | Typescript variations are available, for emphasis or presentation. For example <u>underlining</u>, *italics* or **emboldening.** |
| Styles | Style sheets enable a selected typeface/font style/justification to be given a name and stored for later use. |

**BPP** PUBLISHING

| Aid | Comment |
|---|---|
| Mail merge | *Mail merge* is a process where the typist need only enter names and addresses, and calls up a proforma letter, for a number of standard letters to be printed, for example reminders to debtors. |
| Importing | *Importing* data from other programs such as spreadsheets or databases (or exporting data to them) is very easy with modern packages like Word and Wordperfect. |
| Compatibility | Major packages are now very similar and highly *compatible*. For example, it is possible to open a Wordperfect document with Word, edit it, and save it, either in Word or Wordperfect format. |

### Activity 13.1

What are the advantages of word processing over a manual or simple electronic typewriter for producing text?

## Desktop publishing (DTP)

> **KEY TERM**
>
> **Desktop publishing (DTP)** is the use of office computers to implement computerised typesetting and composition systems.

3.9 Some DTP packages are suitable for the general PC user producing an occasional document. Others are appropriate for full-time in-house publishing departments, producing **brochures, price lists, bulletins and company reports and advertisements,** with sophisticated photography and artwork for output onto professional typesetting printers.

3.10 DTP systems pull **graphics and text** together from other programs and it enables the page, both graphics and text, to be seen as the 'artwork' image for editing and production. A space for a picture can be moved around the page, like 'cut and paste' artwork. This **cuts out the intermediate stage in publishing** or sending material to a phototypesetter to make up pages for printing.

### Activity 13.2

Give examples of how a business organisation might use DTP.

## Computer graphics

3.11 Another use of computers is the production of information in the form of **pictures or diagrams**. A widely used package is Coreldraw.

3.12 **Spreadsheets** and **word processing packages** also commonly incorporate **graphics facilities**, and these are useful for presenting complex numerical data in a more user-friendly form such as a bar chart or pie charts, or a map.

## Presentation graphics

3.13 Programs for presentation graphics are programs which allow the user to build up a series of graphical displays or images which can be used for presentation. With additional hardware, this type of software can be used to produce **35 mm slides** for an on-screen slideshow or storyboard (which can be synchronised with a sound track). The slides that your lecturer uses on the **overhead projector** may well be produced by similar means using, for example, the **Microsoft PowerPoint** package.

## Scanners

3.14 Computers can **read words and pictures** from a 'hard-copy' page, using a scanner. A scanner looks at a whole printed page of input or a photograph or illustration, and records and stores a pattern of dots. The image will be fed in to the computer, where it can be enlarged or reduced, and 'cut and pasted' into position alongside printed text on a page.

3.15 Another use of scanning is to 'read' a book and store the text on a complete file. This might be useful where the **original** book or document was **not produced by computerised methods,** but there is now a requirement to computerise the production of future editions.

## 4 COMMUNICATIONS

4.1 We looked at a number of features of telecommunications **hardware** in Chapter 11, and we now need to consider how that hardware is **used** in office work.

**DEVOLVED ASSESSMENT ALERT**

Go back to Chapter 11 and redo Activity 11.5 on the telephone before reading on. It is a piece of technology so much taken for granted now that it is easy to forget to mention it when discussing potential improvements to systems.

## Fax

**KEY TERM**

**Fax** (or **facsimile transmission**) involves the transmission by data link of exact duplicate copies of documents. The original is fed into the fax machine, which 'reads' it and converts it into electronic form so it can be transmitted over the telephone. It is printed by the recipient's fax machine.

4.2 Fax has largely **superseded** systems such as telex and the computerised equivalent 'teletex' (not to be confused with 'teletext').

4.3 The latest fax machines can also be used as **scanners** to scan data into a PC, as **printers** for PC output and as **photocopiers**.

4.4 Alternatively a PC can be fitted with a **fax modem,** allowing data to be transmitted directly from the PC without going through a separate fax machine.

4.5     However, users of PCs fitted with fax modems can not receive fax messages when the PC is switched off.

---

### Activity 13.3

Which of the following cannot be transmitted *directly* from the UK by a *PC's* internal fax modem to a stand alone *fax* machine in the USA?

(a)   A letter prepared by the sender
(b)   A series of charts, and graphs prepared by the sender using a spreadsheet's graphics facilities
(c)   A copy of an invoice received in this morning's post
(d)   A colour photograph of a product
(e)   An Excel spreadsheet file in electronic form

---

## Electronic mail (E-mail)

4.6     The term 'electronic mail', or **e-mail,** is used to describe various systems of sending data or messages electronically via a telephone or data network and a central computer, without the need to post letters or place memos in pigeon-holes or despatch documents by courier.

4.7     E-mail has the following **advantages**.

(a)   **Speed**. E-mail is far faster than post. It is a particular time-saver when communicating with people overseas.

(b)   **Economy** (no need for stamps etc). E-mail is reckoned to be 20 times cheaper than fax.

(c)   **Efficiency** (a message is prepared once but can be sent to thousands of employees at the touch of a button).

(d)   **Security** (access can be restricted by the use of passwords).

(e)   Documents can be attached from **word-processing,** spreadsheets or other packages.

(f)   Electronic **delivery and read receipts** can be requested.

(g)   Standard footers or 'signatures' can be used to save time.

(h)   People who may regularly receive the same type of messages can be grouped together in a 'distribution list'.

4.8     Typically information is 'posted' by the sender to a central computer which allocates disk storage as a **'mailbox'** for each user. The information is subsequently 'collected' by the receiver from the mailbox.

(a)   Senders of information thus have **documentary evidence** that they have given a piece of information to the recipient and that the recipient has picked up the message.

(b)   Receivers are **not disturbed** by the information when it is sent (as they would be by face-to-face meetings or phone calls), but collect it later at their convenience.

4.9     Each user will typically have **password protected access** to his own inbox, outbox and filing system.

4.10    E-mail systems may be internal only, or may also enable communication to outside organisations via the Internet.

## Activity 13.4

Mis-use of e-mail is regarded as quite a serious problem by many companies.

How do you think employees might mis-use the system? Answer from personal experience if possible.

## Voice mail

4.11 Voice mail (or v-mail) systems enable the **caller's message to be recorded** at the recipient's voice mail box (similar to a mail box in an e-mail system).

4.12 The main **advantage** of the system is that it only requires a telephone to be used. No typing or keying in is necessary. A voice mail message is basically a **spoken memo**: for the person sending the message it is much more convenient than typing it or having it typed and then faxing it.

4.13 Voice mail can be used for different situations.

(a) To leave a message for sales representatives 'in the field'.
(b) To **leave messages** in departments in different time zones.
(c) In organisations where employees might be **working away** at a client's premises.

## Voice messaging

4.14 This is a kind of **switchboard answerphone** that takes the place of a human receptionist, or at least relieves the receptionist of the burden of dealing with common, straightforward calls.

4.15 Typically, when a call is answered a **recorded message** tells the caller to dial the extension they want if they know it, or to hold if they want to speak to the operator. Sometimes other options are offered, such as 'press 2 if you want to know about X service and 3 if you want to know about Y'.

4.16 Such systems **work well** if callers frequently have **similar needs** and these can be accurately anticipated.

4.17 They can be **frustrating** for callers with **non-standard enquiries,** however, and many people find the impersonality of responding to an answerphone unappealing. Badly set up systems can result in the caller being bounced about from one recorded message to another and never getting through to the person they want to deal with.

---

### Case example: Interactive voice response (IVR)

Several pharmaceutical companies have installed sophisticated interactive voice response systems to deal with enquiries from doctors, chemists or patients. For example some allow the caller to press a number on their handset and have details of possible side effects sent back to them by fax.

---

## Computer Telephony Integration (CTI)

4.18 Computer Telephony Integration (CTI) systems **gather information about callers** such as their telephone number and customer account number or demographic information (age, income, interests etc). This is stored on a customer database and can be **called up and sent**

**to the screen** of the person dealing with the call, perhaps before the call has even been put through.

4.19 Thus sales staff dealing with hundreds of calls every day might **appear to remember individual callers** personally and know in advance what they are likely to order. Order forms with key details entered already can be displayed on screen automatically, saving time for both the sales staff and the caller.

4.20 Alternatively a busy manager might note that an **unwelcome call** is coming in on the 'screen pop' that appears on her PC and choose to direct it to her voice mail box rather than dealing with it at once.

4.21 As another example, a bank might use CTI to **prompt sales people** with changes in share prices and with the details of the investors they should call to offer dealing advice.

## Mobile communications

4.22 In theory it is now possible to do any kind of 'office' activity **outside** the office, on the move, although **limitations in battery power** (a technology lagging far behind others described in this book) impose restrictions.

4.23 The mobile services available are increasing all the time. Here are some examples.

(a) **Messaging services** such as: voice mail; short message service (SMS) which allows messages of up to 160 characters to be transmitted over a standard digital phone; and paging services

(b) **Call handling services** such as: call barring, conference calls and call divert

(c) **Corporate services** such as: integrated numbering, so that people have a single contact number for both the phone on their desk and for their mobile; and virtual private networks that incorporate mobile phones as well as conventional desktop phones, so that users can dial internal extension numbers directly.

(d) **Internet access** is possible via some cellular telephones although the speed of transmission is relatively slow at present.

(e) **Dual mode handsets** which allow users to use both cheap cordless technology when in the office and cellular technology when outside.

## 5 CONFERENCING AND DATA INTERCHANGE

### Computer conferencing and bulletin boards

5.1 A computer conferencing system is similar to e-mail but more expensive, in that there is a huge central mailbox on the system where all persons connected to the system can **deposit messages** for everyone to see, and, in turn, **read what other people have left** in the system.

5.2 Computer conferencing can be appropriate for a team of individuals at different locations to compare notes. It becomes a way of keeping track of progress on a **project** between routine team meetings.

5.3 Computer conferencing systems can become **organisation-wide bulletin boards,** where members can leave messages of general import. A bulletin board system can be a way of re-establishing some of the social ties of office life which are alleged to have suffered from computerisation.

# Videoconferencing

5.4 Videoconferencing is the use of computer and communications technology to **conduct meetings** in which several participants, perhaps in different parts of the world, are linked up via **computer and a video system**. (Conference calls on a **telephone system**, where several people can converse at the same time, are a precursor of teleconferencing.)

5.5 Videoconferencing has become increasingly common as the ready availability of chips capable of processing video images has brought the service to desktop PCs at reasonable cost. More expensive systems feature a **separate room with several video screens**, which show the images of those participating in a meeting.

5.6 Even if the technology used is expensive, it is far **cheaper** when compared to the cost in management time and air fares of business **travel**.

---

### Activity 13.5

A video-conference is to take place between company representatives from the US, Spain, Japan and the UK to discuss the results of some market research that has been carried out. Company head office is in the US. The UK representatives believe that the market research data is incorrect. The Japanese feel that it is irrelevant to their market.

What problems might be experienced at this video conference?

---

# Electronic data interchange

5.7 Electronic data interchange (EDI) is a form of computer-to-computer **data** interchange, and so another form of electronic mail. Instead of sending each other reams of paper in the form of invoices, statements and so on, details of inter-company transactions are sent via telecoms links, **avoiding the need for output** and paper at the sending end, and **for re-keying of data** at the receiving end.

5.8 The general concept of having one computer talk directly to another might seem straightforward enough in principle, but in practice there are two major **difficulties**.

(a) Each business wants to produce documents (and hold records on file) to its own **individual requirements** and structure. Thus a computer of X Ltd could not transmit data to a computer of Y Ltd because the records/data transmitted **would not be in a format or structure** to suit Y Ltd.

(b) Businesses may work to differing **time schedules,** especially when they are engaged in international trade. If a London company's computer wants to send a message to a computer in San Francisco, the San Francisco computer might not be switched on or otherwise able to receive the message.

5.9 Until recently different makes of computer could not easily 'talk' to each other. The problem of **compatibility** between different makes of computer was a serious one, and some form of interface between the computers had to be devised to enable data interchange to take place. This is less and less of a problem as businesses adopt common standards and set up sites on the **Internet.**

5.10 Joining an **EDI network** (there are several) is quite **expensive,** but many smaller companies are encouraged to do so by their **suppliers and/or customers**. Many of Marks and Spencer's suppliers have been converted to EDI.

**BPP** PUBLISHING

### Electronic Funds Transfer

5.11 Electronic Funds Transfer (EFT) describes a system whereby a computer user can use his computer system to **transfer funds** - for example make payments to a **supplier,** or pay salaries into **employees'** bank accounts, or transfer funds from one bank account to another account by sending electronic data to his bank. Since businesses keep most of their cash in bank accounts, electronic funds transfer must involve the **banks** themselves.

### *SWIFT*

5.12 A system for the electronic transfer of funds **internationally between banks** themselves is known as SWIFT (the Society for Worldwide Interbank Financial Telecommunications). If X Ltd in the UK wishes to make a payment to a company in, say, Germany, and if his UK bank and the German company's bank are members of the SWIFT network (all the UK clearing banks are members), the settlement between the banks themselves can be made through the SWIFT system.

### *CHAPS and BACS*

5.13 Interbank settlements by the clearing banks **within the UK** are also made by electronic funds transfer, using the CHAPS system (Clearing House Automated Payments System).

5.14 Many large companies now pay the salaries of employees by providing computer data to their bank, using the **BACS (Bankers' Automated Clearing Services)** or BACSTEL service. It has been estimated that switching to BACS can save 90% on transaction charges.

## 6 GROUPWARE, WORKFLOW AND INTRANETS

### Computer Supported Co-operative Working

6.1 Organisations rely upon people working together and co-operating with each other. information systems should be designed to help people to do this. This is the principle behind **Computer Supported Co-Operative Working** (CSCW) .

> **KEY TERM**
>
> **Computer supported co-operative (or 'collaborative') working** is a term which combines the understanding of the way people work in groups with the enabling technologies of computer networking and associated hardware, software, services and techniques.

6.2 Internal telephone networks are perhaps the most obvious example of the use of technology to facilitate group working. Other examples, such as video-conferencing and e-mail, have already been described.

# Groupware

> **KEY TERM**
>
> **Groupware** is a term used to describe a collection of IT tools designed for the use of co-operative or collaborative work groups. Typically, these groups are small project-oriented teams that have important tasks and tight deadlines.

6.3    There are many products and technologies that could be termed groupware. Microsoft Exchange and Lotus Notes are two examples.

6.4    Features might include the following.

(a)    A **scheduler** (or diary or calendar), allowing users to keep track of their schedule and plan meetings with others.

(b)    An electronic **address book** to keep personal and business contact information up-to-date and easy to find. Contacts can be sorted and filed in any way.

(c)    **To do** lists. Personal and business to-do lists can be kept in one easy-to-manage place, and tasks can quickly be prioritised.

(d)    A **journal**, which is used to record interactions with important contacts, record items (such as e-mail messages) and files that are significant to the user, and record activities of all types and track them all without having to remember where each one was saved.

(e)    A **jotter** for jotting down notes as quick reminders of questions, ideas, and so on.

6.5    There are clearly advantages in having information such as this available from the desktop at the touch of a button, rather than relying on scraps of paper, address books, and corporate telephone directories. However, it is when groupware is used to **share information** with colleagues that it comes into its own. Here are some of the features that may be found.

(a)    **Messaging**, comprising an **e-mail** in-box which is used to send and receive messages from the office, home, or the road and **routing** facilities, enabling users to send a message to a single person, send it sequentially to a number of people (who may add to it or comment on it before passing it on), or sending it to every one at once.

(b)    Access to an **information database**, and customisable 'views' of the information held on it, which can be used to standardise the way information is viewed in a workgroup.

(c)    **Group scheduling**, to keep track of colleagues itineraries. Microsoft Exchange Server, for instance offers a 'Meeting Wizard', which can consult the diaries of everyone needed to attend a meeting and automatically work out when they will be available, which venues are free, and what resources are required.

(d)    **Public folders**. These collect, organise, and share files with others on the team or across the organisation.

(e)    **Conferencing** or chat facilities allowing online discussions with others.

(f)    **Assigning tasks**. A task request can be sent to a colleague who can accept, decline, or reassign the task.

(g)    **Voting** type facilities that can, say, request and tally responses to a multiple-choice question sent in a mail message (eg 'Here is a list of options for this year's Christmas party').

(h) **Hyperlinks** in mail messages. The recipient can click the hyperlink to go directly to a Web page or file server.

(i) **Workflow management** (see below) with various degrees of sophistication.

## Workflow

> **KEY TERM**
>
> **Workflow** is a term used to describe the defined series of tasks within an organisation to produce a final outcome.

6.6 Sophisticated workgroup computing applications allow the user to define different **workflows** for different types of jobs. For example, in a publishing setting, a document might be automatically routed from writer to editor to proofreader to production.

6.7 At **each stage** in the workflow, **one individual** or group is **responsible** for a specific task. Once the task is complete, the workflow software ensures that the individuals responsible for the **next** task are notified and receive the data they need to do their stage of the process.

6.8 Workflow systems can be described according to the type of process they are designed to deal with. There are three common types.

(a) **Image-based workflow systems** are designed to automate the flow of paper through an organisation, by transferring the paper to digital "images". These were the first workflow systems that gained wide acceptance. These systems are closely associated with 'imaging' (or 'document image processing' (DIP)) technology, and help with the routing and processing of digitised images.

(b) **Form-based workflow systems** (formflow) are designed to route forms intelligently throughout an organisation. These forms, unlike images, are text-based and consist of editable fields. Forms are automatically routed according to the information entered on them. In addition, these form-based systems can notify or remind people when action is due.

(c) **Co-ordination-based workflow systems** are designed to help the completion of work by providing a framework for **co-ordination** of action. Such systems are intended to improve organisational productivity by addressing the issues necessary to **satisfy customers,** rather than automating procedures that are not closely related to customer satisfaction.

> **DEVOLVED ASSESSMENT ALERT**
>
> Inability to share data that everyone needs is one of main problems faced by modern organisations. You are likely to get credit in your answers to Devolved Assessment tasks if you show an awareness of this and make suggestions for improvements that will help to make sure that people have the information they need to do their jobs.

## Intranets

6.9 The idea behind an 'intranet' is that companies set up their own **mini version of the Internet,** using a combination of the company's own networked computers and Internet technology. Each employee has a browser and access to a server computer holding corporate information on a wide variety of topics, and also offers access to the global Net.

6.10 Potential applications include daily **company newspapers**, **induction material**, online procedure and policy **manuals**, **employee web pages** where individuals post up details of their activities and progress, and **internal databases** of the corporate information store.

6.11 Most of the **cost** of an intranet is the **staff time** required to set up the system.

6.12 The **benefits** of intranets are diverse.

(a) A considerable amount of money can be saved from the **elimination of storage**, **printing** and **distribution** of documents that can be made available to employees on-line.

(b) Documents on-line are **more widely used** than those that are kept on shelves, especially if the document is bulky (for instance company information handbooks, finance manuals and procedures manuals) and needs to be searched. This means that there are **improvements in productivity** and **efficiency**.

(c) It is much **easier to update** information in electronic form.

(d) Wider access to corporate information should open the way to **more flexible working patterns**. For instance if bulky reference materials are available on-line then there is little need to be in the office at all.

---

### Case example: Swiss Bank Corporation

'One of the biggest users of intranets is Swiss Bank Corporation. In fact it has so many - around 100 - that it has just appointed a head of intranets to co-ordinate them all.

At Swiss Bank Corporation intranets are used for:

Corporate accounting and credit information
Publishing research internally, and to a select group of 50 external clients
Trading information
Ordering information technology equipment
IT project management
Informing staff of regulatory changes

The job of Marie Adee, the company's new head of intranets, is to unify the disparate sites so that employees can find information easily. The sites will also be given a common look and feel. All the company's sites can be searched using the Netscape Navigator Web browser, but the company is also standardising on Lotus Domino software.

This software will sit on the server computers that store the intranet information. Domino incorporates Lotus Notes information sharing software. So employees will be able to input information to Web sites either through Notes or through their Web browsers. It will also be possible for SBC to set up workflow applications - which control the flow of work between users in a team.

---

### DEVOLVED ASSESSMENT ALERT

Do read the case examples in this book, because they will often give you ideas what organisations in real life are doing to improve their MIS. If you have time it is even more useful to read the Information Technology pages or supplements in a quality newspaper such as the *Times* or the *Financial Times*. You never know: the organisation in your Devolved Assessment might be experiencing problems that you just happened to read about in the paper the other day.

### Key learning points

- **Spreadsheets** are versatile tools that can be used for a wide variety of tasks, especially at tactical level. There are potential drawbacks due to overuse and poor practice.

- **Word processing** is probably the most widespread feature of the electronic office. It uses a computer system to produce and edit typed letters and documents and store them on magnetic storage media.

- **Computer graphics** allows information to be presented easily in the form of charts or diagrams. **Presentation graphics** software enable the transfer of computer graphics to 35 mm transparencies or overhead projector slides.

- **Desktop publishing** software is used to implement computerised typesetting and composition. A DTP package pulls together **text and graphics** from other programs and is used to 'cut and paste' text and images as required.

- The electronic office may allow **communications** by a number of media including telex, teletex, fax, e-mail, voice mail, computer **conferencing** and teleconferencing.

- **Electronic data interchange** allows the electronic transfer between businesses not just of messages but of trading and commercial documents. In certain sectors, suppliers and customers are adopting EDI to deal with each other.

- **Computer supported co-operative working** combines the understanding of the way people work in groups with the enabling technologies of computer networking and associated hardware, software, services and techniques, including **e-mail**, **group scheduling** and so on.

- **Groupware** and **workflow** software are key products. Internal versions of the Internet called **Intranets** are the current fashion.

### Quick quiz

1    Explain the term 'spreadsheet'.

2    What are the drawbacks of spreadsheets?

3    List six features commonly found in a word processing package.

4    What is a fax modem?

5    What are the advantages of e-mail?

6    What is EDI and what is it used for?

7    What is EFT?

8    Give six examples of how groupware enhances group working.

9    What is an intranet?

### Answers to quick quiz

1    A spreadsheet is a general purpose software package for modelling, 'spreadsheet' being a term loosely derived from the application's likeness to a 'spreadsheet of paper' divided into rows and columns. Modern spreadsheets have added a third dimension to columns and rows so that separate sheets can be manipulated together and linked to one another.

2    They are often badly designed and laid out; they may be difficult for other users to understand; complex macros are difficult to write; it is difficult to keep track of changes.

3    Headers, page numbering, spell checking, presentation features, styles, mail merge, importing and compatibility with other software.

4    It is a device now usually fitted inside a PC that allows the PC user to send faxes directly from the computer, without going through a separate fax machine, and also provides telecommunications links for other purposes such as networking.

5    Speed, economy, efficiency, security, compatibility with WP/graphics packages, delivery and read receipts, attachments.

6    Electronic data interchange is a form of computer-to-computer data interchange, often used instead of paper invoices and statements to exchange details of financial *transactions.* This avoids the need for paper and paper storage and the data only needs to be keyed in once, at the sending end.

7    Electronic funds transfer is a computer-to-computer exchange of *funds,* for instance transferring payment for supermarket purchases from the customer's bank account to the supermarket's account.

8    Messaging, group scheduling, delegating tasks, assigning work, conferencing, voting.

9    A mini-version of the Internet set up using a combination of an organisations internal network and Internet technology such as browsers. Intranets are used to distribute corporate information to all employees.

## Answers to activities

## Answer 13.1

The advantages of word processing for producing text include the following.

(a)    The ability to produce personalised letters of a standard type.
(b)    The ability to amend, correct or update text on screen easily.
(c)    A low error rate in the text.
(d)    Speed of keying in text, and corrections.
(e)    Easy formatting of text.
(f)    Quality is improved.
(g)    Security may be enhanced.

## Answer 13.2

(a)    Design of management reports

(b)    Design and preparation of the annual report

(c)    Design of external documentation, such as press releases and mailshots

(d)    Design of advertisements

(e)    Publication of in-house magazine

(f)    Design of an organisation's standard documentation (for example order forms and quality assurance manuals)

## Answer 13.3

(a)    A letter *can* be sent directly. It will print out at the other end just as if a paper copy of the letter had been passed through the fax machine in the conventional way.

(b)    Likewise the charts and graphs *can* be sent: fax is quite able to cope with images.

(c)    The paper invoice is not stored in electronic form so it *cannot* be sent by the PCs internal modem unless it is converted into that form.

(d)    Likewise a photograph *cannot* be sent directly from the PC unless it is in electronic form. (Colour is not a problem, but if the fax machine in the USA is not capable of printing in colour it will come out in black and white.)

(e)    The electronic file *cannot* be sent to a fax machine. (It could be sent directly to a PC in the USA via e-mail, however.)

## Answer 13.4

E-mail can be mis-used in several ways.

(a)  Employees can look as if they are working at their computers, whereas in fact they are simply 'chatting' to their colleagues.

(b)  It is much harder to convey meaning in written form than it is with the spoken voice. Idle remarks or jokes can easily cause serious offence.

(c)  Sexual harassment via e-mail has been a problem in some organisations.

(d)  Bosses who do not have the strength of character to tell employees off to their faces quite commonly use e-mail to bully their employees. (This is known as 'flame-mail'.)

## Answer 13.5

Possible problems include the following.

(a)  The different time zones might make it difficult to find a time for the meting that was convenient for all the participants.

(b)  Cultural differences might be forgotten. For instance the US representatives may not realise that when the team from Spain sign off for lunch they are unlikely to return for several hours, although then they will be ready to work much later into the evening than, say, the UK representatives.

(c)  Language difficulties are a potential problem, though English would probably be used.

(d)  The meeting is to discuss some detailed figures, which will be circulated in advance, but video-conferencing makes it difficult to pass round data that may be prepared *during* the meeting as a result of ideas put forward.

(e)  The UK representatives, who feel strongly about the issues, may be able to dominate the meeting by shouting the loudest. (Video-conferencing equipment tends to give priority to the loudest voice.)

# Chapter 14  Security

---

## Chapter topic list

---

## Learning objectives

On completion of this chapter you will be able to:

| | Performance criteria | Range Statement |
|---|---|---|
| • Identify improvements/suggest changes to:<br>  ○ physical security of computer hardware<br>  ○ equipment layout, virus safeguards and health and safety issues<br>  ○ passwords<br>  ○ storage and back-up procedures | 21.3.1, 21.3.2 | |
| • Understand the range of computerised MIS | 21.3.1 | 21.3.1 |
| • Identify potential improvements to the MIS and consider them for their impact on the quality of the system and any interrelated systems | 21.3.1 | |
| • Make suggestions for changes supported by a clear rationale as to how they could improve the quality of the system | 21.3.2 | |
| • Assess and clearly state whether assumptions and judgements made are reliable | 21.3.3 | |
| • Present suggestions clearly and in a way which helps people to understand and act on them | 21.3.5 | |
| • Keep confidential information secure from unauthorised people | 21.2.8 | |
| • *Describe an organisation's computer software, systems and networking* | n/a | n/a |

Italicised objectives are areas of knowledge and understanding underlying the elements of competence for Unit 21.

## 1 THE IDENTIFICATION OF RISKS

1.1 Information technology has brought many changes to working practices and procedures in the office. Much information processing is now **faster, more accurate** and **more reliable** than was ever possible using manual processing methods. Computers can tackle **complex** tasks and can handle **huge volumes of data**.

1.2 Computers are used widely in many organisations, and those organisations often **depend entirely** on their IT resources to support the smooth and continuing day-to-day operation of the business.

1.3 A high degree of reliance on computers can mean a **high level of exposure** to computer **failure**. If users do not put adequate security measures and procedures into place, computer failure can result in the **loss of much valuable data**.

**KEY TERM**

**Security** involves the prevention of unauthorised modification, disclosure or destruction of data and the maintenance of uninterrupted computing services.

1.4 Security measures can only be successfully implemented if computer users are aware of the **risks** to the information technology environment. There are many different risks, for instance, accidentally deleting files, the risk of fire, the risk of system breakdown. A useful classification identifies seven types of risk, as follows.

- Human error
- Technical error
- Natural disasters
- Deliberate actions
- Commercial espionage
- Malicious damage
- Industrial action

**Activity 14.1**

See if you can think of examples of risks, in the context of your use of computers, one for each of these categories.

1.5 The risk with the highest incidence is probably **human error**.

1.6 You may have noticed that all the types of risk identified so far are risks to computer **data** or computer **equipment**. There is one other area of risk in the information technology environment to which increasing attention has been paid in recent years, and which does not really fit any of the above categories. When you thought of examples of risks you might have thought of RSI (repetitive strain injury), or eye strain. These are examples of risks to you, the **computer user**.

## 2 RISKS TO THE COMPUTER USER

2.1 Risks to the computer user can be placed in one of two categories.

(a) All those **hazards** to which **any office worker** is exposed, whether or not he or she is using a computer.

(b) Risks which arise from using a **keyboard** (or mouse) and **screen**.

### General risks

2.2 You may be familiar from your earlier studies with the basic **legal** requirements covering **health and safety** in the workplace. As an employee, you are legally obliged to take reasonable care to **avoid injury to yourself and others**. Employers also have a number of duties imposed on them by legislation; **employers' duties** include the provision of certain minimum acceptable standards for the working environment.

- Cleanliness
- Ventilation
- Temperature
- Lighting
- Seating

2.3 Now consider the **workstation** itself. Make sure that your chair has adjustable height and an adjustable back support. Think about how any documents you are using to work from or refer to will fit into your working pattern (for example, do you move things from left to right or from right to left).

### Computer-related risks

2.4 If you have ever worked for long periods at a computer, you may have experienced some **discomfort**. This might have been caused by your use of the **screen** or the **keyboard**.

*The VDU*

2.5 If a screen is too bright, it can cause **eye strain**. There are two common ways of dealing with this problem. The first is to turn the brightness down; all monitors have a brightness and a contrast switch. The second is to fit some kind of anti-glare filter.

2.6 Medical evidence now suggests that working with a VDU does not cause eye defects. It can, however, lead to **sore eyes**, **headaches** or discomfort in the **neck, shoulders and arms**.

2.7 The **position** of the VDU is important in preventing discomfort. Most VDUs are mounted on some kind of **pedestal** and, depending on the desk space available, they may be sited on the surface of the desk itself or may be perched on the base unit of a desktop computer. Health and Safety regulations on 'display screen equipment' require that all VDUs have to have a **swivel and tilt** capability.

*The keyboard*

2.8 Poor positioning of a keyboard can lead to **postural problems**. The angle of keyboards should be adjustable and the workspace in front of them should be of sufficient width for a user to rest his or her forearms. The **angle of typing** can be made more comfortable by placing the wrists on a narrow raised platform in front of the keyboard.

2.9 The most widely discussed keyboard-related complaint is RSI, or **repetitive strain injury**. This is a disorder which affects the upper limbs particularly the forearms and hands. Although there is legal and medical dispute about whether RSI is a genuine condition (because employers tend to settle claims for injury out of court), it seems to arise from poorly designed equipment, environment and posture, which leads to muscles being starved of oxygen, the build up of waste products in the body and the compression of nerves.

*Other computer equipment*

2.10 There are a number of other potential problems which you may encounter if you use computers, or indeed any other **electrical equipment**. The principal risks are injury from **electric shock**, attraction of **static electricity** and the hazard of loose or badly-routed computer **cabling**.

## Minimising risks to the person

2.11 Positive steps can be taken to reduce most of the risks described above. If you are in a job where your remuneration depends on the number of keystrokes you achieve in the working day, you may feel a certain reluctance to adopt some of these measures.

   (a) Ensure that your place of work is **comfortable** and conducive to maintaining a **good posture**.

   (b) Ensure that the **layout** of the workstation will not necessitate **awkward posture** or movements. (You should not need to balance the keyboard on your knees, nor should you need to move you head to be able to see the screen.)

   (c) Take **occasional breaks**, or as a minimum change your posture from time to time to prevent muscle strain.

   (d) Try out different ways of positioning the **keyboard, VDU and input documents** to find one that suits you.

   (e) Reduce the **glare** from your screen in one of the ways described above. Focus should be **sharp**, characters should **not flicker** and there should be **no reflections**.

---

### Activity 14.2

You have to enter a batch of invoices before the accounts department supervisor can close the purchase ledger. Unfortunately a colleague has spilt a cup of coffee over your keyboard and some of the keys are sticking. There is a spare terminal in the office and so you decide to use this. List the adjustments you might wish to make to the computer hardware and office furniture before you start work.

---

## 3 RISKS TO HARDWARE

### Physical threats

3.1 Physical security comprises two sorts of control.

(a) Protection against **natural and man made disasters,** such as fire, flood or sabotage.

(b) Protection against **intruders** obtaining physical access to the system.

3.2 The physical environment has a major effect on information system security, and so planning it properly is an important precondition of an adequate security plan.

*Fire and flood*

3.3 **Fire** is a **serious hazard** to computer systems. Destruction of **data** can be even more costly than the destruction of **hardware.** In a well publicised fire at the Open University some years ago, a portable office was burned down. It contained a computer, and several years' work was lost. There was no back up held!

3.4 A proper fire safety plan is an essential feature of security procedures, in order to prevent fire, detect fire and put out the fire. Fire safety includes:

(a) Site preparation (for example, appropriate building **materials,** fire doors).

(b) **Detection** (for example, smoke detectors).

(c) **Extinguishing** (for example, sprinklers).

(d) **Training** for staff in observing fire safety procedures (for example, no smoking in the computer room).

3.5 **Water** is a serious hazard. Flooding and water damage are often encountered following **firefighting** activities elsewhere in a building. This problem can be countered by the use of waterproof ceilings and floors together with the provision of adequate drainage. In some areas **flooding** is a natural risk, for example in parts of central London and many other towns and cities near rivers or coasts.

*Weather*

3.6 The weather may be a threat. **Wind, rain and storms** can all cause substantial damage to buildings. In certain areas the risks are greater, for example the risk of typhoons in parts of the Far East. Many organisations make heavy use of prefabricated and portable offices, which are particularly vulnerable. Cutbacks in **maintenance** expenditure may lead to **leaking roofs** or **dripping pipes,** which can invite problems of this type.

3.7 **Lightning** and electrical storms pose an additional threat, as they can play havoc with power supplies, causing **power failures** coupled with **power surges** as services are restored. Minute adjustments in power supplies may be enough to affect computer processing operations (these are characterised by lights which dim as the country's population turns on electric kettles following a popular television program).

3.8 One way of combating this is by the use of **uninterrupted (protected) power supplies** (or **UPS**). This will protect equipment from fluctuations in the supply. Power failure can be protected against by the use of a **separate generator.**

*Theft*

3.9 Office break-ins are common. Although the petty cash tin may be the most obvious target, PCs can offer a tempting alternative. A **laptop computer** will fit easily into a briefcase or bag. One person can carry a laser printer or a Pentium desktop processor equally well.

3.10 Another risk is **chip theft**. Some organisations have reported dozens of computers being opened up and the microchips removed. Since a good Pentium chip costs well over £100, a large office with lots of PCs becomes a very attractive target for the criminal.

3.11 Another problem is that much equipment is specifically **designed** for **use off-site** (for example laptops, notebooks, handhelds) and so control procedures have to incorporate the fact that items will be held at many locations.

*Security procedures*

3.12 A **log of all equipment** should be maintained. This may already exist as a part of the fixed asset register. The log should include the **make**, **model** and **serial number** of each item, together with some other **organisation-generated code** which identifies the **department** which owns the item, the **individual responsible** for the item and its **location**. Anyone taking any equipment off-site should **book it out** and book it back in.

3.13 Computer theft may be carried out by persons who have official access to equipment. It may equally be carried out by those who do not. **Burglar alarms** should be installed.

3.14 Smaller items of equipment, such as laptop computers and floppy disks, should always be **locked securely away**. Larger items cannot be moved with ease and one approach adopted is the use of **bolts** to secure them to desks. This discourages 'opportunity' thieves. Larger organisations may also employ site **security guards** and install closed circuit **camera systems**.

*Impact*

3.15 Most computers look pretty solid, but they are actually very delicate pieces of equipment. This means that they **should not be dropped or knocked**. A jolt could do anything from cracking the screen to knocking the hard disk out of alignment, meaning that it is not possible to retrieve the data and programs stored on it.

*Other risks*

3.16 The 'coffee and keyboards' risk was noted earlier. Next time you are in a computing environment, spend a few minutes looking around and see what risks to hardware you can identify. Is the equipment shielded from direct **sunlight**? Do the computers have protective **dust covers**? Are there any dangerously sited **pot plants**?

3.17 In this section we have examined some of the more common risks to computer **hardware**. It should be clear to you that some of these can also affect **software and data**. Later we will examine some of the risks to **storage media** - the disks and tapes on which software and data are held.

## Activity 14.3

Your department is located in an open-plan office, has five networked desktop PCs, a laser printer and a dot matrix printer.

You have just read an article suggesting that the best form of security is to lock hardware away in fireproof cabinets, but you feel that this is impracticable. Make a note of any alternative security measures which you could adopt to protect the hardware.

## Activity 14.4

Your company is in the process of installing a mainframe computer, and because your department will be the primary user, you have been co-opted onto the project team with responsibility for systems installation. You have a meeting at which the office services manager will be present, and you realise that no-one has yet mentioned the risks of fire or flooding in the discussions about site selection. Make a note of the issues which you would like to raise under these headings.

## 4 PHYSICAL ACCESS CONTROL

4.1 The way to minimise many of the risks discussed in the above section is to introduce a series of physical **access** controls, to prevent intruders getting near the computer **equipment** or storage media. Methods of controlling human access include:

- Personnel (security guards)

- Mechanical devices (eg keys, whose issue is recorded)

- Electronic identification devices (eg card-swipe systems)

4.2 Obviously, the best form of access control would be one which **recognised** individuals immediately, without the need for personnel, who can be assaulted, or cards, which can be stolen. However, machines which can identify a person's fingerprints or scan the pattern of a retina are extremely **expensive**, and not widely used.

4.3 It may not be cost effective or convenient to have the **same type** of access controls around the **whole building** all of the time. Instead, the various security requirements of different departments should be estimated, and appropriate boundaries drawn. Some areas will be **very restricted**, whereas others will be **relatively open**.

4.4 Guidelines for data security which should be applied within the office are as follows.

(a) **Fireproof cabinets** should be used to store files, or lockable boxes for floppy disks and CD-ROMs. If files contain confidential data, they should beheld in a lockable room or cabinet.

(b) Computer terminals should be **sited carefully**, to minimise the risk of unauthorised use.

(c) If a computer printout includes confidential data, it should be **shredded** before it is eventually thrown away after use.

(d) **Disks** containing valuable data should not be left lying around an office. They can get lost or stolen. More likely still, they can get damaged, by spilling **tea or coffee** over them, or allowing the disks to gather **dust**, which can make them unreadable.

(e) The computer's environment should **not be excessively hot**.

### Personal identification numbers (PINs)

4.5    In some organisations staff might have a special **personal identification number,** or PIN. PINs may be required to be keyed into keypads to gain entry to the building, and to areas within the building. The staff member be **allowed access** to certain areas, but **forbidden access** to other parts.

### Door locks

4.6    Conventional door locks are of value in certain circumstances, particularly where users are only required to pass through the door a **couple of times a day**. If the number of people using the door increases and the frequency of use is high, it will be difficult to persuade staff to lock a door every time they pass through it.

4.7    If this approach is adopted, a 'good' lock must be accompanied by a **strong door,** otherwise an intruder may simply bypass the lock. Similarly, other points of entry into the room/complex must be as well protected, otherwise the intruder will simply use a **window** to gain access.

4.8    One difficulty with conventional locks is the matter of **key control**. Inevitably, each person authorised to use the door will have a key and there will also be a master key maintained by security. Cleaners and other contractors might be issued with keys. Practices such as lending out keys or taking duplicate keys may be difficult to prevent.

4.9    One approach to this is the installation of **combination locks**, where a numbered keypad is located outside the door and access allowed only after the correct 'code', or sequence of digits has been entered. This will only be effective if users keep the combination **secret** and the combination is **changed** frequently. (This differs from a PIN system as one combination is used by all.)

### Card entry systems

4.10    There is a range of card entry systems available. This is a more sophisticated means of control than the use of locks, as **cards can be programmed** to allow access to certain parts of a building only, between certain times.

4.11    These allow a high degree of monitoring of staff movements; they can for example be used instead of clock cards to record details of time spent on site. Such cards can be incorporated into **identity cards,** which also carry the photograph and signature of the user and which must be 'displayed' at all times.

### Activity 14.5

What are the relative advantages and disadvantages of security guards and electronic identification devices?

## 5    CONTROLS OVER PERSONNEL

### Personnel selection

5.1    The vast majority of employees are **honest** and have good intentions.

5.2 However, a small minority of employees may inflict **deliberate damage** on a system. The issues arising for organisations simply reflect best practice in personnel management and organisational control, and are not the exclusive preserve of the management of information systems.

5.3 Controls related to personnel include the following.

(a) Checks and balances so that a security violation must **pass through several steps** before being implemented.

(b) **Segregation of duties** (division of responsibilities).

(c) **Job rotation,** so that employees change jobs at random intervals, thus making it uncertain that an individual will be able to set up a breach of security in the time available.

(d) Enforced **vacations**.

(e) Access to information granted not on rank in the management hierarchy or precedent, but on a **need-to-know** basis.

(f) Careful **selection** of personnel. IT staff should be recruited with care. They should be honest and should have the qualities and/or experience to do their job well.

## Division of responsibilities

5.4 Some employees have to be in a **position of trust** although a well-designed security system puts as few people in this powerful position as possible. The computer security officer's nightmare when it comes to personnel is when a member of staff who has expertise in the design of the system (and so knows of its vulnerabilities) and a member of staff who uses the information system (and so has day to day procedural knowledge as to how it works, other personnel involved) combine to create a breach of security.

5.5 Dividing up responsibilities, as far as **security** is concerned, has two purposes.

(a) To assign the **responsibility** for certain tasks to specific jobs and individuals. A person in a given job has the responsibility for ensuring that certain controls are applied, and knows that he will be blamed if they are not.

(b) To prevent **deliberate error**. It is easier for a person to commit fraud if he can input data, write programs and operate the computer all by himself. By dividing up the work, it is more difficult to commit fraud or tamper with data, except in collusion with others.

5.6 Desirable as such controls may be, especially where accounting systems are concerned, they conflict with modern ideas about **multi-skilled employees** and widespread **sharing of information**.

## Fraud

5.7 Computer frauds come from disgruntled employees, organised crime (which bribes an employee to breach the organisation's defences) and hackers. Networks, and the fact that many employees can have access to the computer system, make certain types of fraud easier.

5.8 Two **types** of frauds can be identified.

(a) Single **large scale frauds,** usually involving large amounts of money.

(b) Small-scale, but **long term frauds**. If an organisation has 20,000 employees, then five pence sliced off the monthly salary cheque for each employee (the 'salami' technique) would net the fraudster £1,000 per month, or, over a year, £12,000.

5.9 Examples of **methods** of fraud are given below.

(a) Creation of **fictitious supplier accounts** and submission of false invoices, usually for services rather than goods, so that payments are sent to the fictitious supplier.

(b) Abuse of corporate **credit card facilities**, for example to purchase more fuel than is used in the employee's company car.

(c) **Corruption and bribery**, particularly where individuals are in a position of authority as regards making decisions on suppliers or selecting between tenders.

(d) **Misappropriation** of incoming cheques from bona fide customers.

(e) **Theft** of portable fixed assets.

(f) Giving **unauthorised discounts** to customers.

(g) **Stock losses,** including short deliveries by driver (for example in the catering trade) or stock 'wastage' (for example of vehicle parts or unused vehicle service books).

(h) **Fictitious staff** on the payroll. This was reported as prevalent in newspaper publishing some years ago, with wages being paid to Mr Mickey Mouse and others.

5.10 These frauds do not all involve computers, but many could be detected by appropriate use of computer controls, perusal of exception reports, analysis of expenditure ratios and the like.

# 6 RISKS TO STORAGE MEDIA

6.1 We have examined some of the more common risks to computer **hardware** and the computer environment and it should be clear to you that some of these can also affect the **physical things** on which data and software are held. The most widely used forms of storage medium are **disks and tapes**.

## Handling floppy disks, CDs and tapes

6.2 Floppy **disks** are not so floppy these days and CDs are fairly sturdy. However, both should be handled with care, just as you would treat a valuable music CD with care.

(a) They will break or be seriously damaged if you are strong enough to **bend them,** or if you **tread on them** or **run them over** with the castors of your chair.

(b) They do not take kindly to having **hot drinks** spilled over them or to being left on sunny windowsills.

(c) CDs in particular should be protected from **dust** and **scratches** and **finger prints**: hold them along the outer edge or by the centre hole. *Never* touch the surface of the disk inside a floppy disk's casing.

(d) For floppy disks write on the label **before** you stick it on to the disk and write only with a **felt tip pen,** never a ball point. If you write on a CD you should only write on the 'label' side - again only with a felt-tip pen.

(e) Floppy disks are 'magnetic' disks so they are affected by **magnets**. (CDs are optical disks so magnets are not a problem.)

6.3 **Tapes** can be snipped with scissors, or get knotted up, and they can also be damaged by magnets and heat and liquid. Treat them with care.

---

### Activity 14.6

The diagram shows an illustration found on a CD-R. What does it mean?

---

## 7 RISKS TO DATA

7.1 Risks to **data** can be in the form of deliberate or accidental:

- Destruction (or alteration)
- Theft
- Unauthorised disclosure

7.2 Data can be protected from the risk of theft or unauthorised disclosure by suitable controls. There are two forms of access control; the first (as described earlier) prevents **physical** access to the hardware and the second prevents access from the hardware to the software. This is known as **logical** access control.

7.3 In its commonest form, logical access control consists of a password system. Data destruction can be protected against by taking **back-ups** and the risk of alteration of data minimised by a variety of basic precautions.

### Passwords

> **KEY TERM**
>
> **Passwords** are a set of characters which may be allocated to a person, a terminal or a facility which are required to be keyed into the system before further access is permitted.

7.4 **Passwords** can be applied to data files, program files and to parts of a program.

(a) One password may be required to **read a file**, but another to **write new data** to it.

(b) The terminal user can be **restricted** to the use of certain files and programs (eg in a banking system, junior grades of staff are only allowed to access certain routine programs).

7.5 In order to access a system the user needs first to enter a string of characters. If what is entered **matches** a password issued to an authorised user or valid for that particular terminal the system permits access. Otherwise the system **shuts down** and may record the attempted unauthorised access.

7.6 Keeping track of these attempts can alert managers to **repeated efforts** to break into the system; in these cases the culprits might be caught, particularly if there is an apparent pattern to their efforts.

7.7 The restriction of access to a system with passwords is effective and widely used. Requirements for system security must be balanced by the operational requirements for access: a rigidly enforced isolation of the system may significantly reduce the value of the system.

## Problems with passwords

7.8 Passwords ought to be effective in keeping out unauthorised users, but they are **by no means foolproof**.

(a) By **experimenting** with possible passwords, an unauthorised person can gain access to a program or file by **guessing** the correct password. This is not as difficult as it may seem when too many computer users specify 'obvious' passwords. In addition **computer programs** are available that run through millions of possible combinations at lightning speed until the correct one is found.

(b) Someone who is authorised to access a data or program file may **tell an unauthorised person** what the password is, perhaps through carelessness, or because it seems convenient on a particular occasion.

(c) An unauthorised person may simply **observe** someone else keying in their password. Most systems display **asterisks** instead of the actual characters typed, to try to prevent this, although this may not help if the password is a short simple one and the user types very slowly.

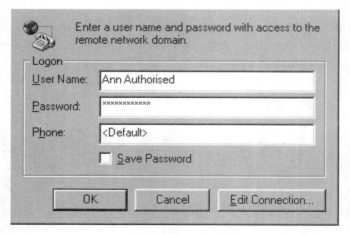

(d) Many password systems come with **standard passwords** as part of the system, such as LETMEIN. It is essential for these to be removed if the system is to be secure.

(e) Password systems rely upon users to use them **conscientiously**. A password system requires both a software system and strong organisational policies if it is to be effective.

(f)   A good password, in a form such as **f146PQzH7364** (numbers and letters, upper and lower case), would be very difficult to guess, but it is also very **difficult to remember!** Valuable information may become totally inaccessible if the user assigns a password (to a spreadsheet or database, say) and then forgets it.

Ways of avoiding this include using **mnemonics** for the letters and using numbers that are **significant** to the user for another reason (a cash card PIN number in reverse, say), but not easily guess-able by others.

---

**BPP - Best Password Practice**

Here is a checklist of points to be observed by computer users to whom passwords have been allocated.

- **Keep your password secret**. Do *not* reveal it to anyone else.

- **Do *not* write it down**. The second easiest way of revealing a password is to write it on an adhesive label and stick this to the VDU, the desk beneath the keyboard, the inside of a desk drawer or the underside of an overhead filing cabinet.

- **Change your password regularly.**

- Change and use your password **discreetly**. Even though a password does not show up on screen, it is easy for onlookers to see which keys are being used. (FRED is a popular password for this reason; the relevant keys are close together on a QWERTY keyboard.)

- **Do not use an obvious password**. (FRED is an obvious password. Your name or nickname is another)

- **Change** your password if you **suspect** that anyone else knows it.

---

7.9   In a logical access system, data and software, or individual computer systems, will be **classified** according to the **sensitivity** and **confidentiality** of data.

(a)   Thus **payroll** data or details of the draft corporate budget for the coming year may be perceived as highly sensitive and made available to identified individuals only.

(b)   Other financial information may be made **available to certain groups** of staff only, for example members of the finance function or a certain grade of management.

(c)   Other data may be **unrestricted.**

7.10  A logical access system performs three operations when access is requested and a password entered.

- **Identification** of the user.
- **Authentication** of user identity.
- Check on user **authority.**

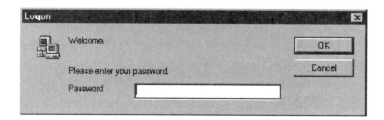

---

**Activity 14.7**

Your company's standard password screen requires users to enter two pieces of data - their user ID (based on their surname) and their password. User IDs are allocated centrally and are up to 10 characters in length, while 8-character passwords are chosen by the user. When you log on your ID is displayed as you enter it and a row of asterisks is displayed as you enter the password. One day, working in your open plan office, you inadvertently enter your password in the user ID field. You look round, but no-one behind you appears to have noticed. What do you do?

## Telecommunications dangers

7.11   When data is transmitted over a network or **telecommunications link** (especially the **Internet**) there are numerous security dangers.

(a)   Corruptions such as **viruses** on a single computer can spread through the network to all of the organisation's computers. (Viruses are described at greater length later in this chapter.)

(b)   Disaffected employees have much greater potential to do **deliberate damage** to valuable corporate data or systems because the network could give them access to parts of the system that they are not really authorised to use.

(c)   If the organisation is linked to an external network, persons outside the company (**hackers**) may be able to get into the company's internal network, either to steal data or to damage the system.

Systems can have **firewalls** (which disable part of the telecoms technology) to prevent unwelcome intrusions into company systems, but a determined hacker may well be able to bypass even these. (There is more on hackers below.)

(d)   Employees may **download inaccurate information** or imperfect or **virus-ridden software** from an external network. For example 'beta' (free trial) versions of forthcoming new editions of many major packages are often available on the Internet, but the whole point about a beta version is that it is not fully tested and may contain bugs that could disrupt an entire system.

(e)   Information transmitted from one part of an organisation to another may be **intercepted**. Data can be 'encrypted' (scrambled) in an attempt to make it unintelligible to eavesdroppers.

(f)   The **communications link itself may break down or distort data**. The worldwide telecommunications infrastructure is improving thanks to the use of new technologies, and there are communications 'protocols' governing the format of data and signals transferred.

## Encryption and other safety measures

7.12   **Encryption** is the only secure way to prevent eavesdropping (as eavesdroppers avoid password controls by tapping the line that data is transmitted across.

### KEY TERM

**Encryption** involves scrambling the data at one end of the line, transmitting the scrambled data, and unscrambling it at the receiver's end of the line.

7.13   **Authentication** is a technique of making sure that a message has come from an authorised sender. Authentication involves adding an extra field to a record, with the contents of this field derived from the remainder of the record by applying an algorithm that has previously been agreed between the senders and recipients of data.

296

7.14 **Dial-back security** operates by requiring the person wanting access to the network to dial into it and identify themselves first. The system then dials the person back on their authorised number before allowing them access.

7.15 All attempted **violations of security** should be automatically **logged** and the log checked regularly. In a multi-user system, the terminal attempting the violation may be automatically disconnected.

## Hacking

7.16 A hacker is a **person who attempts to invade the privacy of a system**.

7.17 Hackers use programming and communications knowledge to gain unauthorised access to a system. Hackers, in the past, have mainly been concerned to **copy** information, but a recent trend has been their desire to **corrupt it**.

7.18 Phone numbers and passwords can be guessed by hackers using **electronic phone directories** or number generators and by software which enables **rapid guessing** using hundreds of permutations per minute.

7.19 **Default passwords** are also available on some electronic bulletin boards and sophisticated hackers could even try to 'tap' messages being transmitted along phone wires.

7.20 The **Computer Misuse Act 1990** makes hacking an offence, but clearly this does not **prevent** it.

## Viruses

> **KEY TERM**
>
> A **virus** is a piece of software which infects programs and data and possibly damages them, and which replicates itself.

7.21 Viruses need an **opportunity to spread**. The programmers of viruses therefore place viruses in the kind of software which is most likely to be copied. This includes:

 (a) **Free software** (for example from magazine covers and the Internet).
 (b) **Pirated software** (cheaper than original versions).
 (c) **E-mail attachments** (easily copied to everyone in an organisation).

*The effect of viruses*

7.22 Viruses may cause **damage to files** or attempt to **destroy files** and damage hard disks.

7.24 An activated virus can **show itself** in a number of ways.

 • The **Stoned** virus displays a **message** saying 'This computer is stoned - legalise marijuana.'

 • **Cascade** causes letters on the **screen** to 'fall' to the bottom of the screen and may reformat the hard disk.

- **Casino** displays a one-armed bandit game on screen; if you fail to win the jackpot, your **hard disk is wiped**.

7.25 The most serious type of virus is one which **infects an operating system** as this governs the whole execution of a program.

7.26 Viruses can spread via floppy disk or e-mail and have been known to copy themselves over whole **networks**. When transmitted over a network into a clean system, the virus continues to reproduce, thus infecting that system.

| Type of virus | Explanation/Example |
| --- | --- |
| File viruses | File viruses infect program files. When you run an infected program the virus runs first, then passes control to the original program. While it has control, the virus code copies itself to another file or to another disk, replicating itself. |
| Macro viruses | A macro virus is a piece of self-replicating code written in an application's 'macro' language. Many applications have macro capabilities including all the programs in **Microsoft Office**.<br><br>The distinguishing factor which makes it possible to create a virus with a macro is the existence of **auto-execute events**. Auto-execute events are opening a file, closing a file, and starting an application. Once a macro is running, it can copy itself to other documents, delete files, and create general havoc in a person's system. These things occur without the user explicitly running the macro. The Melissa virus is a macro virus |
| Boot sector viruses | The boot sector is the part of every hard disk and diskette which is read by the computer when it starts up. Most PCs are set up to attempt to boot from the A: drive first. If the boot sector of a diskette is infected, the virus runs when you attempt to boot from the diskette, and infects the hard disk. |
| Overwriting viruses | An overwriting virus simply overwrites each file it infects with itself, so the program no longer functions. |
| Worms | A worm is a program which spreads (usually) over network connections. Unlike a virus, it does not attach itself to a host program. Worms are not normally associated with PC systems. |
| Dropper | A dropper is a program, not a virus itself, that installs a virus on the PC while performing another function. A typical example is a utility that formats a floppy disk, complete with Stoned virus, on the boot sector. |

*Trojans*

7.27 A Trojan or Trojan Horse is a program intended to perform some covert and usually malicious act. It differs from a virus in that it **doesn't reproduce** (though this distinction is by no means universally accepted).

(a) **A logic bomb** is a **type of trojan** that is **triggered by certain events**. A program will behave normally until a certain event occurs, for example when disk utilisation reaches a certain percentage. A logic bomb, by responding to set conditions, maximises damage. For example, it will be triggered when a disk is nearly full, or when a large number of users are using the system.

(b) A **time bomb** is similar to a logic bomb, except that it is **triggered at a certain date**. Companies have experienced virus attacks on April Fool's Day and on Friday 13th. These were released by time bombs.

### *Bugs*

7.28 A **bug** is an **unintentional fault** in a program, and can be misinterpreted as a virus. Virtually all complex software contains bugs. Minor bugs merely cause inconvenience, while major bugs can cause catastrophic data loss. There is no way of detecting bugs in advance, and the only defence is to ensure you back up your important data regularly.

### *Jokes and hoaxes*

7.29 Some programs claim to be doing something destructive to your computer, but are actually harmless jokes. For example, a message may appear suggesting that your hard disk is about to be reformatted. Unfortunately, it is **easy to over-react** to the joke and cause more damage by trying to eradicate something that is not, in fact, a virus.

7.30 There are a number of common hoaxes, which are widely believed. The most common of these is **Good Times**. This hoax has been around for a couple of years, and usually takes the form of a virus warning about viruses contained in e-mail. People pass along the warning because they are trying to be helpful, wasting the time of all concerned.

---

### Case example: the Good Times hoax

Here is the text of one version (of many) of the well-known 'Good Times' hoax. Read this, see if you can spot the flaws in the argument, and be sure to do Question 7. (*Note.* 'an nth-complexity infinite binary loop' is sheer gobbledegook!)

**V I R U S - W A R N I N G**

There is a computer virus that is being sent across the Internet. If you receive an email message with the subject line "Good Times," DO NOT read the message, DELETE it immediately.

DON'T DOWN LOAD THE FILE!

It has a virus that rewrites your hard drive, obliterating anything on it.

Please be careful and forward this message to anyone you care about.

WARNING!!!!!!! INTERNET VIRUS

Apparently a new computer virus has been engineered by a user of AMERICA ON LINE that is unparalleled in its destructive capability.

What makes this virus so terrifying, is the fact that no program needs to be exchanged for a new computer to be infected. It can be spread through the existing email systems of the Internet. Once a Computer is infected, one of several things can happen. If the computer contains a hard drive, that will most likely be destroyed. If the program is not stopped, the computer's processor will be placed in an nth-complexity infinite binary loop--which can severely damage the processor.

Luckily, there is one sure means of detecting what is now known as the "Good Times" virus. It always travels to new computers the same way in a text email message with the subject line reading "Good Times." The bottom line is:

If you receive a file with the subject line "Good Times", delete it immediately! Do not read it" Rest assured that whoever's name was on the "From" line was surely struck by the virus.

Warn your friends and local system users of this newest threat to the Internet! It could save them a lot of time and money. Could you pass this along to your global mailing list as well?

---

### Identification of a virus

7.31 There are two ways of identifying a virus. The first is to identify it before it does any damage. The second is to identify it when it is activated.

7.32 It is difficult for the typical user to identify the presence of a virus. There are sometimes **tell-tale signs,** such as slight changes in file lengths as displayed in the directory, or additional disk activity before a program is run, but **more sophisticated controls** than this are needed.

(a) **Anti-virus software** such as Dr Solomon's is capable of detecting and eradicating a vast number of viruses before they do any damage. Upgrades are released regularly to deal with new viruses. The software will run whenever a computer is turned on and will continue to monitor in the background until it is turned off again.

(b) Organisations must have **procedures** to guard against the introduction of unauthorised software to their systems. Many viruses and trojans have been spread on pirated versions of popular computer games and via 'joke' e-mail attatchments

(c) Organisations, as a matter of routine, should **ensure that any disk received from outside is virus-free** before the data on the disk is downloaded.

(d) Any **flaws in a widely used program** should be rectified as soon as they come to light.

---

### Case example: Viruses

**Melissa** is a Microsoft Word **Macro** virus. The virus has spread rapidly around the world, and has infected thousands.

Melissa can infect a system when it is received from another infected user via the e-mail program **Microsoft Outlook**. It reads the list of members from the Outlook Global Address Book. An email message is created and sent to the first 50 names in the list. The message is created with the subject

"Important Message From - <User Name>".

The message reads

"Here is that document you asked for ... don't show anyone else ;-)".

Once the system is infected all documents that are opened are infected.

The **CIH.Spacefiller** virus or ('**Chernobyl**') originated in Taiwan and within one week was worldwide.

Chernobyl mainly infects Windows 95/98 executable files (ie programs). When an infected program is run the virus will infect the computer's **memory**. CIH then infects new files when they are opened. The virus infects by first looking for empty, **unused spaces** in a file; then breaking itself up into saller pieces, and **hiding** in these unused spaces.

Chernobyl will **write-over** the first 1MB of the hard-disk with **random data**. It will also attempt to modify or corrupt certain types of 'Flash **BIOS**', software that initialises and manages the relationships and data flow between the system devices, including the hard drive, serial and parallel ports and the keyboard. By overwriting part of the BIOS program, the virus can **stop a computer from starting up** when the power is turned on.

Some variants of the virus activate on **April 26th** (the anniversary of the Chernobyl nuclear reactor disaster, hence the nickname) or June 26th, while other variants will activate on the 26th of **every** month.

---

### Activity 14.8

Your company's sales force take laptop computers on sales trips, as this improves efficiency. After each field trip, orders are downloaded to the central sales order processing system. One of your responsibilities is to perform a monthly 'health check' on the laptops. This involves asking the sales team if they are aware of any problems and carrying out a few routine tests, including checking the keyboard, the screen, the password protection, the software loaded and the existence of back-ups.

One week you switch on a laptop and look at the file directory. The display is shown below. What do you do next?

```
☐    C:\
    ☐ DOS
    ☐ EXCEL
    ☐ GAMES
    ☐ GOLF
    ☐ FLTSIMUL
    ☐ WINDOWS
    ☐ WINWORD
```

---

### Activity 14.9

A **hoax** is not a virus at all, but simply a spoof warning that such and such a document or program contains a virus. Hoaxes are sent by e-mail to unsuspecting persons and they encourage people to forward the message to anybody else they can think of that might be affected by the spoof virus.

What is the point of this?

---

## 8 BACK-UP PROCEDURES

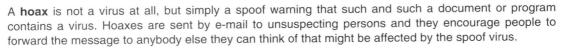

> **KEY TERM**
>
> **Back-up** means to make a copy which would enable recovery in the case of future failure or corruption. A back-up copy of a file is a duplicate copy kept separately from the main system and only used if the original fails.

### Re-creating file data when a file is lost or corrupted

8.1 The worst things that could happen in data processing by computer are either the loss of data, or the loss of a program. Files can be **physically deleted,** and it is also possible for a file to become **corrupted.** A file might also be **physically damaged** and become unreadable.

8.2 An important set of procedural controls is therefore to enable a data or program file to be **recreated** if the original is lost or corrupted.

*Grandfather-father-son security*

8.3 The reconstruction of files can be achieved by use of the grandfather-father-son technique. This technique usually involves the files being copied from the network server, mainframe or PC to magnetic tape.

8.4 It is common to keep three generations (grandfather, father and son) of master files, and sufficient transaction files to re-create the father from the grandfather master file. If the 'son' tape is found to contain corrupted data, a corrected son file can be recreated by going back to the 'father' and redoing whatever processing has been done since the father was created. (This requires either copies of input documents or printouts of processed transactions to be held.)

PUBLISHING

*Other techniques*

8.5     Some non-transaction based files may be backed-up by being periodically '**dumped**' on to a back-up tape, disk or CD. For example, spreadsheet files held on the hard disk of a PC may be copied to tape using a tape streamer unit.

## Procedures

8.6     Creating back-up files is now a regular routine with PC systems in many offices. The computer's **operating system** will have a back-up command for creating back-up files, although these are often intended to be used with floppy disks, which given their small capacity, is not practical.

8.7     With networks and larger systems the system can be set up to back up everything, or certain selected files, **automatically** at a regular time each day (say, midnight).

8.8     All **program** disks or CDs should be kept to enable re-installation if required.

8.9     Backing up a complete **hard disk** on to floppy disks is not practical, because a hard disk has a much larger capacity than a floppy disk. Backing up a hard disk on to a tape is quicker and more convenient, although the user has to go to the expense of buying a **tape streamer** unit. It is possible to back up onto **CD-R** or onto a separate hard disk or a Zip disk.

8.10    Many back-up routines use some kind of **compression** program so that the backed-up data takes up less space than the original. If the back-up has to be used a **restore** program has to be run to **expand** the data into useable format.

## Storage of back-ups

8.11    Back-up copies should be stored **off-site.** This means that if there is a fire or a burglary at the business premises the back up copies will not be damaged. In practice many organisations keep one set of back-ups on-site (for speed of access) and a second set at a separate location.

## The effectiveness of backups

8.12    The backing-up of data is a critical requirement for systems security. However, data on a back-up file will not itself be entirely secure unless some **additional measures** are used.

8.13    If there is a **hardware fault** which causes data loss of corruption the fault must be diagnosed and corrected before the correct data is put at risk in the system. The usefulness of archived data would be entirely negated if it were fed mindlessly into a faulty system. Systems will need to be repaired and fully tested to ensure that the real data will not be corrupted.

## 9       THE DATA PROTECTION ACT

### Why is privacy an important issue?

9.1     In recent years, there has been a growing popular fear that **information** about individuals which was stored on computer files and processed by computer could be **misused**.

9.2 In particular, it was felt that an individual could easily be harmed by the existence of computerised data about him or her which was inaccurate or misleading and which could be **transferred to unauthorised third parties** at high speed and little cost.

9.3 In the UK the current legislation is the **Data Protection Act 1998**. This Act replaced the earlier Data Protection Act 1984.

## The Data Protection Act 1998

9.4 The Data Protection Act 1998 is an attempt to protect the **individual**.

## Definitions of terms used in the Act

9.5 In order to understand the Act it is necessary to know some of the technical terms used in it.

(a) **Personal data** is information about a living individual, including expressions of opinion about him or her. Data about other organisations (eg supplier or customer companies) is not personal data, unless it contains data about individuals who belong to those other organisations.

(b) **Data users** are organisations or individuals who control the contents of files of personal data and the use of personal data which is processed (or intended to be processed) automatically - ie who use personal data which is covered by the terms of the Act.

(c) A **data subject** is an individual who is the subject of personal data.

## The data protection principles

9.6 There are certain Data Protection Principles which data users must comply with.

---

### DATA PROTECTION PRINCIPLES (1998 ACT)

Schedule 1 of the Act contains the revised data protection principles.

1 Personal data shall be processed fairly and lawfully and, in particular, shall not be processed unless:

   (a) at least one of the conditions in Schedule 2 is met (see item (d) above), and

   (b) in the case of sensitive personal data, at least one of the conditions in Schedule 3 is also met (see item (e) above).

2 Personal data shall be obtained only for one or more specified and lawful purposes, and shall not be further processed in any manner incompatible with that purpose or those purposes.

3 Personal data shall be adequate, relevant and not excessive in relation to the purpose or purposes for which they are processed.

4 Personal data shall be accurate and, where necessary, kept up to date.

5 Personal data processed for any purpose or purposes shall not be kept for longer than is necessary for that purpose or those purposes.

6 Personal data shall be processed in accordance with the rights of data subjects under this Act.

7 Appropriate technical and organisational measures shall be taken against unauthorised or unlawful processing of personal data and against accidental loss or destruction of, or damage to, personal data.

8 Personal data shall not be transferred to a country or territory outside the European Economic Area unless that country or territory ensures an adequate level of protection for the rights and freedoms of data subjects in relation to the processing of personal data.

---

*BPP* PUBLISHING

9.7    In July 1995 the European Parliament adopted a **Directive on Data Protection**, with two main purposes.

(a)    To protect **individual privacy**. Previous UK law only applied to **computer-based** information. The directive applies to **all personal data, in any form.**

(b)    To **harmonise data protection legislation** so that, in the interests of improving the operation of the single European market, there can be a **free flow of personal data** between the member states of the EU.

This directive led to the introduction of the new Data Protection Act in 1998.

## The coverage of the Act

9.8    Key points of the Act can be summarised as follows.

(a)    With certain exceptions, all **data users** and all computer bureaux have had to **register** under the Act with the **Data Protection Registrar**.

(b)    **Individuals** (data subjects) are awarded certain **legal rights**.

(c)    **Data holders** must adhere to the **data protection principles**.

### *Registration under the Act*

9.9    The Data Protection Registrar keeps a Register of all data users. Each entry in the Register relates to a data user or computer bureau. Unless a data user has an entry in the Register he may not hold personal data. Even if the data user is registered, he must only hold data and use data for the **purposes** which are registered. A data user must apply to be registered.

### *The rights of data subjects*

9.10    The Act establishes the following rights for data subjects.

(a)    A data subject may seek **compensation** through the courts for damage and any associated distress caused by the **loss, destruction** or **unauthorised disclosure** of data about himself or herself or by **inaccurate data** about himself or herself.

(b)    A data subject may apply to the courts for **inaccurate data** to be **put right** or even **wiped off** the data user's files altogether. Such applications may also be made to the Registrar.

(c)    A data subject may obtain **access** to personal data of which he is the subject. (This is known as the 'subject access' provision.) In other words, a data subject can ask to see his or her personal data that the data user is holding.

(d)    A data subject can **sue** a data user (or bureau) for any **damage or distress** caused to him by personal data about him which is **incorrect** or **misleading** as to matter of **fact** (rather than opinion).

9.11    Features of the 1998 legislation are:

(a)    Everyone now has the right to go to court to seek redress for **any breach** of data protection law, rather than just for certain aspects of it.

(b)    Filing systems that are structured so as to facilitate access to information about a particular person now fall within the legislation. This includes systems that are **paper-based** or on **microfilm** or **microfiche**. Personnel records meet this classification.

(c)    Processing of personal data is **forbidden** except in the following circumstances.

    (i)    With the **consent** of the subject. Consent cannot be implied: it must be by freely given, specific and informed agreement.

    (ii)    As a result of a **contractual arrangement.**

    (iii)    Because of a **legal obligation.**

    (iv)    To **protect the vital interests** of the subject.

    (v)    Where processing is in the **public interest.**

    (vi)    Where processing is required to exercise **official authority.**

(d)    The processing of 'sensitive data' is forbidden, unless express consent has been obtained or there are conflicting obligations under employment law. Sensitive data includes data relating to **racial origin, political opinions, religious beliefs,** physical or mental **health, sexual proclivities** and **trade union** membership.

(e)    If data about a data subject is **obtained from a third party** the data subject must be given.

    (i)    The identity of the **controller** of the data.
    (ii)    The **purposes** for which the data are being processed.
    (iii)    **What data** will be disclosed and **to whom.**
    (iv)    The existence of a right of subject **access** to the data.

(f)    Data subjects have a right not only to have a **copy of data** held about them but also the right to know **why** the data are being processed and **what is the logic** behind the processing.

9.12    The new Act provided for a transitional period for data controllers to bring systems into line with the new law. The Act came finally came into force on March 1 2000.

## Key learning points

- There are many different risks in the IT environment, both to computer hardware and to the organisation's data. **Human error** is probably the most common.

- Risks to the computer **user** include the usual office hazards, and some particularly associated with computers such as eye strain and back and arm injuries through poor equipment and poor posture.

- **Physical threats** to security may be natural or man made. They include fire, flooding, weather, lightning, terrorist activity and accidental damage.

- **Physical access control** attempts to stop **intruders** or other unauthorised persons getting near to computer equipment or storage media.

- Important aspects of physical access control are **door locks** and **card entry systems**. Computer theft is becoming more prevalent as equipment becomes smaller and more portable. All computer equipment should be tagged and registered, and portable items should be logged in and out.

- **Personnel** who will work with computers need to be carefully selected especially if they are to work with confidential data.

- **Computer fraud** usually involves the theft of funds. The opportunities for people to commit fraud are growing as computers become more widespread and computer literacy increases.

- Storage media such as **disks, tapes** and **CDs** are vulnerable to physical damage, through **coffee spills**, excess **heat**, accidental **mishandling.**

- **Passwords** can be applied to protect **data** files. A password is a set of characters which are required to be keyed into a system before further access is permitted. Although password systems can be extremely sophisticated, they all depend on user discipline.

- A **logical access system** is concerned with preventing those persons who have gained physical access from gaining unauthorised access to data or software.

- When data is transmitted over **telecommunications links**, there are a number of security risks. One method of preventing eavesdropping is **encryption**, which scrambles up data while it is being transmitted. Authentication ensures that a message has come from an authorised user.

- A **hacker** is a person who attempts to invade the privacy of a system by circumventing logical access controls.

- **Viruses** are currently the cause of much concern. A virus is a piece of software which corrupts the operation of programs and, given the opportunity, replicates itself throughout a system. Virus protection should be a standard part of the internal control system of any organisation.

- **Back-up procedures** are essential to guard against deliberate or accidental damage to data. Methods include the grandfather-father-son approach and dumping.

- At least some back-ups should be **stored off-site.**

- The Data Protection Act aims to protect the rights of individuals in relation to information organisations held about them.

## Quick quiz

1. Why is it important to identify risks?

2. How can you improve your working environment?

3. Why should organisations keep logs of computer equipment?

4. What is the difference between physical access control and logical access control?

5. When is a strong door lock of limited value?

6. Why should employees be forced to go on holiday?

7. What happens if you run a magnet over a CD-ROM?

8    Draw up a checklist of Best Password Practice.

9    What is dial-back security?

10   What is a virus?

11   Why is a compression program sometimes used in conjunction with back-ups?

## Answers to quick quiz

1    Because organisations often depend entirely on their IT resources to be able to function.

2    By adjusting furniture and equipment height, layout and angles until it is comfortable and convenient to use. By taking regular breaks. By avoiding screen glare, reflections etc.

3    Because otherwise they will not know what assets they possess or where they are, and so they may not notice if they are stolen.

4    Physical access control stops people from getting near computer **equipment**. Logical access control stops them from getting near **data**.

5    When the door is unlocked (obviously!). When a window is left open, or is insecure. When the door itself is a flimsy one.

6    Not simply because they deserve it! Employees who never go on holiday could be covering up some damage they are doing to the organisation's data by making sure that nobody else stands in for them and does their job.

7    It will probably get scratched. The magnetic qualities of the magnet will not harm the CD-ROM, though.

8    Keep it secret, don't write it down, change it regularly and discreetly (and immediately if you suspect someone else knows it), and don't use an obvious word.

9    Dial-back security operates by requiring the person wanting access to the network to dial into it and identify themselves first. The system then dials the person back on their authorised number before allowing them access.

10   A piece of software that infects programs and data and possibly damages them, and which replicates itself.

11   To store back-up copies of data in a format that takes up less storage space than the uncompressed data.

## Answers to activities

## Answer 14.1

Examples might be as follows.

(a)  *Human error.* Entering data in the wrong period, using the wrong data or getting up from your desk leaving the computer in edit mode.

(b)  *Technical error.* Computer not reading a disk properly, bugs in a software package or failed communications links between computers.

(c)  *Natural disasters.* Fire, flooding or lightning.

(d)  *Deliberate actions.* Fraud, perhaps involving electronic transfer of funds to private accounts or alterations to salary data on the payroll master file.

(e)  *Commercial espionage.* Certain financial institutions in the City of London have coated their windows with a reflective substance so that their screens cannot be seen from neighbouring buildings.

(f)  *Malicious damage.* There are well documented cases of disgruntled employees destroying data or introducing viruses just before leaving an organisation.

(g)   *Industrial action.* Loss of use of the processing function, even for a short time, can cause severe disruption.

## Answer 14.2

You should consider whether any of the following are necessary.

(a)   *Adjustment of chair* (height of seat and angle of back support).

(b)   *Layout of desk.* There should be space for input documents (both those processed and those to be processed) and the keyboard should be positioned to allow you to adopt a natural typing posture.

(c)   *Position of screen.* The screen should be angled so that you can see it without having to move or stretch.

(d)   *'Look' of screen.* There should be no reflections visible on the screen and you should minimise glare by adjusting the brightness/contrast and by fitting an anti-glare filter if necessary.

(e)   *Other.* Check that there are no electric cables which you might trip over.

## Answer 14.3

(a)   'Postcode' all pieces of hardware. Invisible ink postcoding is popular, but visible marking is a better deterrent. Soldering irons are ideal for writing on plastic casing.

(b)   Mark the equipment in other ways. Some organisations spray their hardware with permanent paint, perhaps in a particular colour (bright red is popular) or using stencilled shapes.

(c)   Hardware can be bolted to desks. If bolts are passed through the desk and through the bottom of the hardware casing, the equipment can be rendered immobile.

(d)   Ensure that the organisation's standard security procedures (magnetic passes, keypad access to offices, signing-in of visitors etc) are followed.

## Answer 14.4

(a)   *Fire.* Fire security measures can usefully be categorised as preventative, detective and corrective. Preventative measures include siting of the computer in a building constructed of suitable materials and the use of a site which is not affected by the storage of inflammable materials (stationery, chemicals). Detective measures involve the use of smoke detectors. Corrective measures may include installation of a sprinkler system (water-based or possibly gas-based to avoid electrical problems), training of fire officers and good siting of exit signs and fire extinguishers.

(b)   *Flooding.* Water damage may result from flooding or from fire recovery procedures. The golden rule is to avoid siting the computer in a basement.

## Answer 14.5

Security guards can get to know the staff and can act on their own initiative if intruders are spotted. On the other hand, they are expensive and they may become lax about security procedures.

Electronic identification devices are cheap to run and always apply controls to the same standard. On the other hand, they cannot show initiative, and a device which reads a card cannot tell if a card has been stolen and is being used by an intruder.

## Answer 14.6

(a)   Hold the CD by its edges.
(b)   Do not touch the surface of the CD with your fingers.
(c)   Do not allow the CD to get dirty or dusty.
(d)   Do not scratch the surface of the CD.
(e)   Do not bend the CD.
(f)   Store below 40°C (104°F).
(g)   Only write on the label side and only use a felt-tip pen.

## Answer 14.7

If there is any possibility at all that someone may have seen your password appear on the screen, you should change it immediately. Since users can select their own passwords, there will be a 'change password' option somewhere in the menu hierarchy. Use it discreetly, and be sure to remember the new password you have chosen.

## Answer 14.8

You should speak to the salesperson concerned to establish where the files in directory 'Games' and the subdirectories 'Golf' and 'Fltsimul' originated from. You should then remove those directories completely and notify the person concerned that you have done this. It is acknowledged that computer games are a potential source of viruses, particularly if they are not loaded from the 'official' CD-ROM or disks. You should also run an anti-virus program such as Dr Solomon's Toolkit or Norton Anti-Virus.

If necessary rules do not exist already, you should draft appropriate guidelines for computer users to ensure that the risk of introduction of viruses on to the company's PCs is minimised.

## Answer 14.9

Hoaxes do not do any harm in themselves and there is *no* point - unless you believe that it is amusing or desirable to create panic and waste the time of organisations. This is precisely what some of the perpetrators do believe. Recent reports suggest that hoaxes are more of a problem now than real viruses.

BPP PUBLISHING

# List of Key Terms and Index

**BPP**
PUBLISHING

*BPP* PUBLISHING

## ORDER FORM

Any books from our AAT range can be ordered by telephoning 020-8740-2211. Alternatively, send this page to our address below, fax it to us on 020-8740-1184, or email us at **publishing@bpp.com.** Or look us up on our website: www.bpp.com

We aim to deliver to all UK addresses inside 5 working days; a signature will be required. Order to all EU addresses should be delivered within 6 working days. All other orders to overseas addresses should be delivered within 8 working days.

### To: BPP Publishing Ltd, Aldine House, Aldine Place, London W12 8AW

**Tel: 020-8740 2211**          **Fax: 020-8740 1184**          **Email: publishing@bpp.com**

Mr / Ms (full name): _____

Daytime delivery address: _____

_____

Postcode: _____     Daytime Tel: _____

Please send me the following quantities of books.

| | 5/00 Interactive Text | 8/00 DA Kit | 8/00 CA Kit |
|---|---|---|---|
| **FOUNDATION** | | | |
| Unit 1 Recording Income and Receipts | ☐ | ☐ | |
| Unit 2 Making and Recording Payments | ☐ | ☐ | |
| Unit 3 Ledger Balances and Initial Trial Balance | ☐ | ☐ | |
| Unit 4 Supplying information for Management Control | ☐ | ☐ | |
| Unit 20 Working with Information Technology (8/00 Text) | ☐ | | |
| Unit 22/23 Achieving Personal Effectiveness | ☐ | | |
| **INTERMEDIATE** | | | |
| Unit 5 Financial Records and Accounts | ☐ | | ☐ |
| Unit 6 Cost Information | ☐ | | ☐ |
| Unit 7 Reports and Returns | ☐ | ☐ | |
| Unit 21 Using Information Technology | ☐ | ☐ | |
| Unit 22: see below | | | |
| **TECHNICIAN** | | | |
| Unit 8/9 Core Managing Costs and Allocating Resources | ☐ | | ☐ |
| Unit 10 Core Managing Accounting Systems | ☐ | ☐ | |
| Unit 11 Option Financial Statements (Accounting Practice) | ☐ | | ☐ |
| Unit 12 Option Financial Statements (Central Government) | ☐ | | ☐ |
| Unit 15 Option Cash Management and Credit Control | ☐ | ☐ | |
| Unit 16 Option Evaluating Activities | ☐ | ☐ | |
| Unit 17 Option Implementing Auditing Procedures | ☐ | | |
| Unit 18 Option Business Tax FA00(8/00 Text) | ☐ | | |
| Unit 19 Option Personal Tax FA00(8/00 Text) | ☐ | | |
| **TECHNICIAN 1999** | | | |
| Unit 17 Option Business Tax Computations FA99 (8/99 Text & Kit) | ☐ | ☐ | |
| Unit 18 Option Personal Tax Computations FA99 (8/99 Text & Kit) | ☐ | | |
| TOTAL BOOKS | ☐ + | ☐ + ☐ = | ☐ |

**Postage and packaging:**                                                                                      └ @ £9.95 each = £ ☐

**UK:** £2.00 for each book to maximum of £10

**Europe (inc ROI and Channel Islands):** £4.00 for first book, £2.00 for each extra ───── P & P £ ☐

**Rest of the World:** £20.00 for first book, £10 for each extra

Unit 22 Maintaining a Healthy Workplace Interactive Text (postage free)     ☐ @ £3.95 £ ☐

                                                                                         **GRAND TOTAL** £ ☐

I enclose a cheque for £ _____ (cheques to BPP Publishing Ltd) or charge to **Mastercard/Visa/Switch**

**Card number** ☐☐☐☐ ☐☐☐☐ ☐☐☐☐ ☐☐☐☐ ☐☐☐☐

**Start date** _____     **Expiry date** _____     **Issue no. (Switch only)** ___

**Signature** _____

## REVIEW FORM & FREE PRIZE DRAW

All original review forms from the entire BPP range, completed with genuine comments, will be entered into one of two draws on 31 January 2001 and 31 July 2001. The names on the first four forms picked out on each occasion will be sent a cheque for £50.

Name: _____    Address: _____

_____

_____

**How have you used this Interactive Text?**
*(Tick one box only)*

☐ Home study (book only)

☐ On a course: college _____

☐ With 'correspondence' package

☐ Other _____

**Why did you decide to purchase this Interactive Text?** *(Tick one box only)*

☐ Have used BPP Texts in the past

☐ Recommendation by friend/colleague

☐ Recommendation by a lecturer at college

☐ Saw advertising

☐ Other _____

**During the past six months do you recall seeing/receiving any of the following?**
*(Tick as many boxes as are relevant)*

☐ Our advertisement in *Accounting Technician* magazine

☐ Our advertisement in *Pass*

☐ Our brochure with a letter through the post

**Which (if any) aspects of our advertising do you find useful?**
*(Tick as many boxes as are relevant)*

☐ Prices and publication dates of new editions

☐ Information on Interactive Text content

☐ Facility to order books off-the-page

☐ None of the above

**Have you used the companion Assessment Kit for this subject?**     ☐ Yes     ☐ No

**Your ratings, comments and suggestions would be appreciated on the following areas**

|  | Very useful | Useful | Not useful |
|---|---|---|---|
| Introductory section (How to use this Interactive Text etc) | ☐ | ☐ | ☐ |
| Chapter topic lists | ☐ | ☐ | ☐ |
| Chapter learning objectives | ☐ | ☐ | ☐ |
| Key terms | ☐ | ☐ | ☐ |
| Assessment alerts | ☐ | ☐ | ☐ |
| Examples | ☐ | ☐ | ☐ |
| Activities and answers | ☐ | ☐ | ☐ |
| Key learning points | ☐ | ☐ | ☐ |
| Quick quizzes and answers | ☐ | ☐ | ☐ |
| List of key terms and index | ☐ | ☐ | ☐ |
| Icons | ☐ | ☐ | ☐ |

|  | Excellent | Good | Adequate | Poor |
|---|---|---|---|---|
| Overall opinion of this Text | ☐ | ☐ | ☐ | ☐ |

**Do you intend to continue using BPP Interactive Texts/Assessment Kits?** ☐ Yes   ☐ No

**Please note any further comments and suggestions/errors on the reverse of this page.**

**Please return to: Nick Weller, BPP Publishing Ltd, FREEPOST, London, W12 8BR**

## REVIEW FORM & FREE PRIZE DRAW (continued)

**Please note any further comments and suggestions/errors below**

### FREE PRIZE DRAW RULES

1   Closing date for 31 January 2001 draw is 31 December 2000. Closing date for 31 July 2001 draw is 30 June 2001.

2   Restricted to entries with UK and Eire addresses only. BPP employees, their families and business associates are excluded.

3   No purchase necessary. Entry forms are available upon request from BPP Publishing. No more than one entry per title, per person. Draw restricted to persons aged 16 and over.

4   Winners will be notified by post and receive their cheques not later than 6 weeks after the relevant draw date.

5   The decision of the promoter in all matters is final and binding. No correspondence will be entered into.